Joint 15th Linguistic Annotation Workshop and 3rd Designing Meaning Representations Workshop (LAW-DMR 2021)

Online
11 November 2021

ISBN: 978-1-7138-9168-0

Printed from e-media with permission by:

Curran Associates, Inc.
57 Morehouse Lane
Red Hook, NY 12571

Some format issues inherent in the e-media version may also appear in this print version.

Printed with permission by Curran Associates, Inc. (2024)

Association for Computational Linguistics
209 N. Eighth Street
Stroudsburg, Pennsylvania 18360

Phone: 1-570-476-8006
Fax: 1-570-476-0860

acl@aclweb.org

Additional copies of this publication are available from:

Curran Associates, Inc.
57 Morehouse Lane
Red Hook, NY 12571 USA
Phone: 845-758-0400
Fax: 845-758-2633
Email: curran@proceedings.com
Web: www.proceedings.com

LAW-DMR 2021

The Joint 15th Linguistic Annotation Workshop (LAW) and 3rd Designing Meaning Representations (DMR) Workshop

Proceedings of the Workshop

November 11, 2021

Introduction to the Workshop

Linguistic annotation of natural language corpora is the backbone of supervised methods of statistical natural language processing and has contributed to breakthroughs in practical natural language applications, most notably in Machine Translation, Machine Reading, Question Answering, and Recognizing Textual Entailment. Nonetheless, challenges remain in developing systems that can actually "understand" human language, including the ability to track entities in a text, understand the relations between these entities, track events and their participants described in a text, understand how events unfold in time, and distinguish events that have actually happened from events that are planned or intended, are uncertain, or did not happen at all. The fifteenth LAW and third DMR workshops have been combined for the first time to provide a forum for presentation and discussion of innovative research on all aspects of linguistic annotation, with a special focus on the design and annotation of representations of the various elements of meaning contributing to understanding. These proceedings include papers presented at LAW-DMR on November 11, 2021, held online in conjunction with the 2021 Conference on Empirical Methods in Natural Language Processing in Punta Cana, Dominican Republic.

This premier iteration of the joint LAW-DMR workshop received 35 submissions, out of which 18 papers have been accepted to be presented at the workshop—8 as talks and 10 as posters. In addition to oral and poster paper presentations, LAW-DMR also featured invited talks by Joyce Chai (University of Michigan) and Stephan Oepen (University of Oslo), and a panel session discussion of the topic, "What is the future of linguistic annotation?"

We thank the Association for Computational Linguistics' Special Interest Group for Annotation (ACL SIGANN), our organizing committee, for its continuing organization of the LAW workshops, and the EMNLP 2021 workshop chairs for their support. We are grateful to all of the authors for submitting their papers to the workshop and our program committee members for their dedication and their thoughtful reviews. Finally, we thank our invited speakers and panelists for making the workshop a uniquely valuable discussion of linguistic annotation research.

Special Theme: Multi-layered and Multi-modal Annotations

Given that this is the first joint LAW and DMR workshop, this year's theme was to explore multi-layered annotations, and how different types of annotations can be brought together to enhance progress towards true understanding. This includes papers on the broadening and deepening existing annotation schemas, as well as annotations going beyond text to mark up head movements.

Workshop Chairs

Claire Bonial, DEVCOM U.S. Army Research Laboratory
Nianwen Xue, Brandeis University

Organizing Committee

Stefanie Dipper, Ruhr University Bochum
Annemarie Friedrich, Bosch Center for Artificial Intelligence
Chu-Ren Huang, The Hong Kong Polytechnic University
Nancy Ide, Vassar College
Lori Levin, Carnegie-Mellon University
Adam Meyers, New York University
Antonio Pareja-Lora, Universidad Complutense de Madrid / ATLAS, UNED
Massimo Poesio, University of Essex
Sameer Pradhan, University of Pennsylvania and cemantix.org
Ines Rehbein, Leibniz Science Campus, Institute for German Language and Heidelberg University
Manfred Stede, University of Potsdam
Katrin Tomanek, OpenTable
Fei Xia, University of Washington
Heike Zinsmeister, University of Hamburg

Invited Speakers

Joyce Chai, University of Michigan
Stephan Oepen, University of Oslo

Program Committee

Ron Artstein, USC Institute for Creative Technologies
Johan Bos, University of Groningen
Nicoletta Calzolari, ILC-CNR
Emmanuele Chersoni, Hong Kong Polytechnic University
Kathryn Conger, Universitiy of Colorado Boulder
William Croft, University of New Mexico
Valeria de Paiva, Topos Institute
Stefanie Dipper, Ruhr University Bochum
Lucia Donatelli, Saarland University
Jonathan Dunn, University of Canterbury
Kilian Evang, Heinrich Heine University Düsseldorf
Federico Fancellu, Samsung AI Research Canada
Annemarie Friedrich, Bosch Research
Kim Gerdes, Université Paris-Saclay
Jan Hajic, Charles University
Jena D. Hwang, Allen Institute for AI

Table of Contents

Workshop Program

Thursday, 11 November 2021

08:45–09:00 Introduction

09:00–11:00 Session A: Oral presentations:

09:00–10:00 Invited talk by Stephan Oepen: Linguistic Structure beyond Strings and Trees

10:00–10:15 *Zero-shot cross-lingual Meaning Representation Transfer: Annotation of Hungarian using the Prague Functional Generative Description*
Attila Novák, Borbála Novák and Csilla Novák

10:15–10:30 *Theoretical and Practical Issues in the Semantic Annotation of Four Indigenous Languages*
Jens E. L. Van Gysel, Meagan Vigus, Lukas Denk, Andrew Cowell, Rosa Vallejos, Tim O'Gorman and William Croft

10:30–10:45 *Representing Implicit Positive Meaning of Negated Statements in AMR*
Katharina Stein and Lucia Donatelli

10:45–11:00 *AutoAspect: Automatic Annotation of Tense and Aspect for Uniform Meaning Representations*
Daniel Chen, Martha Palmer and Meagan Vigus

11:30–13:30 Session B: Poster presentations:

Thursday, 11 November 2021 (continued)

11:30–12:00	**Overview of poster presentations**
12:00–12:45	*Can predicate-argument relationships be extracted from UD trees?* Adam Ek, Jean-Philippe Bernardy and Stergios Chatzikyriakidis
12:00–12:45	*Classifying Divergences in Cross-lingual AMR Pairs* Shira Wein and Nathan Schneider
12:00–12:45	*A Linguistic Annotation Framework to Study Interactions in Multilingual Healthcare Conversational Forums* Ishani Mondal, Kalika Bali, Mohit Jain, Monojit Choudhury, Ashish Sharma, Evans Gitau, Jacki O'Neill, Kagonya Awori and Sarah Gitau
12:00–12:45	*Sister Help: Data Augmentation for Frame-Semantic Role Labeling* Ayush Pancholy, Miriam R L Petruck and Swabha Swayamdipta
12:00–12:45	*A Corpus Study of Creating Rule-Based Enhanced Universal Dependencies for German* Teresa Bürkle, Stefan Grünewald and Annemarie Friedrich
12:00–12:45	*Subcategorizing Adverbials in Universal Conceptual Cognitive Annotation* Zhuxin Wang, Jakob Prange and Nathan Schneider
12:00–12:45	*Simplifying annotation of intersections in time normalization annotation: exploring syntactic and semantic validation* Peiwen Su and Steven Bethard
12:00–12:45	*Overcoming the challenges in morphological annotation of Turkish in universal dependencies framework* Talha Bedir, Karahan Şahin, Onur Gungor, Suzan Uskudarli, Arzucan Özgür, Tunga Güngör and Balkiz Ozturk Basaran
12:00–12:45	*Automatic Entity State Annotation using the VerbNet Semantic Parser* Ghazaleh Kazeminejad, Martha Palmer, Tao Li and Vivek Srikumar
12:00–12:45	*On Releasing Annotator-Level Labels and Information in Datasets* Vinodkumar Prabhakaran, Aida Mostafazadeh Davani and Mark Diaz

Thursday, 11 November 2021 (continued)

12:45–13:30 Panel discussion: what's the future of linguistic annotation?

14:00–16:00 Session C: Oral presentations:

14:00–15:00 Invited talk by Joyce Chai: Intuitive Physics in Commonsense Language Understanding

15:00–15:15 *Increasing Sentence-Level Comprehension Through Text Classification of Epistemic Functions*
Maria Berger and Elizabeth Goldstein

15:15–15:30 *Towards a Methodology Supporting Semiautomatic Annotation of HeadMovements in Video-recorded Conversations*
Patrizia Paggio, Costanza Navarretta, Bart Jongejan and Manex Agirrezabal

15:30–15:45 *Intensionalizing Abstract Meaning Representations: Non-Veridicality and Scope*
Gregor Williamson, Patrick Elliott and Yuxin Ji

15:45–16:00 *WikiGUM: Exhaustive Entity Linking for Wikification in 12 Genres*
Jessica Lin and Amir Zeldes

16:00–16:15 Concluding remarks

Zero-shot cross-lingual Meaning Representation Transfer: Annotation of Hungarian using the Prague Functional Generative Description

Attila Novák and **Borbála Novák** and **Csilla Novák**
MTA-PPKE Hungarian Language Technology Research Group,
Pázmány Péter Catholic University, Faculty of Information Technology and Bionics
Práter u. 50/a, 1083 Budapest, Hungary
{surname.firstname}@itk.ppke.hu

Abstract

In this paper, we present the results of our experiments concerning the zero-shot cross-lingual performance of the PERIN sentence-to-graph semantic parser. We applied the PTG model trained using the PERIN parser on a 740k-token Czech newspaper corpus to Hungarian. We evaluated the performance of the parser using the official evaluation tool of the MRP 2020 shared task. The gold standard Hungarian annotation was created by manual correction of the output of the parser following the annotation manual of the tectogrammatical level of the Prague Dependency Treebank. An English model trained on a larger one-million-token English newspaper corpus is also available, however, we found that the Czech model performed significantly better on Hungarian input due to the fact that Hungarian is typologically more similar to Czech than to English. We have found that zero-shot transfer of the PTG meaning representation across typologically not-too-distant languages using a neural parser model based on a multilingual contextual language model followed by a manual correction by linguist experts seems to be a viable annotation scenario.

1 Introduction

Two workshops on Cross-Framework Meaning Representation Parsing (MRP) hosted by the 2019 and 2020 editions of the Conference on Computational Natural Language Learning (CoNLL), featured two editions of a shared task, where implementations of parsers turning raw text into different flavors of meaning representation graphs competed with each other.

The first MRP 2019 task (Oepen et al., 2020) involved only English as the object language, and 5 frameworks of meaning representation were featured: DM, PSD, EDS, UCCA and AMR. Two of these frameworks, DM (DELPH-IN MRS Bi-Lexical Dependencies, Ivanova et al., 2012), and PSD (Prague Semantic Dependencies Hajič et al., 2012; Miyao et al., 2014) are simple bi-lexical dependency graphs generated from core predicate-argument structure of a rich syntactic-semantic annotation based on general theories of grammar. The underlying linguistic theory is Head-Driven Phrase Structure Grammar (HPSG, Pollard and Sag, 1994) with Minimal Recursion Semantics (MRS, Copestake et al., 2005) for DM and Prague Functional Generative Description (FGD, Sgall et al., 1986) for PSD.

In DM and PSD, the nodes are surface word forms. The other three frameworks feature more complex graphs that contain nodes not in one-to-one relation to input words. Elementary Dependency Structures (EDS) are based on English Resource Grammar (Flickinger et al., 2017) aka English Resource Semantics (ERS) (Flickinger et al., 2014) annotation[1] that was turned into a variable-free semantic dependency graph consisting of labeled graph nodes representing logical predications and edges representing labeled argument positions. The conversion from ERS to EDS discards information on semantic scope. The nodes are anchored to spans of the input string.

Universal Conceptual Cognitive Annotation (UCCA, Abend and Rappoport, 2013) is an abstract annotation featuring only purely semantic categories and structure. The foundational layer of UCCA (featured in the shared task) consists of a very basic set of semantic categories like Process, Argument, State, "Adverb" (modifier) etc., that are used as labels on edges linking unlabeled nodes representing semantic units and surface word forms.

Finally, Abstract Meaning Representation (AMR, Banarescu et al., 2013) features graphs comparable to EDS, but with more abstract predication labels due to application of lexical decomposition

[1] This is the same HPSG/MRS-based formalism DM is based on

Proceedings of the Joint 15th Linguistic Annotation Workshop (LAW) and 3rd Designing Meaning Representations (DMR) Workshop, pages 1–11
November, 2021.

and normalization towards verbal senses e.g., representing ‘similar’ as the verbal sense ‘resemble’. In contrast to EDS (and the rest), AMR nodes are not explicitly anchored to spans of the surface form.[2]

The graphs in the MRP shared tasks were presented in a JSON-lines-based Uniform Graph Interchange Format, and participants were asked to design and train systems that predict sentence-level meaning representations in all frameworks in parallel to foster transfer and multi-task learning.

In the MRP 2020 shared task (Oepen et al., 2020), DM was dropped, as EDS is a richer representation derived from the same resource. PSD was also replaced by a richer meaning representation, Prague Tectogrammatical Graphs (PTG, Zeman and Hajic, 2020), derived from the same Prague Functional Generative Description (FGD), but retaining more of the original Tectogrammatical annotation than PSD.

EDS, UCCA, and AMR were retained, and Discourse Representation Graphs (DRG, Abzianidze et al., 2020) were added as a new meaning representation. DRG is a graph encoding of Discourse Representation Structures (DRS), the meaning representations at the core of Discourse Representation Theory (DRT; Kamp and Reyle, 1993). This model handles many challenging semantic phenomena from quantifiers to presupposition accommodation, and discourse structure.

In addition to English data, the MRP 2020 task covered new languages, one for each of four of the five covered formalisms (except EDS): Czech for PTG, German for UCCA and DRG, and Chinese for AMR.

Training and evaluation data of the MRP shared task was only available to shared task participants distributed to them by the Linguistic Data Consortium (LDC), since part of the data is based on LDC-owned material, the WSJ part of the Penn Treebank (PTB). The shared task site states that, upon completion of each competition, subsets of task data that are copyright-free (including system submissions and evaluation results) will be made available for public, open-source download. However, unfortunately, we have not found a public release of the data.

However, one of the top performing systems at MRP 2020, the PERIN parser (Samuel and Straka, 2020), which was developed at the Institute of Formal and Applied Linguistics (ÚFAL), Faculty of Mathematics and Physics, Charles University, Prague, was made available at the ÚFAL GitHub repo[3] including pretrained models for the PERIN submission to the shared task. There is also a link to an Interactive demo on Google Colab. This facilitated testing the models on various inputs. Positive subjective impressions of the performance of the English and especially the Czech PTG model of the parser on Hungarian input prompted us to perform the experiment described here evaluating the zero-shot cross-lingual performance of the model. Of the models available, we selected PTG, because

- the categories/concepts it operates with looked immediately familiar,
- the annotation it generated seemed reasonable and detailed,
- the non-English model covers Czech, a language sharing many typological features with Hungarian (rich morphology, relatively free word order, pro drop etc.),
- the model was trained on a sizable 740k-token corpus,
- a rather detailed 1255-page annotation manual (Mikulová et al., 2006) of the underlying Prague tectogrammatical annotation is available in English, and
- performance of the parsers (also of PERIN, in particular) on the Czech PTG data reported in the MRP 2020 task results was relatively high.

Concerning the other formalisms featured in the MRP 2020 task, we had the following impressions, further motivating our model selection:

- Annotation in the UCCA foundational layer is rather coarse-grained compared to PDT (a handful of edge label types, no annotation on nodes).[4] In spite of this, all systems participating in MRP 2020 performed relatively poorly ($F_1 < 0.5$ on edge labels) on UCCA. This might indicate consistency problems with the UCCA annotation.
- While reported performance of the best parsers is generally good on DRG, our impression of DRG output generated from our Hungarian test corpus was that it made rela-

[2]When decomposition is applied, anchoring of individual component nodes becomes non-trivial.

[3]`https://github.com/ufal/perin`

[4]On the positive side, some distinctions present in UCCA, such as state vs. process are orthogonal to those in other annotation schemes, and these would be worth porting.

tively little sense.

- Performance of the best parsers was also good on EDS. However, an EDS-style model is trained only for English. The model struggles on Hungarian input completely misinterpreting important constructions. This seems to be due to typological differences between Hungarian and English. E.g., grammatical relations expressed by prepositions and word order are mainly expressed by suffixes in Hungarian, the latter being an agglutinative language. The EDS model often fails to properly recognize most of these relations (locations, times, possessive constructions, constituents not in canonical positions for English etc.), because suffixes are not independent tokens in Hungarian.[5] There is also pro drop in Hungarian, and this phenomenon affects a high proportion of clauses (see section 4.3.1), but the EDS model fails to recover all such covert pronouns.

The PTG annotation the Czech PERIN model was trained on is derived from the Prague Tectogrammatical Annotation, an elaborate system of deep linguistic analysis based on a many-decade-long tradition of dependency-grammar-based linguistic research. The Prague Dependency Treebank (PDT) and the Prague Czech–English Dependency Treebank (PCEDT; Hajič et al., 2012), from which PTG data was derived, embody an awe-inspiringly immense amount of decade-long annotation work. In addition to the deep syntactic annotation we review here, P(CE)DT annotation includes morphological annotation and a dependency-based shallow 'analytical' syntactic annotation of the underlying text. The tectogrammatical analysis was generated based on these surface-level representations, and then manually checked and corrected.

2 Related Work

Although the MRP 2020 shared task featured a "cross-lingual" track, it only meant in practice that parsers were trained and tested on data in more than one language for meaning representations that had such annotation available. Transfer from one language to another was not tested there.

The Prague dependency annotation scheme has been ported to languages other than Czech or English, examples including the Slovak Dependency Treebank (Gajdošová et al., 2016), the PAWS Treebank (including Polish and Russian in addition to English and Czech, Nedoluzhko et al., 2018), and the Prague Arabic Dependency Treebank (Hajič and Zemánek, 2004). However, all these syntactic annotations have been created manually.

At the same time, there is a significant body of research literature describing work concerning cross-lingual transfer using deep-neural-network-based models. Multilingual pre-training of contextual language models like multilingual BERT (Devlin et al., 2019) and XLM-RoBERTa (Conneau et al., 2020) facilitated this kind of knowledge transfer. These models have been used to train massively multilingual syntactic dependency parsers (Kondratyuk and Straka, 2019), zero-shot named entity recognizers (Wu et al., 2020) etc, with even specific multilingual benchmarks prepared for testing the cross-lingual generalization capability of models on various tasks such as sentence-pair classification, structured prediction (POS tagging, NER), question answering, natural language inference and sentence retrieval (Hu et al., 2020).

In this paper, we examine a zero-shot approach to meaning representation transfer, which belongs to the structured prediction problem class. Few studies address this topic, because evaluation requires tedious manual work.

3 Method

The approach we took was the following. We had a 150-sentence Hungarian corpus annotated by the PERIN Czech PTG model. We turned this into a gold standard Hungarian annotation by manually correcting the output of the parser following the annotation manual of the tectogrammatical level of the Prague Dependency Treebank (Mikulová et al., 2006). Members of the annotation team had solid training in theoretical and computational linguistics and cognitive science encompassing both dependency syntax and formal semantics. However, we had to understand and learn details of the annotation scheme during the process, which required substantial effort. Fortunately, examples in the Annotation Guidelines have English translation. However, only a few illustrative examples have a full tree representation. We had to reiterate and rediscuss our solutions several times to converge on an annotation that we considered consistent with

[5]Note, however, that the English PTG model, which utilizes a rich set of edge label categories to encode grammatical relations, seems to be much less affected by typological differences.

what is described in the PDT annotation guidelines. 50-sentence folds were annotated, discussed and reannotated several times, as our understanding of the annotation scheme evolved during the process. Access to PCEDT would have been very helpful, however, only the Czech part of treebank is available on line,[6] so we could not take a look at the English translations, or efficiently search for specific constructions not being speakers of Czech.

When doing the manual annotation correction, we had to refrain from making modifications to the annotation scheme if we 'disliked' the way a specific phenomenon is handled (or ignored) in the original scheme. We also tried to refrain from interpreting dubious situations 'the way we would have made it', we tried to figure out instead, how ÚFAL experts would do it. We assumed that if the parser more-or-less consistently generates some sort of sufficiently sensible annotation for a specific construction, it reflects a deliberate annotation pattern in the training data.

The serialized JSON lines graph representations output by the parser cannot be edited themselves, although they can be visualized using `mtool`,[7] the Swiss Army Knife for Graph-Based Meaning Representation. We thus created a converter from the JSON lines graph representations to CoNLL-U[8] (using anchors to project the data) and vice versa, and we edited the graphs in the CoNLL-U format. We used `mtool` to visualize our gold standard solutions while we edited the annotations and also to evaluate the zero-shot output of the parser against the edited gold standard version. Based on the graph configurations, `mtool` creates potential node-to-node mappings between the two graphs, so the fact that the ordering of nodes is changed during conversions is not a problem from the point of view of evaluation and visualization.

3.1 The PERIN parser

The name of the parser, PERIN, is motivated by the fact that it embodies a permutation-invariant model that predicts all nodes at once in parallel and is trained using a permutation invariant loss function that is not sensitive to the ordering of nodes (Samuel and Straka, 2020).

The language model the parser uses as neural input 'features' when inferring the graph annotation based on the input tokens is XLM-RoBERTa (base). XLM-R (Conneau et al., 2020) is the encoder part of a transformer model pretrained originally on 2.5TB of filtered CommonCrawl data in 100 languages including Czech and Hungarian to predict masked word forms. This underlying multilingual neural language model makes an essential contribution to the decent zero-shot cross-lingual performance we encountered possible, enabling the parser to output sensible annotation for input in a language the parser itself was not trained to handle originally.

The model uses relative string encodings to predict node labels that map anchored token strings onto label strings. Specifically, in the PTG model, lemmata ('t-lemmata') are used as node labels. This mechanism performs well (as shown by MRP 2020 evaluation results) when parsing text in the same language the model was trained on. However, in our case, applying Czech lemmatization patterns to Hungarian input unsurprisingly resulted in funny lemmata. Nevertheless, since PTG is a 'Flavor-1' model, i.e. nodes are anchored to spans in the input (practically to tokens), external lemmatization can be used to fix the node labels. Since tokens could be linked to nodes, we could also evaluate the annotation ignoring the ill-formed lemmata.

In contrast, our initial probing of the model indicated that grammatical/semantic relations among content words (edge labels in the graph, 'functors' and 'subfunctors' in PDT terminology) seem to carry over relatively well to Hungarian. And it was this aspect of the annotation that we wanted to concentrate on.

4 Results

In addition to visualization, we also used `mtool` to evaluate the zero-shot output of both the Czech and the English PTG models against the edited gold standard version of the test corpus. English PTG has less node features than the Czech model, and also the edge labels generally contain no subfunctor annotation. The English model also uses different patterns to generate node labels (lemmata), so the performance of the models would not be comparable without applying some sort of normalization

[6] `https://lindat.mff.cuni.cz/services/pmltq/#!/treebank/pcedt20_cz/query/`

[7] `https://github.com/cfmrp/mtool`

[8] The files have the same fields as CoNLL-U , but category and dependency labels are, of course, the ones coming from the PTG model rather than UD-compliant labels. We use the `deps` field to store graph edges, `upos` to store the POS label and `feats` to store other node features. We used a special *mrg* relation to link function words (e.g., determiners, postpositions, subordinating conjunctions) to the head content word anchored to the same graph node.

PTG-en	P	R	F
tops	1	1	1
labels	0.843	0.763	0.801
properties	0.558	0.222	0.317
anchors	0.864	0.839	0.852
edges	0.682	0.558	0.614
attributes	0.714	0.546	0.619
all	0.734	0.499	0.594
PTG-cz	P	R	F
tops	1	1	1
labels	0.842	**0.857**	**0.849**
properties	0.932	0.943	0.937
anchors	0.844	0.854	0.849
edges	**0.704**	**0.690**	**0.697**
attributes	**0.745**	**0.665**	**0.703**
all	0.849	0.849	0.849

Table 1: Zero-shot performance of the English and Czech PTG models (PTG-en vs. PTG-cz) on the Hungarian test set. Ignore the apparent performance gap in node properties, as these have not been corrected or normalized.

to the annotations before comparison. The normalization we performed included a) replacement of node labels (lemmata) by the sequence of tokens anchored to the node (with the exception of unanchored tokens, which retained their labels), and b) removal of subfunctor annotation from edge labels (except for subtypes of *coref* and *bridging* relations, as these also have subfunctors in the English annotation).

Performance of the normalized output of the models as returned by `mtool` is compared in Table 1. Node properties have not been corrected or normalized (see Section 4.1), so that row can be ignored. But the Czech model definitely performs better at identifying grammatical relations (edges, attributes) and the difference in node label recall reflects mainly its advantage at identifying zero nodes (due to handling of pro drop and richer annotation of argument coreference relations in light verb constructions).

Below we discuss specific details of the performance of the Czech model on Hungarian input.

4.1 Node properties

The PTG graph representations used in the MRP 2020 shared task were created by automatic conversion from tectogrammatical trees in P(CE)DT. English data comes from the Prague Czech-English Dependency Treebank 2.0 (Hajič et al., 2012) while the source of Czech data was the Prague Dependency Treebank 3.5. (Hajič et al., 2020). Zeman and Hajic (2020) state that 'The Prague treebanks, especially the Czech PDT, contain a number of grammatemes that were assigned semi-automatically without much human intervention. Such properties were omitted and only the manually assigned (or checked) ones were carried over to PTG.' What we see in fact, is that, with the exception of part of speech, and the `tfa` feature (see Section 4.1.2) all we have in terms of node properties ('grammatemes' in the Prague terminology) are the features that were introduced during the upgrade of the treebanks from version 2.0/2.5 to version 3.0. These properties are consequently not described in the PDT 2.0 annotation manual (Mikulová et al., 2006), but their description can be found in Mikulová et al. (2013). The latter source states that these properties were converted from previous annotation by semiautomatic procedures. Moreover, some of the features that remained (*typgroup, diatgram*) have limited or no relevance from our cross-lingual point of view.

At the same time, we really miss the very important grammatical properties that were omitted (number, person, tense, modality, degree etc.). This results in that almost all relevant information is lost in the annotation of e.g., covert pronouns (see Section 4.3.1) or modal auxiliaries (corresponding to *can, must, will* etc.). The latter are not represented in PDT annotation as independent nodes: they only contribute a feature to the node of verb they combine with. This feature, however, is lost in conversion. Technical rather than practical considerations may have played the major role in the selection of the properties kept. Should another conversion of PDT to PTG ever be performed, we would be very happy to see the missing features in the new version. Moreover, the lack of crucial grammatical features in the representation may play an important role in the parser making errors like establishing coreference relations between pronouns and noun phrases of different person/number (e.g., between 'she' and 'I' in the parse of *Eljön, mert szeretem őt.* 'She will come because I love her.' instead of linking 'she' and 'her'.).

Since much of what we would like to see there is not there, and some of what we do have is irrelevant, we have not performed an exhaustive quantitative evaluation of the mapping of node features. Nevertheless, we make some qualitative observations concerning the performance of the parser with regard to specific node features present in the annotation in the following sections.

4.1.1 Part of speech

Lexical nodes have at least a part-of-speech property, which is termed 'semantic' in PDT terminology, but it is much less semantic than what you would expect. E.g., nominalized verbs are 'semantic' nouns. There are just a few deviations from syntactic part of speech: deadjectival adverbs corresponding to English *-ly* adverbs are tagged 'semantic' adjectives, and numerals as adjectival or nominal quantifiers. Morphological negation is a feature reflected in the part of speech category set that does not apply to Hungarian. Also non-ly adverbs are sometimes tagged as adjectives, but otherwise part of speech is accurately identified by the model.

4.1.2 Topic-focus articulation

The Czech model also contains a feature related to topic-focus articulation (`tfa`). This is an advanced feature rarely found in computational meaning representations. However, topic-focus articulation has been one of the major research directions of the Prague school of linguistics behind PTD, so the presence of a feature like this is not so surprising after all. We would have, however, expected four possible values instead of the actual three: *t* = contextually bound expression (topic), *f* = contextually non-bound expression (new information) , *c* = (contextually bound) contrastive expression. We think that it would be relevant to distinguish contextually non-bound contrastive elements (focus proper) from contextually bound contrastive elements (contrastive topic). We could not determine from the limited description in the annotation manual how specific constructions (e.g., contrasting predicates) should fit into the annotation scheme used in PDT. The parser often assigns values to this feature that seem reasonable, but there are also cases where the annotation is obviously wrong (e.g., assignment of the *f* value to definite expressions). The source of these problems could be among others that word order constraints concerning contrastive elements (focus/contrastive topic) are quite different in Czech and Hungarian (Czech: clause final, Hungarian: preverbal) and that there is no definite article in Czech.

4.1.3 Factual and sentence modality

The model is able to differentiate appeals, requests and questions from assertions, however, quite surprisingly, it often fails to identify potential ('would') and contrafactual ('would have')[9] modalities.

4.2 Identification of grammatical/semantic relations

Although an F score of around 0.7 for edges/attributes (see Table 1) might not seem very great at first sight, this is not bad in fact (especially considering the rich variety of possible labels), and not very much worse than the performance of the same parser model for Czech input (F=0.84/0.78, Samuel and Straka, 2020). The model is especially good at identifying adjuncts (time, place, directional and manner adverbials).

What was a bit disappointing for us is the annotation of predicate argument relations in PDT, which in most cases is limited to two relations called *act* and *pat*. These have nothing to do with real thematic roles like *agent* or *patient*, but are mostly simply placeholders for the first two arguments of any predicate. E.g., the subject of *the window broke* is *act*, while the predicate argument in the valency frame of the copula (i.e., *blue* in *my hat is blue*) is marked as *pat*. But PTG is not alone having uninformative argument labels among the meaning representation schemes in MRP 2020: others have ARG0, ARG1 etc.

4.3 Empty elements

In addition to edge labels, the model also relatively successfully predicts empty elements, such as dropped pronouns and ellipsis as long as similar patterns apply to both the source and the target language.

4.3.1 Pro drop

For example, Czech, similarly to Hungarian, features pro drop: i.e. subject pronouns may optionally be omitted in neutral sentences, as shown in the two side-by-side one-word sentences in (1). In the case of Hungarian, there is a lack of overt subject pronouns in most cases when the pronoun is not emphasized. It is a nice feature of the model that it includes existentially bound optional arguments in the analyses it generates (e.g., *Olvasok.* is interpreted as 'I am reading (something).')

[9] In PDT the value 'irreal' is used.

(1) *Olvasok.* *Čtu.*
read.Prs.1Sg read.Prs.1Sg
'I am reading. = I am reading (something).'

In Hungarian, the same sentence with an overt pronoun has different interpretations depending on the intonation pattern (2).

(2) *Én olvasok.*
'I am reading.' (neutral, rare)
'It is me who is reading.' (focus)
'As for me, I do read.' (contrastive topic)

However, in cases where the same phenomenon (i.e. pro drop) does not apply to certain pronouns in the source language, the model always fails to predict such covert pronouns in the target language. In Hungarian, for example, object pronouns also undergo pro drop. What makes this possible is that verbal morphology encodes not only subject agreement but also the definiteness of the object, as illustrated in (3). If the morphology of verb form implies the presence of a definite object, then the lack of an overt object implies the presence of an object pronoun (4a). In contrast, there is no object pro drop in Czech (4b), thus the model fails to predict covert object pronouns for Hungarian. Instead, we get the same interpretation with an existentially bound object that we get for *Olvasok* (1).

(3) a. ***Olvasok*** ***egy*** *könyvet.*
read.Prs.1Sg a book.Sg.Acc
'I am reading a book.'

b. ***Olvasom*** ***a*** *könyvet.*
read.Prs.Def.1Sg the book.Sg.Acc
'I am reading the book.'

(4) a. *Olvasom.*
read.Prs.Def.1Sg

b. *Čtu* *to.*
read.Prs.1Sg that.Acc
'I am reading it.'

4.3.2 Possessive constructions involving pronouns

The same applies to possessive constructions involving personal pronouns. The Czech (or English) version of these constructs involves a possessive pronoun determiner followed by a noun, optionally modified by adjuncts (5b). In Hungarian (and many similar agglutinating languages), the construct involves possessive suffixes attached to the noun as inflection, and the presence of an overt pronoun is optional, and, again, is mostly limited to cases of emphasis on the pronoun (5a). Since the possessive pronoun is obligatory in Czech (it is the key element of the construction), the parser trained on Czech data always fails to predict empty personal pronouns involved in possessive constructions in Hungarian, too.

(5) a. *az* *(én)* *anyám*
the (I) mother.Poss.1Sg

b. *moje* *matka*
my.Fem.Sg.Nom mother.Fem.Sg.Nom
'my mother'

4.3.3 Ellipsis

The model also performs reasonably well predicting and reconstructing elliptical structures as long as a similar elliptical construction is present in the language the model was trained on. Both Czech and Hungarian feature gapping in the second clause in coordinated clauses. However, in Hungarian (similarly to e.g., Turkish), gapping in the first clause is also a frequently used construction. As shown in Fig. 1, the parser fails to properly recognize the elliptical structure if the gap is in the first clause (not an option in Czech or English). For the given examples, we get a perfect parse only if the gap is in the second clause, and word order in the first clause is SVO (Fig. 1c).

4.3.4 Zero copula

PDT much predates the Universal Dependencies (UD) project, and in contrast to the lexical content head solution to copula constructions there, the copula is the head in PDT/PTG. In Hungarian, there is a zero copula in the default 3rd person singular present indicative case, so we needed to introduce a new zero copula (`#zerocop`) item to accommodate the annotation of zero copula constructions to the scheme applied in PDT and PTG. As it is, the model fails to parse zero copula constructions due to the analysis above and the fact that there is always an overt copula in Czech.

4.4 Coordination/parataxis

In contrast to subordination, coordination (in the PDT annotation manual: parataxis) is problematic

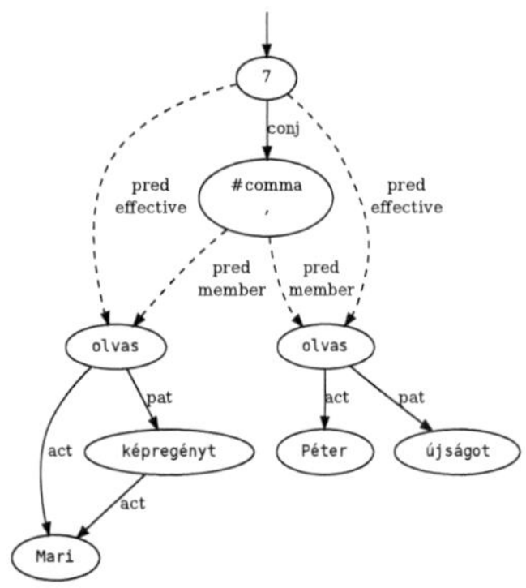

(a) *Péter újságot olvas, Mari képregényt.* 'Peter is reading a newspaper, Mary a comic.' – Gap in second clause, SOV word order in first clause. Minor error in the analysis.

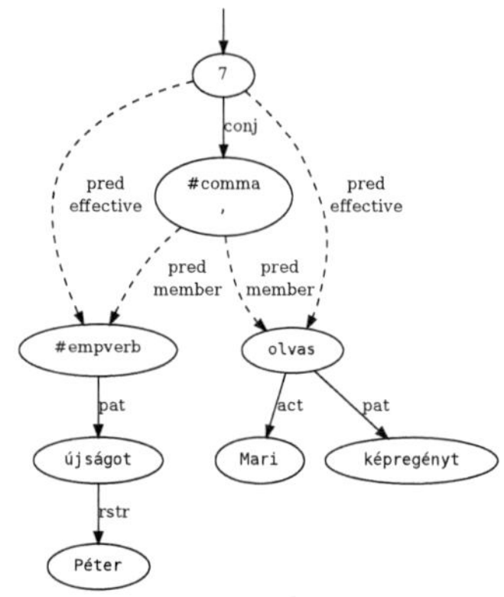

(b) *Péter újságot, Mari képregényt olvas.* – Gap in first clause, SOV word order in second clause. Wrong analysis of first clause.

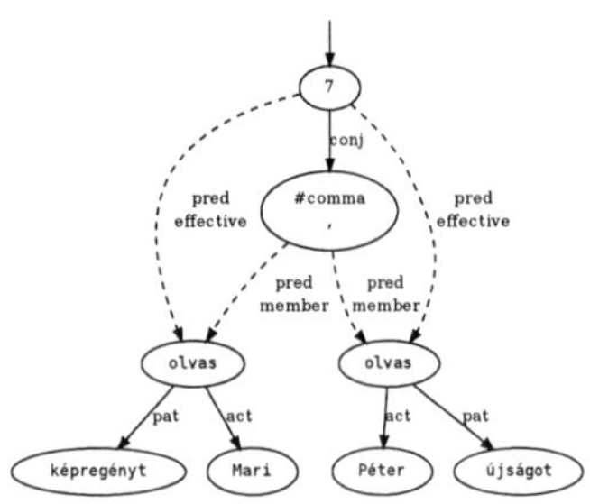

(c) *Péter olvas újságot, Mari képregényt.* – Gap in second clause, SVO word order in first clause. Perfect analysis.

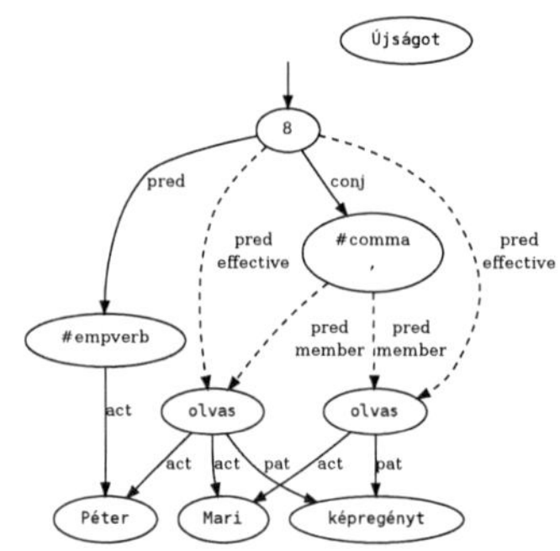

(d) *Újságot Péter, képregényt Mari olvas.* – Gap in first clause, OSV word order in second clause. Wrong analysis.

Figure 1: Output of the Czech PTG grammar for various Hungarian gapping constructions. Only the analysis in 1c is completely correct.

for dependency-based annotation schemes because it is not an endocentric construction. The solution applied in the PTG implementation of PDT structures makes coordinating conjunctions or, in the absence of these, punctuation (commas) the head of coordinate structures, as shown in Fig. 1c. The coordinated predicates there (the two *olvas* 'read' nodes) are *pred–members* of the `#comma` node (technical head of the coordinate structure), and they are also linked directly by *pred–effective* edges to the node dominating the whole structure, here the root of the sentence graph. The technical head (`#comma`) is attached using a relation characterizing the paratactic structure (e.g., conjunction, disjunction, apposition etc., here: *conj*) to the node dominating the coordinate structure. This solution is again different from the one applied in UD, however, it is analogous to the way coordination is represented, e.g., in EDS.

However, two aspects of this solution are problematic. Certain types of coordination express an asymmetric relation like cause, consequence or confrontation, and these types of relations were doubled in the annotation scheme only because they also have a subordinating variant (coordinating *confr, reas* vs. subordinating *contrd, caus*). The distinction is purely syntactic and 99.5% of speakers would have an extremely hard time distinguishing the subordinating variant from the coordinating one. However, the analyses are very different. What is even worse, the representation of the paratactic variant of these constructions completely fails to distinguish which conjunct plays which role, e.g., what is the cause and what is the consequence. These unnecessary syntactic distinctions gave us a hard time during correction of the gold standard data.

Coordinated predicates involving covert subject pronouns were analyzed by the model as verb phrase coordination sharing a single covert subject pronoun rather than assuming two coreferring covert pronouns. We accepted this solution assuming that similar constructions must have been analyzed analogously in the Czech PDT treebank.

4.5 Further problems

The model sometimes fails to integrate parts of the analysis into the whole structure, or, in some cases, completely ignores some part of the input. This often seems to be related to covert elements not attested in the source language like a zero copula or gapping in the first conjunct.

Short function words are sometimes confused with short frequent function words in the source language, and this may result in wrong analysis. E.g., Hungarian *s* 'and' and *a* 'the' are sometimes confused with Czech *s* 'with' and *a* 'and', respectively.

Function words (articles, postpositions, subordinating conjunctions, auxiliaries) are normally merged with content words (the node is anchored on several tokens), but in some cases a partial merge is performed (the function word is anchored both to an independent node of its own and to the node of a content word). This is an error.

The model tokenizes at hyphens, and the hyphen remains unanchored. This is quite problematic for Hungarian, because suffixes (e.g., case endings) are often attached with a hyphen to the stem, and such case endings become independent tokens in the analysis.

5 Conclusion

In this paper we presented our experiment investigating the zero-shot cross-lingual performance of neural parser models based on the PDT/PTG meaning representation formalism. The model yields reasonable performance, and it can be feasibly applied in a semi-automatic annotation scenario. The specific language pairs were Czech–Hungarian vs. English–Hungarian. The former model performs better because the source and the target language share more typological characteristics like rich morphology, free word order, pro drop etc. even though they belong to different language families. Moreover, the PDT/PTG annotation scheme utilizing a rich set of dependency relations as edge labels seems to perform much better than, e.g., EDS where edge labels are completely abstract.

Fortes of the PDT/PTG model:

- some aspects of the model are extremely rich,
- detailed classification and still efficient recognition of adjuncts and covert pronouns, including control, quasi-control, other coreference relations and existentially bound arguments,
- most analyses are easy to interpret.

Points that could be improved:

- important features were discarded in the PDT-to-PTG conversion,
- the *act* and *pat* argument relations are semantically empty (real thematic roles would be very much welcome),
- problems with some asymmetric coordinating structures (unreasonable contrast between e.g., *caus* and *reas*),
- too flat structures (e.g., the attachment of 'rhematizers' to the predicate instead of to what they modify).

Acknowledgements

This research was implemented with support provided by grants FK 125217 and PD 125216 of the National Research, Development and Innovation Office of Hungary financed under the FK 17 and PD 17 funding schemes.

References

Omri Abend and Ari Rappoport. 2013. UCCA: A semantics-based grammatical annotation scheme. In *Proceedings of the 10th International Conference on Computational Semantics (IWCS 2013) – Long Papers*, pages 1–12, Potsdam, Germany. Association for Computational Linguistics.

Lasha Abzianidze, Johan Bos, and Stephan Oepen. 2020. DRS at MRP 2020: Dressing up discourse representation structures as graphs. In *Proceedings of the CoNLL 2020 Shared Task: Cross-Framework Meaning Representation Parsing*, pages 23–32, Online. Association for Computational Linguistics.

Laura Banarescu, Claire Bonial, Shu Cai, Madalina Georgescu, Kira Griffitt, Ulf Hermjakob, Kevin Knight, Philipp Koehn, Martha Palmer, and Nathan Schneider. 2013. Abstract Meaning Representation for sembanking. In *Proceedings of the 7th Linguistic Annotation Workshop and Interoperability with Discourse*, pages 178–186, Sofia, Bulgaria. Association for Computational Linguistics.

Alexis Conneau, Kartikay Khandelwal, Naman Goyal, Vishrav Chaudhary, Guillaume Wenzek, Francisco Guzmán, Edouard Grave, Myle Ott, Luke Zettlemoyer, and Veselin Stoyanov. 2020. Unsupervised cross-lingual representation learning at scale. In *Proceedings of the 58th Annual Meeting of the Association for Computational Linguistics*, pages 8440–8451, Online. Association for Computational Linguistics.

Ann Copestake, Dan Flickinger, Carl Pollard, and Ivan Sag. 2005. Minimal recursion semantics: An introduction. *Reseach On Language And Computation*, 3:281–332.

Jacob Devlin, Ming-Wei Chang, Kenton Lee, and Kristina Toutanova. 2019. BERT: Pre-training of deep bidirectional transformers for language understanding. In *Proceedings of the 2019 Conference of the North American Chapter of the Association for Computational Linguistics: Human Language Technologies, Volume 1 (Long and Short Papers)*, pages 4171–4186, Minneapolis, Minnesota. Association for Computational Linguistics.

Dan Flickinger, Emily M. Bender, and Stephan Oepen. 2014. Towards an encyclopedia of compositional semantics: Documenting the interface of the English Resource Grammar. In *Proceedings of the Ninth International Conference on Language Resources and Evaluation (LREC'14)*, pages 875–881, Reykjavik, Iceland. European Language Resources Association (ELRA).

Dan Flickinger, Stephan Oepen, and Emily M. Bender. 2017. *Sustainable Development and Refinement of Complex Linguistic Annotations at Scale*, pages 353–377. Springer Netherlands, Dordrecht.

Katarína Gajdošová, Mária Šimková, and et al. 2016. Slovak dependency treebank. LINDAT/CLARIAH-CZ digital library at the Institute of Formal and Applied Linguistics (ÚFAL), Faculty of Mathematics and Physics, Charles University.

Jan Hajič, Eduard Bejček, Jaroslava Hlavacova, Marie Mikulová, Milan Straka, Jan Štěpánek, and Barbora Štěpánková. 2020. Prague dependency treebank - consolidated 1.0. In *Proceedings of the 12th Language Resources and Evaluation Conference*, pages 5208–5218, Marseille, France. European Language Resources Association.

Jan Hajič, Eva Hajičová, Jarmila Panevová, Petr Sgall, Ondřej Bojar, Silvie Cinková, Eva Fučíková, Marie Mikulová, Petr Pajas, Jan Popelka, Jiří Semecký, Jana Šindlerová, Jan Štěpánek, Josef Toman, Zdeňka Urešová, and Zdeněk Žabokrtský. 2012. Announcing Prague Czech-English Dependency Treebank 2.0. In *Proceedings of the Eighth International Conference on Language Resources and Evaluation (LREC'12)*, pages 3153–3160, Istanbul, Turkey. European Language Resources Association (ELRA).

Jan Hajič and Petr Zemánek. 2004. Prague arabic dependency treebank: Development in data and tools. In *In Proc. of the NEMLAR Intern. Conf. on Arabic Language Resources and Tools*, pages 110–117.

Junjie Hu, Sebastian Ruder, Aditya Siddhant, Graham Neubig, Orhan Firat, and Melvin Johnson. 2020. Xtreme: A massively multilingual multi-task benchmark for evaluating cross-lingual generalization. *CoRR*, abs/2003.11080.

Angelina Ivanova, Stephan Oepen, Lilja Øvrelid, and Dan Flickinger. 2012. Who did what to whom? a contrastive study of syntacto-semantic dependencies. In *Proceedings of the Sixth Linguistic Annotation Workshop*, pages 2–11, Jeju, Republic of Korea. Association for Computational Linguistics.

Hans Kamp and Uwe Reyle. 1993. *From Discourse to Logic: Introduction to Model-theoretic Semantics of Natural Language, Formal Logic and Discourse Representation Theory*, volume 42 of *Studies in Linguistics and Philosophy*. Springer, Dordrecht.

Dan Kondratyuk and Milan Straka. 2019. 75 languages, 1 model: Parsing Universal Dependencies universally. In *Proceedings of the 2019 Conference on Empirical Methods in Natural Language Processing and the 9th International Joint Conference on Natural Language Processing (EMNLP-IJCNLP)*, pages 2779–2795, Hong Kong, China. Association for Computational Linguistics.

Marie Mikulová, Alevtina Bémová, Jan Hajič, Eva Hajičová, Jiří Havelka, Veronika Kolářová, Lucie Kučová, Markéta Lopatková, Petr Pajas, Jarmila Panevová, Magda Razímová, Petr Sgall, Jan Štěpánek, Zdeňka Urešová, Kateřina Veselá, and Zdeněk Žabokrtský. 2006. Annotation on the tectogrammatical level in the prague dependency treebank. annotation manual. Technical Report 30, ÚFAL MFF UK, Prague, Czech Rep.

Marie Mikulová, Eduard Bejček, Jiří Mírovský, Anna Nedoluzhko, Jarmila Panevová, Lucie Poláková, Pavel Straňák, Magda Ševčíková, and Zdeněk Žabokrtský. 2013. From PDT 2.0 to PDT 3.0 (modifications and complements). Technical report, ÚFAL MFF UK, Prague, Czech Rep.

Yusuke Miyao, Stephan Oepen, and Daniel Zeman. 2014. In-house: An ensemble of pre-existing off-the-shelf parsers. In *Proceedings of the 8th International Workshop on Semantic Evaluation (SemEval 2014)*, pages 335–340, Dublin, Ireland. Association for Computational Linguistics.

Anna Nedoluzhko, Michal Novák, and Maciej Ogrodniczuk. 2018. PAWS: A multi-lingual parallel treebank with anaphoric relations. In *Proceedings of the First Workshop on Computational Models of Reference, Anaphora and Coreference*, pages 68–76, New Orleans, Louisiana. Association for Computational Linguistics.

Stephan Oepen, Omri Abend, Lasha Abzianidze, Johan Bos, Jan Hajic, Daniel Hershcovich, Bin Li, Tim O'Gorman, Nianwen Xue, and Daniel Zeman. 2020. MRP 2020: The second shared task on cross-framework and cross-lingual meaning representation parsing. In *Proceedings of the CoNLL 2020 Shared Task: Cross-Framework Meaning Representation Parsing*, pages 1–22, Online. Association for Computational Linguistics.

Carl Pollard and Ivan A. Sag. 1994. *Head-Driven Phrase Structure Grammar*. The University of Chicago Press, Chicago.

David Samuel and Milan Straka. 2020. ÚFAL at MRP 2020: Permutation-invariant semantic parsing in PERIN. In *Proceedings of the CoNLL 2020 Shared Task: Cross-Framework Meaning Representation Parsing*, pages 53–64, Online. Association for Computational Linguistics.

Petr Sgall, Eva Hajičová, and Jarmilla Panevová. 1986. *The Meaning of the Sentence in Its Semantic and Pragmatic Aspects*. Reidel, Dordrecht.

Qianhui Wu, Zijia Lin, Börje F. Karlsson, Biqing Huang, and Jian-Guang Lou. 2020. Unitrans : Unifying model transfer and data transfer for cross-lingual named entity recognition with unlabeled data. In *Proceedings of the Twenty-Ninth International Joint Conference on Artificial Intelligence, IJCAI-20*, pages 3926–3932. International Joint Conferences on Artificial Intelligence Organization. Main track.

Daniel Zeman and Jan Hajic. 2020. FGD at MRP 2020: Prague tectogrammatical graphs. In *Proceedings of the CoNLL 2020 Shared Task: Cross-Framework Meaning Representation Parsing*, pages 33–39, Online. Association for Computational Linguistics.

Theoretical and Practical Issues in the Semantic Annotation of Four Indigenous Languages

Jens E. L. Van Gysel [1], Meagan Vigus[1], Lukas Denk [1], Andrew Cowell[2], Rosa Vallejos[1], Tim O'Gorman[3], and William Croft[1]

[1]Department of Linguistics, University of New Mexico
[2]Department of Linguistics, University of Colorado, Boulder
[3]Thorn

{jelvangysel,mvigus, ldenk,rvallejos,wcroft}@unm.edu,
tim.ogorman@wearethorn.org, james.cowell@colorado.edu

Abstract

Computational resources such as semantically annotated corpora can play an important role in enabling speakers of indigenous minority languages to participate in government, education, and other domains of public life in their own language. However, many languages – mainly those with small native speaker populations and without written traditions – have little to no digital support. One hurdle in creating such resources is that for many languages, few speakers would be capable of annotating texts – a task which requires literacy and some linguistic training – and that these experts' time is typically in high demand for language planning work. This paper assesses whether typologically trained non-speakers of an indigenous language can feasibly perform semantic annotation using Uniform Meaning Representations, thus allowing for the creation of computational materials without putting further strain on community resources.[1]

1 Introduction

Over the last few decades, there has been a call to enable speakers of indigenous minority languages to participate in government, education, and other domains of public life in their own language. Computational resources can play an important role in such efforts (Probst et al., 2002). For example, semantically annotated corpora for minority languages can be used for information extraction to obtain situational awareness in disaster situations (Griffitt et al., 2018), to link unstructured text in various languages to structured knowledge bases (Zhang and Rettinger, 2014), and as scaffolding for machine translation into these languages . As of 2019, only 1705 out of the 7795 languages in Simons and Thomas (2019), 22%, had any digital support. Even for languages with large native speaker populations and considerable political standing such as Farsi, computational resources are often limited (Feely et al., 2014).

The limited availability of (digital) data in such minority languages is only one hurdle to the creation of computational resources. Wherever data are available, they need to be provided with semantic annotations in order to be made maximally useful for the purposes described above.

Semantic annotation allows unstructured text to be linked to representations such as Abstract Meaning Representations (AMR, Banarescu et al., 2013) or Discourse Representation Structures (DRS, Kamp and Reyle, 2013; Bos et al., 2017). Such annotation schemes have become more cross-linguistically informed over the years. The DARPA Low Resource Languages for Emerging Incidents project (LORELEI), for one, has conducted shared annotation tasks with languages such as Tagalog, Yoruba and Somali (Griffitt et al., 2018). The Uniform Meaning Representation project, on the other hand, aims to make English-based AMR cross-linguistically applicable (Van Gysel et al., 2021).

In practice, however, current annotation workflows have little chance of being applied to truly "no-resource" languages. Semantic annotation is typically done by speakers of the target language, as it is assumed that (native) speaker intuitions are necessary to make judgments required for semantic annotation. This may be feasible for "low-resource" languages with millions of speakers such as Oromo, Tigrinya, Uyghur, and Ukrainian – the "incident languages" in Griffitt et al. (2018). For many others, including most of the 1500 languages with fewer than 1000 speakers (Eberhard et al., 2020), such annotators are unlikely to be available for several reasons (see section 2). This paper therefore has two main goals. Firstly, it assesses whether the structure of UMR indeed makes it scalable to languages with a different typological profile than traditionally well-represented languages in NLP such as English and Mandarin. Secondly, it assesses whether

[1]The sixth author was affiliated with the University of Massachusetts Amherst at the time this work was done.

Proceedings of the Joint 15th Linguistic Annotation Workshop (LAW) and 3rd Designing Meaning Representations (DMR) Workshop, pages 12–22
November, 2021.

non-speakers of an indigenous language trained in typological linguistics can successfully perform UMR semantic annotation of such languages based on morpheme-level glosses, utterance-level free translations, grammars, and dictionaries.

Specifically, we present quantitative results of two annotation experiments using UMR to annotate texts in Kukama (Tupían, Peru), and Arapaho (Algonquian, US), and qualitative results of initial annotation efforts with Sanapaná (Enlhet-Enenlhet, Paraguay) and Navajo (Athabaskan, US). These four languages were chosen because (1) they represent a range of resource availability from no-resource (Sanapaná) to low-resource (Arapaho, see Sections 2.1-2.4), (2) they are typologically diverse, representing more isolating (Kukama), agglutinating (Sanapaná), and polysynthetic (Arapaho, Navajo) types, and (3) co-authors of this paper have significant expertise in them. In section 2, the advantages of a workflow using linguistically trained non-speakers as annotators are laid out, and its necessity is illustrated through sociolinguistic sketches of the four languages at hand. Section 3 introduces UMR. Section 4 presents an overview of theoretical issues relating to the UMR guidelines encountered during the annotation of these four languages. Sections 5-6 present the inter-annotator agreement and adjudication results of the Kukama and Arapaho annotation experiments. Section 7 presents an overview of difficulties with the annotation workflow used in these two experiments.

2 Limitations on current semantic annotation procedures

Regardless of how large a corpus is available and how typologically informed an annotation scheme is, trained and qualified annotators are vital to successful annotation. These are often hard to come by in low-resource language contexts. Linguists working on such languages have the training required to familiarize themselves with semantic values and concepts used by annotation schemes. Since they are often still in the process of studying the language, however, their semantic judgments may be less than reliable. Native speakers can provide the most accurate interpretations of the meanings of forms in their language. From this point of view, they make "better" annotators. However, they vary with respect to various "literacies".

According to Eberhard et al. (2020), 3982 of the world's languages – slightly over half – have a writing system. However, only 15-20% of languages have an actual written tradition (Borin, 2009). Therefore, native speaker consultants often have limited literacy in their own language, although they may have literacy in regional or national linguae francae. Many low-resource languages are spoken in remote areas where people may not yet have easy access to or familiarity with digital technology. They are also likely to have more limited access to formal linguistics training than the national societies surrounding them.

In contexts of advanced language shift (which many indigenous language-speaking communities face), these factors may form correlated continua, and may be related to age. There may be a continuum of multilingualism so that younger speakers are more likely to be dominant in a lingua franca, while older generations are near-monolingual in the local language. Similarly, the speakers most fluent in an endangered language are likely to have gone through less formal education, be less literate, and be less comfortable with digital tools.

These factors conspire to create a situation where few speakers of low-resource indigenous languages are currently well-equipped to conduct semantic annotation projects on their language. Furthermore, wherever there are qualified local language experts, their time is typically in high demand for language planning projects such as curriculum development and teaching, which are typically given higher priority in language maintenance efforts. The following brief sociolinguistic sketches of Kukama, Arapaho, Sanapaná, and Navajo illustrate these points.

2.1 Kukama (Tupian, Peru)

Among the Kukama, most of the around 1,000 native speakers are over 60, and live scattered across many remote villages, limiting their opportunities to use the language with each other. Many have not received formal education in either Kukama or Spanish. Adults in their 40s and 50s may have passive knowledge of Kukama. Through revitalization projects, young people have started learning Kukama as a heritage language and training as bilingual teachers. Several orthographies have been proposed, but the implementation and consolidation of an official one is still ongoing. It is unlikely that the heritage speakers have sufficient command of the language to perform semantic annotation by themselves, or that the elderly native speakers can be sufficiently trained in linguistics to do so.

2.2 Arapaho (Algonquian, USA)

Among the Northern Arapaho (Wyoming), there are about 100 native speakers, all over 65, only a handful of whom have strong literacy skills in Arapaho. Several hundred have native passive knowledge, and several hundred second language learners exist, though only a handful of younger people have acquired significant (but non-fluent) productive knowledge. Some second language learners with good literacy and technology skills could do annotation using the existing semantically labeled and translated corpus, but may need to collaborate with native speakers to capture all nuances.

This context may be better described as low-resource than no-resource, and is one of the few indigenous language contexts where annotation might happen without direct participation of a linguist. A linguist would likely still have to train annotators. Even here, the very small numbers of literate native speakers and reasonably productive second-language speakers poses issues: there are high demands on the time of both groups to engage in basic teaching and curriculum development.

2.3 Sanapaná (Enlhet-Enenlhet, Paraguay)

Sanapaná is spoken by around 1000 people in Paraguay. There is still intergenerational transmission in two communities. In the other Sanapaná communities, most people have shifted to Paraguayan Guaraní or Spanish for daily communication. Even where children still learn Sanapaná in the home, they go through formal education in Spanish and Guaraní, and tend to be more literate in these national languages than in Sanapaná. Young people often have smartphones, but few people have experience working with computers. No native speakers have formal training in linguistics, so it is unlikely that even most of the younger generation of native speakers would be able to perform semantic annotation independently.

2.4 Navajo (Athabaskan, USA)

With around 170.000 speakers, Navajo is the least endangered Native North American language. Although younger generations are becoming less fluent, their language and culture are part of curricula in high schools and colleges across the reservation (e.g. Diné College; Navajo Technical University), and various pedagogical and linguistic materials are available to promote research on the language. Furthermore, the University of New Mexico offers a graduate degree in Navajo Linguistics and employs native speakers as professors and instructors. Navajo scholars from this environment would be able to do semantic annotation of their language.

2.5 Takeaways

For communities whose language is threatened, the role of dictionaries, teaching materials, and text collections in language development projects may seem more obvious than that of semantic annotation. Therefore, the few speakers who would be qualified for annotation (multilingual, literate, linguistically trained native speakers; field linguists with some degree of proficiency in the language), as well as speech communities as a whole, may prefer to spend their limited time and resources in ways that contribute more directly to these tangible goals. An annotation workflow where non-speakers of the language (e.g. research assistants who are unable to spend time in the field) can do semantic annotation would facilitate the creation of computational resources without drawing on the limited and valuable time of local experts.

3 Uniform Meaning Representation (UMR)

Uniform Meaning Representation (UMR) is a semantic annotation scheme designed to meet the needs of a wide range of NLP applications which require intermediate meaning representations. UMR is based on Abstract Meaning Representation (Banarescu et al., 2013). AMR captures the meanings of natural language sentences as single-rooted, directed, node- and edge-labelled graphs, and focuses on predicate-argument structure, named entities, and word sense disambiguation. It was mainly designed for the annotation of English. The usefulness of AMR and its amenability to machine learning have been repeatedly proven (Cai and Lam, 2020; Li et al., 2020).

3.1 Goals of UMR annotation

Potential downstream uses of UMR include applications of interest to the NLP community, and applications of use to speech communities. One the one hand, the use of AMR as an intermediate representation for e.g. inferencing for question answering (Sachan and Xing, 2016; Kapanipathi et al., 2021) and human-robot interaction (Bastianelli et al., 2013) has been proven. So far, inferencing from AMRs has necessarily remained limited to sentence-level information, or has been based on ad-hoc meaning representations spanning multiple sentence-level AMRs. UMR's document-level structure (see Section 3.2) is expected to aid such applications. Supervised machine learning systems for morphological analysis can be trained on small datasets (as small as 3000 annotated word tokens, Moeller and Hulden, 2018; Moeller, 2021) collected during language documentation. Application of such methodologies to semantic annotation could allow for the expansion of such downstream applications to low-resource language contexts.

On the other hand, UMR-annotated corpora would be useful to more typical language documentation endeavors. UMR is designed as a "road map" to help research teams develop PropBank-style frame files during the process of annotation. The annotation process may thus help enrich lexicons with argument structure information (Croft and Sutton, 2017). The inclusion of such information in lexicons can facilitate the learning of the language by new speakers, especially in contexts of advanced language endangerment where most learners are adults and have limited opportunities to acquire usage patterns through immersion.

3.2 Structure of UMR

UMR nodes represent concepts (e.g. word senses, named entity types, attribute values), while edges between nodes represent relations between those concepts (e.g. participant roles, attribute types such as aspect, person, and number, and general semantic relations). Sample UMRs for Kukama sentences can be found in the supplementary materials.

UMR builds on AMR by extending it to new semantic domains, such as aspect, coreference, and temporal and modal dependencies (Van Gysel et al., 2021). Most semantic domains are captured in a sentence-level graph structure, while co-reference, temporal relations, and modality are captured in a document-level graph. This paper deals only with the sentence-level structure: we annotated (and calculated IAA for) predicate-argument structure, aspect, and other non-participant role relations within the phrase and the clause (e.g. possession, quantification). UMR specifications for these semantic domains can be found in Van Gysel et al. (2021).[2] Temporal and modal relations were not annotated, nor was cross-sentence co-reference. UMR also aims to extend AMR to new languages by basing its structure soundly on insights of linguistic typology (Van Gysel et al., 2019), and by making its annotation workflows amenable to low-resource contexts often encountered in work with the world's endangered languages (Vigus et al., 2020).

One way in which UMR was made flexible for low-resource languages is a roadmap approach (Van Gysel et al., 2021). Languages without existing computational resources start at "Stage 0". Annotation here operates at the word level, so that annotators do not have to morphologically decompose words - they do, however, have to consider the semantics of inflectional morphology. Since different semantic domains annotated by UMR are somewhat independent, annotators for "Stage 0" languages may choose to only annotate categories for which they are confident in their analysis - likely categories expressed by independent words. They may, for instance, choose to annotate argument structure and tense, but not aspect. Annotators are more likely to use coarse-grained categories on annotation lattices (Van Gysel et al., 2019). "Stage 1" of UMR annotation is based on the existence of a lexicon with PropBank-style frame files and advanced semantic analysis of the language. There is somewhat of a continuum between the two stages: as semantic analysis of the language advances, more categories will be able to be annotated, and they will be annotated at a more fine-grained level, moving the language closer to Stage 1. For the annotation task described in this paper, annotators used Stage 0 UMR as the languages did not have existing lexicons with frame files.

4 UMR Applied to Four Indigenous Languages

The UMR annotation scheme and its guidelines were designed with cross-lingual variation in mind. We tested UMR on narrative texts in two indigenous languages, Navajo and Sanapaná. 107 lines of Sanapaná text were annotated by the first author, amounting to 332 Sanapaná words and 600 words in the free Spanish translation. 261 lines of Navajo text were annotated by the third author, amounting to 2044 Navajo words and 5020 words in the free English translation. In addition, issues that arose in the Kukama and Arapaho experiments (Sections 5-6) also tested the UMR annotation scheme. UMR adds semantic structure to AMR annotation, specifically aspect, general participant roles, quantifi-

[2]The current UMR guidelines can be found at `https://umr4nlp.github.io/web`.

cation, scope, and temporal and modal structure (including polarity). We focus on the annotation of those categories here.

4.1 Extensions to Current UMR

Many semantic categories remain unannotated in the current version of UMR (or standard AMR). The annotators of the four indigenous languages encountered some of these categories, even in the short texts they annotated. These categories are targets for future development of UMR.

These categories pertain to discourse-level phenomena, including interactional categories. UMR includes coreference relations to entities and events. However, it does not annotate the relative discourse prominence of referents. Arapaho partly encodes discourse prominence through a grammatical distinction between proximate and obviative noun phrases. UMR does not currently annotate coreference between a pronoun and a section of prior discourse (also known as "discourse deixis") either, as with the Sanapaná anaphoric construction in (1), where *apkeleyvoma enyatav'a* 'how our ancestors lived/the lives of our ancestors' is equated to a whole paragraph of preceding discourse.

(1) *ahlta=n-t-em-ak*
PHOD=2/3F-COP-PST/HAB-V2.NFUT
apk-el-eyv-om-a
2/3M-DSTR-live-PST/HAB-NMLZ
en-yata-v'a
1PL-grandfather-PL
'That is how our ancestors lived.'

Another category not currently annotated is clause-level information structure, specifically the distinction between topic-comment, thetic and identificational (focus) sentences (Lambrecht, 1994). The last sentence type includes focus operators such as 'just' and 'only' as in (2) from Sanapaná.

(2)
apk-el-v-ay'-aye=hlta
2/3M-DSTR-arrive-PST/HAB-V1.NFUT=PHOD
vanhla' valayo sokhoye'
only Paraguayan at.first
'Only the Paraguayans arrived at first.'

Finally, interactional grammatical constructions such as speech act constructions and vocatives occurred in reported speech in the narratives.

UMR has adopted AMR's large set of named entity categories. However, the set needs to be extended to include named entities not found in large industrialized societies. In the annotated texts, named entities were found referring to clans (Navajo), age-grade societies (Arapaho) and supernatural beings (Kukama).

4.2 The Sentence-Level to Document-Level Annotation Pipeline

Issues in the application of UMR to specific constructions in the four languages raised more general issues in semantic annotation across languages.

The first issue is the relation between sentence-level and document-level annotation (across sentences). The standard pipeline is to annotate individual sentences before document-level annotation. Aspect is annotated at the sentence level, while modal dependencies are annotated at the document level, as hypothetical "worlds" or mental spaces (Fauconnier, 1985) containing unrealized events, that may be referred to across sentences. For unrealized events, such as the Arapaho imperatives in (3), we annotate aspect at the sentence level as the event would be realized in the mental space of the speaker's command.

(3) *wohei cei-te'e be! cei-koohu!*
okay to.here-this.side friend to.here-run
'Wohei come this way, friend! Run this way!'

However, the annotation of the mental space as the unrealized space of the speaker's command is done at the document level. Following this standard pipeline means that document-level context is not considered during sentence-level annotation, which is somewhat counterintuitive to linguist annotators.

4.3 Semantic Annotation and Lexical Semantic Differences

Another broad issue arose with the annotation of general participant roles, which are used for arguments of predicates before frame files are developed for a language. This allows for the annotation of basic clause structure at the outset, since developing frame files for a lexicon is a long-term task. The general participant roles are defined in UMR by broad semantic event classes: mental events have Experiencer and Stimulus roles, motion/location events have Theme and Location/Goal/Source roles, change of state events have Actor and Undergoer roles, and transfer events have a Recipient role as well as Agent and Theme roles. But some roles vary within and across languages with respect to the agentivity of participants.

For example, the subject of 'stay' is annotated as Actor in UMR since the subject of English *stay* is more active/agentive than *be (at)*. Kukama *yuti* is translated as'stay', but is more stative, so Actor is not an appropriate label. Conversely, the subject of 'know' is annotated as Experiencer in UMR, because the subject of English *know* is not agentive. The Arapaho verb *he'in-* is typically loosely glossed 'know'; however, it can also mean 'find out about' and 'remember, keep in mind', and it can be used in imperatives as 'know/remember it!'. This verb could be better glossed as 'actively remember/understand and act thereon' and involves agency on the part of the subject. In contrast, Arapaho *hee3obee-* means 'know' or 'feel' in the sense of information acquired via sensory input of any kind, and the subject is not agentive.

The first issue here is that participant roles are event-specific, and fixing a general participant role for events such as 'stay' or 'know' is arbitrary to some extent. But the cross-lingual issue is that events are categorized or conceptualized in different ways in different languages: Kukama *yuti* is construed as less active than English *stay*, and Arapaho has two different verbs covering some of the same set of events as English *know*, but not precisely. Semantic annotation of certain grammatical categories, including participant roles and aspect, is closely tied to lexical semantics. We cannot assume that verbs in other languages are semantically identical to their English translation equivalents. Yet research in lexical semantic typology is much less far advanced than in the semantic typology of grammatical categories (Koptjevskaja-Tamm and Vanhove, 2012).

A solution is the development of verb-specific frame files, with enough semantic detail to capture differences as well as similarities in meaning across languages. As these verb-specific frame files are developed, every verb-specific participant role will be linked to the relevant general participant role previously used in this language, so as to not render "Stage 0" participant role annotations obsolete. As noted above, that is a major task, and in the meantime, general participant role annotation must be taken with a large grain of salt.

4.4 Preserving Language-Particular Semantic Subtleties

Finally, a general observation of the language experts that adjudicated the annotation experiments described in sections 5 - 6 is a concern that cross-lingual semantic annotation may be too coarse-grained to capture important semantic subtleties encoded in particular languages. For example, in Arapaho, *heyeih-* is a prefix meaning 'almost [to a location], almost [finished], etc.' with the action still ongoing and the assumption that it will be or at least could be completed successfully. In contrast, *too-* is a prefix meaning 'almost [did it, but not quite], 'almost [but just missed], etc.' with the action now ended but unsuccessful. English *almost* does not distinguish these senses, and a semantic representation based on *almost* does not capture the meaning of each Arapaho translation equivalent. We suggest extending the idea of lattices of semantic values proposed by Van Gysel et al. (2019) to semantic categories such as that expressed by *almost*, *heyeih-* and *too-*, to capture language-particular semantic subtleties while retaining cross-lingual comparability.

5 Annotation Experiment 1: Kukama

5.1 Annotation procedure and materials

60 lines of Kukama text were taken from a traditional narrative collected by the fifth author of this paper, a linguist with extensive knowledge of Kukama, but little UMR experience. This dataset amounted to 223 words of Kukama text, and 360 words in the English free translation. These data were annotated according to the current UMR guidelines (Van Gysel et al., 2021) by the first and second author of this paper, both of whom have extensive experience with UMR and training in typological and/or descriptive linguistics, but little to no previous knowledge of Kukama.

The first ten lines were annotated by both annotators separately as a trial, after which they convened and adjudicated their disagreements. This adjudicated version was then discussed with the expert linguist. The following 50 lines were then annotated by both annotators independently, and constitute the sample over which inter-annotator agreement was calculated. Annotators took an average of 5.8 and 6.7 minutes per line for these 50 lines, respectively. Annotators had at their disposal a transcription of the Kukama text, a morpheme breakdown, morpheme-level glosses in English and Spanish, and intonation unit-level free translations in English and Spanish. They could also draw on a Kukama grammar (Vallejos, 2016), and a dictionary (Vallejos and Amías, 2015).

5.2 Evaluation procedure

Inter-annotator agreement (precision, recall, and F-score) between the two annotators was calculated using Smatch (Cai and Knight, 2013). Two sets of agreement scores are presented in section 5.3: the first one represents the exact agreement between the sets of annotations, while the second one represents the "compatibility" of the annotations on the typological lattices in which the UMR annotation categories are organized; see Van Gysel et al. (2019). If one annotator chooses a fine-grained value (e.g. Performance, for aspect) that is a subvalue of the value chosen by the other annotator (e.g. Process), this triple counts as a disagreement for the set of identity scores, but as an agreement for the set of compatibility scores.

In addition to IAA scores, we present accuracy scores for both annotators. A gold standard annotation was constructed by discussing the annotation of each of the 50 lines of data with the language expert. First, the two annotators established an adjudicated graph for each line between themselves, which was subsequently adjusted as deemed necessary by the language expert. Both annotators' original graphs were then compared with this established gold standard using Smatch. Once again, both identity and compatibility scores are reported.

5.3 Annotation results

The IAA scores of the Kukama annotation experiment can be seen in the first two lines of Table 1. IAA is rather high, approaching the 0.8 threshold for precision, recall, and F-score. Treating compatible-but-not-identical annotations as agreement increases precision by 0.01, but does not affect recall and F-score. This result can be interpreted as indicating that both annotators were able to apply the UMR annotation guidelines to Kukama in rather systematic and consistent ways, and were able to use annotation categories at the same level of granularity, even though neither of them had significant previous knowledge of the morphosyntactic or morphosemantic characteristics of Kukama.

Lines 3-6 show both annotators' agreement with the gold standard established after adjudication with the language expert. In both cases, precision surpasses the threshold of 0.8, while recall approaches it, and F-score surpasses it for one annotator. The compatibility scores show only a marginal increase in F-score, and only for one annotator.

	Precision	**Recall**	**F-score**
Ann. 1 - Ann. 2 Identity	0.77	0.79	0.78
Ann. 1 - Ann. 2 Compatibility	0.78	0.79	0.78
Ann. 1 - Gold Identity	0.81	0.76	0.78
Ann. 1 - Gold Compatibility	0.81	0.76	0.78
Ann. 2 - Gold Identity	0.85	0.78	0.81
Ann. 2 - Gold Compatibility	0.85	0.78	0.82

Table 1: Kukama IAA and Accuracy scores

6 Annotation Experiment 2: Arapaho

6.1 Annotation procedure and materials

35 lines of Arapaho text were taken from a traditional narrative collected by the fourth author of this paper, a linguist with extensive knowledge of Arapaho. This dataset amounted to 128 words of Arapaho text, and 310 words in the English free translation. The data were annotated by the same two annotators as experiment 1, following the same procedure. The first 10 lines were again used as a pilot, followed by annotation of 25 lines for the purposes of IAA calculation. Annotators took an average of 11 and 8.2 minutes per line for these 25 lines, respectively. Annotators had similar resources at their disposal as for Kukama: transcription, morpheme breakdown, and morpheme and sentence-level translations in English. They could draw on an online Arapaho-English lexical database (Cowell, 2021), and a grammar (Cowell and Moss Sr, 2008).

6.2 Evaluation procedure

Inter-annotator agreement was calculated in the same way as described for Kukama in 5.2, and is reported in Table 2. Again, gold standard annotations were constructed for each line by first adjudicating between the two main annotators, and subsequently discussing every annotation with the language expert, who adjusted this adjudicated annotation as necessary. Both for IAA calculation and comparison with the gold standard, Smatch was used.

6.3 Annotation results

The IAA scores of the Arapaho experiment are listed in the first two lines of Table 2. The scores for identity are somewhat lower than those for Kukama, even though they are still in the mid 0.7 range.

	Precision	Recall	F-score
Ann. 1 - Ann. 2 Identity	0.79	0.73	0.76
Ann. 1 - Ann. 2 Compatibility	0.81	0.74	0.77
Ann. 1 - Gold Identity	0.79	0.74	0.76
Ann. 1 - Gold Compatibility	0.80	0.75	0.77
Ann. 2 - Gold Identity	0.90	0.92	0.91
Ann. 2 - Gold Compatibility	0.90	0.92	0.91

Table 2: Arapaho IAA and Accuracy scores

Considering compatible annotations as agreements has a more pronounced impact on IAA than in Kukama, bringing them up into the same 0.8-region as Kukama IAA. This somewhat lower agreement score, at least before factoring in compatibility, together with the higher average annotation time per line, indicates that the annotators had more difficulty annotating Arapaho than Kukama and were more cautious, opting for more coarse-grained annotation values more often. Nevertheless, the fairly high precision, recall, and F-scores show that both annotators were again able to apply the UMR guidelines to Arapaho in consistent ways.

Lines 3-6 of Table 2 again show the Smatch scores comparing each annotator's initial result with the final gold standard annotation. Once again, accuracy is high, with scores approaching 0.80 for one annotator, and surpassing this threshold for the other. This discrepancy may be at least partially explained by the fact that the higher-scoring annotator took significantly more time per line – more thorough consultation of the reference materials may, unsurprisingly, correspond to higher annotation accuracy.

7 Discussion: Implications for Annotation Workflows

This paper set out to assess whether a typologically trained linguist can semantically annotate languages they do not speak or otherwise have expertise in, in order to facilitate the creation of computational resources for indigenous languages without having to further burden field linguists or communities. The IAA scores for the experiments discussed in sections 5-6 suggest that this is relatively possible: we were able to reach fairly high agreement between annotators, and between each annotator and an expert in the target language, with a minimal amount of practice. In other words, Kukama and Arapaho morpheme-by-morpheme glosses and free translations, together with reference materials such as a dictionary and grammar, allowed annotators to interpret the meanings of sentences in these languages fairly accurately. However, the types of disagreements between annotators, and between annotators and language experts, point towards a number of ways in which there is still room for improvement regarding the workflow described here.

On the one hand, a fair number of disagreements between annotators, and inaccuracies on their part, stemmed from inconsistencies and/or gaps in the available materials. For example, in the Kukama sentence in Figure 1, the Spanish and English free translations are not internally consistent – the English translation does not contain the word 'almost', and in the Spanish version, the word for 'wanted' is between brackets to indicate the wanting is implied. Even though Vallejos (2016) details the use of *iyara* as both an adverb meaning 'almost' and a desiderative marker, these inconsistent translations would lead annotators to make different decisions.

Issues like these are likely to be quite frequent when working from materials collected in language documentation projects. These materials are often collected over multiple years and by multiple people, and analyses often change throughout these periods and are not always automatically updated in materials collected earlier.

Other disagreements and inaccuracies stemmed from notational and content-based common practice in language description and grammar writing. For instance, meanings of derived stems or compounds are often not transparently clear from the sum of the glosses of the component parts: the Kukama stem *itsi-kaka* is glossed in the annotated text as 'be scared-REC', but is listed in Vallejos (2016, p. 202) as one of a set of verbs with which the reciprocal marker takes on an inchoative function ('become scared'). Since the transcriber/translator of the text opted for 'idiomatic' translations on the utterance-level rather than a more 'literal' translation ('my daughters call scared,' rather than something like 'my daughters call, having become scared'), such nuances of meaning slip between the cracks of the morpheme-level gloss and the utterance-level translation. This lost information can have important ramifications for annotation choices, in this case for the aspect annotation of this predicate.

Line ID: 2 go

Words	tsamɨmɨrakunia	karuaranu	muna	iyaratsuriay
Morphemes	tsa- mɨmɨrakunia	karuara -nu	muna	iyara -tsuriay
Morpheme Gloss(English)	1F.SF- daugther.woman	aquatic.being -PL.F	steal	almost -PAS3
Morpheme Gloss(Spanish)	1F.SF- hijademujer	ser.acuático -PL.F	robar	casi -PAS3

Free(en) the karuaras wanted to steal my daugther

Free(es) los yacurunas (quisieron) casi roban a mi hija

Figure 1: Kukama, Line 2 of annotated text

Regarding content, many Arapaho noun incorporation and associated motion constructions were difficult to annotate, since UMR guidelines for event and participant identification rest on syntactic tests that are not always discussed in detail in reference grammars, such as the ability of a verb with incorporated object to co-occur with an independent NP co-referential with this object, (Vigus et al., 2020).

Even though it is unrealistic to expect field linguists to gear their grammar-writing practices specifically towards creating materials with maximal usefulness for semantic annotation, there may be ways in which the impact of these issues can be limited. For example, the issue of meanings slipping between the cracks of morpheme-level glosses and utterance-level translations could partially be remedied by providing an intermediate level of granularity in translations – translations at the word level. Many field linguists provide the texts they collect with word-level translations in the early stages of their analysis (before they have a thorough understanding of the morphological structure of the language). For certain types of languages (e.g. languages with complex and irregular morphophonemics, or languages that make extensive use of derivation and compounding with idiosyncratic semantics for word-formation), linguists may continue producing these word-level translations in their databases even at more advanced stages of analysis. These word-level translations are usually not exported when texts are published or cited as examples in linguistics publications. However, providing them to semantic annotators would be likely to significantly improve inter-annotator agreement and overall accuracy.

For those aspects of descriptive linguistic practice which are harder to influence, it may be easier to compromise on the side of the annotation workflow. A workflow where annotators are given time to read a grammar of the language and familiarize themselves with its structure before annotating, rather than using the grammar only as a reference work to look up constructions and their functions in an ad-hoc way during annotation is likely to result in higher agreement and accuracy scores. And, rather than hoping that annotators can reach a high enough accuracy to establish gold standard annotations by themselves, allowing for consultation and adjudication with a language expert is likely to remain necessary.

8 Summary and conclusions

This paper has aimed to raise awareness among computational linguists that the languages currently treated in NLP research and shared tasks as low-resource languages, and especially no-resource languages lacking any digital presence to speak of, do not just present problems of scale in comparison to major world languages. They also present qualitatively different challenges, especially regarding the recruitment of qualified annotators. The numerous languages with small speaker numbers and limited resources, which are often spoken in more remote areas, pose unique challenges for creating digitally robust and cross-linguistically comparable semantic annotation projects. Nevertheless, this paper showed that workflows can be designed which allow for semantic annotation without placing an undue burden on the limited resources of native speaker communities. Semantically annotated corpora developed in this way, and computational resources derived from them, have the potential to both provide benefits to indigenous communities, and to allow us to progress in our understanding of lexical and grammatical semantics.

9 Ethical Considerations

In recent years and decades, indigenous and other scholars have cautioned against the "mining" of indigenous language data – the use of such data for research purposes without consultation with the community that speaks the language and without sharing benefits with that community. Even though this paper shows that non-speakers of a language can be recruited to do semantic annotation, we strongly recommend that such projects be designed and conducted in collaboration with community members.

References

Laura Banarescu, Claire Bonial, Shu Cai, Madalina Georgescu, Kira Griffitt, Ulf Hermjakob, Kevin Knight, Philipp Koehn, Martha Palmer, and Nathan Schneider. 2013. Abstract Meaning Representation for sembanking. In *Proceedings of the 7th Linguistic Annotation Workshop and Interoperability with Discourse*, pages 178–186, Sofia, Bulgaria. Association for Computational Linguistics.

Emanuele Bastianelli, Giuseppe Castellucci, Danilo Croce, and Roberto Basili. 2013. Textual inference and meaning representation in human robot interaction. In *Proceedings of the Joint Symposium on Semantic Processing. Textual Inference and Structures in Corpora*, pages 65–69, Trento, Italy.

Lars Borin. 2009. Linguistic resources for the languages of the world. Paper presented at the GF Summer School, Gothenburg, 26 August 2009.

Johan Bos, Valerio Basile, Kilian Evang, Noortje J Venhuizen, and Johannes Bjerva. 2017. The Groningen Meaning Bank. In *Handbook of Linguistic Annotation*, pages 463–496. Springer.

Deng Cai and Wai Lam. 2020. AMR parsing via graph-sequence iterative inference. In *Proceedings of the 58th Annual Meeting of the Association for Computational Linguistics*, pages 1290–1301, Online.

Shu Cai and Kevin Knight. 2013. "Smatch: An evaluation metric for semantic feature structures". In *"Proceedings of the 51st Annual Meeting of the Association for Computational Linguistics (Volume 2: Short Papers)"*, pages 748–752, Sofia, Bulgaria. Association for Computational Linguistics.

Andrew Cowell. 2021. Arapaho Lexical Database, Version 2021. Boulder, CO: University of Colorado. Available at https://verbs.colorado.edu/arapaho/public/view_search).

Andrew Cowell and Alonzo Moss Sr. 2008. *The Arapaho Language*. University Press of Colorado.

William Croft and Logan Sutton. 2017. Construction grammar and lexicography. In Patrick Hanks and Gilles-Maurice de Schryver, editors, *International Handbook of Modern Lexis and Lexicography*. Springer, Berlin.

David M Eberhard, Gary F. Simons, and Charles D. Fennig. 2020. "Ethnologue: Languages of the World. Twenty-third Edition". http://www.ethnologue.com.

Gilles Fauconnier. 1985. *Mental Spaces: Aspects of Meaning Construction in Natural Language*. Cambridge University Press, Cambridge.

Weston Feely, Mehdi Manshadi, Robert E Frederking, and Lori S Levin. 2014. The CMU METAL Farsi NLP approach. In *LREC*, pages 4052–4055.

Kira Griffitt, Jennifer Tracey, Ann Bies, and Stephanie Strassel. 2018. Simple semantic annotation and situation frames: Two approaches to basic text understanding in LORELEI. In *Proceedings of the Eleventh International Conference on Language Resources and Evaluation (LREC 2018)*.

Hans Kamp and Uwe Reyle. 2013. *From discourse to logic: Introduction to modeltheoretic semantics of natural language, formal logic and discourse representation theory*, volume 42. Springer Science & Business Media.

Pavan Kapanipathi, Ibrahim Abdelaziz, Srinivas Ravishankar, Salim Roukos, Alexander Gray, Ramón Fernandez Astudillo, Maria Chang, Cristina Cornelio, Saswati Dana, Achille Fokoue, Dinesh Garg, Alfio Gliozzo, Sairam Gurajada, Hima Karanam, Naweed Khan, Dinesh Khandelwal, Young-Suk Lee, Yunyao Li, Francois Luus, Ndivhuwo Makondo, Nandana Mihindukulasooriya, Tahira Naseem, Sumit Neelam, Lucian Popa, Revanth Gangi Reddy, Ryan Riegel, Gaetano Rossiello, Udit Sharma, G P Shrivatsa Bhargav, and Mo Yu. 2021. Leveraging Abstract Meaning Representation for knowledge base question answering. In *Findings of the Association for Computational Linguistics: ACL-IJCNLP 2021*, pages 3884–3894, Online. Association for Computational Linguistics.

Maria Koptjevskaja-Tamm and Martine Vanhove. 2012. New directions in lexical typology. *Linguistics, Special issue*, 50.3.

Knud Lambrecht. 1994. *Information Structure and Sentence Form. Topic, Focus, and the Mental Representation of Discourse Referents*. Cambridge University Press, Cambridge.

Xinjian Li, Siddharth Dalmia, Juncheng Li, Matthew Lee, Patrick Littell, Jiali Yao, Antonios Anastasopoulos, David R Mortensen, Graham Neubig, Alan W Black, et al. 2020. Universal phone recognition with a multilingual allophone system. In *ICASSP 2020-2020 IEEE International Conference on Acoustics, Speech and Signal Processing (ICASSP)*, pages 8249–8253. IEEE.

Sarah Moeller. 2021. *Integrating Machine Learning into Language Documentation and Description*. Ph.D. thesis, University of Colorado at Boulder.

Sarah Moeller and Mans Hulden. 2018. Automatic glossing in a low-resource setting for language documentation. In *Proceedings of the Workshop on Computational Modeling of Polysynthetic Languages*, pages 84–93, Santa Fe, New Mexico, USA. Association for Computational Linguistics.

Katharina Probst, Lori Levin, Erik Peterson, Alon Lavie, and Jaime Carbonell. 2002. MT for minority languages using elicitation-based learning of syntactic transfer rules. *Machine Translation*, 17(4):245–270.

Mrinmaya Sachan and Eric Xing. 2016. Machine comprehension using rich semantic representations. In *Proceedings of the 54th Annual Meeting of the Association for Computational Linguistics (Volume 2: Short Papers)*, pages 486–492.

Gary Simons and Abbey Thomas. 2019. Assessing digital language support as a factor in language vitality. *6th International Conference on Language Documentation and Conservation. University of Hawai'i at Manoa, 28 February - 3 March 2019.*

Rosa Vallejos. 2016. *A Grammar of Kukama-Kukamiria: A language from the Amazon*. Brill.

Rosa Vallejos and Rosa Amías. 2015. *Diccionario kukama-kukamiria castellano*. FORMABIAP.

Jens E. L. Van Gysel, Meagan Vigus, Jayeol Chun, Kenneth Lai, Sarah Moeller, Jiarui Yao, Tim O'Gorman, Andrew Cowell, William Croft, Jan Huang, Chu-Ren Hajič, James H. Martin, Stephan Oepen, Martha Palmer, James Pustejovsky, Rosa Vallejos, and Nianwen Xue. 2021. Designing a uniform meaning representation for natural language processing. *Künstliche Intelligenz*, pages 1–18.

Jens E. L. Van Gysel, Meagan Vigus, Pavlina Kalm, Sook-kyung Lee, Michael Regan, and William Croft. 2019. Cross-linguistic semantic annotation: Reconciling the language-specific and the universal. In *Proceedings of the First International Workshop on Designing Meaning Representations*, pages 1–14, Florence, Italy. Association for Computational Linguistics.

Meagan Vigus, Jens E. L. Van Gysel, Tim O'Gorman, Andrew Cowell, Rosa Vallejos, and William Croft. 2020. Cross-lingual annotation: a road map for low- and no-resource languages. In *Proceedings of the Second International Workshop on Designing Meaning Representations*, pages 30–40, Barcelona Spain (online). Association for Computational Linguistics.

Lei Zhang and Achim Rettinger. 2014. X-LiSA: Cross-lingual semantic annotation. *Proceedings of the VLDB Endowment*, 7(13):1693–1696.

Representing Implicit Positive Meaning of Negated Statements in AMR

Katharina Stein **Lucia Donatelli**
Department of Language Science and Technology
Saarland Informatics Campus
Saarland University, Germany
{kstein, donatelli}@coli.uni-saarland.de

Abstract

Abstract Meaning Representation (AMR) has become popular for representing the meaning of natural language in graph structures. However, AMR does not represent scope information, posing a problem for its overall expressivity and specifically for drawing inferences from negated statements. This is the case with so-called "positive interpretations" of negated statements, in which implicit positive meaning is identified by inferring the opposite of the negation's focus. In this work, we investigate how potential positive interpretations (PPIs) can be represented in AMR. We propose a logically motivated AMR structure for PPIs that makes the focus of negation explicit and sketch an initial proposal for a systematic methodology to generate this more expressive structure.

1 Introduction

There has been a recent and growing interest in representing the meaning of natural language in graph structures. One semantic framework that has become popular is the semantic representation language of Abstract Meaning Representation (AMR) (Banarescu et al., 2013). AMRs are attractive for their ease of readability, and they are intuitive representations due to their focus on predicate-argument structures. Additionally, annotating meaning with graph structures is easier than following many traditional formal semantic frameworks (Bos, 2016) and often allows for increased expressive capacity.

An important application for meaning representations are inference tasks that play a crucial role in many NLP tasks such as information extraction and question answering (Abzianidze and Bos, 2019). Such inference tasks are where AMR often falls short due to its lack of precise scope representation. For example, from (1-a) it can be inferred that *"The boy stole the money"* and hence the boy is a thief; from (1-b), it can be inferred that *"The boy did not steal the money"* and is likely not a thief.

(1) a. The boy stole the money yesterday.
b. The boy did not steal the money yesterday.

Yet, the information provided by the scope of the negation alone is not sufficient when drawing inferences. Negated statements can convey implicit positive meaning, or Potential Positive Interpretation (PPI) (Blanco and Moldovan, 2011), that is usually understood intuitively by humans. For example, an intuitive interpretation for (1-b) is that "***someone other than*** *the boy stole the money yesterday*" (and the boy is not a thief). It could also be inferred, however, that "*the boy stole* ***something other than*** *money*," (and is still a thief) depending on whether *the boy* or *the money* is the focus of the negation. As a third alternative, if the focus of the negation is *yesterday*, we can indeed infer that "*the boy stole the money,*" though we do not know when. Both scope and focus of negation need to be detected to understand these nuanced interpretations and draw correct inferences, an exisitng weakness in many current Natural Language Inference (NLI) tasks (Naik et al., 2018).

The goal of this paper is therefore (i) to investigate how the PPIs of negative statements can be represented in AMRs and (ii) to investigate whether these structures can be generated from the AMR of the negated sentence in a systematic way based on the work by Blanco and Sarabi (2016) and Sarabi and Blanco (2016). To this end, we propose a novel, logically-motivated AMR structure that makes both scope and focus of negation explict. We additionally sketch an initial proposal for how to transform existing AMRs into this more expressive format. Initial assessment results support previously made observations that AMR lacks expressive capacity when it comes to scope. This lack of expressivity is especially problematic for PPIs whose concrete meaning results from an interaction of the negation and information structure. Our methodology

Proceedings of the Joint 15th Linguistic Annotation Workshop (LAW) and 3rd Designing Meaning Representations (DMR) Workshop, pages 23–35

	Semantic Role	Dependency	Potential Positive Interpretations
1	ARG_0	*nsubj*	[Someone] stole my money yesterday, *but not the young boy*
2	ARG_1	*obj*	The young boy stole [something] yesterday, *but not my money*
3	*verb*	*root*	The young boy [some verb] my money yesterday, *but not stole*
4	ARGM -TMP	*obl:tmod*	The young boy stole my money [at some point in time], *but not yesterday*
5		*nsubj*	The young [some person] stole my money yesterday, *but not the young boy*
6		*amod*	The [some adjective] boy stole my money yesterday, *but not the young boy*
7		*nmod:poss*	The young boy stole [someone's] money yesterday, *but not my money*
8		*obj*	They young boy stole my [something] yesterday, *but not my money*
Positive Counterpart: The young boy stole my money yesterday.			

Table 1: The PPIs generated using semantic roles (1-4) and syntactic dependencies (1-8) for the negated statement: *"The young boy did not steal my money yesterday"*.

enables us to express the negation's foci in AMR without modifying the original AMR. To our knowledge we are the first to propose a representation of both scope and focus in AMR in order to express the full meaning of negated statements.

This paper is structured as follows. Section 2 presents background about focus of negation, previous work on generating PPIs and about scope in AMR. Based on this, we propose an approach to represent the PPIs of a negated statement in AMRs and a methodology to systematically generate these AMRs (Section 3) which we then verify with corpus examples (Section 4). In Section 5 we conclude and discuss next steps.

2 Background and Related Work

2.1 Focus of Negation

Deriving the meaning of negated statements in NLP tasks is more challenging than for statements lacking negation. This complexity is due in part to the ambiguity of negation with respect to its scope and focus. According to Huddleston and Pullum (2002), the focus is the part of the scope that is intended to be interpreted as being false. Blanco and Moldovan (2011, 2014) state that negated statements can carry implicit positive meaning. For example, *"cows do not eat **meat**"* has the implicit meaning that *"cows eat something other than meat"*. They state that implicit positive meaning arises because of a speaker's specific choice to formulate the negated statement, i.e. if the positive implication is not intended the speaker would say something different (for example, *"cows do not eat"*).

The ability to detect the positive meaning by detecting the scope and focus of negation yields valuable information for NLP tasks, especially for those involving inferences (Blanco and Moldovan, 2011, 2014). Selecting the smallest suitable focus, i.e. a fine-grained focus, often yields a larger amount of positive meaning (Blanco and Moldovan, 2012, 2014). Indeed, this has been found in NLI benchmarks: strong negation words are often responsible for models prediction contradiction for neutral or entailed statements (Naik et al., 2018). Representing scope and focus in a more precise manner can further assist in fact detection, building correct timelines, and identifying discourse structure (Altuna et al., 2017; Anand and Martell, 2012).

2.2 Positive Interpretations of Negated Statements

Blanco and Sarabi (2016) and Sarabi and Blanco (2016) developed methodologies that make the implicit positive meaning of a negated statement, or all positive interpretations derived from potential foci of negation, explicit by automatically generating its PPIs based on the focus.

Focusing on verbal negation the positive counterpart is first generated by removing negation; each PPI is then generated by selecting one of the potential foci of the negation and replacing it with an "existential placeholder". The potential foci get identified based on the semantic roles (Blanco and Sarabi, 2016) or the syntactic dependents (Sarabi and Blanco, 2016) of the verb. Table 1 shows both the coarse-grained (1-4) and the fine-grained PPIs (5-8). Sarabi and Blanco (2017) extend the syntactic dependency based methodology to address the negation of nouns and adjectives.

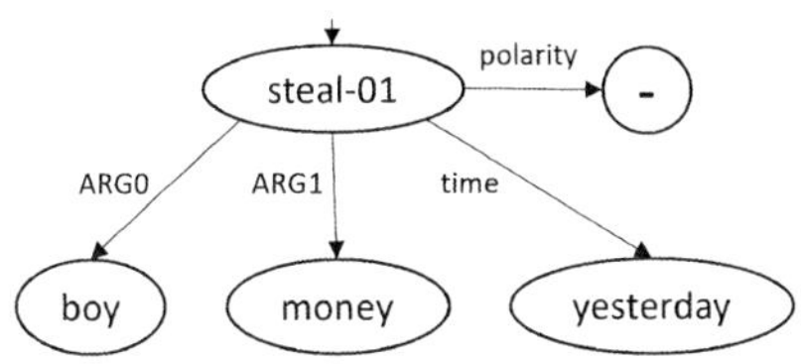

(a) Graph representation

$$\text{instance}(s, \text{steal}-01) \wedge \text{instance}(b, \text{boy}) \wedge \text{instance}(m, \text{money}) \wedge \text{instance}(y, \text{yesterday}) \wedge \text{ARG0}(s, b) \wedge \text{ARG1}(s, m) \wedge \text{time}(s, y) \wedge \text{polarity}(s, -)$$

(b) Conjunction of Logical Triples

Figure 1: AMR representations for the sentence *"The boy did not steal the money yesterday."* Information about negation's scope and focus is not captured.

2.3 Abstract Meaning Representation

AMRs are single-rooted, directed, labeled acyclic graphs whose nodes represent the predicate and the arguments of the represented sentence and the edges represent the semantic relations between the concepts. Figure 1a shows the graphical AMR for the sentence *"The boy did not steal the money yesterday."* Negation is represented with a `:polarity` relation between the negated concept and the polarity constant "-". This representation does not provide any information about the scope of the negation, seen clearly when represented as a conjunction of logical triples helpful to draw inferences (Figure 1b).

Without negation, this logical representation of an AMR can successfully be used to draw inferences by applying the conjunction elimination rule. However, as negation is represented as a conjunct, the elimination rule can yield wrong results when drawing inferences. As already stated by Bos (2020), applying the rule allows us to erroneously drop the negation. From Figure 1b, it could be inferred that *"The boy stole the money yesterday"*. Dropping one of the other conjuncts can lead to wrong inferences, as well, if the focus of the negation is dropped but not the negation itself.

Several approaches have been proposed to address the lack of scope information in AMR (Bos, 2016, 2020; Pustejovsky et al., 2019). Pustejovsky et al. (2019) propose an extended version of AMR that introduces a node for scope that can be added on top of the AMR structure and represents the relative scope between two other nodes, e.g. a quantifier and negation. Bos (2016) defines a recursive translation function that maps an AMR into first-order logic (FOL). The resulting formulas include existential quantifiers and the negation as a logical operator that scopes over the sub-formula corresponding to the sub-graph it is attached to. However, none of these approaches addresses the representation of focus of negation.

The overall focus of a statement can be represented in AMR by making the corresponding node the root and re-arranging the rest of the graph using inverse roles. However, the expressiveness of this focus representation is limited. Specifically, only a single node can be be the focus, posing a problem for PPIs where the focus of the negation consists of several nodes. Additionally, leaving the negation at the original position does not make clear that focus of the negation is expressed.

Bos (2016) shows that his translation function can derive formulas where the logical negation scopes only over a sub-formula when moving the negation in the AMR to the corresponding subgraph. For example, the formula for *"It was not a boy who stole the money yesterday"* could be correctly derived by moving the negation to `boy`. However, the resulting AMR and the corresponding FOL formula do not explicitly represent that there exists another person who is the agent of this stealing event. Furthermore, moving only the negation does not allow to differentiate between the representation of coarse-grained PPIs and PPIs where the focus is a single, internal node.

3 Method

The goal of this exploratory work is to investigate (i) how the PPIs of a negated statement can be represented in AMRs and (ii) if it is possible to generate them systematically from the original AMR of the negated statement for increased expressivity. We employ a combination of the semantic role based (Blanco and Sarabi, 2016) and the syntactic dependency based approach (Sarabi and Blanco, 2016) as the starting point for this investigation. For simplicity, we ignore tense as well as semantic differences between definite and indefinite determiners.

3.1 Representing PPIs in AMRs

The main question regarding PPIs in AMRs concerns the representation of *"but"*. Specifically, we must decide where the subgraph for the *"but not* [original text of focus]" part of the PPI should be inserted. A manual investigation of AMRs for simi-

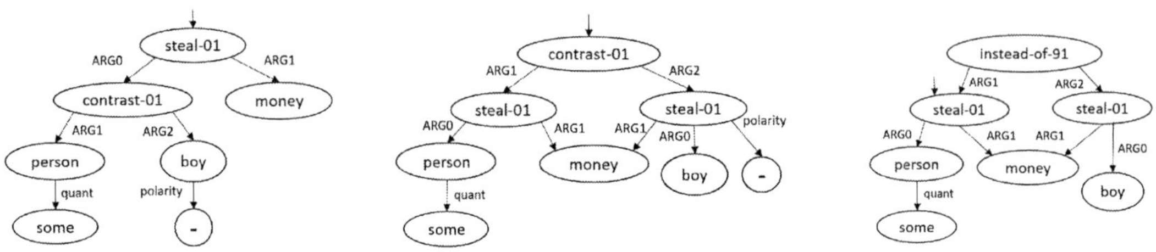

(a) Inner Contrast version (b) Outer Contrast version (c) Instead version

Figure 2: The three representation structures considered for representing PPIs for the example ARG0 PPI *"Some person stole the money but not the boy"*.

	Inner Contrast	**Outer Contrast**	**Instead**
Pro	• "but" similar to "and" • logically motivated • makes focus explicit	• most frequent way to encode "but" in similar cases	• `instead-of-91` to express "A but not B"
Con	• only very few examples in AMR corpora with an inner `contrast-01` node	• Negation attached to main predicate • focus not explicit, can only be inferred from not shared arguments	• no polarity relation • only implicit negation in AMR

Table 2: The advantages and disadvantages of the three considered AMR versions with respect to the current work.

lar sentence structures in AMR corpora[1] resulted in three potential representations (see Figure 2). Two of them represent *"but"* using `contrast-01`: *Inner Contrast* with `contrast-01` as an inner node and *Outer Contrast* with `contrast-01` as the root node. *Instead* represents *"but"* with the `instead-of-91` concept.

Consider the negated statement in (2) with its potential PPIs based on different foci of the negation:

(2) The boy did not steal the money.

a. ARG0: Some person stole the money but not the boy.

b. ARG1: The boy stole something but not the money.

c. ROOT: The boy did something with the money but not steal

The AMR for the negated statement corresponds to the one in Figure 1 without the `:time` relation. Figure 2 illustrates the three different AMR versions considered for the ARG0 PPI interpretation (2-a) (when ARG0 is the focus); Table 2 summarizes the main advantages and disadvantages of the versions with respect to the current work.

The `instead-of-91` relation was considered because the AMR dictionary[2] lists *"not A but B"* as an example use and the PPIs can be rephrased to e.g. *"The boy stole not the money but something yesterday"*. The main difference compared to the *Contrast* versions is the absence of the `:polarity` relation, as the negation is implicitly included in the ARG2 role by definition. As one of the motivations for this work is to make the meaning of negation explicit, it would be counterintuitive to use a representation that expresses negation implicitly.

The *Inner Contrast* and the *Outer Contrast* versions have quite different overall structures. The *Outer Contrast* AMR has the `contrast-01` concept as its root and its two arguments are themselves AMRs for a complete sentence each. In particular, the ARG2 subgraph corresponds to the original negated AMR and the ARG1 subgraph to the AMR for the PPI without the "*but not* [original text of focus]" part, with re-entrancies for shared arguments. In the *Inner Contrast* version on the other hand, the `contrast-01` concept replaces the node that is the root of the chosen focus, e.g. the ARG0 argument for the ARG0 PPI. The AMR for the placeholder is the ARG1 argument of the `contrast-01` concept and the original ARG0 subgraph, (here *boy*), becomes the ARG2 argument with the negation directly attached to it instead of to the root predicate. The structure of this graph and the representation of "but" are similar to "and" and how *"Some person and not the boy stole the money"* gets represented.

Interestingly, in a manual survey of similar ex-

[1]https://amr.isi.edu/download/amr-bank-struct-v3.0.txt, https://amr.isi.edu/download/2018-01-25/amr-release-bio-v3.0.txt

[2]https://amr.isi.edu/doc/amr-dict.html

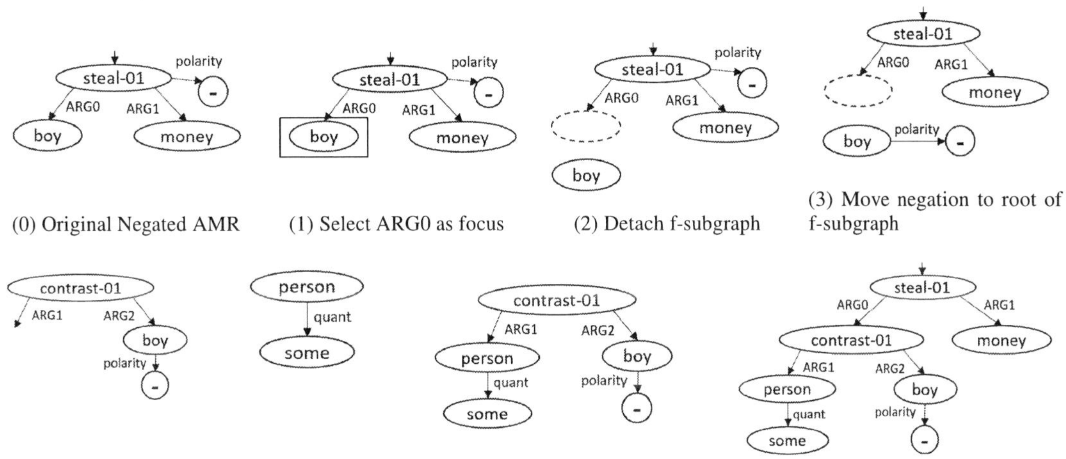

(0) Original Negated AMR (1) Select ARG0 as focus (2) Detach f-subgraph (3) Move negation to root of f-subgraph

(4) Attach f-subgraph to `contrast-01` as ARG2 (5) Subgraph for placeholder (6) Attach p-subgraph to `contrast-01` as ARG1 (7) Attach `contrast-01` subgraph to original AMR at empty ARG0 position

Figure 3: The steps of the initial version of the methodology to generate the AMR for the ARG0 PPI *"Some person stole the money but not the boy"* (7) from the AMR of the original negated statement (0).

amples encountered in AMR corpora, almost all representations correspond to the *Outer Contrast* version. Nevertheless, the *Inner Contrast* version has two advantages for the current work. First, the structure is more logically motivated than the *Outer Contrast* structure, as *"but"* often gets represented as *"and not"* in logic and hence a similar structure in AMRs seems to be preferable. Additionally, the *Inner Contrast* version makes the focus of the negation explicit as the negation is attached directly to the concept that is intended to be interpreted as false. For these reasons, we choose the *Inner Contrast* version to represent PPIs.

3.2 Generating the PPI Representations

Based on the general structure of the *Inner Contrast* AMRs and Sarabi and Blanco (2016)'s methodology, we propose to systematically generate PPI AMRs. As an initial step (0), the original AMR is traversed, starting at the node the polarity is attached to; all subgraphs rooted at the visited nodes are considered as potential foci (subgraphs), except for the polarity node. We then proceed as follows:

1. We select the focus of negation;
2. The chosen focus subgraph (f-subgraph) is detached from the original AMR;
3. The negation is moved to the root of the f-subgraph;
4. The f-subgraph is attached to a `contrast-01` node as ARG2;
5. We create a subgraph for the placeholder (p-subgraph);
6. The p-subgraph is attached to a `contrast-01` node as ARG1;
7. The `contrast-01` subgraph is then attached at the original position of the f-subgraph.

Figure 3 illustrates these steps graphically. This transformation can be executed directly on the original AMR of the negated statement and hence no positive counterpart needs to be derived as an intermediate step. As AMRs do not represent tense, inflection and auxiliaries required by the syntax, only the negatively-oriented polarity-sensitive items have to be exchanged with their positively-oriented counterparts.

4 Findings

In the following section, the validity of the initial proposal for the representation of PPIs of negated statements in AMRs and for the methodology to generate them will be verified by means of examples and extended and adapted if necessary. For reasons of space, only some of the PPIs are presented for the example statements.

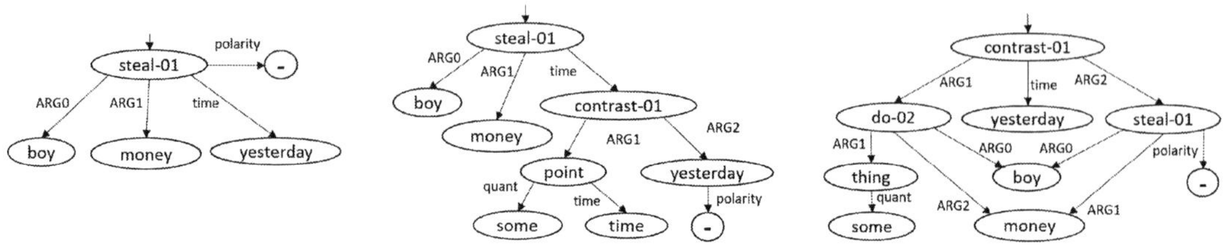

(a) The boy did not steal the money yesterday.

(b) TIME: The boy stole the money at some point in time but not yesterday.

(c) ROOT: The boy did something with the money yesterday but not steal.

Figure 4: Verbal negation: AMRs for *"The boy did not steal the money yesterday"* and two of its PPIs.

(a) The young boy did not steal my money yesterday.

(b) ARG1: The young boy stole my something yesterday but not my money.

(c) ARG0: Some young person stole my money yesterday but not the young boy.

(d) MOD: Some boy stole my money yesterday but not the young boy.

Figure 5: Fine-grained PPIs: AMRs for *"The young boy did not steal my money yesterday"* and three of its PPIs.

4.1 Verbal Negation

Figure 3 illustrates how to generate the AMR for an ARG0 PPI. Example (3) extends (2) with the non-core relation `:time` (Figure 4a).

(3) The boy did not steal the money yesterday.

(4) The young boy did not steal my money yesterday.

Figure 4b shows that the AMR for the PPI generated from `:time` has the same overall structure as when choosing a core relation as focus. When the negated verb itself is chosen as the focus, the AMR for the corresponding ROOT PPI looks different (see Figure 4c). In order to generate the AMR for ROOT PPIs, the predicate and all its arguments need to be considered as the f-subgraph and two additional steps must be added to the transformation between step (6) and (7). First, *boy* and *money* are the ARG0 and ARG1 arguments of both predicates of the PPI respectively and hence need to be shared. Second, non-core relations modifying a complete conjunction are pulled-out in AMRs and therefore *yesterday* is moved to the root node.

Example (4) (Figure 5a) adds the modifier *young* and the possessive pronoun *my* to the ARG0 and ARG1 arguments of (3) respectively, leading to four additional, fine-grained PPIs. Figure 5b shows the AMR for the ARG1 fine-grained PPI. Similar to ROOT PPIs, fine-grained foci can be internal nodes and therefore one has to take care of the required re-entrancies, e.g. the two `:poss` relations in 5b need to link to the same entity (i.e. *"I"*).

Whereas the previous case works similar to the coarse-grained PPIs, it gets more difficult when adjectives are involved. The two fine-grained PPIs that Sarabi and Blanco (2016)'s methodology generates for the ARG0 argument *the young boy* are *"The young some person stole my money yesterday but not the young boy"* and *"The some_adjective boy stole my money yesterday ..."*. Instead of *some_adjective*, we use *some* as a general placeholder for adjectives. Still, both PPIs sound rather unsuitable because of the co-occurrence of the determiner and *some*. Possible solutions would be to remove the determiner or to exchange it with an indefinite determiner and to remove *some* completely. To ensure consistency with negated statements not including a determiner, e.g. *"Young boys did not steal my money"*, we decided to discard the determiner which also never is represented in AMR (see Figure 5c, 5d).

In case of the MOD PPI yet another issue comes up. The AMR generated by the proposed transformation steps represents only one boy that "*has some property but is not young*" because the contrast subgraph is attached at the original position of `young` beneath `boy`. However, in the MOD PPI two different boys are referenced. Therefore, the methodology in Figure 3 has to be adapted in the following way in order to generate the AMR in Figure 5d: In step (1) not only the f-subgraph but also the subgraph covering the complete semantic role to which the fine-grained focus belongs (sr-subgraph) has to be detected. Both subgraphs are equivalent in the case of coarse-grained and ROOT foci. In all steps except for step (3) "f-subgraph" needs to be replaced with "sr-subgraph". Additionally, the sr-subgraph needs to be copied before adding the negation in step (3). The p-subgraph in step (5) replaces the f-subgraph in the copied sr-subgraph and the resulting subgraph is then attached to the contrast subgraph in step (6). For the examples covered so far these modifications do not affect the resulting PPI AMRs. Hence, the adapted methodology is more suitable. (See Appendix for detailed illustrations of the adapted steps for a MOD PPI and a ROOT PPI example.)

4.2 Negated Adjectives

Sarabi and Blanco (2017) extend the methodology from Sarabi and Blanco (2016) to non-verbal negation by modifying the selection of the potential foci. When an adjective is negated, they choose all subtrees rooted in the direct dependents of the negated adjective as well as the adjective itself as potential foci. Here, we only consider the negation of predicative adjectives, i.e. where the adjective concept is the root of the AMR. Predicative adjectives are represented using a PropBank frame whenever one is available, such as for *sad* in Example (5).

(5) The child was not sad at the party.

Hence, the corresponding AMR structures are similar to those for verbal negation (see Figure 6a). However, when exchanging *sad* with *funny* the root is no longer related to `child` with a core relation but with the `:domain` relation because no PropBank frame is available (Figure 6b). Still, generating the AMRs for the PPIs works in the same way as for verbal negation except for the ROOT PPI. For predicative adjectives neither *some_adjective* nor *some* are suitable placeholders. Therefore, in order to generate the ROOT PPIs for negated adjectives first an appropriate concept for the placeholder needs to be determined (see Figure 6c).

4.3 Negated Nouns

Following Sarabi and Blanco (2017), we distinguish two cases when a noun is negated: when the negated noun is the root of the AMR and when this is not the case. If a negated sentence contains a main verb as in Examples (6) and (7) the structure of the AMR depends on the specific meaning. (6) can be rephrased as *"The boy did not steal any money yesterday"* and gets represented with the same AMR as shown in Figure 1a. Hence, it can be treated as an instance of verbal negation. (7) on the other hand cannot be rephrased this way but as *"There was no adult who spoke loudly in the church"* and therefore the noun is the root of the corresponding AMR (Figure 7e). Still, the PPIs and their AMRs are the same as for verbal negation (e.g. Figure 7f). The only adaption required in order to apply the proposed methodology to AMRs with an negated noun as root node is to make the closest predicate the root instead of the noun before selecting the foci and generating the AMRs.

Yet, there is one limitation of the PPIs generated for negated statements with the meaning "there is no X that" which concerns quantification. When generating PPIs from foci different from the negated noun itself it is important that the PPI still expresses the negated existential quantification, e.g. the MANNER PPI for (7) must not express only that "an adult spoke in some manner in church but not loudly" because this does not exclude that "there was also an adult who spoke loudly in church". We decided to replace the negation *no* with a bare plural instead of using an indefinite article as done by Sarabi and Blanco (2017) because the noun phrase needs to be generic and the use of indefinite singular generics is more re-

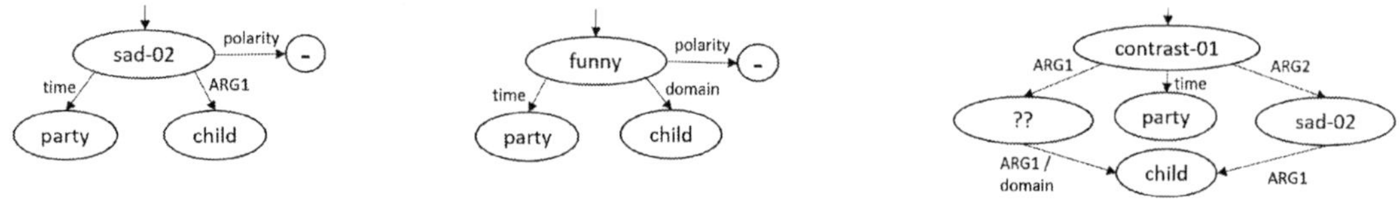

(a) The child was not sad at the party.

(b) The child was not funny at the party.

(c) ROOT: The child was [??] at the party but not sad.

Figure 6: AMRs for the examples of negated adjectives and the overall structure of a ROOT PPI.

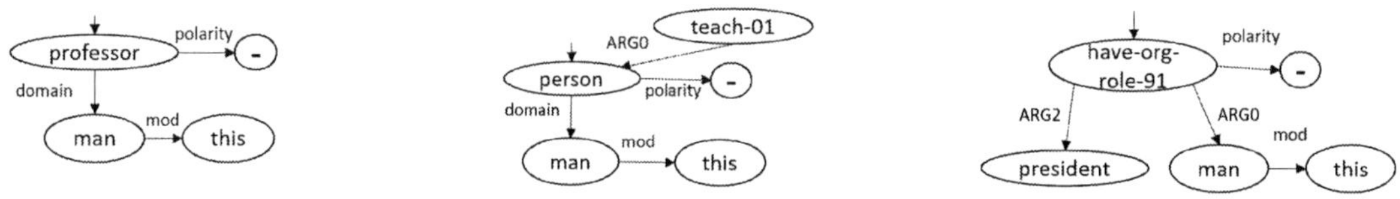

(a) This man is no professor.

(b) This man is no teacher.

(c) This man is no president.

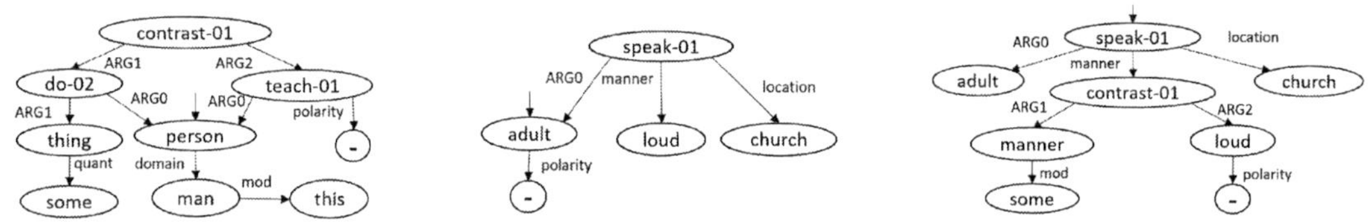

(d) ROOT: This man is a person who does something but not teach.

(e) No adult spoke loudly in the church.

(f) MANNER: Adults spoke in some manner in the church but not loudly.

Figure 7: AMRs for the examples of negated nouns and some of their PPIs.

stricted than the use of bare plural generics (Cohen, 2001). However, this adaption does not solve the issue on the AMR level because AMRs do not represent (most) determiners and do not have a deep representation for quantifiers (see Figure 7f). For the current work, the problem could be addressed by using the *Outer Contrast* version for the PPIs but nevertheless, this example supports the need to extend the expressiveness of the AMR framework.

(6) The boy stole no money yesterday .

(7) No adult spoke loudly in the church.

(8) This man is no professor.

When a copula verb is involved like in Example (8), the structure of the AMR depends on the representation of the specific noun. When no appropriate frame is available the noun itself is the root (Figure 7a). Exchanging *professor* with *teacher* leads to a different structure because *teacher* gets represented as *a person who teaches* (Figure 7b) and exchanging it with *president* results yet in another graph structure, because *president* gets represented by the `have-org-role-91` frame (Figure 7c).

The PPIs for foci that are not the negated noun itself and their generation do not differ from the examples in the previous sections. However, when the negated noun is chosen as the focus, each of the three examples has its own particularities. For the *president* example the only difference compared to verbal negation is that it does not make sense to select the root as potential focus. Example (8) illustrates again the problem of a suitable placeholder as the AMR for the ROOT PPI *"This man is something but no professor"* is a less-than-ideal solution because of *something*. When the negated noun invokes a predicate this is easier because *"This man is no teacher"* is represented as *"This man is not a person who teaches"*. However, this results in an additional potential focus, i.e. *person*. One approach to deal with this inconsistency would be to consider the predicate and `person` as one unit for nouns that invoke predicates. Additionally, the position where the contrast subgraph gets inserted into the original graph needs to be modified in order to result in the correct AMR (see Figure 7d).

The examples in this section illustrate that representing and generating PPIs for negated statements involving the copula verb *to be* that gets not represented in AMRs is complex due to differences in

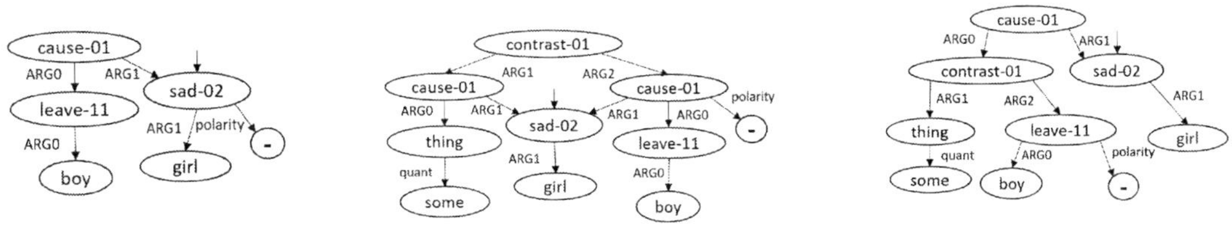

(a) The girl was not sad because the boy left.

(b) CAUSE: The girl was sad because of something but not because the boy left.

(c) The girl was sad because something happened but the boy did not leave.

Figure 8: AMR for Example (9) (a) and the correct CAUSE PPI (b) and the incorrect PPI (c).

the AMR representations of specific nouns.

4.4 Limitation: Negating Causation

In the case of negated statements that include an ARGM-CAU semantic role factuality plays a role when selecting the causation as the focus. In AMRs, causation is represented with the frame `cause-01`. Figure 8a shows the AMR for Example (9).

(9) The girl was not sad because the boy left.

A first attempt to represent the CAUSE PPI *"The girl was sad because of something but not because the boy left"* was to embed `contrast-01` beneath the `cause-01` node in the same way as "because X and because Y" would be represented. However, the resulting graph in Figure 8c represents *"The girl was sad because something happened but the boy did not leave"* which implies that the boy did not leave. In contrast, the leaving of the boy is a factual event in the original sentence and all PPIs need to express that the leaving of the boy indeed happened. Figure 8b shows the correct AMR for the CAUSE PPI where the negation is attached to `cause-01`. In the case of fine-grained PPIs the proposed methodology also leads to problems with respect to the factuality of the "boy-leaving-event". Therefore, further research on investigating the interactions of negation, scope and factuality is needed for representing PPIs in AMRs.

5 Conclusion & Future Work

The way in which negation is represented in AMRs does not allow for accurate interpretation of scope or the ability to disambiguate between the potential foci of the negation. The goal of the current work was therefore, to investigate how the PPIs of negated statements can be represented in AMRs in order to explicitly represent the focus of negation and whether these representations can be generated in a systematical way. We proposed a logically motivated representation for the PPIs where the negation is attached directly to the root node of the focus. As future work, we plan to investigate our proposed approach on sentences from existing AMR corpora.

Working through example negated statements has shown that representing positive meaning adequately in AMRs is a complex task especially when quantifier and scope interactions are involved. The results support the need for an extension of AMR that is able to handle quantifiers and scope phenomena in general, and negation in particular, in a systematic and explicit way that is suitable for inference tasks. Representing focus explicitly in AMRs does not solve the problem that modelling negation simply as a relation is inappropriate for drawing inferences. As a next step, then, we hope to combine our proposed approach with an existing approach that extends AMR's scope capacities, specifically by investigating the use of Pustejovsky et al. (2019)'s approach for determining which nodes to consider as potential foci and by translating the `contrast-01` concept and the existential placeholder subgraphs into FOL.

References

Lasha Abzianidze and Johan Bos. 2019. Thirty musts for meaning banking. In *Proceedings of the First International Workshop on Designing Meaning Representations*, pages 15–27, Florence, Italy. Association for Computational Linguistics.

Begoña Altuna, Anne-Lyse Minard, and Manuela Speranza. 2017. The scope and focus of negation: A complete annotation framework for Italian. In *Proceedings of the Workshop Computational Semantics Beyond Events and Roles*, pages 34–42, Valencia, Spain. Association for Computational Linguistics.

Pranav Anand and Craig Martell. 2012. Annotating the focus of negation in terms of questions under discussion. In *Proceedings of the Workshop on Extra-Propositional Aspects of Meaning in Computational Linguistics*, pages 65–69, Jeju, Republic of Korea. Association for Computational Linguistics.

Laura Banarescu, Claire Bonial, Shu Cai, Madalina Georgescu, Kira Griffitt, Ulf Hermjakob, Kevin Knight, Philipp Koehn, Martha Palmer, and Nathan Schneider. 2013. Abstract Meaning Representation for sembanking. In *Proceedings of the 7th Linguistic Annotation Workshop and Interoperability with Discourse*, pages 178–186, Sofia, Bulgaria. Association for Computational Linguistics.

Eduardo Blanco and Dan Moldovan. 2011. Some issues on detecting negation from text. In *Twenty-Fourth International FLAIRS Conference*. Citeseer.

Eduardo Blanco and Dan Moldovan. 2012. Fine-grained focus for pinpointing positive implicit meaning from negated statements. In *Proceedings of the 2012 Conference of the North American Chapter of the Association for Computational Linguistics: Human Language Technologies*, pages 456–465, Montréal, Canada. Association for Computational Linguistics.

Eduardo Blanco and Dan Moldovan. 2014. Retrieving implicit positive meaning from negated statements. *Natural Language Engineering*, 20(4):501–535.

Eduardo Blanco and Zahra Sarabi. 2016. Automatic generation and scoring of positive interpretations from negated statements. In *Proceedings of the 2016 Conference of the North American Chapter of the Association for Computational Linguistics: Human Language Technologies*, pages 1431–1441, San Diego, California. Association for Computational Linguistics.

Johan Bos. 2016. Expressive Power of Abstract Meaning Representations. *Computational Linguistics*, 42(3):527–535.

Johan Bos. 2020. Separating argument structure from logical structure in AMR. In *Proceedings of the Second International Workshop on Designing Meaning Representations*, pages 13–20, Barcelona Spain (online). Association for Computational Linguistics.

Ariel Cohen. 2001. On the Generic Use of Indefinite Singulars. *Journal of Semantics*, 18(3):183–209.

Rodney Huddleston and Geoffrey K Pullum. 2002. The cambridge grammar of english. *Language. Cambridge: Cambridge University Press*, 1.

Aakanksha Naik, Abhilasha Ravichander, Norman Sadeh, Carolyn Rose, and Graham Neubig. 2018. Stress test evaluation for natural language inference. In *Proceedings of the 27th International Conference on Computational Linguistics*, pages 2340–2353, Santa Fe, New Mexico, USA. Association for Computational Linguistics.

James Pustejovsky, Ken Lai, and Nianwen Xue. 2019. Modeling quantification and scope in Abstract Meaning Representations. In *Proceedings of the First International Workshop on Designing Meaning Representations*, pages 28–33, Florence, Italy. Association for Computational Linguistics.

Zahra Sarabi and Eduardo Blanco. 2016. Understanding negation in positive terms using syntactic dependencies. In *Proceedings of the 2016 Conference on Empirical Methods in Natural Language Processing*, pages 1108–1118, Austin, Texas. Association for Computational Linguistics.

Zahra Sarabi and Eduardo Blanco. 2017. If no media were allowed inside the venue, was anybody allowed? In *Proceedings of the 15th Conference of the European Chapter of the Association for Computational Linguistics: Volume 1, Long Papers*, pages 860–869, Valencia, Spain. Association for Computational Linguistics.

A Appendix

0	Start with original AMR of negated statement
1	a. Select the focus and the corresponding f-subgraph b. Select the sr-subgraph to which the focus belongs
2	Detach the sr-subgraph from the original AMR and copy it
3	Move negation to the root of the f-subgraph within the detached sr-subgraph
4	Attach the resulting negated subgraph to `:ARG2` of `contrast-01`
5	a. Create the appropriate subgraph for the existential placeholder b. Detach the f-subgraph from the copied sr-subgraph c. Attach the subgraph for the existential placeholder at empty position
6	Attach the resulting subgraph to `:ARG1` of `contrast-01` a. Fix re-entrancies for arguments shared between `:ARG1` and `:ARG2` b. Pull-out shared non-core relations
7	Attach the contrast subgraph to the original AMR at empty original position of the sr-subgraph

Table 3: The steps of the proposed methodology to transform the AMR of an negated statement into the AMR of one of its PPIs.

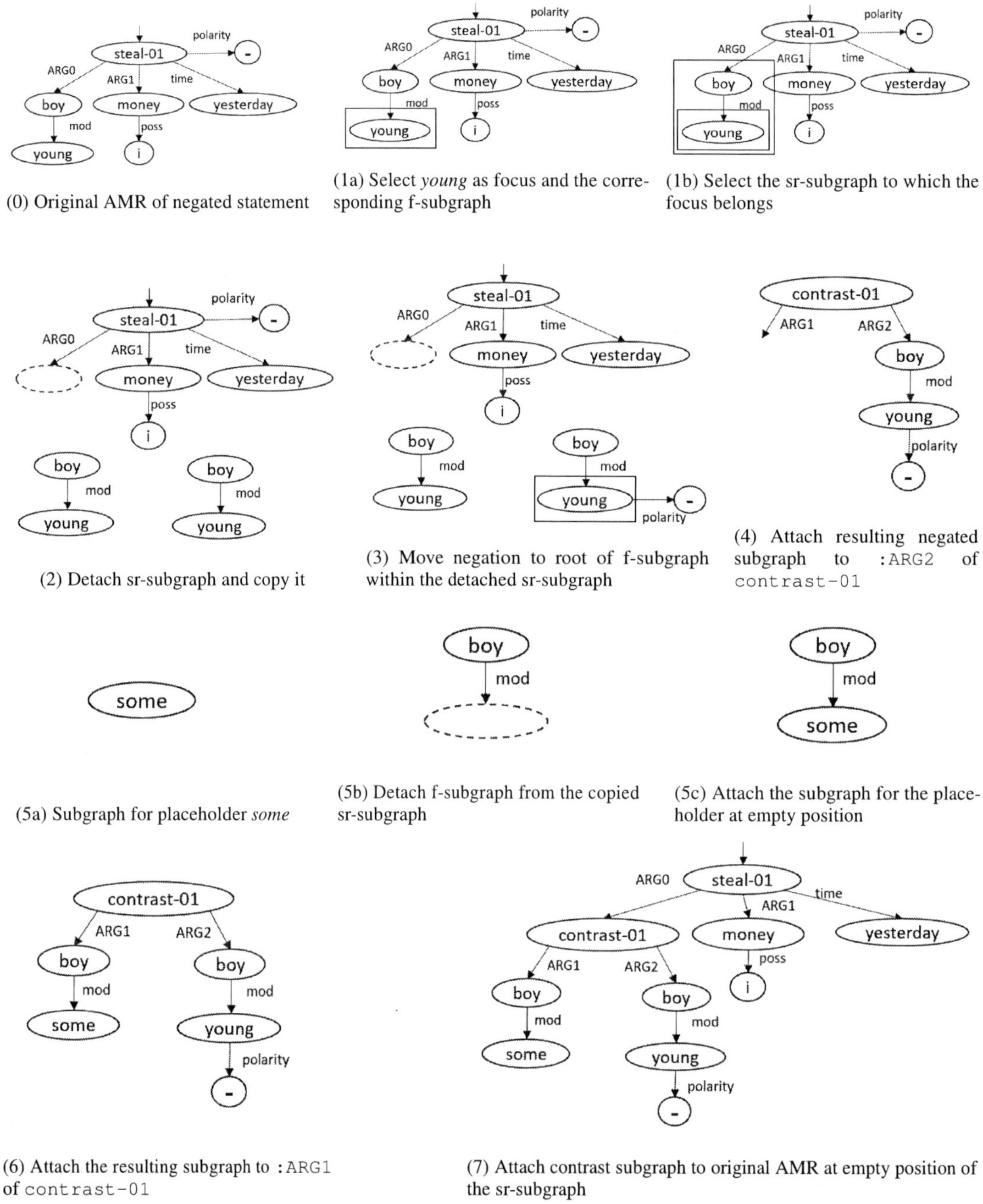

(0) Original AMR of negated statement

(1a) Select *young* as focus and the corresponding f-subgraph

(1b) Select the sr-subgraph to which the focus belongs

(2) Detach sr-subgraph and copy it

(3) Move negation to root of f-subgraph within the detached sr-subgraph

(4) Attach resulting negated subgraph to `:ARG2` of `contrast-01`

(5a) Subgraph for placeholder *some*

(5b) Detach f-subgraph from the copied sr-subgraph

(5c) Attach the subgraph for the placeholder at empty position

(6) Attach the resulting subgraph to `:ARG1` of `contrast-01`

(7) Attach contrast subgraph to original AMR at empty position of the sr-subgraph

Figure 9: Illustration of generating the AMR for the MOD PPI *"Some boy stole my money yesterday but not the young boy"* (7) from the AMR of the negated statement *"The young boy did not steal my money yesterday"* (0).

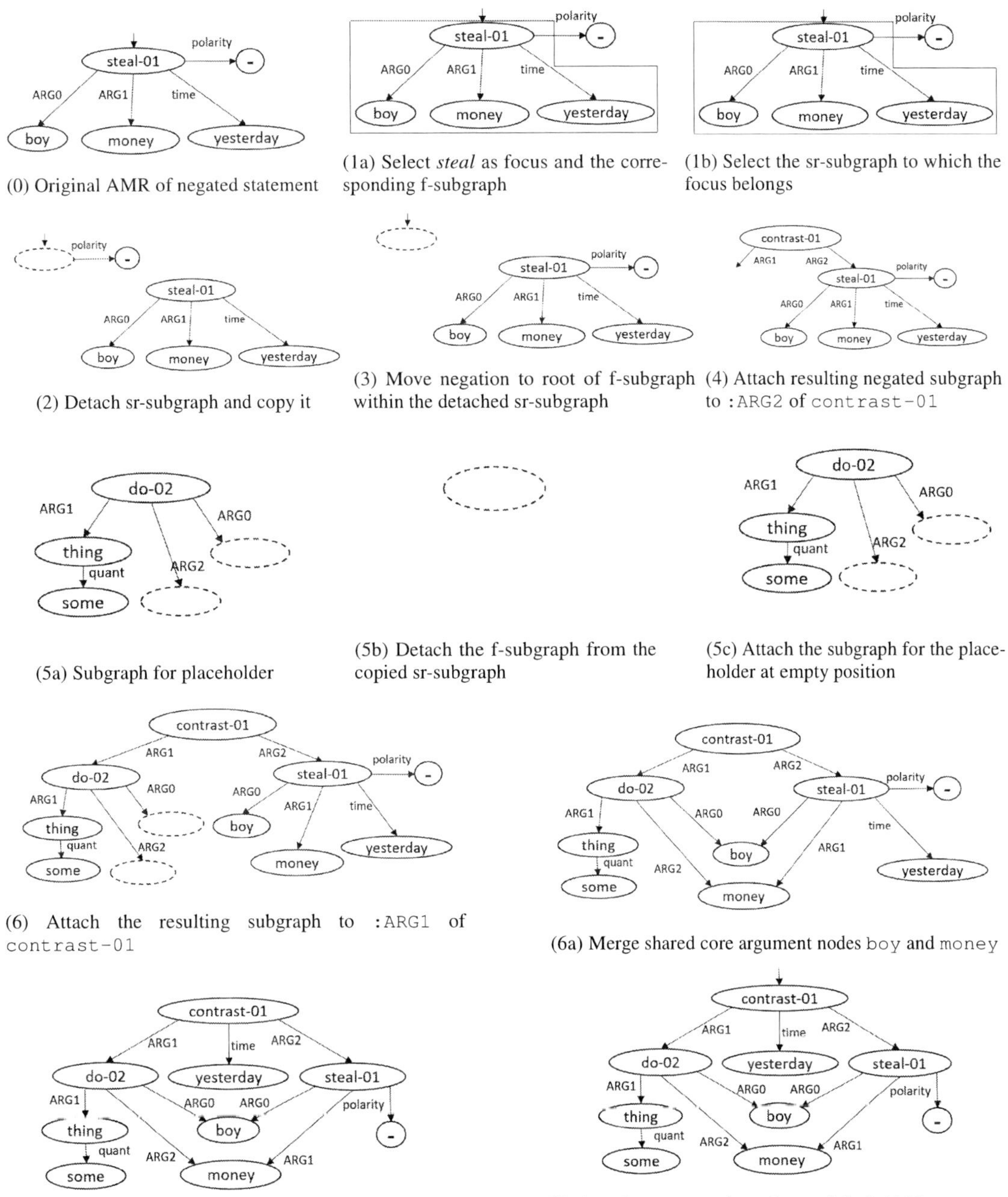

(0) Original AMR of negated statement

(1a) Select *steal* as focus and the corresponding f-subgraph

(1b) Select the sr-subgraph to which the focus belongs

(2) Detach sr-subgraph and copy it

(3) Move negation to root of f-subgraph within the detached sr-subgraph

(4) Attach resulting negated subgraph to `:ARG2` of `contrast-01`

(5a) Subgraph for placeholder

(5b) Detach the f-subgraph from the copied sr-subgraph

(5c) Attach the subgraph for the placeholder at empty position

(6) Attach the resulting subgraph to `:ARG1` of `contrast-01`

(6a) Merge shared core argument nodes `boy` and `money`

(6b) Pull-out non-core relation `:time`

(7) Attach contrast subgraph to original AMR at empty position of the sr-subgraph

Figure 10: Illustration of generating the AMR for the ROOT PPI *"The boy did something with the money yesterday but not steal"* (7) from the AMR of the negated statement *"The boy did not steal the money yesterday"* (0). In the special case of selecting the root / the predicate frame as focus here, the f-subgraph (as well as the sr-subgraph) consists of the predicate and all its arguments except for the negation. For reasons of space the copied sr-subgraph is not shown in step (2) and (3).

AutoAspect: Automatic Annotation of Tense and Aspect for Uniform Meaning Representations

Daniel Chen
University of Colorado at Boulder
Boulder, CO, USA
daniel.chen-1@colorado.edu

Martha Palmer
University of Colorado at Boulder
Boulder, CO, USA
martha.palmer@colorado.edu

Meagan Vigus
University of New Mexico
Albuquerque, NM, USA
mvigus@unm.edu

Abstract

We present AutoAspect, a novel, rule-based annotation tool for labeling tense and aspect. The pilot version annotates English data. The aspect labels are designed specifically for Uniform Meaning Representations (UMR), an annotation schema that aims to encode crosslingual semantic information. The annotation tool combines syntactic and semantic cues to assign aspects on a sentence-by-sentence basis, following a sequence of rules that each output a UMR aspect. Identified events proceed through the sequence until they are assigned an aspect. We achieve a recall of 76.17% for identifying UMR events and an accuracy of 62.57% on all identified events, with high precision values for 2 of the aspect labels.

1 Introduction

As the field of Natural Language Processing advances, there are increasing demands for more sophisticated applications and richer representations. Abstract Meaning Representations (AMR; Banarescu et al. 2013), and their more recent crosslingual incarnation as Uniform Meaning Representations (UMR; Van Gysel et al. 2021), are a response to that demand. AMR/UMRs provide an abstract, directed acyclic graph representation of a complete sentence, focusing on the underlying "who" did "what" to "whom" elements of the events being described. The more information that can be associated with those events, in terms of whether they have been completed, or whether they have achieved their intended results, the better.

The increased richness of UMR Tense, Aspect and Modality annotations, as described below, can more clearly identify the completion and achievement of events in a cross-lingual context, providing a firmer baseline for comparing typologically distinct languages. Automating such a complex semantic processing task provides valuable qualitative and temporal crosslingual features that applications like translation models and virtual assistants can utilize to more accurately capture the semantic nuances of events. Given the substantial amounts of English AMR annotation, the question immediately arises of how to efficiently add these new annotation features to pre-existing English AMRs.

This paper describes an implementation of an automatic system that relies on VerbNet, a rich lexical resource, as the basis for categorizing event descriptions according to the Aspect guidelines discussed below. Our initial results are quite promising, and there are obvious next steps to take.

2 Background Information

Previous automatic annotation models operate on different definitions of aspect. In Friedrich et al. (2016), clauses are annotated for situation entity types, which capture some of the same semantic distinctions as the UMR aspect annotation scheme, including state and habitual. Friedrich et al. (2016) also include modal distinctions in their annotation, such as questions and imperatives. Unlike Friedrich et al. (2016), the UMR aspect annotation distinguishes between different types of dynamic (non-stative) clauses (Activity, Endeavor, and Performance); these are all annotated as Event in Friedrich et al. (2016).

Friedrich and Gateva (2017) annotate a binary telicity distinction: telic vs. atelic. The UMR aspect annotation annotates a three-way distinction for non-stative events, which takes both the qualitative and temporal dimensions of event semantics into account.

The UMR aspect annotation consists of a feature assigned to events that indicates their internal qualitative and temporal structure (Van Gysel et al., 2019, 2021). Every node classified as an "event" in UMR receives an aspect annotation. UMR defines "event" based on the typological prototype of a verb as described in Croft (2001), and Croft (in press). UMR events exhibit either the prototypical information-packaging of a verb, predication (as opposed to modification and reference), or the prototypical semantic class of a verb, a process (as opposed to a property or an entity).

The aspectual distinctions made in UMR are based on Croft (2012)'s two-dimensional analysis of aspect and build on the aspect annotations from Donatelli et al. (2018, 2019). Croft (2012) analyzes aspectual structure as having both a temporal dimension and a qualitative dimension; the temporal dimension measures out the event's unfolding over time and the qualitative dimension measures out the change that occurs (or does not occur) during the event.

The UMR aspectual distinctions do not have a direct correspondence with either specific verbs or specific constructions in a language; instead, they annotate the aspectual structure of an event in its context. In order to ensure the maximum cross-linguistic comparability of annotation values, UMR uses lattices of compatible annotation values for certain annotation categories, including aspect (Van Gysel et al., 2019).

In addition to the lattices, UMR also considers a certain level of specificity in annotation as the base level, corresponding to distinctions that tend to be straightforward to annotate in a majority of languages. For aspect, there are four base-level annotation values: STATE, ACTIVITY, ENDEAVOR, and PERFORMANCE. In addition, there is a HABITUAL value. The annotation of these categories manually relies on a series of decisions that distinguish event types.

First, event nominals are annotated as PROCESS, one of the more coarse-grained categories on the lattice. Processes in reference (i.e., event/action nominals) lack grammatical clues as to their aspectual structure in English and many other languages; therefore, they are simply annotated as PROCESS.

Next, the HABITUAL value applies to all events that are repeated on a regular basis, regardless of the internal aspectual structure of each individual (repeated) event. This means that further aspectual distinctions (including between PROCESS and STATE) are collapsed for habitual events.

The rest of the aspectual values make a distinction between stative and non-stative events. STATE is the base-level value that captures all stative events; non-stative events are divided into ACTIVITY, ENDEAVOR, and PERFORMANCE.

UMR defines stative events as those in which no change occurs on the qualitative dimension during the event (Vendler, 1967; Croft, 2012). In addition to prototypical stative events, UMR extends the STATE value to "nonverbal predication" (*He **is** a teacher. / There **is** a sandwich in the kitchen.*), events modalized by ability modals (*This car can **go** 100mph.*), and modal complement-taking predicates (*She **wants** to eat at noon.*).

In addition, UMR uses the STATE value for a class of events termed "inactive actions" in Croft (2012). Inactive actions are semantically intermediate between states and processes; this class includes verbs of sensation, perception, cognition, emotion, and position. These types of events can variably be construed as either states or processes, even within the same language. Since the construal of an inactive action can be hard to ascertain in context, UMR annotates all inactive actions with the STATE value.

The rest of the base level aspect annotations (ACTIVITY, ENDEAVOR, PERFORMANCE) work to characterize non-stative events (PROCESSES in UMR). These events are defined as those that involve change on the qualitative dimension.

The distinction between the ACTIVITY annotation value and the ENDEAVOR and PERFORMANCE values is based on whether the event is still ongoing at Document Creation Time (DCT), or whether it has ended. Events annotated as ACTIVITY indicate that the event may be ongoing at DCT.

Both ENDEAVOR and PERFORMANCE characterize non-stative events that have ended prior to DCT. The ENDEAVOR and PERFORMANCE values differ from each other in whether the event has been terminated or completed. Events annotated as ENDEAVOR signal that the event has terminated, without reaching completion. This means that the event has not reached a distinct result state on the qualitative dimension. The PERFORMANCE label indicates that an event has been completed, reaching a distinct result state. The UMR PERFORMANCE value corresponds to Vendler's achievements and accomplishments.

UMR also incudes a number of more fine-grained aspectual types on its aspect lattice (see Van Gysel et al. 2019). Many of these fine-grained aspect values make distinctions that cross-cut the base-level annotation values. These include whether an event is punctual or durative, which cross-cuts the ENDEAVOR/PERFORMANCE distinction. For durative ENDEAVORS and PERFORMANCES, in addition to all ACTIVITIES, there is also the cross-cutting distinction of incremental vs. nonincremental change (Dowty, 1991; Croft, 2012).

The base-level UMR aspectual values were selected because they capture the most salient pieces of aspectual structure and they can be consistently annotated, even in languages with minimal grammatical aspect marking like English. The presence or absence of change on the qualitative dimension is captured by the PROCESS vs. STATE distinction. Boundedness on the temporal dimension is captured for processes by the distinction between ACTIVITY and ENDEAVOR/PERFORMANCE. Finally, boundedness on the qualitative dimension is captured by the distinction between ENDEAVOR and PERFORMANCE.

3 Rule-Based Classification

The rule-based classifier[1] follows the sequential manual annotation steps as closely as possible, immediately exiting the sequence as soon as an annotation label has been assigned by a numbered step. The annotation loop processes text by sentence, such that every identified event in a sentence receives an annotation.

3.1 Step 1a: Syntactic Split

Step 1a syntactically separates annotation branches into *verbs* and *event nominals*. Since all event nominals are assigned the same aspect by Step 1b, the *event nominals* branch does not pass through the sequence of rules and is analyzed separately. The *verbs* branch is explored by allowing any tokens that the spaCy English Web Core Large NLP parser (Honnibal et al., 2021) marks as having a part-of-speech (POS) corresponding to any of the Penn Treebank VERB tags[2] to continue on to the sequence of rule-based decisions (Steps 2a-8).

We experimented with various parsers for extracting verbal events, which included running the ClearTAC parser (Myers and Palmer, 2019) and iterating through the list of events SemParse (Gung, 2020; Gung and Palmer, 2021) generates for the input sentence. At this stage, we are able to extract more verbal events using the spaCy NLP parser.

3.2 Step 1b: Event Nominals Branch

While SemParse misses some verbal events, it is the sole parser that can identify nominal tokens that correspond to VerbNet frames. With this functionality, a derived nominal like *explosion* shares the same VerbNet ID as its parent verb *explode*. It can thus be recognized by SemParse as an event nominal. Thus, to follow the *event nominals* annotation branch, we run SemParse separately and only extract spans of text in the sentence that constitute event nominals.

We restrict identification of event nominals to spans of text that do not contain any Penn Treebank VERB tags. Thus, the span *historic visit* is identified as an event nominal because both tokens have a non-verbal POS: adjective and singular noun, respectively. But the span *to lay the groundwork* does not get identified as an event nominal because *lay* has a verbal POS and will thus be handled in the verbal annotation branch. All event nominals receive the PROCESS label from Step 1b, and thus exit the annotation search.

The *event nominals* branch is explored only after the *verbs* annotation branch terminates. The final list of events and corresponding aspects collected for each sentence combines the outputs of the *verbs* and *event nominals* annotation branches.

3.3 Steps 2-3: Verbs Branch

The remaining steps all take place in the *verbs* annotation branch. Step 2a handles non-verbal predication, which analyzes all English copula forms that are followed by predicate nominals, adjectives, and locationals. It assigns all copula forms the aspect STATE, with the condition that the copula does not function as a helping verb, i.e. no verb form directly follows it. Note that UMR annotates the nominal or adjectival predicate rather than the copula, so the sentence *"He is friendly."* results in a UMR aspect annotation for the event *friendly* rather than the verbal token *is*. We compare the aspect results accordingly, not requiring the token that receives the label from AutoAspect to correspond exactly to the predicate token(s) representing

[1] All code can be found at `https://github.com/dchensta/AutoAspect`.

[2] VB (base form), VBD (past tense), VBG (gerund or present participle), VBN (past participle), VBP (non-3rd person singular present, and VBZ (3rd person singular present).

the UMR event.

Step 2b annotates for STATE as well, and it does so based on VerbNet class, requiring a semantic processing tool. We run SemParse and extract the VerbNet senses corresponding to the verbal tokens in the sentence. For each VerbNet sense y in the pre-determined list of VerbNet class IDs that are labeled STATE, we match the SemParse sense x to y by backing off to the most coarse-grained class. For example, the SemParse VerbNet class ID for the lemma *want* is x = *want-32.1-1-1*, but the specified class in the pre-determined list is y = *want-32.1*. We run a regular expressions match to ensure that the class ID y is contained within the span of the more fine-grained class ID x, confirming that x and y belong to the same class. Any verb event that does not receive a STATE label from Steps 2a and 2b receives the umbrella label PROCESS and continues on to Step 4.

3.4 Steps 4-8: Verb Branch

Steps 4-8 subcategorize the umbrella label PROCESS carried over from Step 2b into the labels ACTIVITY, PERFORMANCE, and ENDEAVOR.

Steps 4 and 5 continue to classify based on VerbNet class. Step 4 assigns all verbs that receive a participial[3] Penn Treebank label from spaCy the label ACTIVITY. Verbs with inceptive and continuative auxiliary verbs[4] like *started* and *continued* also receive the ACTIVITY label. Step 5 assigns all completive auxilaries[5] — like *finished* — the label PERFORMANCE and all terminative auxiliaries[6] — like *stopped* — the label ENDEAVOR.

Step 6 assigns verbs that occur in clauses with container adverbials — marked by the preposition *in* — the label PERFORMANCE. Step 6 also assigns verbs that occur in clauses with durative adverbials — marked by the preposition *for* — the label ENDEAVOR. We use the spaCy dependency parser to check that those prepositions occur in the same clause as the verb being analyzed.

Step 7 annotates verbs that occur with non-result paths as ENDEAVOR, marked by prepositions like *around*, *along*, and *past*. A non-result path is defined for the tool as the occurrence of a preposition immediately after the verb it is a dependent of, e.g. in the sentence *"He **walked along** the river."*, where *along* occurs immediately after the main verb *walked*.

Finally, Step 8 assigns any verbal event that has not yet received an annotation the label PERFORMANCE.

4 Results

Many of the annotation steps are themselves complex semantic processing tasks. Therefore, the performance of this rule-based model depends heavily on the limits of the classifier components being utilized. Given the lack of substantial training data that would be required for a machine learning-driven implementation, we focus on specific examples that reveal the linguistic blind spots of our model.

4.1 Annotation Results

The following results were generated from running AutoAspect on four gold standard news articles from the LDC REFLEX English core set of newswire and web text documents (Strassel and Tracey, 2016) that were annotated by our team. Table 1 shows results for the critical subtask of event identification, which yielded a recall of 76.17%, a reasonably high recall for a pilot study with limited gold data. For this specific task, recall is the only appropriate measure for statistical analysis, because precision penalizes the model for annotating an event that is not present in the gold data. Given the variability in using syntactic and semantic cues in the annotation manual, it is more appropriate to see how much of the human-identified labels it is capturing.

For example, AutoAspect analyzes the initial split by analyzing Penn TreeBank verbs separately from Penn TreeBank nominals. In the phrase *investigation of bombing campaign*, it is important to note when AutoAspect only identifies the *investigation* event and fails to identify the *campaign* event. However, a sentence like *"I think the court would be highly politicized."* does not assign an aspect to the verb *think*, but to the event *be_politicized*. Since AutoAspect will analyze every token labeled with a Penn TreeBank VERB part-of-speech, it would be disingenuous to penalize the model for labeling an event that is subsumed by a UMR event purposefully abstracting away from strictly syntactic cues.

[3] VBG (present participle or gerund), VBN (past participle)

[4] *begin-55.1*, *continue-55.3*, and *sustain-55.6*

[5] *complete-55.2*

[6] *stop-55.4*

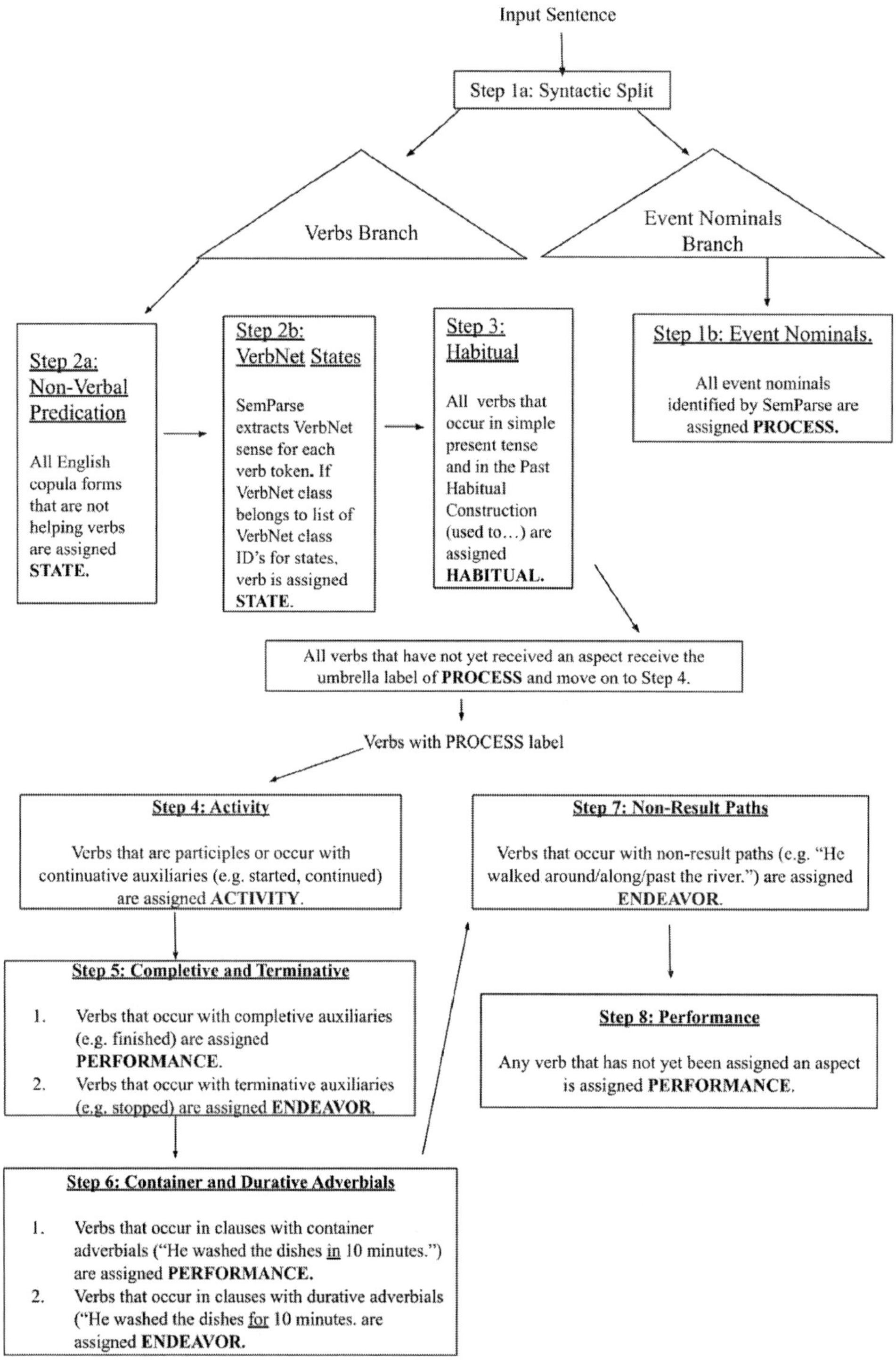

Figure 1: Flow Chart of Automatic Classification

Task	FN	TP	Recall	Acc
Event Nominal ID	56	179	76.17	
ID-ed Events Performance		112		62.57

Table 1: Recall for event identification subtask and performance of model on all gold events that were identified by the model, across all aspect labels.

Of the 235 gold events spread throughout the 4 gold files, the model failed to identify 56, leaving 179 events that were identified. Of those 179, the model correctly labeled 112 gold events out of the 179 it could identify, yielding an accuracy of 62.57%.

Label Error	FP	TP	# Gold	Precision
HABITUAL	27	3	5	10
STATE	7	43	71	86
ACTIVITY	12	6	9	33.33
PROCESS	1	4	56	N/A[7]
PERFORMANCE	15	56	94	78.87
ENDEAVOR	5	0	0	0

[7] Given that almost all of the 56 events the model failed to detect were event nominals, the precision calculation for PROCESS is vacuous.

Table 2: Counts and precision of each type of mislabeled annotation. For each aspect label, FP and TP counts are from the 179 events that AutoAspect successfully detected, number of gold events is from the 235 total gold events.

In Table 2, we show the counts for each type of incorrect label that AutoAspect assigned to an event. This allows us to identify both the linguistic errors made by the model and which errors it makes more frequently. Further development of the tool can thus identify the error-triggering linguistic inputs and improve how a specific rule-based component processes those linguistic inputs.

Table 2 also depicts high precision for STATE and PERFORMANCE, indicating that SemParse is successfully matching VerbNet states to verb tokens and that gold PERFORMANCE tokens are generally able to avoid triggering Steps 2a-7. We did obtain poor precision for HABITUAL and ACTIVITY, showing that the model is too accepting of false positive inputs in Steps 3 and 4.

4.2 Linguistic Analysis

The following linguistic inputs consistently led to errors in the output of AutoAspect.

Sentence	UMR Events
A. Clinton's ***signature*** would be an important symbolic ***gesture***.	sign, be_important, gesture
B. He told survivors of the ***genocide*** there the United States would support the International Court.	tell, genocide, support
C. ***Pleasure.***	be_pleasure
D. Despite American ***objections***, the International Criminal Court enjoys wide support.	object, enjoy
E. ...it will sell weapons to Iran, contrary to the earlier made ***agreement***.	sell, agreement
F. Carla Delponte briefly contemplated an investigation of NATO's bombing ***campaign***.	contemplate, investigate, campaign

Table 3: Missed event nominal corresponding to a gold UMR event in the sentence is bolded and italicized.

Sentence	UMR Events
G. Part of the purpose of this **historic visit** is to lay the groundwork...	visit, be_part, lay
H. It is his **decision**.	decide
I. But the **opposition** here in the United States is intense.	opposition, intense
J. Carla Delponte briefly contemplated an **investigation of NATO's bombing campaign**.	contemplate, investigate, campaign

Table 4: Accurately identified span containing a UMR event nominal is bolded.

1. **Less Explicitly Deverbal Event Nominals:** Failure to detect event nominals made up 45.5% of errors. Table 3 depicts event nominals that SemParse did not detect and Table 4 depicts event nominals that SemParse did detect. Sentence C is notable because it involves a nominal found in a dialogic omission of the main verb. SemParse still fails to identify *pleasure* as an event in the sentence *"It's been a pleasure."*, citing it as an attributive argument of the main verb, the event *seem-109-1-1*.

   These examples indicate that abstracting away from syntactic cues like having a main verb remains a difficult NLP task. SemParse is trained on Unified PropBank corpora, mapping nominal and adjectival predicates to VerbNet roles. Since VerbNet roles are syntactically defined for verbs, mappings exist for linking sentences like *"John has a fear of spiders"* to *"John fears spiders"* and *"John is afraid of spiders"*(Gung, 2020). Thus, an event like *campaign* in Sentence E will not be identified because SemParse currently only

Sentence	UMR Event	AutoAspect	Gold Aspect
K. ...the Pardon Commission, after it has made its decision, **sends** it to the President...	send	HABITUAL	HABITUAL
L. He will spend the next several days at the medical center there before he **returns** home with his wife Sherry.	return	HABITUAL	PERFORMANCE
M. Marsha, thank you very much for **speaking** with us.	speak	ACTIVITY	PERFORMANCE
N. ...they were afraid of the spy mania **rising** in Russia...	rise	ACTIVITY	ACTIVITY

Table 5: Annotation of present tense verb forms.

identifies event nominals/adjectivals that function as arguments of the main verb of the sentence, *contemplated*. A human annotator can identify another argument structure where the noun phrase headed by *investigation* has its own argument roles that could be identified as event nominals, but SemParse identification requires clear sentential structure as input and tends to be more limited to the main verb. Even then, event nominal identification is not guaranteed, given that *survivors* and *genocide* in Sentence B go undetected, despite being the direct object of the main verb *told*.

One possibility is that SemParse handles more explicitly deverbal nominals better. In Table 3, less explicitly deverbal nominals like *signature* and *gesture* are undetected. Table 4 shows that the deriving suffix *-tion* appears to make for more readibly detectable event nominals in *decision*, *opposition*, and *investigation*, all core arguments of their main verb. In F, like *gesture*, the nominal *visit* shares an identical form with its verbal lemma, but SemParse identifies *visit* and not *gesture*. Notably, the event nominal in F also does not occur as part of the core arguments of the main verb *is*, and was successfully identified as its own nominal phrase.

But SemParse also missed *objections* in D and *agreement* in E, both nominals that have a transparently derivative suffix that attaches to the verb lemma. Both of those event nominals occur in adjunct clauses that are not core arguments of the main verb and themselves do not contain a verb.

2. **Dialogic Sentences:** In addition to Sentence C, UMR annotates dialogic sentences like *"One last question."* as a singular event that labels the adjective: *be_last*. The current syntactic split of verbs and nominals does not allow AutoAspect to label predicative nominals and adjectives that lack a main verb. Additionally, multi-sentence coreference is common in dialogue, as in the sentences *"Is this case likely to strain US-Russian relations? I'm afraid it might."*, where an event from the previous clause (*strain*) becomes elided in a successive clause.

3. **Present Tense Verbs:** Table 5 depicts mislabeled and correctly labeled present tense verbs. Mislabeling present tense verbs as HABITUAL was the most common error made by the model aside from the main subtask of event identification, making up 22% of errors. Mislabeling verbs in the present participle form as ACTIVITY was another consistent error, occurring at Step 4. The most common gold label for these erroneous HABITUAL and ACTIVITY labels was PERFORMANCE. For example, in Sentence L, *returns* is mislabeled as HABITUAL. The future tense verb *will spend* in the first clause changes the aspect for the successive clauses of L, i.e. the clause *"...before he* ***returns*** *home with his wife Sherry"*.

The prevalence of gold PERFORMANCE labels indicates that Steps 3 and 4 are prematurely assigning an aspect and not letting certain present participles continue throughout the sequence and make it all the way to Step 8. However, AutoAspect also correctly labeled some present tense forms, as seen in Sentences K and N. Experimenting with using tense and aspect annotations[8] from the ClearTAC parser resulted in even more false positives for HABITUAL and ACTIVITY. Reducing the number of false positives for HABITUAL and ACTIVITY necessitates building a semantic parser that can discern between sentences like L with multi-tense contexts and sentences like M with dialogic contexts.

[8]Tenses: present, past, future; Aspects: progressive, perfect, perfect progressive

4. **Container and Durative Adverbials:** The AutoAspect decision-making for container and durative adverbials in Step 6 — as well as the non-resultative paths in Step 7 — currently only checks if specific prepositions like *in* and *for* are found as dependents of the main verb. Thus, the sentence *"They also said this court did not give the lawyers for the defense due procedure."* incorrectly assigns the verb *give* the aspect ENDEAVOR, because the prepositional phrase *for the defense* is incorrectly parsed by the spaCy dependency parser as being a dependent of the verb *give*.

   Future work can incorporate semantic processing of prepositional phrases to help AutoAspect refine its analysis of prepositional dependencies. One such system is SNACS (Schneider et al., 2018), which outputs disambiguated supersenses like TIME and DURATIVE that could match the semantic properties of the container and durative adverbials.

5. **Stativity:** 15 STATIVE verbs such as *expected* and *contemplated* were mislabeled as PERFORMANCE. This implies that the pre-defined list of VerbNet class IDs that correspond to *state* events does not yet fully cover the range of stative verbs, and/or that SemParse isn't able to find all the VerbNet classes. One solution is to pursue development of a stativity annotator, such as SitEnt (Friedrich et al., 2016), which houses training data that annotates verbs as *stative*, *dynamic*, or neither.

   The overall task of classifying SitEnt types achieved an accuracy of 76% using a CRF model that utilizes hand-crafted feature sets. A key difference is that the SitEnt features are accessed simultaneously by the model, while AutoAspect follows the sequential UMR annotation steps. Future research directions could incorporate developing a feature-based model to achieve an accuracy comparable to SitEnt, which also was scored on larger corpora (Brown and MASC) than the 4 gold documents AutoAspect scored.

5 Conclusion

The linguistic blind spots discovered from analyzing the results highlight many areas for future development for the AutoAspect annotator. It is clear that the primarily syntax-driven rules are unable to capture semantic properties like stativity, disambiguation of prepositional phrases, and genre of text. Feeding in input sentence-by-sentence also prevents AutoAspect from properly analyzing multi-sentence events. The tool currently has a recall of 76.17% for identifying events and a 62.57% accuracy for identified events. As more gold UMR data is processed, further linguistic blind spots can be identified for development past the pilot version.

Acknowledgments

We gratefully acknowledge the support of NSF 1764048 RI: Medium: Collaborative Research: Developing a Uniform Meaning Representation for Natural Language Processing. Any opinions, findings, and conclusions or recommendations expressed in this material are those of the authors and do not necessarily reflect the views of NSF or the U.S. government. We thank James Gung and Ghazaleh Kazeminejad for their valuable assistance in teaching us how to use the SemParse tool. We thank Skatje Myers for assisting us with the ClearTAC tool.

References

Laura Banarescu, Claire Bonial, Shu Cai, Madalina Georgescu, Kira Griffitt, Ulf Hermjakob, Kevin Knight, Philipp Koehn, Martha Palmer, and Nathan Schneider. 2013. Abstract meaning representation for sembanking. In *Proceedings of the 7th linguistic annotation workshop and interoperability with discourse*, pages 178–186.

William Croft. 2001. *Radical construction grammar*. Oxford University Press, Oxford.

William Croft. 2012. *Verbs: Aspect and causal structure*. Oxford University Press, Oxford.

William Croft. in press. *Morphosyntax: Constructions of the World's Languages*.

Lucia Donatelli, Michael Regan, William Croft, and Nathan Schneider. 2018. Annotation of tense and aspect semantics for sentential AMR. In *Proceedings of the Joint Workshop on Linguistic Annotation, Multiword Expressions and Constructions (LAW-MWE-CxG-2018)*, pages 96–108.

Lucia Donatelli, Nathan Schneider, William Croft, and Michael Regan. 2019. Tense and aspect semantics for sentential amr. *Proceedings of the Society for Computation in Linguistics*, 2(1):346–348.

David Dowty. 1991. Thematic proto-roles and argument selection. *Language*, 67:547–619.

Annemarie Friedrich and Damyana Gateva. 2017. Classification of telicity using cross-linguistic annotation projection. In *Proceedings of the 2017 Conference on Empirical Methods in Natural Language Processing*, pages 2559–2565, Copenhagen, Denmark. Association for Computational Linguistics.

Annemarie Friedrich, Alexis Palmer, and Manfred Pinkal. 2016. Situation entity types: automatic classification of clause-level aspect. In *Proceedings of the 54th Annual Meeting of the Association for Computational Linguistics (Volume 1: Long Papers)*, pages 1757–1768.

James Gung. 2020. *Abstraction, Sense Distinctions and Syntax in Neural Semantic Role Labeling*. Ph.D. thesis, University of Colorado at Boulder.

James Gung and Martha Palmer. 2021. Predicate representations and polysemy in verbnet semantic parsing. In *14th International Conference on Computational Semantics (IWCS)*, online.

Matthew Honnibal, Ines Montani, Sofie Van Landeghem, and Adriane Boyd. 2021. spaCy: Industrial-strength Natural Language Processing in Python.

Skatje Myers and Martha Palmer. 2019. Cleartac: Verb tense, aspect, and form classification using neural nets. In *Proceedings of the First International Workshop on Designing Meaning Representations*, pages 136–140.

Nathan Schneider, Jena D Hwang, Vivek Srikumar, Jakob Prange, Austin Blodgett, Sarah R Moeller, Aviram Stern, Adi Bitan, and Omri Abend. 2018. Comprehensive supersense disambiguation of english prepositions and possessives. *arXiv preprint arXiv:1805.04905*.

Stephanie Strassel and Jennifer Tracey. 2016. Lorelei language packs: Data, tools, and resources for technology development in low resource languages. In *Proceedings of the Tenth International Conference on Language Resources and Evaluation (LREC'16)*, pages 3273–3280.

Jens E. L. Van Gysel, Meagan Vigus, Pavlina Kalm, Sook-kyung Lee, Michael Regan, and William Croft. 2019. Cross-linguistic semantic annotation: Reconciling the language-specific and the universal. In *Proceedings of the First International Workshop on Designing Meaning Representations*, pages 1–14, Florence, Italy.

Jens EL Van Gysel, Meagan Vigus, Jayeol Chun, Kenneth Lai, Sarah Moeller, Jiarui Yao, Tim O'Gorman, Andrew Cowell, William Croft, Jan Huang, Chu-Ren Hajič, James H. Martin, Stephan Oepen, Martha Palmer, James Pustejovsky, Rosa Vallejos, and Nianwen Xue. 2021. Designing a uniform meaning representation for natural language processing. *Künstliche Intelligenz*, pages 1–18.

Zeno Vendler. 1967. *Linguistics in philosophy*, chapter Verbs and times. Cornell University Press, Ithaca.

A Supplementary Material

A.1 List of VerbNet classes corresponding to the aspect STATE

- want-32.1
- long-32.2
- try-61.1
- intend-61.2
- wish-62
- allow-64.1
- let-64.2
- admit-64.3
- forbid-64.4
- tingle-40.8.2
- pain-40.8.1
- stimulus_subject-30.4
- keep-15.2
- support-15.3
- contain-15.4
- being_dressed-41.3.3
- simple_dressing-1.3.1
- function-105.2.1
- lodge-46
- exist-47.1
- bulge-47.5.3
- meander-47.7
- contiguous_location-47.8
- terminus-47.9
- put_spatial-9.2-1
- cling-22.5
- entity_specific_modes_being-47.2
- light_emission-43.1
- smell_emission-43.3
- sound_emission-43.2
- sound_existence-47.4
- substance_emission-43.4-1
- swarm-47.5.1-1
- animal_sounds-38
- carve-21.2-1
- modes_of_being_with_motion-47.3
- snooze-40.4
- body_internal_states-40.6
- spatial_configuration-47.6
- peer-30.3
- see-30.1

Can predicate-argument relationships be extracted from UD trees?

Adam Ek **Jean-Philippe Bernardy** **Stergios Chatzikyriakidis**
Centre for Linguistic Theory and Studies in Probability
Department of Philosophy, Linguistics and Theory of Science
University of Gothenburg
{adam.ek,jean-philippe.bernardy,stergios.chatzikyriakidis}@gu.se

Abstract

In this paper we investigate the possibility of extracting predicate-argument relations from UD trees (and enhanced UD graphs). Concretely, we apply UD parsers on an English question answering/semantic-role labeling data set (FitzGerald et al., 2018) and check if the annotations reflect the relations in the resulting parse trees, using a small number of rules to extract this information. We find that 79.1% of the argument-predicate pairs can be found in this way, on the basis of Udify (Kondratyuk and Straka, 2019). Error analysis reveals that half of the error cases are attributable to shortcomings in the dataset. The remaining errors are mostly due to predicate-argument relations not being extractible algorithmically from the UD trees (requiring semantic reasoning to be resolved). The parser itself is only responsible for a small portion of errors. Our analysis suggests a number of improvements to the UD annotation schema: we propose to enhance the schema in four ways, in order to capture argument-predicate relations. Additionally, we propose improvements regarding data collection for question answering/semantic-role labeling data.

1 Introduction

Universal Dependencies (UD), can be seen as a compromise, a balancing act between six principles, referred to as Manning's law (Nivre et al., 2016):

1. UD needs to be satisfactory for analysis of individual languages
2. UD needs to be good for linguistic typology
3. UD must be suitable for rapid, consistent annotation
4. UD must be suitable for computer parsing with high accuracy
5. UD must be easily comprehended and used by a non-linguist
6. UD must provide good support for downstream language understanding tasks

Support for natural language understanding downstream tasks in the UD schema has been shown in a number of studies including event extraction, negation scope detection and opinion analysis (Fares et al., 2018), information extraction (Angeli et al., 2015), image retrieval (Schuster et al., 2015), question-answering (Reddy et al., 2017), and Natural Language Inference (Mishra et al., 2020), among many others.

However, certain syntactic dependencies relevant to semantics are not included in the original formulation of UD. For example, a word may be the subject of two conjoined verbs, but in UD the subject is only connected to one of the verbs. To discover that the word is the subject of two verbs it has to be inferred from the conjunction. However, this creates unnecessary burdens for models using the UD schema. The *enhanced UD schema* (EUD) (Schuster and Manning, 2016) includes such edges, with the aim to make semantics more explicit. Recently there has been a surge of interest and development of EUD, spurred on by its applicability on semantic downstream tasks such as information extraction (Tiktinsky et al., 2020; Sun et al., 2020). Research into EUD has also be facilitated recently by two shared tasks on EUD parsing (Bouma et al., 2020, 2021), which has resulted in a mix of machine learning and rule-based approaches for producing EUD graphs. We come back to an evaluation of the EUD schema in Section 5.1.

The support provided by UD w.r.t. downstream NLU tasks raises the question of how much "semantics" UD actually contains, or better put, how much semantic reasoning can one perform by using just the information provided by UD. This is also related to the question of whether UD dependencies

Proceedings of the Joint 15th Linguistic Annotation Workshop (LAW) and 3rd Designing Meaning Representations (DMR) Workshop, pages 46–55
November, 2021.

should be seen as semantic, syntactic, or maybe something between the two. To some extent all three possibilities have been considered. One way to approach this question is to check the amount of semantic knowledge that UD exhibits, explicitly or implicitly, in relation to specific semantic tasks or features. Silveira (2016) argues that the way to see UD is as a representation "for" semantics, not "of" semantics. Under this view, UD can be seen as a kind of scaffolding where some proper semantic backbone will be built upon. Again, however, this begs the question of the nature of the scaffolding. Silveira (2016) claims that UD has implicit semantic role information and also shows that their enhanced version, which, as they argue, mirror semantic relations more closely, perform better than normal UD in an event extraction task involving a model that extracts dependency features from different parses. Previous research has shown the opposite to be the case, i.e. UD performing better than the enhanced version in this task Miwa et al. (2010a,b); Buyko and Hahn (2010), even though these pieces of work are not directly tested on enhanced UD, but on previous related efforts to expand basic UD (Silveira, 2016). UD has been also criticized by researchers working in Theoretical Linguistics (Osborne and Gerdes, 2019). According to them, UD fails to observe Manning's first desideratum because "UD annotation choices are not satisfactory on linguistic analysis grounds because they result from a mixture of semantic and syntactic criteria". Lastly, one could argue that approaches that attempt to combine UD with an explicit logical semantics interface implicitly assume that UD is syntactic and/or missing crucial semantic information.

In this paper, we propose a way to test the semantic capabilities of UD *parsers* for English by using their output to infer answers in a Question-Answering task. More precisely, what we want to investigate is the question of whether predicate-argument relations are correctly captured by UD parsers. We believe that this is an important question to be posed, because, if this is the case and there is enough ground/scaffolding, then a more fine-grained semantic representation may be build on top of UD (for example, some correspondence between UD syntactic trees and logical semantics). A related question is to what extent enhanced dependencies are better, if at all, in precisely encoding predicate-argument relations.

2 Dataset

We perform experiments on the question-answering/semantic-role-labeling dataset of (FitzGerald et al., 2018), which is based on the work of (He et al., 2015), simply referred to as "QA-SRL" below. The rationale is that, in the QA-SRL dataset, question-answers pairs are directly concerning predicate-argument structures. Each question has a passage which it refers to. For example, the dataset might contain the passage "UN published a report" together with the question "What did something publish?". The answers are provided by annotators selecting a contiguous span of text in the passage which answers the question, in this case the object "a report".

The dataset contains passages from 3 domains in English: Wikipedia, Wikinews and science, with questions and answers generated by crowdsourcing. For each verbal predicate in the passage, questions about one of the arguments are constructed by the annotators using question templates. In total the dataset contain 265156 valid questions over 76397 passages. The QA-SRL dataset also contains an automatically generated dataset. However, we have not included this part and only consider the crowdsourced part.

3 Task and Method

The most obvious way to test whether UD parsers can correctly identify the semantic arguments of verbs would be to map the form of a QA-SRL question to an UD role, then retrieve the subtree of the argument from the UD tree and check if it matches the human annotations.

Unfortunately it is not easy to map the argument types of the QA-SRL dataset to UD roles. One difficulty is the mismatch of passive and active voice between questions and answers. Another problem is that the non-subject UD roles (obj/obl/advcl/etc) are in n-to-n correspondence with the QA-SRL argument types (locations, time, etc). Converting these relationship to a functional mapping would require the use of some statistical model to extract these features from the sentence. Using a statistical model would make unclear whether it is UD that captures argument-predicate relationships, or the model. Thus, to keep the method simple we resort to checking if the UD trees obtained from a parser contains the annotated QA-SRL argument. To avoid the question of *which* semantic role should be extracted, we check if *any* of the children of the verb matches the answer. We make two further amendments to the task: 1. we enhance UD trees with EUD arcs and 2. we check for arguments in the parent position.

The second amendment helps with cases when the sentence has the form of a copula or when the verb plays the role of adjectival phrase. For example, given the passage "Paleontologists are interested in fossils" and the question "Who is interested in something?", then one should be able to recover "Paleontologists" as an argument. However, in the UD tree, "Paleontologists" is the parent of "interested". Likewise, given "The observed animals were tortoises." and the question "What was observed?" should point to "animals"; which is the parent of "observed" in the UD tree.

The first amendment is to use the EUD schema rather than plain UD. While the state-of-the-art UD parsers do not provide this information, it is possible to automatically add most EUD edges using a number of rules (Silveira, 2016; Ek and Bernardy, 2020). Thus our pipeline consists in first running a plain UD parser, we test both the Stanza parser (Qi et al., 2020) and the Udify parser (Kondratyuk and Straka, 2019), and then we apply the following enhancements to the UD trees, using the system developed in (Ek and Bernardy, 2020):

1. Propagation of incoming dependencies to conjuncts;
2. Propagation of outgoing dependencies from conjuncts;
3. Propagation of subject relations for direct control and raising constructions;
4. Addition of co-reference arcs in relative clause constructions

To recapitulate, after adding enhanced edges for each question in the test set, we proceed to:

1. Find the verb index relevant to the question. Generally this information is given by the QA-SRL data. In rare cases some adjustments need to be made, for example if the parser counted words differently than the dataset we adjust the verb index accordingly;
2. Collect all possible arguments according to the EUD graph;
3. Extract the constituent for each argument by following the child edges;
4. Normalize the text of each constituent by removing punctuation, leading prepositions, and determiners. Indeed, the annotations are inconsistent regarding whether prepositions and determiners should be part of the argument or not;
5. If any of the gold answers match any of the arguments retrieved, we consider the argument retrieval a success

4 Results and Analysis

In this section we present the results obtained from extracting predicate-argument relations, and provide an analysis of the errors observed.

4.1 Baseline

As a side experiment, we have attempted to find if the argument can be found *anywhere* as a constituent in the UD parse tree.

Model	Upper bound
Udify	98.9%
Stanza	98.6%

Table 1: Dependency parsers upper bound performance.

Table 1 shows that in 98.9 and 98.6 of the cases, it is possible to extract the semantic arguments from the syntactic structure by finding an appropriate root of the tree. Thus, the above numbers place a theoretical upper bound on the method, as the accuracy that we could achieve if arguments were always correctly attached to their predicate. This means that the above numbers provide a sanity check for the approach: in 98.9% of the cases, the gold correspond to something which Udify has identified *somewhere* in the sentence.

4.2 Extracting predicate-argument relations

In Table 2 we report the accuracy for both parsers, with and without the applying the enhancements described in Section 3. The results show a clear

Parser	Plain UD	EUD
Udify	0.683	0.791
Stanza	0.722	0.744

Table 2: Accuracy of UD trees with and without enhancements using the Udify and Stanza parsers.

superiority for Udify, which is more than 4 percentage points above Stanza in both configurations.

Taking into account enhancement edges gives a large benefit to Udify parser, and a small benefit to Stanza.

To get a better sense of where the errors are coming from, we have performed manual analysis as follows. Focusing on the best performing configuration (Udify with enhanced dependencies), we picked 100 test cases at random, and, by manual inspection, we determined if the error is imputable to either the parser, the dataset or the method. Our classification criteria are as follows:

Parser If the used UD parser produced a wrong parse tree.

Dataset If either the passage or the question is incorrect, either syntactically or semantically; or if the annotations do not contain the answer according to the question and passage.

Method If both the dataset and the parse tree are correct, but the argument is not related to the verb in the UD tree.

We found the following results: out of 100 cases, 49 errors were attributable to the dataset, 13 to the parser and 38 to the method. In terms of percentage points of lost accuracy, this means that 10.2 points are attributable to the dataset, 2.7 points to the parser and 7.9 points to the method. We further analyze error cases below.

4.3 Shortcomings of the data set

We found 49 errors imputable to shortcomings in the QA-SRL dataset in our sample. In 20 cases out of those, we found that the annotators chose an answer which is a semantic superset of the answer found in the passage. This situation is illustrated in Section 4.3.

(1) An error due to a superset relation between the gold and the retrieved answer

Passage: Placards on the courtyard wall explain it served as headquarters for Field marshal Kollowrat-Krakowsky battling Napoleonic forces in the 1796 Siege of Kehl

Question: Where was someone battling?

Gold: 'Siege of Kehl'

Retrieved: in the 1796 Siege of Kehl

In this example, the correct answer is only "Kehl", as the "siege of" indicates something which happened at "Kehl". Thus, the gold provided by the annotators include the actual gold answer, but provide additional information.

Another issue that arises in the dataset (7 cases in our sample) is incorrect or incomprehensible questions. This is frequently caused by considering a word which is a noun or an adjective in the passage as verb (or part of a verb, e.g. a past participle in a passive verbal form) about which to ask questions. This concerns either homophonous forms or forms that can be formed by using a base form which is a homophone to the word in the passage. An example is shown below:

(2) An error due to changing the POS of a word in the passage

Passage: In 1977 a swamp created by heavy rains was found to contain 8 toxic materials, including 11 suspected cancer-causing chemicals

Question: When was something being swamped?

Gold: 'in 1977'

In this example the noun 'swamp' is turned to a past participle, part of the passive past continuous verbal form "was being swamped".

In the following example the incomprehensibility is caused by plain ungrammaticality:

(3) An error due to an ungrammatical question

Passage: A Texas man was rescued earlier this week after being adrift at sea for 31 hours, according to media reports on Monday

Question: Who was something according to?

Gold: 'media reports'

Lastly, in 9 cases the actual answer is just not in the provided passage. Despite this problem, annotators did provide a gold answer. The following is such an example:

(4) An example where the answer is not in the passage

Passage: What this entails is a more complex relationship to technology than either techno-optimists or techno-pessimists tend to allow.

Question: What isn't being allowed?

Gold: 'complex relationship to technology', 'a more complex relationship to technology', more complex relationship to technology'

Here the passage tells us that "techno-optimists" allow do not allow *simple (or less complex) relationships to technology*. However neither the word "less" or "simple" or equivalent are found in the passage. Thus, the gold simply cannot be annotated as a span in the passage, even though annotators did attempt to do so.

Another notable issue is the incorrect identification of a verb occurrence which occurs more than once in the passage (the question is about one occurrence and the answer about another), accounting for two cases in our sample. In another two cases, the syntax of the passage was plainly incorrect, and thus the parser could not recover any useful UD tree.

4.4 Shortcomings of the parser

In most cases, parsing errors are attributable to difficulty in handling punctuation (in particular quotes)- and attachment errors.

In 5 out of the 13 parse error cases in our sample, Udify interpreted quotation marks as sentence final markers and terminated the parsing, as in the sentence: *After summarizing his career , Matisse refers to the possibilities the cut-out technique offers , insisting " [...] "* where the parser stops after the first quotation mark.

Another common error (6 cases out of 13) is incorrect attachment. That is, a subtree of the dependency tree is attached to the wrong head, as in: *Churchill was a prolific writer, often under the pen name " Winston S. Churchill " , which he **used** [...]* where "used" is attached to "writer" rather than "name". Of course, in this case, a correct attachment demands a fine understanding of the sentence, so one might wonder if this it reasonable to expect such precision from the parser. Indeed, this is precisely what we intend to estimate by our experiment.

4.5 Shortcomings of the method

Seen as a way to test parsers, our method relies on the assumption that predicate-argument relationships are either directly encoded in the UD syntax, or can be directly inferred from it. Thus, conversely, the predicate-argument relationship can serve as a proxy for testing UD parser. Even though the assumption generally holds (not withstanding parsing errors), it sometimes fails. In the rest of the section we analyze the cases when this happens.

Insufficient propagation of arguments The first class of issues is related to the propagation of argument to all the predicates where they apply. This sort of situation accounts roughly for one third of the errors attributable to shortcomings of the method. While EUD mandates subject control propagation, there are other kinds of argument propagation which can apply.

The first main case occurs when purpose clauses are present. Consider the following passage and question: "Public officials in Texas have urged citizens to receive a flu shot. Who receives something?" Here the answer can be retrieved from a relation between *citizens* and *receive*, but the relationship is not direct: it is mediated by a purpose clause, and this mediation is not identified explicitly in the UD representation.

The second main case involves topicalization of prepositional phrase. The following example illustrates. "In the summer, the glacier melts rapidly, producing a thick deposit of sediment. When is something produced?" In this case the temporal clause is not syntactically attached to *producing*. Rather, it is topicalized and thus attached to the top level node.

Semantic or pragmatic reasoning is necessary In the second class of issues, some sort of semantic and/or pragmatic reasoning is necessary to understand the relationship between arguments and their predicates. The following passage illustrates the problem: "New South Wales premier Mike Baird said people should leave work early and arrive home before dark, as storms were predicted to intensify. Why did someone say something?" Here the cause is not syntactically related to the verb "say". Furthermore, locating the cause cannot be a matter of traversing the syntax tree, using *any* method. Instead, proper identification of the answer relies on the lexical semantics of the passage. We attribute roughly one fourth of the shortcomings of the methods to this class. We stress however that the lines are blurred between various classes of errors. Even though the classification is done according to the best of our judgement it is not easy to make the difference between this case and the previous one.

Anaphora resolution Another cause of errors is the lack of anaphora resolution layer in the processing pipeline. For example, the search for syntactic arguments may find the pronoun "it", but the annotators could have resolved the anaphora to a noun phrase (say "the power plant"). This class of errors causes only a tenth of the method shortcomings. This low number may come as a surprise. Its relatively low weight can be explained by two factors: the first one is that annotators are allowed to point to pronouns when identifying arguments. In this case anaphora resolution plays no role. Additionally, each passage is only one sentence long. Therefore, the possibilities for anaphora resolution are limited.

Shortcomings of the parent heuristic When the answer is one of the children, we consider the whole subtree as a candidate answer. When the answer should be looked up in the parent node, we cannot do the same thing: the parent node would contain the whole phrase, which is wrong. For example, when trying to answer "Who observed?" given "The observed animals were tortoises", the parent is "animals", which is the root of the sentence. The heuristic that we apply is to subtract the subtree which contains the verb to obtain the candidate answer. Often, this works well, but in this example we obtain nonsense. This problem accounts roughly for 15 percent of method errors.

Other issues The above list covers roughly 80 percent of errors. The remaining issues include various idiosyncratic interpretations of passages and questions (parataxis, non-deterministic selection of non-specific relative clauses, etc.). Some of them seem as if they could be handled by special rules to identify arguments, but we have preferred not to implement such rules in order to keep the results more directly linked to the syntactic trees which we analyze.

5 Suggested improvements to annotation schemes

In this section we leverage our understanding of EUD and QA-SRL, and provide advice to creators of datasets featuring either annotation schema.

5.1 EUD

While the main UD format prescribes dependency *trees*, UD also specifies an enhanced format which allows for additional semantically relevant edges to be added (thus obtaining a graph). As Candito et al. (2017) among others note, different tasks seem to require different semantic representations. Thus, our suggestions to the EUD schema focus on how to extract arguments indicated by some question.

Our analysis shows that EUD is able to model the predicates and arguments in QA-SRL to a high degree (when probed with our fairly straightforward rule-based system) providing an appreciable increase in accuracy compared to plain UD, see Table 2. Yet, as far as we understand, the EUD annotation standard is lacking in clarity when it comes to how much semantic relations should be reflected in the structure. The standard reference appears to be the UD website[1], where all enhancements seem to be deducible algorithmically from the plain UD tree. However, as seen in Section 4.5, certain predicate-argument relationships are not present in the dependency structure, even after applying the algorithmic enhancements.

We believe that a variant of the EUD scheme with full reflection of predicate-argument structure would be beneficial for many downstream tasks. In the light of our experiment, we propose a number of following arcs to be added, as we list below.

EUD mandates the propagation of subjects through control verbs. As an illustration, consider the sentence "John wants to eat.". The UD tree contains the arcs in black, and EUD mandates to add the blue arc:

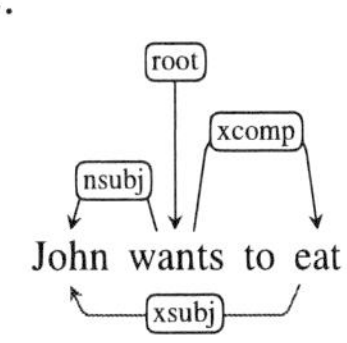

However, we have found that the predicate, the argument and the control verb are not arranged in fixed syntactic patterns, which makes adding the relevant arcs difficult. The main source of difficulties appear to be that the relationship between

[1]https://universaldependencies.org/u/overview/enhanced-syntax.html

the argument and predicate can be mediated by a purpose clause.

To illustrate the complexity of the problem, we show two typical examples.

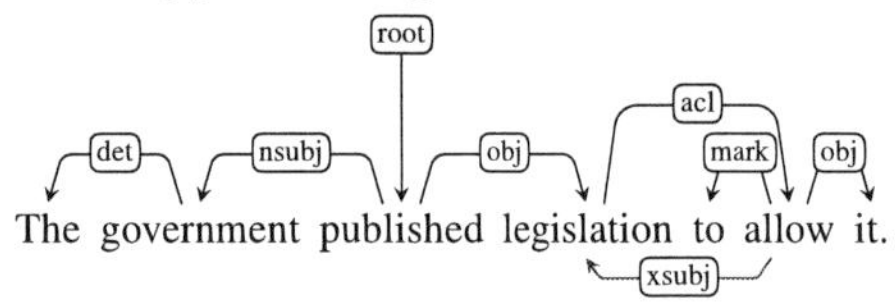

Above, the (semantic) subject of "allow" is "government", which is syntactically a grandfather node of allow. ("Legislation" is another candidate, but it also cannot be identified using a simple syntactic pattern.)

In the example below, we face two difficulties. First, "take" is not a control verb. Second, even though the desired argument of "maintain" (which is "arrangement") can be identified as an argument of "take", this can only be done *via* a relative clause. Third, the roles do not match (a subject becomes an object).

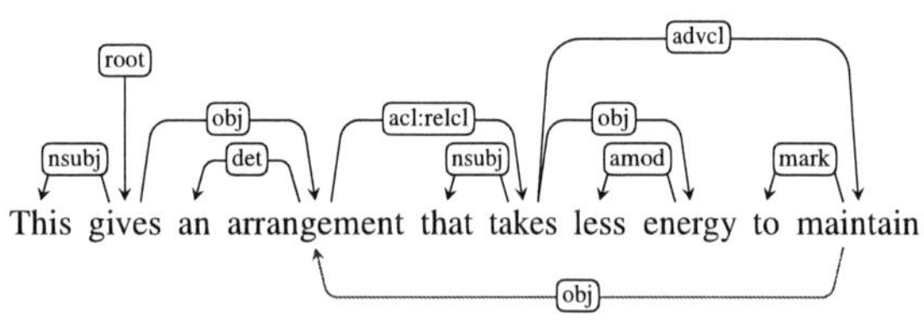

In sum, we purport that, in general, the semantic subject (or object) of a predicate can be found anywhere in the sentence.

Another shortcoming observed is regarding topicalization. Topicalization occurs when a phrase in a sentence is moved to the front of the sentence, to make the phrase more prominent. In the case of prepositional phrases, often indicating semantic roles pertaining to the location, time, or manner in which something happens, is typically expressed with the role obl. However, two verbs may be associated with a prepositional phrase indicating time. Thus, the obl argument should be propagated similarly to how the subject and object roles are propagated in control-like verb construction. An example from the dataset, with out proposed enhancement in blue:

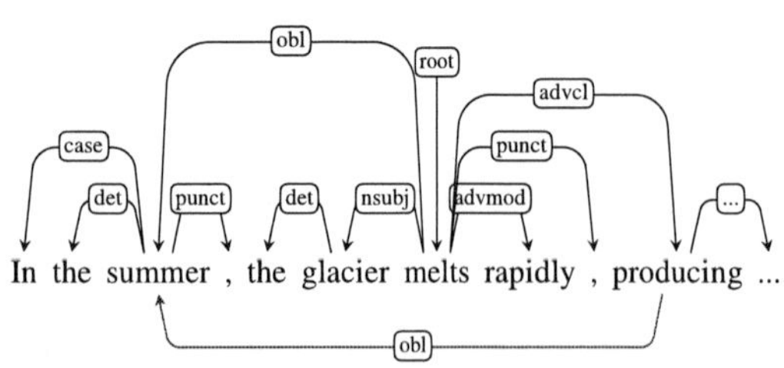

This addition allows for a straightforward interpretation of "when" things happen, by associating both "melts" and "producing" (which is a consequence of "melts") with the phrase "in the summer". This allows us to more easily extract the answer to the question: "when was something produced?".

Finally, anaphoric relationships should be noted as well. This is a well-studied topic which we won't comment further upon, however, we refer readers to the Universal Anaphora project (Poesio et al., 1999).

It should be noted that, contrary to the algorithmic transformations of UD trees, some of the above arcs cannot be deduced without a certain amount of semantic understanding of the sentence (in the sense that substituting lexemes by others with the same POS would change the structure). However, this kind of effect is already present when deciding the attachment of constituents, and therefore already affects plain UD.

5.2 QA-SRL

We have discovered several possible improvements regarding the QA-SRL data collection.

One prevalent source of ambiguity regards the selection of a general or specific phrase, as in Example (1). A way to remedy this ambiguity in future versions of the QA-SRL datasets is to give annotators more specific instructions for cases like these. A solution that seems to be viable is to instruct annotators to give the most specific answer as this is found in the text, which correctly answers the question. In plain words, this is the longest possible substring that correctly answers the question. In the case of Example (1), that would be the substring "in the 1796 Siege of Kehl". Note that the relations subset and superset have a more restricted meaning here, as they are bound by the specific syntax found in the passage. As such, the gold and the retrieved answer stand in a subset relation, if the former is a superstring (thus, more specific) of the latter and, vice versa, in a superset relation, if the former is a substring of the latter. An instruction to select the longer string would also lift the ambiguity inherent to selection of non-specific relative clauses. To illustrate, consider the passage-question pair "Matisse's wife Amélie , who suspected that he was having an affair, ended their 41-year marriage. Who ended something?" For this example the annotators marked 'Amélie' and 'Matisse's wife Amélie' as possible answers, but 'Matisse's wife Amélie , who suspected that he was having an affair' is the longest acceptable string.

To prevent incomprehensible questions (like Section 4.3), additional validation tests should be run to safeguard against the formation of ungrammatical questions. One way to do this is to validate at least part of the questions in the dataset using a syntactic acceptability task. This helps identify the ungrammatical questions and replace them with grammatical ones. We observed that annotators tend to make attempts at such meaningless questions as well as questions which do not have an answer in the passage. This is presumably caused by annotators "trying their best", but results in bogus answers. One idea to filter those would be to turn proposed answers into inference problems, as suggested by Demszky et al. (2018). If the constructed problem is not an entailment, then the answer should be rejected. For instance, Example 4 would be turned into the following problem:

(5) NLI pair for Example (4)

Premise: What this entails is a more complex relationship to technology than either techno-optimists or techno-pessimists tend to allow.

Hypothesis: Complex relationship to technology isn't being allowed.

Even though the double-negation complicates reasoning, in this case, one can reasonably expect that the absence of entailment could be detected. This could be done by another round of annotations, perhaps helped by a statistical model which would select doubtful cases.

6 Related Work

In addition to our suggestions, there has been several other proposals to extend syntactic dependency trees to more explicitly cover semantic phenomena, including the work of Silveira (2016), already discussed in the introduction.

Additionally, Candito et al. (2017) notably propose additions to the EUD schema mainly focusing on extracting the arguments of non-finite verbs and dealing with syntactic alterations in a French treebank.

The Universal Decompositional Semantics project (White et al., 2016; Zhang et al., 2017) is another attempt at extending the UD framework to cover semantic phenomena. They develop the Semantic proto-role labeling protocol (SPR1 and SPR2), to find proto-semantic roles by decomposing semantic roles such as "Agent" into more fine-grained properties.

Working more generally on dependency trees, Stanovsky et al. (2016) develop a framework to enhance dependency trees such that semantic propositions are more easily recoverable which includes a similar propagation of subjects and objects as in EUD. However they do not appear to take any special note of purpose clauses or topicalization.

7 Conclusion and Future Work

We have found that a state-of-the-art UD parser such as Udify only fails to produce a semantically correct UD trees in rare cases. If we exclude difficulties in handling quotes, only 8 cases out of 100 errors are imputable to the parser.

However, in a lot of cases the semantic relationship cannot possibly be present in the UD format, due to its tree structure. To express this, enhancing the structure with additional arcs is needed. Some of those arcs can be found by algorithmic means (as listed in Section 3), boosting the accuracy by a several points, see Table 2. One could expect that the EUD schema would mandate the addition of all semantically relevant arcs, but this is not the case. We have advocated for an update to the EUD standard which fills this gap, as discussed in Section 5.1.

While the goals of the QA-SRL appear to align perfectly with ours, and the annotation for QA-SRL was both effective and relatively cheap, we notice some shortcomings in the annotations (Section 4.3). Sometimes annotators get something wrong because of a tricky phenomena or they are presented with a badly formulated question about the passage. We have proposed a number of strategies to improve data collection for future similar datasets (Section 5.2). Another point to consider is that it is much cheaper to annotate QA-SRL than full EUD parse trees. Therefore QA-SRL could be a proxy for training EUD parsers on predicate-argument structures, together with for example multi-task learning. That is, in addition to training a system to predicting arcs, the system would be optimized on selecting the spans of text corresponding to the arguments of predicates.

Acknowledgements

We would like to thank the reviewers for their helpful comments. The research reported in this paper was supported by a grant from the Swedish Research Council (VR project 2014-39) for the establishment of the Centre for Linguistic Theory and Studies in Probability (CLASP) at the University of Gothenburg.

References

Gabor Angeli, Melvin Jose Johnson Premkumar, and Christopher D. Manning. 2015. Leveraging linguistic structure for open domain information extraction. In *Proceedings of the 53rd Annual Meeting of the Association for Computational Linguistics and the 7th International Joint Conference on Natural Language Processing (Volume 1: Long Papers)*, pages 344–354, Beijing, China. Association for Computational Linguistics.

Gosse Bouma, Djamé Seddah, and Daniel Zeman. 2020. Overview of the iwpt 2020 shared task on parsing into enhanced universal dependencies. In *Proceedings of the 16th International Conference on Parsing Technologies and the IWPT 2020 Shared Task on Parsing into Enhanced Universal Dependencies*, pages 151–161.

Gosse Bouma, Djamé Seddah, and Daniel Zeman. 2021. From raw text to enhanced universal dependencies: The parsing shared task at iwpt 2021. In *Proceedings of the 17th International Conference on Parsing Technologies (IWPT 2021)*, pages 146–157.

Ekaterina Buyko and Udo Hahn. 2010. Evaluating the impact of alternative dependency graph encodings on solving event extraction tasks. In *Proceedings of the 2010 Conference on Empirical Methods in Natural Language Processing*, pages 982–992.

Marie Candito, Bruno Guillaume, Guy Perrier, and Djamé Seddah. 2017. Enhanced UD dependencies with neutralized diathesis alternation. In *Proceedings of the Fourth International Conference on Dependency Linguistics (Depling 2017)*, pages 42–53, Pisa,Italy. Linköping University Electronic Press.

Dorottya Demszky, Kelvin Guu, and Percy Liang. 2018. Transforming question answering datasets into natural language inference datasets. *CoRR*, abs/1809.02922.

Adam Ek and Jean-Philippe Bernardy. 2020. How much of enhanced UD is contained in UD? In *Proceedings of the 16th International Conference on Parsing Technologies and the IWPT 2020 Shared Task on Parsing into Enhanced Universal Dependencies*, pages 221–226, Online. Association for Computational Linguistics.

Murhaf Fares, Stephan Oepen, Lilja Øvrelid, Jari Björne, and Richard Johansson. 2018. The 2018 shared task on extrinsic parser evaluation: On the downstream utility of English Universal Dependency parsers. In *Proceedings of the CoNLL 2018 Shared Task: Multilingual Parsing from Raw Text to Universal Dependencies*, pages 22–33, Brussels, Belgium. Association for Computational Linguistics.

Nicholas FitzGerald, Julian Michael, Luheng He, and Luke Zettlemoyer. 2018. Large-scale QA-SRL parsing. In *Proceedings of the 56th Annual Meeting of the Association for Computational Linguistics (Volume 1: Long Papers)*, pages 2051–2060, Melbourne, Australia. Association for Computational Linguistics.

Luheng He, Mike Lewis, and Luke Zettlemoyer. 2015. Question-answer driven semantic role labeling: Using natural language to annotate natural language. In *Proceedings of the 2015 Conference on Empirical Methods in Natural Language Processing*, pages 643–653, Lisbon, Portugal. Association for Computational Linguistics.

Dan Kondratyuk and Milan Straka. 2019. 75 languages, 1 model: Parsing universal dependencies universally. In *Proceedings of the 2019 Conference on Empirical Methods in Natural Language Processing and the 9th International Joint Conference on Natural Language Processing (EMNLP-IJCNLP)*, pages 2779–2795, Hong Kong, China. Association for Computational Linguistics.

Anshuman Mishra, Dhruvesh Patel, Aparna Vijayakumar, Xiang Li, Pavan Kapanipathi, and Kartik Talamadupula. 2020. Reading comprehension as natural language inference:a semantic analysis. In *Proceedings of the Ninth Joint Conference on Lexical and Computational Semantics*, pages 12–19, Barcelona, Spain (Online). Association for Computational Linguistics.

Makoto Miwa, Sampo Pyysalo, Tadayoshi Hara, and Jun'ichi Tsujii. 2010a. Evaluating dependency representations for event extraction. In *Proceedings of the 23rd International Conference on Computational Linguistics (Coling 2010)*, pages 779–787, Beijing, China. Coling 2010 Organizing Committee.

Makoto Miwa, Sampo Pyysalo, Tadayoshi Hara, and Jun'ichi Tsujii. 2010b. A comparative study of syntactic parsers for event extraction. In *Proceedings of the 2010 Workshop on Biomedical Natural Language Processing*, pages 37–45.

Joakim Nivre, Marie-Catherine de Marneffe, Filip Ginter, Yoav Goldberg, Jan Hajič, Christopher D. Manning, Ryan McDonald, Slav Petrov, Sampo Pyysalo, Natalia Silveira, Reut Tsarfaty, and Daniel Zeman. 2016. Universal Dependencies v1: A multilingual treebank collection. In *Proceedings of the Tenth International Conference on Language Resources and Evaluation (LREC'16)*, pages 1659–1666, Portorož,

Slovenia. European Language Resources Association (ELRA).

Timothy Osborne and Kim Gerdes. 2019. The status of function words in dependency grammar: A critique of universal dependencies (ud). *Glossa (Online)*.

Massimo Poesio, Florence Bruneseaux, and Laurent Romary. 1999. The mate meta-scheme for coreference in dialogues in multiple languages. In *ACL'99 Workshop Towards Standards and Tools for Discourse Tagging*, pages 65–74.

Peng Qi, Yuhao Zhang, Yuhui Zhang, Jason Bolton, and Christopher D. Manning. 2020. Stanza: A Python natural language processing toolkit for many human languages. In *Proceedings of the 58th Annual Meeting of the Association for Computational Linguistics: System Demonstrations*.

Siva Reddy, Oscar Täckström, Slav Petrov, Mark Steedman, and Mirella Lapata. 2017. Universal semantic parsing. In *Proceedings of the 2017 Conference on Empirical Methods in Natural Language Processing*, pages 89–101, Copenhagen, Denmark. Association for Computational Linguistics.

Sebastian Schuster, Ranjay Krishna, Angel Chang, Li Fei-Fei, and Christopher D. Manning. 2015. Generating semantically precise scene graphs from textual descriptions for improved image retrieval. In *Proceedings of the Fourth Workshop on Vision and Language*, pages 70–80, Lisbon, Portugal. Association for Computational Linguistics.

Sebastian Schuster and Christopher D Manning. 2016. Enhanced english universal dependencies: An improved representation for natural language understanding tasks. In *Proceedings of the Tenth International Conference on Language Resources and Evaluation (LREC'16)*, pages 2371–2378.

Natalia G Silveira. 2016. *Designing syntactic representations for NLP: An empirical investigation*. Ph.D. thesis, Stanford University.

Gabriel Stanovsky, Jessica Ficler, Ido Dagan, and Yoav Goldberg. 2016. Getting more out of syntax with props. *arXiv preprint arXiv:1603.01648*.

Mingming Sun, Wenyue Hua, Zoey Liu, Xin Wang, Kangjie Zheng, and Ping Li. 2020. A predicate-function-argument annotation of natural language for open-domain information expression. In *Proceedings of the 2020 Conference on Empirical Methods in Natural Language Processing (EMNLP)*, pages 2140–2150.

Aryeh Tiktinsky, Yoav Goldberg, and Reut Tsarfaty. 2020. pybart: Evidence-based syntactic transformations for ie. *arXiv preprint arXiv:2005.01306*.

Aaron Steven White, Drew Reisinger, Keisuke Sakaguchi, Tim Vieira, Sheng Zhang, Rachel Rudinger, Kyle Rawlins, and Benjamin Van Durme. 2016. Universal decompositional semantics on universal dependencies. In *Proceedings of the 2016 Conference on Empirical Methods in Natural Language Processing*, pages 1713–1723.

Sheng Zhang, Rachel Rudinger, and Benjamin Van Durme. 2017. An evaluation of predpatt and open ie via stage 1 semantic role labeling. In *IWCS 2017—12th International Conference on Computational Semantics—Short papers*.

Classifying Divergences in Cross-lingual AMR Pairs

Shira Wein Nathan Schneider
Georgetown University
{sw1158, nathan.schneider}@georgetown.edu

Abstract

Translation divergences are varied and widespread, challenging approaches that rely on parallel text. To annotate translation divergences, we propose a schema grounded in the Abstract Meaning Representation (AMR), a sentence-level semantic framework instantiated for a number of languages. By comparing parallel AMR graphs, we can identify specific points of divergence. Each divergence is labeled with both a type and a cause. We release a small corpus of annotated English-Spanish data, and analyze the annotations in our corpus.

1 Introduction

A variety of factors come into play in translating from one language into another (Dorr, 1990; Dorr and Voss, 1993). The resulting parallel texts are not always completely equivalent in meaning. Differences, or *divergences*, between the source and target may reflect lexical or grammatical differences between the two languages, stylistic considerations, or simply the translator's preference for idiomatic phrasing.

Identifying translation divergences may enable more nuanced use of parallel text in applications; for example, it has been shown that translation divergences have a measurable impact on machine translation (Vyas et al., 2018). This information on the types and causes of divergence enables these parallel texts to be more fully utilized in cross-lingual natural language processing tasks. Specifically, different types of semantic divergences impact the performance of neural machine translation systems differently (Briakou and Carpuat, 2021), which motivates work to categorize and describe divergences in parallel texts.

Taking advantage of the fact that Abstract Meaning Representation (AMR) (Banarescu et al., 2013, 2019) resources and tools have been developed for a variety of languages (§2.3) and given the usefulness of AMR for downstream multilingual tasks such as machine translation (Song et al., 2019; Nguyen et al., 2021), we signal the need for categorization and detection of divergences in cross-lingual AMR pairs.

The structure of an AMR reflects the semantic relations of the sentence, so structural divergences (a difference in the structure of an AMR graph, whether it be the label or role) between multilingual AMR pairs serve as a reflection of semantic differences between a sentence and its translation.

We develop and present a categorization schema to identify both the type and the cause of the divergence as being due to semantic divergence, annotation divergence, or syntactic divergence; this schema annotates both the type and cause of a structural divergence, to (1) make the data more adaptable to cross-lingual NLP applications, (2) identify non-literal translations, (3) make AMR more cross-linguistically consistent (Song et al., 2019), and (4) investigate the ways in which annotation, semantics, and syntax play a role in cross-lingual AMR parsing (Damonte, 2019).

We then annotate a set of 50 parallel English-Spanish AMRs annotations from *The Little Prince* (Migueles-Abraira, 2017) using our divergence schema and make these annotations available online. Using this small set of gold annotated data, we are able to explore the comprehensiveness and meaningfulness of this annotation schema.

Our contributions include:

- A novel annotation schema for the classification of semantic and translation divergences between cross-lingual pairs of AMRs (§3)
- A small corpus of English-Spanish parallel AMRs annotated with our schema (§4)
- An analysis of the ways in which cross-lingual parallel AMRs may differ in annotation, which poses a problem for cross-lingual AMR parsing (§4.3)

We release the dataset for this work to enable

Proceedings of the Joint 15th Linguistic Annotation Workshop (LAW) and 3rd Designing Meaning Representations (DMR) Workshop, pages 56–65
November, 2021.

cross-lingual Spanish-English analysis of AMR pairs, as well as promote expansion of this work to other languages.[1]

2 Background and Related Work

2.1 Semantic Divergences

Translation divergences occur when translation from one language to another results in a different meaning or structure (Dorr, 1994). These translation divergences can appear due to translation choices or to syntactic differences between the languages (Dorr, 1990; Dorr and Voss, 1993). The implications of these translation divergences include difficulties when using parallel texts for downstream tasks, because it can be difficult to identify why or how parallel sentences differ.

For example, a parallel corpus, such as a work of fiction, likely contains some non-literal translations. When training a machine translation system on this parallel corpus, these divergences present a problem if looking to produce as literal a translation as possible. An example of this from our corpus is shown in figure 1. The English sentence "Which is your planet?" is aligned to "¿De qué planeta eres?" which literally translates to "What planet are you from?" The Spanish sentence is less awkward than the original English sentence, and more explicitly asks about planet of origin, as opposed to ownership of a planet. This is a semantic divergence (due to translation choice), resulting in the Spanish AMR having a different focus (root).

Divergences have been explored with respect to synonymy (Gaillard et al., 2010) and diachronically (Montariol and Allauzen, 2021).

Other approaches have addressed whether and how given sentence pairs diverge. Carpuat et al. (2017) identify divergences in parallel corpora using a cross-lingual textual entailment system to identify less equivalent sentence pairs. Relatedly, work has been done to identify semantic divergences in parallel texts, classifying sentences as being divergent or non-divergent (Vyas et al., 2018).

Prior work which both categorically annotated and modeled semantic divergences includes the REFreSD dataset of English-French sentence pairs annotated with three types of divergences (subtree deletion, phrase replacement, and lexical substitution) based on a tree model (Briakou and Carpuat, 2020). Similarly, an attempt to classify these divergences automatically includes the hierarchical alignment scheme of Chinese and English parse trees which enables the identification and quantification of translation divergences (Deng and Xue, 2017).

These divergences have also been considered for downstream tasks. Prior work includes fine-tuning approach to account for non-literal translations in the pre-training of cross-lingual language models (Zhai et al., 2020).

2.2 AMR for Cross-linguistic Divergences

The Abstract Meaning Representation (AMR) is a framework for expressing the meaning of a whole sentence as a semantic graph (Banarescu et al., 2013, 2019). The semantically-oriented AMR framework has been extended to and studied in multiple languages, as well as cross-linguistically. However, it has not been used to formalize different kinds of translation divergences in cross-lingual parallel texts. We explore the use of Abstract Meaning Representations in formalizing the study of semantic translation divergences across parallel texts.

Abstract Meaning Representations (AMRs) are a type of semantic representation designed to pair a whole sentence with its meaning. AMRs are rooted, labeled graphs where each node is an instance of a semantic unit. The general purpose of the semantic representation is to capture the core logical elements of meaning. Annotation of AMR is lightweight as it does not represent morphology, articles, or tense, but does require a fair amount of training. Inter-annotator agreement is measured using Smatch, which calculates semantic overlap

English: Which is your planet?

```
(p / planet
    :poss (y / you)
    :domain (a / amr-unknown))
```

Spanish: ¿ De qué planeta eres ?
Literal translation: What planet are you from?

```
(s / ser-de-91
   :ARG1 (t / tú)
   :ARG2 (p / planeta
       :campo (a / amr-desconocido)))
```

Figure 1: Example of a focus,sem divergence.

[1]The dataset for this work can be found at: https://github.com/shirawein/spanish-english-amr-corpus

between two AMRs (Cai and Knight, 2013). The root of the AMR is the **focus**, an attribute marked with `:argN` is a **core argument role** (where `N` is some number ≥0), and any other attribute (e.g., `:opN`, `:domain`, `:manner`) is a **non-core role**.

2.3 Use of AMR in Many Languages and Cross-linguistically

Abstract Meaning Representation is not an interlingua, but has since been studied in multiple languages and cross-linguistically (Xue et al., 2014; Li et al., 2016; Migueles-Abraira, 2017; Linh and Nguyen, 2019; Sobrevilla Cabezudo and Pardo, 2019; Choe et al., 2019).

AMR annotations of *The Little Prince* have been presented in English, Chinese (Li et al., 2016), Spanish (Migueles-Abraira, 2017), and Vietnamese (Linh and Nguyen, 2019). Additional work has been done to adapt AMR annotation (Sobrevilla Cabezudo and Pardo, 2019) and alignment (Anchiêta and Pardo, 2020) to Portuguese, and Korean (Choe et al., 2019).

Cross-lingual studies of AMR primarily compare the structures between two AMRs representative of a parallel text, which may partially be due to the fact that AMR is not designed to be interlingual (Xue et al., 2014). *AMRICA* visualizes and automatically aligns AMRs, including two AMRs of a sentence and its translation, designed to facilitate research into cross-lingual AMRs (Saphra and Lopez, 2015). We take this as inspiration to use AMR pairs as a starting point for divergence classification between parallel texts.

Cross-lingual approaches to AMR parsing explore transfer learning techniques to generate parallel AMR annotations in multiple languages, and suggest that AMR can serve as a cross-lingual semantic representation capable of overcoming linguistic differences (Damonte and Cohen, 2018; Zhu et al., 2019; Blloshmi et al., 2020).

Additional work has explored whether structural differences across cross-lingual Chinese/English and English/Czech AMR pairs are due to syntactic idiosyncrasies (Xue et al., 2014), which can be of use in machine translation (Song et al., 2019; Nguyen et al., 2021).

3 Cross-lingual AMR Divergence Annotation Schema

We develop a categorization schema to be able to identify with granularity the type of structural divergence as well as the cause of the divergence between the two AMRs. Next, we annotate 50 Spanish-English AMR pairs using this schema.

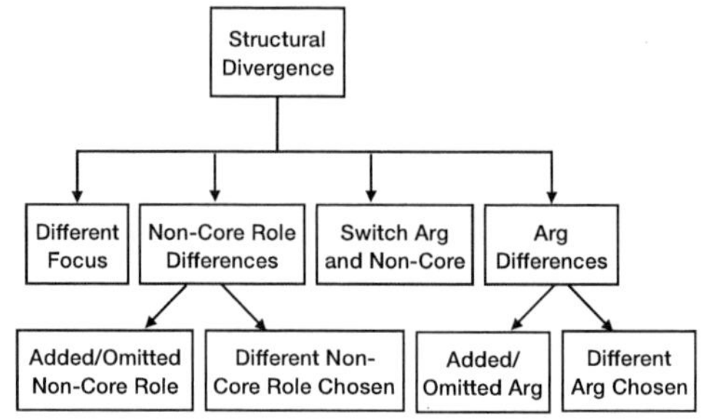

Figure 2: Types of structural divergence.

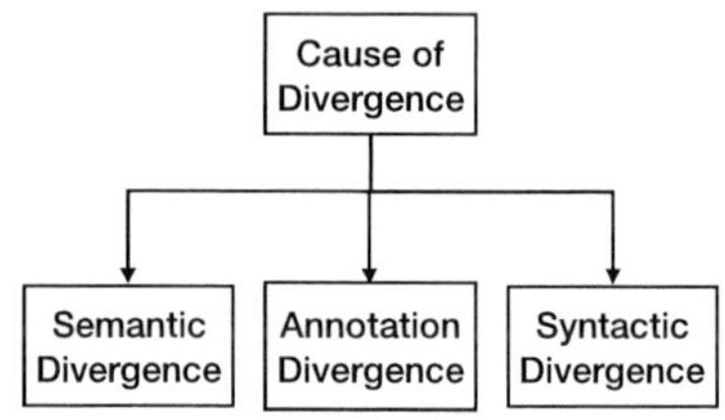

Figure 3: Causes of structural divergence.

If an AMR pair has a structural divergence, meaning there is some difference in the way that the two AMRs are structured, there must be both a type of divergence (figure 2) and a cause for the divergence (figure 3).

3.1 Cause of Divergence

The cause of the divergence can be:

- semantic divergences ("sem," due to translation choice)
- annotation divergences ("anno," due to annotation choice)
- or, syntactic divergences ("synt," inherent differences between the languages)

In semantic divergences, the Spanish translation is an inexact, non-literal, translation of the English sentence. For annotation divergences, the Spanish translation is a literal translation of the English sentence but the AMR was annotated differently nonetheless. Syntactic divergences arise because of some feature of either English or Spanish, the Spanish translation of the English sentences diverges in some way causing a structural divergence in the AMR.

3.2 Type of Divergence

As shown in figure 2, the type of structural divergence can be a:

1. different focus ("focus")

2. a difference between the arguments / core roles ("diffarg" or "omitarg")
3. the same label/feature being an argument in one AMR and a non-core role in the other AMR ("switch")
4. a difference between non-core roles ("diffnon-core" or "omitnoncore")

These four subcategories are listed by decreasing degree of granularity and effect on the structure of the rest of the AMR.

If the focus is different between the two AMRs, then the entire rest of the structure differs by definition, because the arguments and non-core roles that the focus can take on differ. Therefore, if an AMR pair is annotated with each having a different focus, then it is not possible to then annotate argument differences or non-core role differences.

In the subsections that follow, we include and explain the annotation of 7 illustrative examples.

3.3 Example of focus,sem

One example of a focus difference due to translation, as described in §2, is shown in figure 1. The focus, or root of the AMR graph, is the head/first node in the AMR. Here the focus differs because of the translation from the awkward "Which is your planet?" to the Spanish "¿De qué planeta eres?" which more explicitly asks about the geographic origin of the person being asked the question. The translation is a non-literal translation and the Spanish AMR reflects the Spanish sentence.

3.4 Example of focus,anno

An example of a different focus due to annotation choice includes the AMR pair for the English sentence *Volcanic eruptions are like fires in a chimney* . and the parallel Spanish sentence *las erupciones volcánicas son como el fuego de una chimenea* . The focus difference here, where in the English sentence the focus is *erupt* and in the Spanish sentence the focus is *paracer = seem*, is due to annotation divergence in these gold annotations. The Spanish translation is a very literal translation of the English sentence. There are no other inherent language differences that place more emphasis on the "seeming" in the Spanish sentence either. Therefore, the difference is due to neither semantic divergence, being a literal translation, nor due to syntactic divergence; the difference is due to annotator discrepancy.

English: Volcanic eruptions are like fires in a chimney .

```
(e / erupt-0
  :ARG1 (v / volcano)
  :ARG1-of (r / resemble-01
    :ARG2 (f / fire
      :location (c / chimney))))
```

Spanish: Las erupciones volcánicas son como el fuego de una chimenea .
Literal translation: Volcanic eruptions are like the fire of a chimney.

```
(p / parecer
  :ARG0 (e / erupción
    :mod (v / volcánico))
  :ARG1 (s / ser-de-91
    :ARG1 (f / fuego)
    :ARG2 (c / chimenea)))
```

Similarly, if an argument is added/omitted or the label for an argument and non-core role are switched, then it is not possible to annotate a non-core role difference. It is still possible to have more than one structural divergence in an AMR pair because there are often multiple arguments and non-core roles in an AMR, so multiple differences may occur which do not explicitly encompass the others (as in §3.8).

3.5 Example of switch,anno

An AMR pair with English sentence: *To forget a friend is sad* . and Spanish sentence *Olvidar a un amigo es triste* . is an example of the infrequent "switch." This pair annotates *forget* in English as an `:ARG0`, while *olvidar = forget* in Spanish is annotated as `:domain`. This is due to an annotation divergence. The English PropBank entry for sad-02 denotes `:ARG0` as the being the causer of the sadness which makes it an appropriate choice for the English, and the same guidelines were being referenced for the Spanish AMR annotation. Therefore this is due to annotation divergence, and likely is an annotation error in the Spanish AMR.

Additionally, an argument difference can be due to adding/omitting an argument, or because for the same argument label (e.g. `:arg0`) different arguments are chosen. If the same part of the sentence / feature of the AMR is featured as an `:arg0` in one AMR and an `:arg1` in the other AMR, this counts as two added/omitted arguments because the annotator judged that there was sufficient evidence for an `:arg0`, but this was omitted in the other AMR, and vice versa.

3.6 Example of diffarg,synt

English: The fourth planet belonged to a businessman .

```
(b / belong-01
  :ARG0 (p / planet
    :ord (o / ordinal-entity :value 4))
  :ARG1 (b3 / businessman))
```

Spanish: El cuarto planeta era de un hombre de negocios .
Literal translation: The fourth planet was of a businessman.

```
(p / pertenecer
  :ARG0 (p2 / planeta
    :ord (e / entidad-ordinal :valor 4))
  :ARG1 (h / hombre
    :mod (n / negocio)))
```

Here the `:ARG1`, *businessman* in English and *hombre* = *man* in Spanish, is due to syntactic divergence. *Hombre de negocios* is the Spanish translation of *businessman*, and literally means "man of business." Therefore it is structured in the AMR as *hombre* = *man*, `:mod` *negocio* = *business*.

Similarly, a non-core role difference can be due to adding/omitting a non-core role, or because for the same argument label difference non-core roles are chosen.

3.7 Example of diffnoncore,sem

English: " I think it is time for breakfast , " she added an instant later .

```
(a / add-01
  :ARG0 (s / she)
  :ARG1 (t / think-01
    :ARG0 s
    :ARG1 (t2 / time
      :purpose (b / breakfast-01)))
  :time (l / late
    :degree (m / more
      :quant (i / instant))))
```

Spanish: " Creo que es la hora de desayunar " , añadió ella al instante .
Literal translation: "I think it's time for breakfast," she added instantly.

```
(a / añadir
  :ARG0 (e / ella)
  :ARG1 (c / creer
    :ARG0 e
    :ARG1 (h / hora
      :propósito (d / desayunar)))
  :tiempo (a2 / al-instante))
```

This difference in the non-core attribute (`:time` / `:tiempo`) is due to semantic divergences, being a non-literal Spanish translation. The English sentence says "an instant later," while the Spanish translation literally says "instantly." Therefore, the English AMR reflects the time as being an instant later and the Spanish AMR reflects the time as being at that instant.

3.8 Example of omitnoncore,synt omitnoncore,synt (2)

English: That is funny!

```
(f2 / funny
  :domain (t2 / that))
```

Spanish: ¡ Qué gracioso !
Literal translation: How funny!

```
(g / gracioso
  :grado (t / tan))
```

`:grado` corresponds to the English `:degree`, so the degree is included in the Spanish sentence, but the domain is included in the English sentence. This is due to syntactic divergence because a natural Spanish translation of "that is funny" would literally translate in English to "how funny," making degree more appropriate than domain.

3.9 Example of no divergence

English: Draw me a sheep ...

```
(d / draw-01
  :ARG0 (y / you)
  :ARG1 (s / sheep)
  :ARG2 (i / i)
  :mode imperative)
```

Spanish: Dibújame una oveja ...
Literal translation: Draw me a sheep ...

```
(d / dibujar
  :ARG0 (t / tú)
  :ARG1 (o / oveja)
  :ARG2 (y / yo)
  :modo imperativo)
```

These AMRs are equivalent in every way, having equivalent sets of labels / relations, as well as the same arguments for each label.

4 Annotated Corpus

In order to demonstrate the scope, effectiveness and use of this annotation schema, we decide to annotate a small corpus of English-Spanish sentences within the domain of literary works. We use a set of 50 English-Spanish AMR pairs, representing parallel sentences from *The Little Prince* (Migueles-Abraira et al., 2018). The work from which these 50 English-Spanish AMR pairs are derived also presents relevant linguistic issues hindering Spanish AMR annotation: NP ellipses, third person possessive pronouns, third person clitic pronouns, and the usage of *se* (Migueles-Abraira et al., 2018).

We annotated the 50 Spanish-English AMR pairs with a divergence classification, being empty if there is no structural divergence, or with at least one type,cause pair. It is possible to have more than one structural divergence so any structural divergence is listed with its cause.

Figure 5 shows the breakdown of cause of divergence for the 50 pairs in our corpus, as well as the relationship between type of divergence and cause. While different focus and different `arg` chosen are regularly due to annotation choice, different non-core role chosen or omitted non-core role are much more often due to translation choice.

4.1 The Annotation Process

All sentence pairs were annotated by the designer of the annotation scheme, who is fluent in both English and Spanish. There were few apparent difficulties in applying the scheme. The primary question was whether divergences that seemed like they were due to syntactic divergences were in fact inherent properties of the language, because this relies on expert knowledge of both languages. Ultimately this did not pose an issue because each of the three causes of structural divergence are mutually exclusive, so confirming that the property in question is in fact a feature inherent to the language can be validated by ensuring that there is not a difference in translation or annotation. The examples of language difference in §3.6 and §3.8 include justification for two instances of this classification. Reliability of the annotations could be validated by extending the study to include additional annotators and calculating inter-annotator agreement.

4.2 Distribution of Corpus

Of the 50 multilingual AMR pairs, 13 pairs had no structural divergence, 11 pairs had multiple divergences (9 pairs with 2 divergences and 2 pairs with 3 divergences), and 26 pairs have one structural divergence. There were 49 divergences in total.

Figure 5 shows the number of instances of every structural divergence caused by each of the three causes, with the types of structural divergences in rows and the causes of structural divergences in columns. Related information can also be seen in the form of a bar chart (Figure 4), which shows the proportion of instances for which a structural divergence is due to each cause.

Figures 5 and 4 show that there is a considerable discrepancy between type of divergence and cause. While non-core role divergences tend to be primarily due to semantic divergences, argument divergences tend to be due to annotation divergences or syntactic divergences. Change in focus tends to be due to an annotation divergence. The root serves as a representation of the central focus or topic of the sentence, so this relationship suggests that the central topic of the sentence is not changing between the parallel texts and instead the different focus annotation is due to annotator discrepancy.

4.3 Implications for AMR Parsing & Cross-lingual Tasks

The results of this study indicate that cross-lingual AMR pairs actually do sometimes inherently differ because of properties of the language, so these differences need to be accounted for when developing cross-lingual AMR systems.

As (Xue et al., 2014) identifies divergences between Czech, Chinese, and English annotations in parallel texts which affect the degree to which AMR is an interlingua, we similarly investigate the causes and ways in which AMR is an interlingua, tested on the cross-lingual case of Spanish and English. Notably, due to the granularity of our annotation schema, we are able to both describe and quantify the divergence. We identify pairs of AMRs as being more than solely divergent, by rigorously classifying each type of divergence, as well as attributing each divergence to one of three causes: semantics, annotation, or syntax.

Additionally, we show that the structure provided in AMR allows many divergences to be identified and categorized by an annotator, even cross-lingually. This motivates future work leveraging

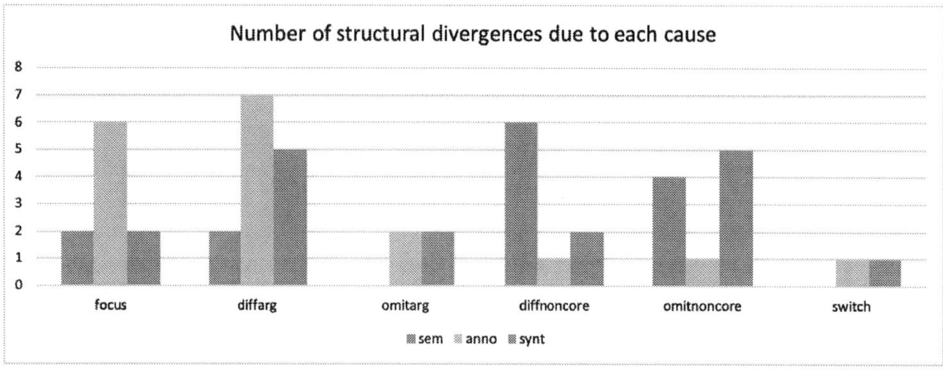

Figure 4: Bar chart reflecting the percent of instances for which each structural divergence was semantic, annotation, or syntactic.

	sem	anno	synt	
focus	2	6	2	10
diffarg	2	7	5	14
omitarg	0	2	2	4
diffnoncore	6	1	2	9
omitnoncore	4	1	5	10
switch	0	1	1	2
	14	18	17	

Figure 5: Number of instances of each structural divergence, and the number of times they were due to each cause of divergence. Greener cells indicate higher numbers and redder cells indicate lower numbers of instances. Sums across rows (types of divergence) and columns (causes of divergence) are found in clear cells to the right and bottom, respectively.

the semantic information captured by cross-lingual AMR pairs to identify sentences as being divergent or equivalent.

5 Related Work on Cross-lingual Meaning Representations

Related work has been done on cross-lingual adaptations of other meaning representations, including the development and analysis of cross-lingual semantic annotation schemes (Van Gysel et al., 2019). The Universal Dependencies framework has also been useful in the analysis of cross-lingual syntactic divergences (Nikolaev et al., 2020). Universal Conceptual Cognitive Annotation (UCCA) annotates grammatical meaning while abstracting away from the syntax of the language (Abend and Rappoport, 2013).

The Uniform Meaning Representation framework extends AMR with a focus on quantification and scope, as well as uniformity across languages (Van Gysel et al., 2021).

The Parallel Meaning Bank is a corpus of parallel texts with corresponding linguistic annotations and Discourse Representation Structure annotations projected from English (Abzianidze et al., 2017). Prior work towards the production of parallel meaning banks focused on the alignment of informative translations—translations where more details are included in the target translation than the source text—through an inclusion relation symbol (Bos, 2014). Work on the Parallel Meaning Bank also includes a comparison of translations as being meaning-preserving or not, and these discrepancies as being largely due to: human annotation error, syntactic differences in definite articles, translation of proper names, or non-literal translations (van Noord et al., 2018).

Alignment for multilingual meaning representations has also been studied in relation to FrameNet, including recent work looking to unify a Multilingual FrameNet with alignments between all dozen FrameNet languages (Baker and Lorenzi, 2020).

The Prague Czech-English Dependency Treebank (PCEDT) similarly considers the adaptation of an English framework to a non-English extension, focusing on dependency annotation for the Czech translations of the Penn Treebank. PCEDT highlights some of the issues that arise out of automatically transferring annotation schema to another language. Ultimately, the authors find that the annotation schema are not sufficiently fine-grained to provide for a seamless conversion from annotation in one language to annotation in the other, and the difficulty of developing an annotation schema capable of this seamless transformation is unknown (Čmejrek et al., 2004).

XL-AMR has used transfer learning to automatically produce AMR annotations for Chinese, German, Italian, and French, and provides qualitative analysis suggesting that even with limited training data, the parser is able to manage many structural divergences across languages (Blloshmi et al., 2020).

6 Conclusion

We have presented our annotation schema for classification of structural divergences in cross-lingual meaning representations and released 50 Spanish-English annotated examples. We demonstrate with our annotation schema and analysis of the annotated dataset that structural divergence in pairs of cross-lingual meaning representations can serve as a meaningful proxy of divergences between parallel texts. Therefore, tools which rely on highly literal translations, such as pre-trained machine translation systems, would benefit from applying this structural divergence annotation schema to cross-lingual Abstract Meaning Representations of the data.

The scope of our empirical study was limited, however, because there are currently only 50 pairs of Spanish-English AMR annotations publicly available. Studying language pairs with more gold AMR data, or adapting the approach to alternate meaning representation formalisms, would further test the utility of our approach.

Acknowledgments

We thank reviewers for helpful feedback. This work is supported in part by a Clare Boothe Luce Scholarship.

References

Omri Abend and Ari Rappoport. 2013. UCCA: A semantics-based grammatical annotation scheme. In *Proceedings of the 10th International Conference on Computational Semantics (IWCS 2013) Long Papers*, pages 1–12, Potsdam, Germany. Association for Computational Linguistics.

Lasha Abzianidze, Johannes Bjerva, Kilian Evang, Hessel Haagsma, Rik van Noord, Pierre Ludmann, Duc-Duy Nguyen, and Johan Bos. 2017. The Parallel Meaning Bank: Towards a multilingual corpus of translations annotated with compositional meaning representations. In *Proceedings of the 15th Conference of the European Chapter of the Association for Computational Linguistics: Volume 2, Short Papers*, pages 242–247, Valencia, Spain. Association for Computational Linguistics.

Rafael Anchiêta and Thiago Pardo. 2020. Semantically inspired AMR alignment for the Portuguese language. In *Proceedings of the 2020 Conference on Empirical Methods in Natural Language Processing (EMNLP)*, pages 1595–1600, Online. Association for Computational Linguistics.

Collin F. Baker and Arthur Lorenzi. 2020. Exploring crosslinguistic frame alignment. In *Proceedings of the International FrameNet Workshop 2020: Towards a Global, Multilingual FrameNet*, pages 77–84, Marseille, France. European Language Resources Association.

Laura Banarescu, Claire Bonial, Shu Cai, Madalina Georgescu, Kira Griffitt, Ulf Hermjakob, Kevin Knight, Philipp Koehn, Martha Palmer, and Nathan Schneider. 2013. Abstract Meaning Representation for sembanking. In *Proceedings of the 7th Linguistic Annotation Workshop and Interoperability with Discourse*, pages 178–186, Sofia, Bulgaria. Association for Computational Linguistics.

Laura Banarescu, Claire Bonial, Shu Cai, Madalina Georgescu, Kira Griffitt, Ulf Hermjakob, Kevin Knight, Philipp Koehn, Martha Palmer, and Nathan Schneider. 2019. Abstract Meaning Representation (AMR) 1.2.6 specification. `https://github.com/amrisi/amr-guidelines/blob/master/amr.md`.

Rexhina Blloshmi, Rocco Tripodi, and Roberto Navigli. 2020. XL-AMR: Enabling cross-lingual AMR parsing with transfer learning techniques. In *Proceedings of the 2020 Conference on Empirical Methods in Natural Language Processing (EMNLP)*, pages 2487–2500, Online. Association for Computational Linguistics.

Johan Bos. 2014. Semantic annotation issues in parallel meaning banking. In *ACL 2014*.

Eleftheria Briakou and Marine Carpuat. 2020. Detecting fine-grained cross-lingual semantic divergences without supervision by learning to rank. In *Proceedings of the 2020 Conference on Empirical Methods in Natural Language Processing (EMNLP)*, pages 1563–1580, Online. Association for Computational Linguistics.

Eleftheria Briakou and Marine Carpuat. 2021. Beyond noise: Mitigating the impact of fine-grained semantic divergences on neural machine translation. *CoRR*, abs/2105.15087.

Shu Cai and Kevin Knight. 2013. Smatch: an evaluation metric for semantic feature structures. In *Proceedings of the 51st Annual Meeting of the Association for Computational Linguistics (Volume 2: Short Papers)*, pages 748–752, Sofia, Bulgaria. Association for Computational Linguistics.

Marine Carpuat, Yogarshi Vyas, and Xing Niu. 2017. Detecting cross-lingual semantic divergence for neural machine translation. In *Proceedings of the First Workshop on Neural Machine Translation*, pages 69–79, Vancouver. Association for Computational Linguistics.

Hyonsu Choe, Jiyoon Han, Hyejin Park, and Hansaem Kim. 2019. Copula and case-stacking annotations for Korean AMR. In *Proceedings of the First International Workshop on Designing Meaning Representations*, pages 128–135, Florence, Italy. Association for Computational Linguistics.

Martin Čmejrek, Jan Cuřín, and Jiří Havelka. 2004. Prague Czech-English Dependency Treebank: Any hopes for a common annotation scheme? In *Proceedings of the Workshop Frontiers in Corpus Annotation at HLT-NAACL 2004*, pages 47–54, Boston, Massachusetts, USA. Association for Computational Linguistics.

Marco Damonte. 2019. *Understanding and Generating Language with Abstract Meaning Representation*. Ph.D. thesis, University of Edinburgh.

Marco Damonte and Shay B. Cohen. 2018. Cross-lingual Abstract Meaning Representation parsing. In *Proceedings of the 2018 Conference of the North American Chapter of the Association for Computational Linguistics: Human Language Technologies, Volume 1 (Long Papers)*, pages 1146–1155, New Orleans, Louisiana. Association for Computational Linguistics.

Dun Deng and Nianwen Xue. 2017. Translation divergences in Chinese–English machine translation: An empirical investigation. *Computational Linguistics*, 43(3):521–565.

Bonnie Dorr. 1990. Solving thematic divergences in machine translation. In *Proceedings of the 28th Annual Meeting on Association for Computational Linguistics*, ACL '90, page 127–134, USA. Association for Computational Linguistics.

Bonnie J. Dorr. 1994. Machine translation divergences: A formal description and proposed solution. *Computational Linguistics*, 20(4):597–633.

Bonnie J. Dorr and Clare R. Voss. 1993. Constraints on the space of MT divergences.

Benoît Gaillard, Yannick Chudy, Pierre Magistry, Shu-Kai Hsieh, and Emmanuel Navarro. 2010. Graph representation of synonymy and translation resources for crosslinguistic modelisation of meaning. In *Proceedings of the 24th Pacific Asia Conference on Language, Information and Computation*, pages 819–830, Tohoku University, Sendai, Japan. Institute of Digital Enhancement of Cognitive Processing, Waseda University.

Bin Li, Yuan Wen, Weiguang Qu, Lijun Bu, and Nianwen Xue. 2016. Annotating The Little Prince with Chinese AMRs. In *Proceedings of the 10th Linguistic Annotation Workshop held in conjunction with ACL 2016 (LAW-X 2016)*, pages 7–15, Berlin, Germany. Association for Computational Linguistics.

Ha Linh and Huyen Nguyen. 2019. A case study on meaning representation for Vietnamese. In *Proceedings of the First International Workshop on Designing Meaning Representations*, pages 148–153, Florence, Italy. Association for Computational Linguistics.

Noelia Migueles-Abraira. 2017. A study towards Spanish Abstract Meaning Representation. Master's thesis, University of the Basque Country.

Noelia Migueles-Abraira, Rodrigo Agerri, and Arantza Diaz de Ilarraza. 2018. Annotating Abstract Meaning Representations for Spanish. In *Proceedings of the Eleventh International Conference on Language Resources and Evaluation (LREC 2018)*, Miyazaki, Japan. European Language Resources Association (ELRA).

Syrielle Montariol and Alexandre Allauzen. 2021. Measure and evaluation of semantic divergence across two languages. In *Proceedings of the 59th Annual Meeting of the Association for Computational Linguistics and the 11th International Joint Conference on Natural Language Processing (Volume 1: Long Papers)*, pages 1247–1258, Online. Association for Computational Linguistics.

Long HB Nguyen, Viet H Pham, and Dien Dinh. 2021. Improving neural machine translation with AMR semantic graphs. *Mathematical Problems in Engineering*, 2021.

Dmitry Nikolaev, Ofir Arviv, Taelin Karidi, Neta Kenneth, Veronika Mitnik, Lilja Maria Saeboe, and Omri Abend. 2020. Fine-grained analysis of cross-linguistic syntactic divergences. In *Proceedings of the 58th Annual Meeting of the Association for Computational Linguistics*, pages 1159–1176, Online. Association for Computational Linguistics.

Naomi Saphra and Adam Lopez. 2015. AMRICA: an AMR inspector for cross-language alignments. In *Proceedings of the 2015 Conference of the North American Chapter of the Association for Computational Linguistics: Demonstrations*, pages 36–40, Denver, Colorado. Association for Computational Linguistics.

Marco Antonio Sobrevilla Cabezudo and Thiago Pardo. 2019. Towards a general Abstract Meaning Representation corpus for Brazilian Portuguese. In *Proceedings of the 13th Linguistic Annotation Workshop*, pages 236–244, Florence, Italy. Association for Computational Linguistics.

Linfeng Song, Daniel Gildea, Yue Zhang, Zhiguo Wang, and Jinsong Su. 2019. Semantic neural machine translation using AMR. *Transactions of the Association for Computational Linguistics*, 7:19–31.

Jens E. L. Van Gysel, Meagan Vigus, Jayeol Chun, Kenneth Lai, Sarah Moeller, Jiarui Yao, Tim O'Gorman, Andrew Cowell, William Croft, Chu-Ren Huang, Jan Hajič, James H. Martin, Stephan Oepen, Martha

Palmer, James Pustejovsky, Rosa Vallejos, and Nianwen Xue. 2021. Designing a Uniform Meaning Representation for natural language processing. *KI - Künstliche Intelligenz*.

Jens E. L. Van Gysel, Meagan Vigus, Pavlina Kalm, Sook-kyung Lee, Michael Regan, and William Croft. 2019. Cross-linguistic semantic annotation: Reconciling the language-specific and the universal. In *Proceedings of the First International Workshop on Designing Meaning Representations*, pages 1–14, Florence, Italy. Association for Computational Linguistics.

Rik van Noord, Lasha Abzianidze, Hessel Haagsma, and Johan Bos. 2018. Evaluating scoped meaning representations. In *Proceedings of the Eleventh International Conference on Language Resources and Evaluation (LREC 2018)*, Miyazaki, Japan. European Language Resources Association (ELRA).

Yogarshi Vyas, Xing Niu, and Marine Carpuat. 2018. Identifying semantic divergences in parallel text without annotations. In *Proceedings of the 2018 Conference of the North American Chapter of the Association for Computational Linguistics: Human Language Technologies, Volume 1 (Long Papers)*, pages 1503–1515, New Orleans, Louisiana. Association for Computational Linguistics.

Nianwen Xue, Ondřej Bojar, Jan Hajič, Martha Palmer, Zdeňka Urešová, and Xiuhong Zhang. 2014. Not an interlingua, but close: Comparison of English AMRs to Chinese and Czech. In *Proceedings of the Ninth International Conference on Language Resources and Evaluation (LREC'14)*, pages 1765–1772, Reykjavik, Iceland. European Language Resources Association (ELRA).

Yuming Zhai, Gabriel Illouz, and Anne Vilnat. 2020. Detecting non-literal translations by fine-tuning cross-lingual pre-trained language models. In *Proceedings of the 28th International Conference on Computational Linguistics*, pages 5944–5956, Barcelona, Spain (Online). International Committee on Computational Linguistics.

Huaiyu Zhu, Yunyao Li, and Laura Chiticariu. 2019. Towards universal semantic representation. In *Proceedings of the First International Workshop on Designing Meaning Representations*, pages 177–181, Florence, Italy. Association for Computational Linguistics.

A Linguistic Annotation Framework to Study Interactions in Multilingual Healthcare Conversational Forums

[♡]Ishani Mondal, [♡]Kalika Bali, [♡]Mohit Jain, [♡]Monojit Choudhury, [♠]Ashish Sharma,[*]
[◇]Evans Gitau, [◇]Jacki O' Neill, [◇]Kagonya Awori, [◇]Sarah Gitau
[♡]Microsoft Research Labs, Bangalore, India
[♠]Paul G. Allen School of Computer Science and Engineering, University of Washington
[◇]Microsoft Africa Research Institute, Nairobi, Kenya
{t-imonda, kalikab, monojitc, jacki.oneill}@microsoft.com

Abstract

In recent years, remote digital healthcare using online chats has gained momentum, especially in the Global South. Though prior work has studied interaction patterns in online (health) forums, such as TalkLife, Reddit and Facebook, there has been limited work in understanding interactions in small, close-knit community of instant messengers. In this paper, we propose a linguistic annotation framework to facilitate the analysis of health-focused WhatsApp groups. The primary aim of the framework is to understand interpersonal relationships among peer supporters in order to help develop NLP solutions for remote patient care and reduce the burden of overworked healthcare providers. Our framework consists of fine-grained peer support categorization and message-level sentiment tagging. Additionally, due to the prevalence of multilinguality in such groups, we incorporate word-level language annotations. We use the proposed framework to study two WhatsApp groups in Kenya for youth living with HIV, facilitated by a healthcare provider.

1 Introduction

Good communication between patients and healthcare providers as a part of patient-centered care, where the patient is an equal partner in their healthcare decisions, has been shown to improve medical adherence (Schoenthaler et al., 2009; Ciechanowski et al., 2001) (i.e., the practice of consistently taking the medicines as prescribed) . However in the Global South, i.e. the countries, located primarily in the southern hemisphere, that have historically been identified as third world due to perceptions of their socio-economic status, technological advancements, and global dominance, high patient volumes and a need for cost-effective solutions can make patient-centered care difficult. In recent years, various online chat applications such as WhatsApp and WeChat are being increasingly used to ensure smooth access to both patient-provider communication and peer support beyond formal healthcare system (Karusala et al., 2021; Bhat et al., 2021; Karusala et al., 2020). Even though these peer support groups are effective in providing patient-centered care, they can be taxing for already overworked healthcare providers (Viswanathan et al., 2020). There is therefore a necessity for designing technology to support both the providers and patients using such groups.

Prior work on online health forums focuses on analyzing participation (Schultz et al., 2019; Sadeque et al., 2015; van Campen and Iedema, 2007), social connection and engagement (Sharma et al., 2020a; Kushner and Sharma, 2020; Smith-Merry et al., 2019; Halder et al., 2017), and modelling user behavior (Hosseini and Caragea, 2021; Sharma et al., 2020b; Buechel et al., 2018; Elliott et al., 2018; Pérez-Rosas et al., 2017; Choudhury et al., 2016; Gibson et al., 2016; Choudhury and De, 2014). Further, existing research focuses on the linguistic analysis of conversations in social media platforms like Facebook (Dehouche, 2020; Tian et al., 2017; Vyas et al., 2014; Das and Gambäck, 2013), Reddit and Twitter (Zomick et al., 2019; Rudra et al., 2019; Kiesling et al., 2018; Rijhwani et al., 2017; Tran and Ostendorf, 2016; Rudra et al., 2016; Celli and Rossi, 2012; Bak et al., 2012; Gouws et al., 2011), but has paid little attention to analyzing the conversations in small, close-knit WhatsApp communities. In this paper, we propose a hierarchical annotation framework to facilitate the analysis of health-focused WhatsApp groups.

Our proposed hierarchical framework consists of fine-grained peer support categorization and message-level sentiment tagging. Additionally, we address the prevalence of code-mixing in such

[*] This work was done when the author was a Research Fellow at Microsoft Research Lab India.

Proceedings of the Joint 15th Linguistic Annotation Workshop (LAW) and 3rd Designing Meaning Representations (DMR) Workshop, pages 66–77
November, 2021.

WhatsApp groups by incorporating word-level language annotation. We evaluate our framework on chat logs of two WhatsApp groups of Kenyan youth living with HIV, moderated by a healthcare provider. We also develop a user-friendly annotation interface to facilitate annotation. In the rest of the paper, we describe the annotation process using the framework, the challenges faced and our learnings. Our annotation study shows that the annotators achieve high agreement for all categories, thereby indicating the efficacy of our linguistic annotation framework. We believe that this framework can be used to analyze inter-personal relationships among group members and is the first step towards developing NLP solutions to support healthcare workers providing remote patient care.

While developing the framework, we emphasized on code-mixing. Multilingualism in Kenya contributes to a considerable linguistic diversity in a population that speaks Kiswahili, Kikiyu and English fluently (Dwivedi, 2015; Chumbow, 2010). This leads to a high prevalence of code-mixing in their linguistic interactions. This is further enriched by the use of Sheng, a Swahili and English-based cant (a mixed language or creole), by the urban youth in Kenya. It emerged as a result of urbanization and globalization (Githiora, 2002; ABD). Any annotation framework for such conversations, therefore, has to take into account this multilinguality.

Several annotation schemas have been proposed for multilingual code-mixed messages on social media platforms (Chakravarthi et al., 2021, 2020; Sirajzade et al., 2020; Vijay et al., 2018; Swami et al., 2018; Dhar et al., 2018; Jamatia et al., 2016; Begum et al., 2016; Maharjan et al., 2015; Barman et al., 2014; Bergsma et al., 2012). However, to the best of our knowledge, none of these look into instant-messaging based interactions among peer supporters using code-mixed African languages like Kiswahili, Sheng.

We developed our annotation framework to support an ethnomethodologically-informed ethnographic analysis of the chat: a qualitative approach used in Human-Computer Interaction (HCI) research to understand social interactions (Button and Sharrock, 1997; Hughes et al., 1994). Such analysis has proven useful in the design of computer systems as it reveals the practices and methods of those who will use these systems and which need to be designed for (Crabtree, 2003); being used to examine text interactions such as instant messages (O'Neill and Martin, 2003), internet forums (Martin et al., 2014) and chat messages (Wang et al., 2020; Jain et al., 2018a). The annotation framework was designed to be used to support and inform the ethnographic analysis, with the aim of identifying ways in which we might support both the healthcare provider and participants in these chat groups.

Additionally, the framework would be useful for sociolinguistic studies of multilingual conversations and the schema could be extended to understand other peer support settings such as mental health forums. Another area where the framework might prove useful is for research around improving human-machine conversational agents (Ashktorab et al., 2019; Jain et al., 2018b) by leveraging data annotated using these categories.

2 Dataset

We studied WhatsApp chat logs from two peer-support groups for Kenyan youth, living with HIV. There were a total of 1,655 messages in Group-1 (28 members, 14 female, 14 male, age=14-17 years) and 4,901 messages in Group-2 (27 members, 21 female, 6 male, age=18-24 years). Both the groups were facilitated by a healthcare provider with a background in public health, HIV testing, and counselling. The facilitator sent weekly messages on a range of topics, such as future goals, strategies for medical adherence, etc., responded to queries (within 12 hours), clarified any misinformation posted on the group, and referred medical-questions to a clinic. The chat records were in Kiswahili, English and Sheng, sometimes a mix of these languages in a single message. All the messages were anonymized and translated into English by a native speaker. Each chat message in the dataset had the following information: anonymized speaker ID, timestamp, original message and English-translated message. The data contains sensitive content dealing with people's deeply personal lives and tragedies, and therefore, even with anonymization there are ethical reasons for not making the dataset public. However, anyone wanting access to the data for research purposes can get in touch with the authors.

3 Annotation Framework

The primary objective of our proposed linguistic annotation framework is to facilitate studies

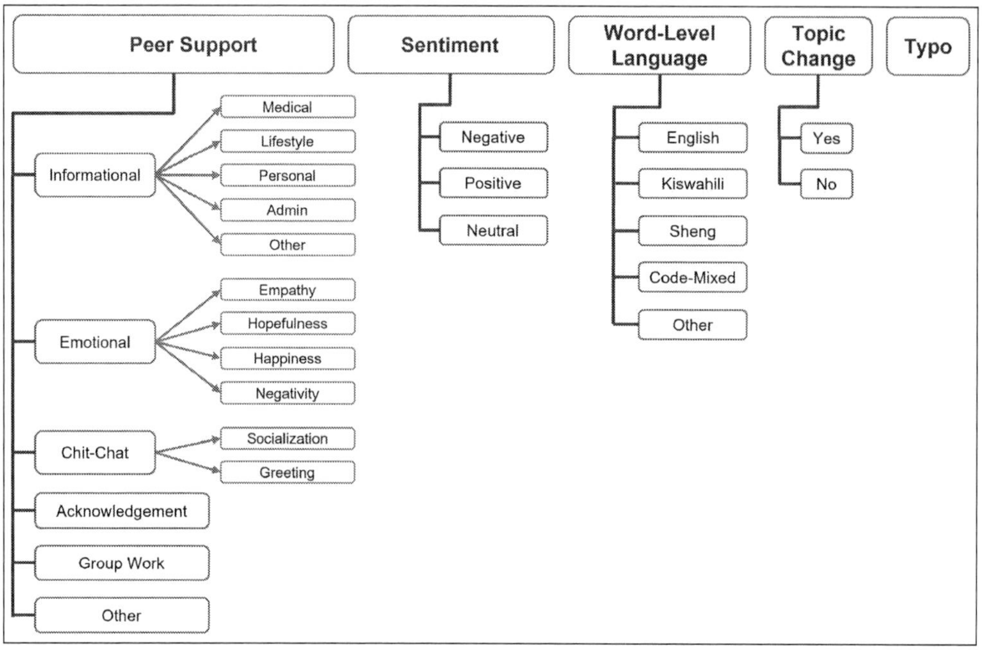

Figure 1: An overview of the linguistic annotation framework.

on inter-personal relationships among the peer-supporters. In order to satisfy the above objective, the framework is governed by the following guiding principles. 1) We want to model the conversational intent of the peer supporters behind the act of sending messages. 2) We need to assess the psychology of their behavior by understanding their sentiments and emotions. This is even more critical in a healthcare setup where it is important to maintain an overall positive outlook. 3) We also want to capture the morphosyntactic level of linguistic information which can be used to help us tease apart deeper interaction patterns and stylistic features of conversations. The framework (Figure 1) has a hierarchical schema with five top-level categories that deal with linguistic and pragmatic phenomena observed in the chat. The categories include *Peer Support* (principle 1, 3.1), *Sentiment* (principle 2, 3.2), *Word-Level Language*, *Topic Change*, and *Typo* (principle 3, 3.3, 3.4, 3.5). Note that this framework can be further augmented to include more linguistic features and can be extended to perform similar studies on other peer support groups. In this section, we define the broader and fine-grained categories.

3.1 Peer Support

Peer support refers to members using their own experiences to help others feel accepted and understood. Our framework defines the following sub-categories of peer support as:

3.1.1 Informational

The group members either seek or provide factual information, advice, or warning. These are further classified as:

- **Seek Information:** A group member is seeking information from fellow group members. E.g., "*explain further about circumcision*".
- **Provide Information:** A group member is providing information. E.g., "*Yeah, it might be a sign. Also it increases when you are stressed.*".

The informational sub-category is further divided into the following sub-types:

Medical: Seeking or providing factual information, advice, or warning about medicine, treatment, or disease.
E.g., [Original] "*Most people infected with the bacteria that cause tuberculosis don't have symptoms. When symptoms do occur, they usually include a cough (sometimes blood-tinged), weight loss, night sweats and fever*".

Lifestyle: Healthy lifestyle related information such as exercise and food.
E.g., [Original] "*You can take a lot of soup, njahe, omena. These works well for new moms. Don't*

drink coffe or majani. Tumia to cocoa".
[Translated] "You can take a lot of soup, turtle beans, fish. These work well for new moms. Don't drink coffee or tea. Use only cocoa".

Personal: Information regarding relationships with partner or other family members.
E.g., [Original] "*The problem is I have a partner na ajue my status am afraid day nitamwambia he can even kill himself*"
[Translated] "*The problem is that I have a partner who doesn't know my status and am afraid the day I decide to say he might kill himself.*"

Admin: Administrative information such as rules and regulations of the group and formal meetings.
E.g., [Original] "*We shall respect all members and not use words like HIV, ART, CD4 So that people feel comfortable*".

Other: This contains any information not included in the above categories.
E.g., [Original] "*Hi....This is a big warning...my mother in law has just lost over Kes. 70,000 to M-Shwari and KCB-MPESA con-women...*".

3.1.2 Emotional

This sub-category deals with seeking emotional support, or communicating empathy, love or concern towards fellow group members.
E.g., [Original] "*Haki usichoke mm pia nilipoteza hapitite BT ilirudi tu lakini jaribu uone daktari, saa zing one inakuwanga type ya drugdrug kukeep time yakutake drug pole dia*".
[Translated] "Please don't be am also loosing appetite but it come back just go see a doctor, sometimes it's usually the type of drug and your timing for your medication, sorry my dear".

The emotional sub-category of messages are further sub-categorized into the following:
Empathy: An explicit mention of the difficulty experienced by the seeker that validates his/her distress or an attempt to see things from the seekers' perspective.
E.g., [Original] "*pia Mimi na shida ingine Niko na mimba yake*".
[Translated] "Same here also and another problem is that he got me pregnant".

Hopefulness: A response encouraging others to stay hopeful and optimistic in difficult situations.
E.g., [Original] "*Sorry for this dear. Like 5002 has said some things need sacrifice and time. Never give up. Just try and overcome the hurdle, all will be fine.*"

Happiness: A response that indicates a happy mood or excitement.
E.g., [Original] "*Early this month, we were blessed with a baby girl and we thank God for His mercies on us*".

Negativity: A response that indicates a mournful mood or shows any negative emotion (such as anger/sorrow/frustration). E.g., [Original] "*Hello guys nfeel so bad today c ski poa nko n headache n pia cna strength pray 4 me*".
[Translated] "Hello guys am feeling so bad today i have a headache and I also dont have energy please pray for me".

3.1.3 Chit-Chat

The messages in this category include introductions, greetings and other responses that promote social interactions or demonstrate friendliness.
E.g., [Original] "*Lunch ilipita sasa ni supper*"
[Translated] "Lunch is over it's now supper time".

It can be further sub-categorized as: **Socialization** (E.g., [Original] "*Karibuni lunch guys*", [Translated] "Welcome for lunch guys") and **Greeting** (E.g. [Original] "*Happy Easter guys*").

3.1.4 Acknowledgement

Responses used to affirm, acknowledge and/or backchannel communication, are tagged under this category. .
E.g., [Original] "*Santy...pia ww doz poa*".
[Translated] "Thanks..you too sleep well".

3.1.5 Group Work

A response wherein members encourage each other to work as a group.
E.g., [Original] "*Let's bring topics even on the contemporary experiences so that we can continue keeping the group more active as it should be guys!*"

3.1.6 Other

Any response that does not belong to any of the above categories (like emoji, a system-generated message, etc).
E.g., [Original] "*Waiting for this message*". (a default system-generated message in WhatsApp)

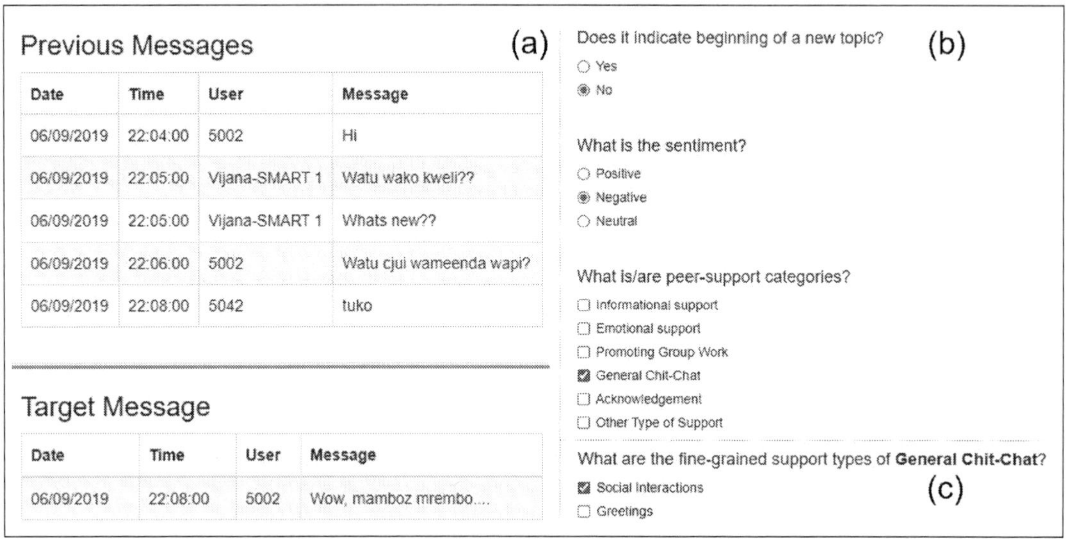

Figure 2: An overview of the annotation interface to annotate WhatsApp chat messages.

3.2 Sentiment

Sentiment is a view or opinion that is held or expressed by an individual. The sentiments are further categorized into the following:

Negative: It expresses a negative view or opinion. E.g., [Original] "*Uko na shida ya kichwa c siri*". [Translated] "You have a mental problem it's no secret".

Positive: A message is classified as positive if the speaker expresses a strongly positive opinion on something or someone. Note: Greetings are not included in this category.
E.g., [Original] "*I'm much happy to interact and share with you guys!*"

Neutral: When neither positive nor negative sentiment is expressed, the message is labelled as neutral. This could include a general comment, acknowledgement, chitchat or a simple greeting.
E.g., [Original] "*I suggest that we should try and at least do this for our health.*"

3.3 Word-Level Language

To understand the code-mixed interactions in the chat, word-level language annotation is needed. For our dataset, we used five language identification codes: *En* for English, *Sw* for Kiswahili, *Sh* for Sheng, *CM* for Code-Mixed words or phrases (E.g., '*nfeel*', '*tutawash*'), and *Oth* for miscellaneous (e.g., emojis, any other language).
E.g., [Original] "*Mimi Nilichukua my siz tukalost*".
[Language] (Sw) (Sw) (En) (En) (CM)
[Translated] "I took my sister and I got lost".
If a particular word is tagged as *Oth*, the annotators were asked to explain the reason behind choosing this particular tag. For instance, *Kyole 2* (name of a hospital) is assigned the language tag *Oth*, and the reason specified is *Named Entity*. Also, if the language is different from *En*, *Sh* and *Sw*, that needs to be specified in the reason correctly. Thus, our schema can be further extensible to annotate more languages.

3.4 Topic Change

Each message is labeled with a binary flag (Yes/No) to indicate a change in topic.

3.5 Typo

Shortened words, abbreviations and misspellings are pervasive in informal conversations, especially in instant messaging such as WhatsApp. It is important to identify and normalize such typos. The annotators were asked to correctly normalize the typos found during the annotation process. It is worthy to note that the typos and abbreviations need to be separately tagged and identified. E.g.,
1. [Original] "***Fuine** and how are you..*"
2. [Original] "*We shall respect all members and not use words like **HIV**, **ART**, **CD4**, **VL**. So that people feel comfortable.*"
The spelling mistake and abbreviations in the

above examples are written in bold.

4 Annotation Interface Overview

We developed an annotation interface (Figure 2) to facilitate user-friendly annotation. The annotators were provided with detailed guidelines on how to use the interface for annotating the chat messages based on our proposed annotation framework. Django framework (Python) was used on the server-side for implementing this interface. This interface can be also used to annotate the peer support conversations in the mental health chat forums such as Reddit, TalkLife. The annotators need to login into the interface with their credentials to start the annotation process as outlined in the guidelines provided to them. On logging in, a target message is displayed along with ten (or less) previous messages to provide context (Figure 2a). The right side of the screen shows question related to top-level categories: peer support, sentiment, and change in topic (Figure 2b). The annotators then have to choose appropriate labels. For the peer support category, the annotators have to further choose subcategory labels as well (Figure 2c).

As a message can be associated with multiple subcategories, the annotators are asked to highlight specific portions of the message for each subcategory. E.g., in the message *"Hi...he got me pregnant..."*—*"Hi"* is tagged as *Chit-Chat → Greeting* and *"he got me pregnant"* is tagged as *Informational → Personal*.

For *Typo*, the annotators are asked to highlight spelling mistakes and abbreviations, and correct them wherever possible. For instance, in the message *"Morning members from today, hence forth untill further notice am the S.T.O (sitting allowance officer) ask any querry you get the right answer"* the annotators needs to highlight the typos (*"untill"*, *"querry"*) and normalize those (*"until"*, *"query"*) using the interface. Moreover, they should also annotate the abbreviation (*"S.T.O"*).

The annotation requires a language tag for each word in the message. Instead of specifying a language label for each word, the annotators are asked to highlight the word spans for each language category, facilitating quicker and less error-prone language identification. For example, in the message *"Wow, mamboz mrembo"* ([Translated]: *"Wow, Hello beautiful"*)—*"Wow"* is highlighted as *English* and the word span *"mamboz mrembo"* is highlighted as *Kiswahili*.

The annotators are expected to completely annotate each message before moving on to the next message. The submitted annotations are saved in a cloud database. The annotators have an option to revise and modify their current or previously submitted annotations during the process. If the annotators are unsure of how to annotate a particular message, the interface allows them an option to note and skip that message. This annotation interface can be leveraged easily to annotate any complex hierarchical annotation schema comprising of multiple levels.

5 Annotation Experiments and Observations

The annotation was conducted in three phases. In Phase-1, a small sample of 395 English-translated messages (105 messages from Group-1, 290 messages from Group-2) were annotated, and the corresponding original multilingual messages of the same set were annotated in Phase-2. In Phase-3, the entire multilingual dataset was annotated. Below we discuss the challenges faced and the learnings from all the annotation phases.

5.1 Annotation Phase-1

The Phase-1 study was designed to ensure that the entire annotation process as well the guidelines were well-understood by the annotators. In this phase, the short-listed 395 chat messages were annotated by one of the co-authors, an expert English speaker, who led the development of the proposed annotation framework. The co-author, not being able to understand Swahili or Sheng, found it easier to initially develop the schema using the English-translated messages (this translation was manually carried out by a native speaker). We consider that as the gold standard annotation for Phase-1, and use it to assess the quality of the rest of the pilot annotations in Phase 1. Though the English-translations were not of great quality, but that did not affect our interpretations since we have carried out the final annotation on the multilingual messages (Phase-2 and Phase-3).

Three annotators (graduate students proficient in English) were asked to annotate the same 395 messages using the annotation guidelines. For quality estimation, Cohen's Kappa (κ) (Vieira et al., 2010) was used to assess inter-annotator agreement (IAA) between each annotator and the expert annotator. We observed an average of 0.67 κ agreement for the fine-grained peer support subcategory tags and 0.89 κ for sentiment. While there was strong agreement for sentiment labelling, the peer support subcategories showed only moderate agreement.

We analyzed the data to understand the annotation differences. First, we found the highest annotation disagreement among *Informational* messages—46% of the total disagreements were between *Medical* and *Lifestyle*. Hence, we revised the annotation guidelines such that *Medical* was given priority over *Lifestyle*, i.e., the annotators were asked to select only *Medical*, or both *Medical* and *Lifestyle*, when unsure. For example, in this message, "*Hi? It's GXXX here I think you can try tell a person who has not accepted the status the importance of taking the drugs and how they work in our bodies. Yah remember to eat healthy*", the individual is stressing upon both the importance of medical adherence and consumption of healthy food. Hence, it should be tagged as both *Medical* and *Lifestyle* under *Informational*.

Second, the ambiguity between *Lifestyle* and *Personal* subcategories comprised 12% of the disagreements. For example: "*We should always protect ourselves using a condom during sexual intercourse*". Our guidelines were revised to clarify that the *Personal* tag should be applied only to messages dealing with personal relationships, while the *Lifestyle* tag should only be used to annotate lifestyle habits. Thus, in the above example, only *Lifestyle* tag is applicable.

Third, another source of confusion was between *Group Work* and *Admin* with 24% of total disagreements. To solve this confusion, we provided more examples in the annotation guidelines to clarify the differences between them. These examples were laid out to elucidate that encouraging more activity within the group members belong to *Group Work* whereas *Admin* dealt with the meetings arranged by the moderators or formal group regulations. For example, in "*With this group, we would like to support each other in staying healthy and supported. If you are having problems or questions about your health, please share them with the group, or inbox me individually. We are stronger together.*", the moderator is talking about the rules of communication within the group, thus it should be tagged as *Admin*. Whereas in "*How are we all doing this week? What are you most looking forward to about this group?*", the speaker is encouraging more participation in the group and should be annotated as *Group Work*.

Finally, other minor disagreements originated due to human error (provide versus seek information, *Greetings* versus *Acknowledgement*). This did not require any revision of the guideline.

5.2 Annotation Phase-2

The annotation guidelines were revised based on the learnings from Phase-1 annotations. We have calculated the pairwise Cohens kappa score using the Scikit-learn library of Python. In Phase-1, we wanted to understand how much each of the pilot annotators agree with the expert annotator using Kappa Agreement. Certain portions of annotation guidelines as well as schema were updated and revised based on their understanding.

Two professional annotators, based in Kenya and proficient in English, Kiswahili, Kikuyu and Sheng languages, were then asked to carry another pilot annotation in Phase-2 based on the revised guidelines. In Phase-2 IAA results (as illustrated in Figure-3), we calculate the pairwise agreement between two annotators of Africa for each of the peer support categories on the multilingual chat messages. No gold standard annotation was used to assess the quality of their annotation in Phase-2 unlike Phase-1. The key difference between Phase-1 and Phase-2 was the addition of language tagging as well as the annotation being undertaken on the original messages rather than the translations.

While analyzing IAA, we observed that tags of English-translations differed from those of the original chat logs, which was due to inaccurate language translation. For instance, "*Poa Sana*" ([Translated] "*Very good*") was tagged as *Acknowledgement* and *Socialization* by the annotators, whereas the corresponding English-translation "*Hey*" was tagged as *Greetings* by the expert annotator. Thus, with the help of the Kenyan annotators, a more accurate English translation was also obtained, and accordingly the gold standard annotation was corrected.

The annotators also found the language tags of certain named entities such as food items (e.g., 'soup', 'cocoa') confusing, mainly because some of the named entities can exist as borrowings in *Kiswahili* and *Sheng*. Hence, we modified the instructions to categorize such entities as *English*.

5.3 Annotation Phase-3

In this phase, the same annotators from Phase-2 annotated the entire dataset based on the revised guidelines. An iterative revision of the guidelines was conducted based on any observed confusion in this phase as well, and the annotators were expected to revise their annotations accordingly. Here we describe a few of them.

First, annotators were unsure about tagging specific entities, such as time (e.g., '1100hrs', '1pm'), symbols (e.g., '+'), laughter (e.g., 'hahaha') and numerals (e.g., '2','five'). This was resolved by asking the annotators to tag time, symbols, and numerals as *Other* language, along with specifying the reason as 'time', 'symbols' or 'numerals', respectively. Laughter expressions were tagged in the language they were written in, as different languages have different expressions for laughter, e.g., 'hahaha' was tagged as *English*.

Second, annotators also faced difficulties in tagging language category for typos (e.g., 'realtionships', 'apa', 'nni'). This was resolved by asking them to choose the language category of the normalized word (e.g., 'realtionships' → 'relationships' in *English*, 'apa' → 'hapa' in *Kiswahili*, 'nni' → 'nini' in *Kiswahili*). It is worthy to note that in order to tag the abbreviations and contracted forms of words, the annotators were also asked to tag it to the language category of the expanded form. We did not come across any ambiguities or unclarities regarding this during the annotation process.

Third, emojis posed another challenge for annotating the peer support categories of the chat messages. In the annotation guidelines, the annotators were instructed to tag non-textual content as *Other*. However, for certain messages, decoding the emoji was needed to obtain the correct tag. For example, "*Is* 🥂 *bad?*". The semantics of the message is dependent on decoding the meaning of the emoji ("*Is drinking alcohol bad?*"). Ideally, this message should be annotated as *Lifestyle* and not *Other* in the *Informational* category. Since the point of human annotation is to indeed identify deeper meaning which a naive algorithm might miss, the annotators were asked to tag the messages after decoding the meaning of the emoji.

5.4 Observations

The distribution of peer support category labels for Phase-3 in both the groups are summarized in Table 1. We observed that a majority of the messages in both the groups belong to *Chit-Chat* (65.9% in Group-1 and 66.2% in Group-2), followed by *Informational*. Within *Informational* category, *Medical* stands out as the most prominent for Group-2 (35.0% informational messages) while *Admin* is the most prominent in Group-1 (34.6% informational messages).

It should be noted that the IAA is relatively lower for *Hopefulness*, *Admin*, and *Group Work* indicating disagreement between the annotators. Overall, *Chit-Chat* and *Acknowledgement* are easier to annotate as is reflected in their IAA score. Further, we also observe that most messages are short in length with an average message length of 4.34 words in Group-1 and 5.6 words in Group-2.

Peer Support	Group-1	Group-2
Informational		
Medical	57	445
Lifestyle	24	81
Personal	50	392
Admin	86	195
Other	31	158
Emotional		
Empathy	21	42
Hopefulness	27	93
Happiness	5	31
Negativity	29	51
Chit-Chat		
Socialization	1168	2316
Greetings	232	695
Acknowledgement	242	615
Group Work	17	225
Other	138	304

Table 1: Overall distribution of peer support categories in both the peer support groups after Phase-3.

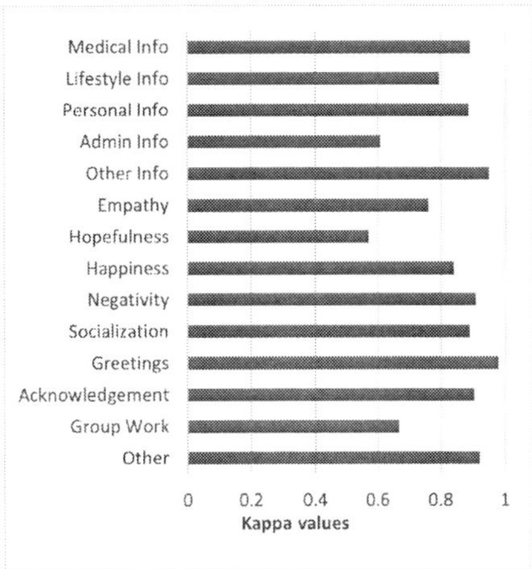

Figure 3: IAA for peer support categories in Phase-2

Word-Level Language	Group-1	Group-2
Monolingual		
En Only	805	2278
Sw Only	262	633
Sh Only	64	142
CM Only	3	9
Multilingual		
En Sw	171	706
En Sh	16	84
En Sw Sh	54	198
En CM	4	17
Sw Sh	70	182
En Sw CM	15	63
En Sh CM	2	5
Sw Sh CM	2	24
Sw CM	14	38
En Sw Sh CM	8	40

Table 2: Overall distribution of the messages containing different language category labels in both the groups after Phase-3. The nature of messages (monolingual or multilingual) is determined by the language tags for each of the words in the messages.

With respect to *Sentiment* labels, most of the messages were tagged as *Neutral* (93.4% in Group-1 and 87.1% in Group-2), followed by *Negative* (5.0% in Group-1 and 4.3% in Group-2) and then *Positive*. It was also found that the annotators agreed mostly on *Negative* sentiment (Phase-2 κ=0.92) and disagreed the most on *Positive* (Phase-2 κ=0.67).

Table 2 describes the results for language tagging after Phase-3. It shows that the IAA score for *English (En)* (κ=0.98) and *Kiswahili (Sw)* (κ=0.98) words is higher compared to those of *Sheng (Sh)* (κ=0.87) and *Code-Mixed phrases (CM)* (κ=0.85). It can also be observed that the messages contain a high amount of code-mixing (23.8% messages are code-mixed in Group-1 and 24.4% in Group-2). While English is the dominant language for the monolingual messages, code-mixed *English Kiswahili (En Sw)* is the dominant language-pair for the multilingual messages.

We found that a change of topic was indicated in 3% and 4% of the chat messages in Group-1 and Group-2, respectively. In Group-1, a topic change was initiated mostly by the admin (89% of topic changes), while in Group-2, other group members have also been found to initiate discussions on new topics (only 39% of total topic changes were triggered by the admin). Further, we observe that a topic change is mostly (95.2%) associated with the *Informational* or *Group Work* subcategories.

Due to the informal nature of WhatsApp conversations, a significant percentage of chat logs contain spelling mistakes (19.4% and 18.7% messages in Group-1 and Group-2, respectively) or abbreviations (15.7% and 10.9% messages in Group-1 and Group-2, respectively).

6 Conclusion and Future Work

In this paper, we presented a comprehensive annotation schema, combining several linguistic and pragmatic phenomena, to enable studies of WhatsApp based conversations of youth living with HIV. Unlike Twitter and Facebook, this requires understanding the content of previous discourse to annotate the sentiment and conversational intent of supporting the peers in specific examples. During the process of annotation, we have learnt that a good percentage of examples require understanding the context. To the best of our knowledge, we are the first to combine several standard annotation schemes to annotate the multilingual conversations in a small, close-knit community.

We believe our schema can be used to flag important messages (based on user concerns) to the healthcare providers. This will in turn help to alleviate the need to scroll through all the messages individually to identify the ones that require a response from the facilitators. Linguists can also use this framework to study the nature of multilingualism in such conversations from both sociolinguistic and structural perspectives. In future, we plan to use the framework to further study the nature of engagement and multilingual interactions in such peer-support groups in healthcare domain with the aim of enhancing remote patient care.

Acknowledgement

We thank Professor Keshet Ronen, Naveena Karusala, and other members from the University of Washington for providing us access to the datasets. We also thank Samuel Maina from Microsoft Africa Research Institute (MARI) for providing his feedback on the work, and the three annotators from Microsoft Research India Lab for putting a considerable amount of time in annotation, and giving us their feedback on the schema. Finally, we acknowledge the efforts of Dr. Seema Mehrotra from the National Institute of Mental Health and Neurosciences (NIMHANS), Bangalore during the initial ideation around an annotation framework on healthcare conversations.

References

Zahra Ashktorab, Mohit Jain, Q. Vera Liao, and Justin D. Weisz. 2019. *Resilient Chatbots: Repair Strategy Preferences for Conversational Breakdowns*, page 112. Association for Computing Machinery, New York, NY, USA.

JinYeong Bak, Suin Kim, and Alice Oh. 2012. Self-disclosure and relationship strength in Twitter conversations. In *Proceedings of the 50th Annual Meeting of the Association for Computational Linguistics (Volume 2: Short Papers)*, pages 60–64, Jeju Island, Korea. Association for Computational Linguistics.

Utsab Barman, Amitava Das, Joachim Wagner, and Jennifer Foster. 2014. Code mixing: A challenge for language identification in the language of social media. In *CodeSwitch@EMNLP*.

Rafiya Begum, Kalika Bali, Monojit Choudhury, Koustav Rudra, and Niloy Ganguly. 2016. Functions of code-switching in tweets: An annotation framework and some initial experiments. In *Proceedings of the Tenth International Conference on Language Resources and Evaluation (LREC'16)*, pages 1644–1650, Portorož, Slovenia. European Language Resources Association (ELRA).

Shane Bergsma, Paul McNamee, Mossaab Bagdouri, Clayton Fink, and Theresa Wilson. 2012. Language identification for creating language-specific Twitter collections. In *Proceedings of the Second Workshop on Language in Social Media*, pages 65–74, Montréal, Canada. Association for Computational Linguistics.

Karthik S. Bhat, Mohit Jain, and Neha Kumar. 2021. Infrastructuring telehealth in (in)formal patient-doctor contexts. *Proc. ACM Hum.-Comput. Interact.*, 5(CSCW2).

Sven Buechel, Anneke Buffone, Barry Slaff, L. Ungar, and João Sedoc. 2018. Modeling empathy and distress in reaction to news stories. In *EMNLP*.

Graham Button and Wes Sharrock. 1997. *The Production of Order and the Order of Production: Possibilities for Distributed Organisations, Work and Technology in the Print Industry*, pages 1–16. Springer Netherlands, Dordrecht.

Fabio Celli and Luca Rossi. 2012. The role of emotional stability in Twitter conversations. In *Proceedings of the Workshop on Semantic Analysis in Social Media*, pages 10–17, Avignon, France. Association for Computational Linguistics.

Bharathi Raja Chakravarthi, Vigneshwaran Muralidaran, Ruba Priyadharshini, and John Philip McCrae. 2020. Corpus creation for sentiment analysis in code-mixed Tamil-English text. In *Proceedings of the 1st Joint Workshop on Spoken Language Technologies for Under-resourced languages (SLTU) and Collaboration and Computing for Under-Resourced Languages (CCURL)*, pages 202–210, Marseille, France. European Language Resources association.

Bharathi Raja Chakravarthi, Ruba Priyadharshini, Vigneshwaran Muralidaran, Navya Jose, Shardul Suryawanshi, Elizabeth Sherly, and John P. McCrae. 2021. Dravidiancodemix: Sentiment analysis and offensive language identification dataset for dravidian languages in code-mixed text.

M. D. Choudhury and Sushovan De. 2014. Mental health discourse on reddit: Self-disclosure, social support, and anonymity. In *ICWSM*.

M. D. Choudhury, Emre Kcman, Mark Dredze, Glen A. Coppersmith, and Mrinal Kumar. 2016. Discovering shifts to suicidal ideation from mental health content in social media. *Proceedings of the 2016 CHI Conference on Human Factors in Computing Systems*.

B. S. Chumbow. 2010. Linguistic diversity, pluralism and national development in africa. *Africa Development*, 34:21–45.

P. Ciechanowski, W. Katon, J. Russo, and E. Walker. 2001. The patient-provider relationship: attachment theory and adherence to treatment in diabetes. *The American journal of psychiatry*, 158 1:29–35.

Andy Crabtree. 2003. *Designing Collaborative Systems: A Practical Guide to Ethnography*. Springer, London.

Amitava Das and Björn Gambäck. 2013. Code-mixing in social media text. the last language identification frontier? *Trait. Autom. des Langues*, 54:41–64.

Nassim Dehouche. 2020. Dataset on usage and engagement patterns for facebook live sellers in thailand. *Data in Brief*, 30:105661.

Mrinal Dhar, Vaibhav Kumar, and Manish Shrivastava. 2018. Enabling code-mixed translation: Parallel corpus creation and mt augmentation approach.

A. Dwivedi. 2015. Linguistic realities in kenya: A preliminary survey.

R. Elliott, A. Bohart, J. Watson, and D. Murphy. 2018. Therapist empathy and client outcome: An updated meta-analysis. *Psychotherapy*, 55:399410.

James Gibson, Dogan Can, Bo Xiao, Zac E. Imel, David C. Atkins, P. Georgiou, and Shrikanth S. Narayanan. 2016. A deep learning approach to modeling empathy in addiction counseling. In *INTERSPEECH*.

Chege Githiora. 2002. Sheng: Peer language, swahili dialect or emerging creole? *Journal of African Cultural Studies*, 15(2):159–181.

Stephan Gouws, Donald Metzler, Congxing Cai, and Eduard Hovy. 2011. Contextual bearing on linguistic variation in social media. In *Proceedings of the Workshop on Language in Social Media (LSM 2011)*, pages 20–29, Portland, Oregon. Association for Computational Linguistics.

Kishaloy Halder, Lahari Poddar, and Min-Yen Kan. 2017. Modeling temporal progression of emotional status in mental health forum: A recurrent neural net approach. In *Proceedings of the 8th Workshop on Computational Approaches to Subjectivity, Sentiment and Social Media Analysis*, pages 127–135, Copenhagen, Denmark. Association for Computational Linguistics.

Mahshid Hosseini and Cornelia Caragea. 2021. It takes two to empathize: One to seek and one to provide. *Proceedings of the AAAI Conference on Artificial Intelligence*, 35(14):13018–13026.

John Hughes, Val King, Tom Rodden, and Hans Andersen. 1994. Moving out from the control room: Ethnography in system design. In *Proceedings of the 1994 ACM Conference on Computer Supported Cooperative Work*, CSCW '94, page 429439, New York, NY, USA. Association for Computing Machinery.

Mohit Jain, Pratyush Kumar, Ishita Bhansali, Q. Vera Liao, Khai Truong, and Shwetak Patel. 2018a. Farmchat: A conversational agent to answer farmer queries. *Proc. ACM Interact. Mob. Wearable Ubiquitous Technol.*, 2(4).

Mohit Jain, Pratyush Kumar, Ramachandra Kota, and Shwetak N. Patel. 2018b. Evaluating and informing the design of chatbots. In *Proceedings of the 2018 Designing Interactive Systems Conference*, DIS '18, page 895906, New York, NY, USA. Association for Computing Machinery.

Anupam Jamatia, Björn Gambäck, and Amitava Das. 2016. Collecting and annotating indian social media code-mixed corpora. In *CICLing*.

Naveena Karusala, David Odhiambo Seeh, Cyrus Mugo, Brandon Guthrie, Megan A Moreno, Grace John-Stewart, Irene Inwani, Richard Anderson, and Keshet Ronen. 2021. *That Courage to Encourage: Participation and Aspirations in Chat-Based Peer Support for Youth Living with HIV*. Association for Computing Machinery, New York, NY, USA.

Naveena Karusala, Ding Wang, and Jacki O'Neill. 2020. *Making Chat at Home in the Hospital: Exploring Chat Use by Nurses*, page 115. Association for Computing Machinery, New York, NY, USA.

Scott F. Kiesling, Umashanthi Pavalanathan, Jim Fitzpatrick, Xiaochuang Han, and Jacob Eisenstein. 2018. Interactional stancetaking in online forums. *Computational Linguistics*, 44(4):683–718.

Taisa Kushner and Amit Sharma. 2020. Bursts of activity: Temporal patterns of help-seeking and support in online mental health forums. In *Proceedings of The Web Conference 2020*, WWW '20, page 29062912, New York, NY, USA. Association for Computing Machinery.

Suraj Maharjan, Elizabeth Blair, Steven Bethard, and Thamar Solorio. 2015. Developing language-tagged corpora for code-switching tweets. In *Proceedings of The 9th Linguistic Annotation Workshop*, pages 72–84, Denver, Colorado, USA. Association for Computational Linguistics.

David Martin, Benjamin V. Hanrahan, Jacki O'Neill, and Neha Gupta. 2014. Being a turker. In *Proceedings of the 17th ACM Conference on Computer Supported Cooperative Work Social Computing*, CSCW '14, page 224235, New York, NY, USA. Association for Computing Machinery.

Jacki O'Neill and David Martin. 2003. Text chat in action. In *Proceedings of the 2003 International ACM SIGGROUP Conference on Supporting Group Work*, GROUP '03, page 4049, New York, NY, USA. Association for Computing Machinery.

Verónica Pérez-Rosas, Rada Mihalcea, Kenneth Resnicow, Satinder Singh, and Lawrence An. 2017. Understanding and predicting empathic behavior in counseling therapy. In *Proceedings of the 55th Annual Meeting of the Association for Computational Linguistics (Volume 1: Long Papers)*, pages 1426–1435, Vancouver, Canada. Association for Computational Linguistics.

Shruti Rijhwani, Royal Sequiera, Monojit Choudhury, Kalika Bali, and Chandra Shekhar Maddila. 2017. Estimating code-switching on Twitter with a novel generalized word-level language detection technique. In *Proceedings of the 55th Annual Meeting of the Association for Computational Linguistics (Volume 1: Long Papers)*, pages 1971–1982, Vancouver, Canada. Association for Computational Linguistics.

Koustav Rudra, Shruti Rijhwani, Rafiya Begum, Kalika Bali, Monojit Choudhury, and Niloy Ganguly. 2016. Understanding language preference for expression of opinion and sentiment: What do Hindi-English speakers do on Twitter? In *Proceedings of the 2016 Conference on Empirical Methods in Natural Language Processing*, pages 1131–1141, Austin, Texas. Association for Computational Linguistics.

Koustav Rudra, Ashish Sharma, Kalika Bali, Monojit Choudhury, and Niloy Ganguly. 2019. Identifying and analyzing different aspects of english-hindi code-switching in twitter. *ACM Trans. Asian Low-Resour. Lang. Inf. Process.*, 18(3).

Farig Sadeque, Thamar Solorio, Ted Pedersen, Prasha Shrestha, and Steven Bethard. 2015. Predicting continued participation in online health forums. In *Proceedings of the Sixth International Workshop on*

Health Text Mining and Information Analysis, pages 12–20, Lisbon, Portugal. Association for Computational Linguistics.

Antoinette Schoenthaler, William F. Chaplin, John P. Allegrante, Senaida Fernandez, Marleny Diaz-Gloster, Jonathan N. Tobin, and Gbenga Ogedegbe. 2009. Provider communication effects medication adherence in hypertensive african americans. *Patient Education and Counseling*, 75(2):185–191.

Rosalie Schultz, Stephen Quinn, Byron Wilson, Tammy Abbott, and Sheree Cairney. 2019. Structural modelling of wellbeing for indigenous australians: importance of mental health. *BMC Health Services Research*, 19(1):488.

Ashish Sharma, M. Choudhury, Tim Althoff, and Amit Sharma. 2020a. Engagement patterns of peer-to-peer interactions on mental health platforms. In *ICWSM*.

Ashish Sharma, Adam Miner, David Atkins, and Tim Althoff. 2020b. A computational approach to understanding empathy expressed in text-based mental health support. In *Proceedings of the 2020 Conference on Empirical Methods in Natural Language Processing (EMNLP)*, pages 5263–5276, Online. Association for Computational Linguistics.

Joshgun Sirajzade, Daniela Gierschek, and Christoph Schommer. 2020. An annotation framework for Luxembourgish sentiment analysis. In *Proceedings of the 1st Joint Workshop on Spoken Language Technologies for Under-resourced languages (SLTU) and Collaboration and Computing for Under-Resourced Languages (CCURL)*, pages 172–176, Marseille, France. European Language Resources association.

Jennifer Smith-Merry, G. Goggin, A. Campbell, Kirsty McKenzie, Brad Ridout, and C. Baylosis. 2019. Social connection and online engagement: Insights from interviews with users of a mental health online forum. *JMIR Mental Health*, 6.

Sahil Swami, A. Khandelwal, Vinay Singh, S. Akhtar, and Manish Shrivastava. 2018. A corpus of english-hindi code-mixed tweets for sarcasm detection. *ArXiv*, abs/1805.11869.

Ye Tian, Thiago Galery, Giulio Dulcinati, Emilia Molimpakis, and Chao Sun. 2017. Facebook sentiment: Reactions and emojis. In *Proceedings of the Fifth International Workshop on Natural Language Processing for Social Media*, pages 11–16, Valencia, Spain. Association for Computational Linguistics.

Trang Tran and Mari Ostendorf. 2016. Characterizing the language of online communities and its relation to community reception. In *Proceedings of the 2016 Conference on Empirical Methods in Natural Language Processing*, pages 1030–1035, Austin, Texas. Association for Computational Linguistics.

Cretien van Campen and Jurjen Iedema. 2007. Are persons with physical disabilities who participate in society healthier and happier? structural equation modelling of objective participation and subjective well-being. *Quality of Life Research*, 16(4):635.

S. Vieira, U. Kaymak, and J. Sousa. 2010. Cohen's kappa coefficient as a performance measure for feature selection. *International Conference on Fuzzy Systems*, pages 1–8.

Deepanshu Vijay, Aditya Bohra, Vinay Singh, Syed Sarfaraz Akhtar, and Manish Shrivastava. 2018. Corpus creation and emotion prediction for Hindi-English code-mixed social media text. In *Proceedings of the 2018 Conference of the North American Chapter of the Association for Computational Linguistics: Student Research Workshop*, pages 128–135, New Orleans, Louisiana, USA. Association for Computational Linguistics.

Ramaswamy Viswanathan, Michael F. Myers, and Ayman H. Fanous. 2020. Support groups and individual mental health care via video conferencing for frontline clinicians during the covid-19 pandemic. *Psychosomatics*, 61(5):538–543. 32660876[pmid].

Yogarshi Vyas, Spandana Gella, Jatin Sharma, K. Bali, and M. Choudhury. 2014. Pos tagging of english-hindi code-mixed social media content. In *EMNLP*.

Ding Wang, Santosh D. Kale, and Jacki O'Neill. 2020. *Please Call the Specialism: Using WeChat to Support Patient Care in China*, page 113. Association for Computing Machinery, New York, NY, USA.

Jonathan Zomick, Sarah Ita Levitan, and Mark Serper. 2019. Linguistic analysis of schizophrenia in Reddit posts. In *Proceedings of the Sixth Workshop on Computational Linguistics and Clinical Psychology*, pages 74–83, Minneapolis, Minnesota. Association for Computational Linguistics.

Sister Help: Data Augmentation for Frame-Semantic Role Labeling

Ayush Pancholy[♦] **Miriam R. L. Petruck**[♥] **Swabha Swayamdipta**[♣]
[♦] University of California, Berkeley
[♥] International Computer Science Institute, Berkeley
[♣] Allen Institute for Artificial Intelligence
{ayush.pancholy@,miriamp@icsi.}berkeley.edu
swabhas@allenai.org

Abstract

While FrameNet is widely regarded as a rich resource of semantics in natural language processing, a major criticism concerns its lack of coverage and the relative paucity of its labeled data compared to other commonly used lexical resources such as PropBank and VerbNet. This paper reports on a pilot study to address these gaps. We propose a data augmentation approach, which uses existing frame-specific annotation to automatically annotate other lexical units of the same frame which are unannotated. Our rule-based approach defines the notion of a **sister lexical unit** and generates frame-specific augmented data for training. We present experiments on frame-semantic role labeling which demonstrate the importance of this data augmentation: we obtain a large improvement to prior results on frame identification and argument identification for FrameNet, utilizing both full-text and lexicographic annotations under FrameNet. Our findings on data augmentation highlight the value of automatic resource creation for improved models in frame-semantic parsing.

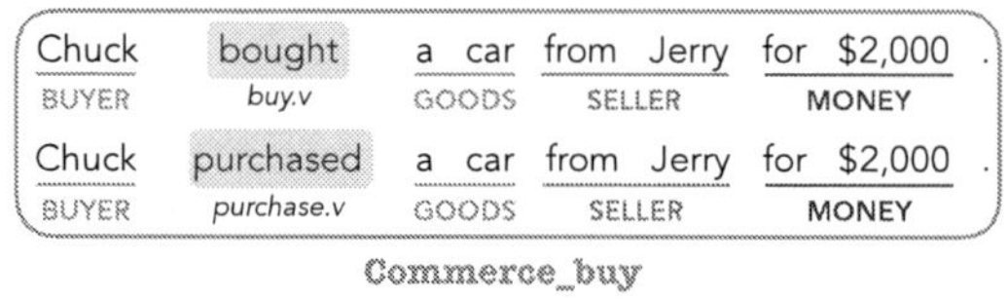

Figure 1: Illustration of Sister Lexical Units (**Sister LUs**) with FrameNet annotation for the verbs *buy* and *purchase*, which are defined in terms of the `Commerce_buy` frame. The arguments of both LUs are identical, both realizing the frame elements (FEs) BUYER, GOODS, SELLER, and MONEY. Targets in the sentence that trigger the frame are the words *bought* and *purchased*, respectively.

1 Introduction

Among the challenges to Natural Language Processing (NLP) systems is access to sufficient and accurate information about the mapping between form and meaning in language (Bender and Koller, 2020). While the number of resources that provide such information has increased in recent decades, producing these resources remains labor-intensive and costly. This is particularly true for FrameNet (**FN**; Ruppenhofer et al., 2016), a rich resource of semantic annotations, popularized for semantic role labeling (**SRL**) since the pioneering work of Gildea and Jurafsky (2002).

Nevertheless, FrameNet still relies (almost exclusively) on expert manual linguistic annotation, resulting in far fewer annotations than other resources that are able to scale up the annotation process easily (FitzGerald et al., 2018). Moreover, the fine-grained annotations in FrameNet make them harder to produce compared to other lexical resources such as PropBank (Palmer et al., 2005) and VerbNet (Kipper et al., 2000). As a result, while SRL has continued to be a mainstay of core NLP, with applications in event extraction, participant tracking, machine translation, and question-answering, far fewer SRL systems use FrameNet for training, in contrast to PropBank.[1]

Our work seeks to address this low resource problem in FrameNet in English by automatic data augmentation. We leverage the FrameNet hierarchy where multiple lexical units are associated with the same frame, but might have a different number of annotations associated with them (§2). We propose a rule-based approach to transfer annotations among sister LUs; see Fig. 1 for an illustration. We implement and extend the proposal by Petruck and Swayamdipta (2019) to generate new annotation for previously unannotated LUs in the same frame, by exploiting the already identified target and frame of a given lemma. We hypothesize that our rule-based approach to transfer *frame-specific* annotation to generate semantic role labels for example

[1]PropBank annotations were also included in CoNLL shared tasks in 2005 (Carreras and Màrquez, 2005) and 2012 (Pradhan et al., 2012), and in OntoNotes (Pradhan et al., 2013).

Proceedings of the Joint 15th Linguistic Annotation Workshop (LAW) and 3rd Designing Meaning Representations (DMR) Workshop, pages 78–84
November, 2021. ©2021 Association for Computational Linguistics

sentences of lexical units (**LUs**) for which none exist, can indeed result in a FrameNet with higher coverage annotations, a state of affairs that can help in training frame-semantic role labeling systems (§3). Our experiments show that this is indeed the case; models trained on augmented data are able to surpass a strong baseline (OPEN-SESAME; Swayamdipta et al., 2017) for frame and argument identification (§4). We also provide a summary of the types of linguistic errors in the augmented data and the SRL task.

While our work provides a proof of concept, its novelty lies in exploiting frame-specific annotation to produce augmented data yielding new annotation. Our implementation and augmented data are publicly available.[2]

2 Background

2.1 FrameNet

FrameNet (Ruppenhofer et al., 2016) is a research and resource development project in corpus-based computational lexicography grounded in the principles of **frame semantics** (Fillmore, 1985). One of the goals of this effort is documenting the **valences**, i.e., the syntactic and semantic combinatorial possibilities of each item analyzed. These valence descriptions provide critical information on the mapping between form and meaning; NLP and more broadly, natural language understanding (NLU) require such mapping.

At the heart of the work is the **semantic frame**, a script-like knowledge structure that facilitates inference within and across events, situations, relations, etc. FrameNet defines a semantic frame in terms of its **frame elements** (FEs), or participants in the scene that the frame captures; a **lexical unit** (LU) is a pairing of a lemma and a frame, thus characterizing that LU in terms of the frame that it evokes. Valence descriptions derive from the annotation of FEs, i.e. **semantic roles**, on example sentences that illustrate the linguistic manifestation of the participants in a scene for the target of analysis. The first sentence in Figure 1 illustrates annotation with respect to the verb *buy*, which FN defines in terms of the `Commerce_buy` frame, whose FEs are a BUYER, SELLER, GOODS, and MONEY.[3]

[2] `https://github.com/ayush-pancholy/sister-help`

[3] Frame names appear in `Typewriter` font; FE names are in SMALL CAPS; and LUs are in *italics*.

The FrameNet[4] database (version 1.7) holds 1,224 frames, 10,478 frame-specific FEs (in lexical frames),[5] over 13,500 LUs. The primary annotations are in the form of nearly 203,000 manually annotated sentences providing information about the mapping between form and meaning in English; these are called the **lexicographic** annotations. A subset of the sentences with lexicographic annotations contain annotations for all possible frames of meaning in them; FrameNet calls this subset full-text annotations. Despite FrameNet's costly annotation efforts, 38% of the over 13,500 LUs in the database remain without annotation. That is, a significant amount of LUs in the database have no associated annotated sentences to serve as training data for downstream NLP applications.

2.2 Frame Semantic Role Labeling

Semantic role labeling (**SRL**) involves automatically labeling who did what to whom in a text document. SRL systems facilitate developing NLP applications, like question answering (Shen and Lapata, 2007), machine translation (Pedersen, 2001), and text summarization (Han et al., 2016), to name but a few. Frame semantic role labeling (**frame-SRL**) is a special type of SRL where the task is to identify target tokens (which evoke a frame of meaning), the frame itself (of target LUs) and FEs, or semantic roles, in text. The relationship between frames and their respective FEs requires that the system first identify the correct frame (FrameID) to identify the correct FEs (ArgID). Identifying the frame incorrectly necessarily means incorrect FE identification.[6] In practice, frame-SRL is usually implemented as a pipeline of structured prediction (Smith, 2011) tasks: identifying targets and LUs, frames, and finally the FEs (Das et al., 2010).

Using an early version of FN data (Johnson et al., 2001), Gildea and Jurafsky (2002) developed the first SRL system, which also initiated SRL as a now well-recognized task in the field. Recent years have seen the development of several (relatively) high-performing SRL systems. SEMAFOR (Das et al., 2014) uses a pipeline of discrete, manually designed feature-based linear clas-

[4] `https://framenet.icsi.berkeley.edu/fndrupal/framenet_request_data`

[5] FrameNet distinguishes between lexical and non-lexical frames, where the latter do not have associated annotation sets.

[6] Baker et al. (2007) also considered correct identification of the spans of a dependent of a lexical unit, even if the frame and by definition the FEs were identified incorrectly.

sifiers for target identification, frame identification (FrameID), and argument identification (ArgID). The core constraints of frame-semantic analyses, e.g. not repeating core FEs, are satisfied via integer linear programming. PathLSTM (Roth and Lapata, 2016) uses neural features to embed path relationships between frames and FEs, in a pipeline similar to that of SEMAFOR. Yang and Mitchell (2017) use a joint model to leverage Propbank SRL annotations to improve frame-SRL. OPEN-SESAME (Swayamdipta et al., 2017, 2018) uses an unconstrained, neural approach in a pipeline like SEMAFOR and PathLSTM. Continuous representations and a sophisticated global model based on semi-Markov conditional random fields (Sarawagi and Cohen, 2004) improve identifying arguments. We employ OPEN-SESAME[7] as the baseline of choice in our experiments (§4). With the exception of a few approaches, like that of Yang and Mitchell (2017), most prior work uses only the full-text annotations for frame-SRL; we present experiments considering the larger set of lexicographic annotations as well.

3 Method: Data Augmentation with Sister LUs

The relationship among LUs in a frame motivates examining their use for paraphrasing, where one LU replaces another resulting in an alternative phrasing of a sentence. Ellsworth and Janin (2007) produced paraphrases based on the relationship among LUs of a frame or closely related frames, augmenting a meager data set for use in speech recognition.

Most importantly, LUs in a frame tend overwhelmingly to follow the same annotation structure: the arguments of a lexical unit in a frame consist of the same FEs, regardless of the LU.[8] Note the parallel annotation for the two sentences in Figure 1 for the verbs, *buy* and *purchase*. We use this critical insight in our work, hypothesizing that existing annotation would inform the automated generation of annotation for **un**annotated LUs in a given frame.

To this end, Petruck and Swayamdipta (2019) defined **Sister Lexical Unit** as any LU for which annotation exists in a frame, and whose annotation can serve as a model to generate new annotation. A **Sister** is the LU with annotation and an **EmptyLU** lacks annotation; the Sister LU and the Empty LU must be of the same part of speech.

To generate augmented labeled data, we first identified all EmptyLUs. For each such LU, we identified a corresponding Sister, specifically, the LU with the greatest number of annotation sets and of the same POS as the EmptyLU in a given frame. We replaced each occurrence of a Sister in an annotated sentence with the EmptyLU. The replacement process included steps to ensure that the newly generated instance included the correct word forms, i.e., singular and plural forms of nouns or conjugated verbs of a Sister LU, following the strategy that Rastogi and Van Durme (2014) employed, which augmented FN using a paraphrase database (Ganitkevitch et al., 2013) to add new lemmas and then rewrote existing annotated sentences with those lemmas.

We transferred each sentence in the annotation set of the Sister into that of each EmptyLU, and replaced instances of the Sister with those of the EmptyLU. The replacement process ensured that newly generated data included correct word forms, i.e., singular and plural forms of nouns, conjugated verbs, or those with tense marking.

Ensuring agreement of tense, person, and number between instances of a sister and an EmptyLU required replacing the original word forms with those of the same grammatical number for nouns and tense, person, and number for verbs. However, this does not always yield correct results, e.g., for lemmas with irregular plural or past tense forms, as in *ox, oxen* and *bring, brought*.

3.1 Candidates for Augmentation

The aforementioned process identified 2,805 previously unannotated LUs, of which approximately 500 either were multiword expressions (MWEs) or had an MWE as a potential Sister. Thus, the process added at least one sentence to each previously empty annotation set, yielding the potential to provide new annotation for (approximately) 45% of the unannotated LUs in FrameNet 1.7. See Table 2 in the Appendix A for a few pairs of sister and empty LU pairs. The replacement process did not always yield grammatically correct results. Sometimes FrameNet (arbitrarily) treats MWEs as single LUs, and using a MWE (as a Sister or an EmptyLU) often resulted in ungrammatical sentences. Thus, we also eliminated MWEs from the data in this

[7]https://github.com/swabhs/open-sesame

[8]Two or more FEs might be part of a *core set*, yet only one will be realized for valid annotation. For a given frame, different LUs may not realize all the same FEs in all examples.

work, resulting in 2,300 previously unannotated LUs, eligible for augmentation.

4 Experiments

To test the idea of leveraging frame-specific annotation to generate new annotation for LUs lacking any, we wish to compare the performance of our approach with a baseline model. This facilitates determining the extent to which our augmentation algorithm would improve SRL performance, and thus (potentially) contribute to the FrameNet corpus. Our augmentation approach is applied to FrameNet version 1.7.

4.1 Training Data

In principle, our data augmentation algorithm (§3) could provide new annotation for 2,300 LUs (§3.1), all of which could be used for training. However, we wish to determine whether using augmented data improves performance on the existing test sets. Additionally, care must be taken to avoid the logical flaw of using augmentation algorithm from producing labeled sentences specifically for the test set: the process would circularly assume that the algorithm offers accurate labelling.

We addressed this issue by adjusting the training data for the baseline: we removed annotation from 1,500 randomly selected LUs from the lexicographic portion of the training data for FN 1.7. Each of these 1,500 LUs functions as Empty-LUs when stripped of their annotation. Our baseline model was trained with the remaining lexicographic annotations. Our full model was trained on data given by the augmentation algorithm to re-annotate the 1,500 LUs, in addition to the data used for the baseline. Note that not all LUs are eligible for training in OPEN-SESAME, which involves a pre-processing step to remove those LUs incompatible with the parser; Table 1 provides the final training data statistics.

In addition to the lexicographic annotations, both the baseline and the augmented setup use all the full-text annotations in FrameNet 1.7. Our training data adjustments above allow using the standard validation and test sets for FrameNet 1.7, following Swayamdipta et al. (2017).

4.2 Model and Hyperparameters

All of our experiments were performed using the non-syntactic model provided in OPEN-SESAME (Swayamdipta et al., 2017, 2018). We follow the basic setup in OPEN-SESAME which assumes gold targets for FrameID and gold frames for ArgID. We left most hyperparameters associated with OPEN-SESAME at their default values, but decreased the learning rate for training the ArgID stage to 0.0001 from its original value of 0.0005. The decrease allowed training ArgID on the entire dataset in three epochs without error, which serves reproducibility requirements.

4.3 Results

Table 1 presents test and validation set performances comparing two OPEN-SESAME models, trained with and without the augmented data for ArgID and FrameID. All measures in the experimental setting outperformed the baseline, highlighting the value of data augmentation. Although our main interest was testing the system's performance for ArgID (i.e., identifying semantic roles / FEs for given frame-LU annotations) of the augmented data, we also observed improvement in the identification of frames. The results in the experimental setting show an absolute improvement of 2.7 in F1 on ArgID and 1.6 in F1 on FrameID.[9]

4.4 Error Analysis and Discussion

At times the augmentation algorithm produced ungrammatical sentences. We do not believe that errors occurred because of ungrammatical sentences. Still, FrameNet would not conjure producing data with ungrammatical sentences.[10] A manual analysis of a random sample of LUs showed three categories of errors: (a) word form mismatch; (b) incorrect or missing marker; and (c) semantic mismatch, examples of which appear in (a) - (c):

(a) *The moon was now *occlude* by clouds.

(b) *And he *complained* the endless squeeze on cash.

(c) ?The faint *flash* from a street light showed him the outline of a hedge.

The semantic mismatch in (c) holds between *faint*.a and *flash*.n, yielding a semantically odd sentence not an ungrammatical one. By definition, a *flash* would not be *faint*.[11]

[9]We further experimented with cross validation settings for both FrameID and ArgID; however, the runtime of OPEN-SESAME was prohibitively slow in this setting.

[10]A complete manual analysis of the data remains to be done. In future extensions of this work, we will report such an analysis, including the percentage of grammatical sentences.

[11]The results showed several types of semantic mismatch. Space limitations preclude discussing all of them here.

	Training Data		Dev		Test			
			ArgID	FrameID	ArgID			FrameID
	#LUs	#Lexicographic Annotations	F1	F1	P	R	F1	F1
OPEN-SESAME	6905	164372	59.3	84.7	61.8	56.9	59.2	81.1
	7944	260292	**61.9**	**85.3**	**63.6**	**60.3**	**61.9**	**82.7**

Table 1: Results comparing the OPEN-SESAME models trained on the original FrameNet 1.7 data for frame identification (FrameID) and argument identification (ArgID) tasks, with OPEN-SESAME models trained on our augmented data. Data augmentation improves performance on both tasks across all metrics; boldface indicates best performance. Note that under both settings we consider full-text annotations, a subset of the lexicographic annotations. Gold-standard frames were used for ArgID, and gold-standard targets for FrameID, in both the baseline and our models. Development set results only include F1 scores; (by default) OPEN-SESAME just reports that score.

Recall that incorrectly identifying a frame necessarily yields incorrect FEs (ArgID). The analysis showed that errors occurred with highly polysemous lemmas, such as *make*.v, where FrameNet has 10 LUs; in (d), OPEN-SESAME misidentified *making*.v as `Manufacturing`, not `Earnings_and_losses`. Similarly, (e) is a misidentification of *gathering* as `Food_gathering`, not `Come_together`. Note the metaphorical use of the verb in (e), compared to literal senses of the lemma *gather*.v.

(d) I like working and *making* money.

(e) ...the debate on welfare reform is *gathering* like a storm at sea...

5 Related Work

Data augmentation in the context of FrameNet and SRL is not novel. Pavlick et al. (2015) created an expanded FN via automatic paraphrasing and crowdsourcing to confirm frame assignment of LUs. Hartmann et al. (2017) used automatically generated training data by linking FrameNet, PropBank, and VerbNet to study the differences among those resources in frame assignment and semantic role classification. The results showed that the augmented data performed as well as the training data for these tasks on German texts. With similar goals to those of this work, Carvalho et al. (2020) proposed augmenting FN annotation using notions of lexical, syntactic, or semantic equivalence, and FN's frame-to-frame relations (Inheritance, Using, SubFrame, etc.) to *infer* annotations across related frames, producing a 13% increase in annotation.

6 Conclusion and Future Work

We outlined an approach to Frame-SRL that seeks to leverage existing annotation in a frame to generate new annotation for previously unannotated LUs in the same frame, by exploiting the already identified target and frame of a given lemma. Further, we demonstrated that augmentation of data improves Frame-SRL performance substantially. While we show the advantages of this approach on the open-SESAME baseline, future work might involve studying if using this type of data augmentation will yield improvements on a state-of-the-art SRL system, e.g. Fei et al. (2021).

Several other interesting directions for future work exist, including the following: refining the augmentation algorithm to produce more grammatical sentences; streamlining open-SESAME's code to run more efficiently; use active-learning to inform the data generation and to assist in the SRL task; and experimentation with other computational techniques, as suggested by Petruck and Swayamdipta (2019). These plans will advance defining processes to include Frame-SRL into FrameNet's development process, the ultimate goal of this work.[12]

Acknowledgements

The authors are grateful to the three anonymous reviewers for their feedback, and to Nathan Schneider for his input on various aspects of the experiment, including very early conversations about pursuing the idea. Collin Baker and Michael Ellsworth have contributed to the completion of the paper in countless ways.

References

Collin F. Baker, Michael Ellsworth, and Katrin Erk. 2007. Semeval-2007 task 19: Frame semantic structure extraction. In *Proceedings of the 4th Inter-*

[12]Rigorous testing of multiple factors will be required to evaluate the viability of including Frame-SRL into FrameNet's existing primarily manual process.

national Workshop on Semantic Evaluations, SemEval@ACL 2007, Prague, Czech Republic, June 23-24, 2007, pages 99–104. The Association for Computer Linguistics.

Emily M. Bender and Alexander Koller. 2020. Climbing towards NLU: On meaning, form, and understanding in the age of data. In *Proceedings of the 58th Annual Meeting of the Association for Computational Linguistics*, pages 5185–5198, Online. Association for Computational Linguistics.

Xavier Carreras and Lluís Màrquez. 2005. Introduction to the CoNLL-2005 shared task: Semantic role labeling. In *Proceedings of the Ninth Conference on Computational Natural Language Learning (CoNLL-2005)*, pages 152–164, Ann Arbor, Michigan. Association for Computational Linguistics.

Breno Carvalho, Aline Paes, and Bernardo Gonçalves. 2020. Augmenting linguistic semi-structured data for machine learning: A Case study using FrameNet. In *Proceedings of the International Conference on Machine Learning Techniques and NLP*, volume 10.12, pages 1–13.

Dipanjan Das, Desai Chen, André F. T. Martins, Nathan Schneider, and Noah A. Smith. 2014. Frame-semantic parsing. *Computational Linguistics*, 40(1):9–56.

Dipanjan Das, Nathan Schneider, Desai Chen, and Noah A. Smith. 2010. Probabilistic frame-semantic parsing. In *Human Language Technologies: The 2010 Annual Conference of the North American Chapter of the Association for Computational Linguistics*, pages 948–956, Los Angeles, California. Association for Computational Linguistics.

Michael Ellsworth and Adam Janin. 2007. Mutaphrase: Paraphrasing with FrameNet. In *Proceedings of the ACL-PASCAL Workshop on Textual Entailment and Paraphrasing*, pages 143–150, Prague. Association for Computational Linguistics.

Hao Fei, Shengqiong Wu, Yafeng Ren, and Donghong Ji. 2021. Second-order semantic role labeling with global structural refinement. *IEEE/ACM Transactions on Audio, Speech, and Language Processing*, 29:1966–1976.

Charles J. Fillmore. 1985. Frames and the semantics of understanding. *Quaderni di Semantica*, 6(2):222–254.

Nicholas FitzGerald, Julian Michael, Luheng He, and Luke Zettlemoyer. 2018. Large-scale QA-SRL parsing. In *Proceedings of the 56th Annual Meeting of the Association for Computational Linguistics (Volume 1: Long Papers)*, pages 2051–2060, Melbourne, Australia. Association for Computational Linguistics.

Juri Ganitkevitch, Benjamin Van Durme, and Chris Callison-Burch. 2013. PPDB: The paraphrase database. In *Proceedings of the 2013 Conference of the North American Chapter of the Association for Computational Linguistics: Human Language Technologies*, pages 758–764, Atlanta, Georgia. Association for Computational Linguistics.

Daniel Gildea and Daniel Jurafsky. 2002. Automatic labeling of semantic roles. *Computational Linguistics*, 28(3):245–288.

Xu Han, Tao Lv, Zhirui Hu, Xinyan Wang, and Cong Wang. 2016. Text summarization using FrameNet-based semantic graph model. *Scientific Programming*, 2016:1–10.

Silvana Hartmann, Éva Mújdricza-Maydt, Ilia Kuznetsov, Iryna Gurevych, and Anette Frank. 2017. Assessing SRL frameworks with automatic training data expansion. In *Proceedings of the 11th Linguistic Annotation Workshop*, pages 115–121, Valencia, Spain. Association for Computational Linguistics.

Christopher R. Johnson, Charles J. Fillmore, Esther J. Wood, Josef Ruppenhofer, Margaret Urban, Miriam R. L. Petruck, and Collin F. Baker. 2001. The FrameNet Project: Tools for Lexicon Building. ICSI Online Publication.

Karin Kipper, Hoa Trang Dang, and Martha Palmer. 2000. Class-based construction of a verb lexicon. In *Proceedings of the Seventeenth National Conference on Artificial Intelligence and Twelfth Conference on Innovative Applications of Artificial Intelligence*, pages 691–696. AAAI Press.

Martha Palmer, Daniel Gildea, and Paul Kingsbury. 2005. The proposition bank: An annotated corpus of semantic roles. *Computational Linguistics*, 31(1):71–106.

Ellie Pavlick, Travis Wolfe, Pushpendre Rastogi, Chris Callison-Burch, Mark Dredze, and Benjamin Van Durme. 2015. FrameNet+: Fast paraphrastic tripling of FrameNet. In *Proceedings of the 53rd Annual Meeting of the Association for Computational Linguistics and the 7th International Joint Conference on Natural Language Processing (Volume 2: Short Papers)*, pages 408–413, Beijing, China. Association for Computational Linguistics.

Bolette S. Pedersen. 2001. Lexical ambiguity in machine translation: Using frame semantics for expressing systemacies in polysemy. In *Recent Advances in Natural Language Processing*.

Miriam R L Petruck and Swabha Swayamdipta. 2019. Automating FrameNet annotation. Pre-Proposal for NSF CISE EAGER Grant.

Sameer Pradhan, Alessandro Moschitti, Nianwen Xue, Hwee Tou Ng, Anders Björkelund, Olga Uryupina, Yuchen Zhang, and Zhi Zhong. 2013. Towards robust linguistic analysis using OntoNotes. In *Proceedings of the Seventeenth Conference on Computational Natural Language Learning*, pages 143–152, Sofia, Bulgaria. Association for Computational Linguistics.

Sameer Pradhan, Alessandro Moschitti, Nianwen Xue, Olga Uryupina, and Yuchen Zhang. 2012. CoNLL-2012 shared task: Modeling multilingual unrestricted coreference in OntoNotes. In *Joint Conference on EMNLP and CoNLL - Shared Task*, pages 1–40, Jeju Island, Korea. Association for Computational Linguistics.

Pushpendre Rastogi and Benjamin Van Durme. 2014. Augmenting FrameNet via PPDB. In *Proceedings of the Second Workshop on EVENTS: Definition, Detection, Coreference, and Representation*, Baltimore, Maryland, USA. Association for Computational Linguistics.

Michael Roth and Mirella Lapata. 2016. Neural semantic role labeling with dependency path embeddings. In *Proceedings of the 54th Annual Meeting of the Association for Computational Linguistics (Volume 1: Long Papers)*, pages 1192–1202.

Josef Ruppenhofer, Michael Ellsworth, Miriam R. L. Petruck, Christopher R. Johnson, Collin F. Baker, and Jan Scheffczyk. 2016. *FrameNet II: Extended Theory and Practice*. ICSI: Berkeley.

Sunita Sarawagi and William W. Cohen. 2004. Semi-markov conditional random fields for information extraction. In *Proc. of NeurIPS*, pages 1185–1192.

Dan Shen and Mirella Lapata. 2007. Using semantic roles to improve question answering. In *Proceedings of the 2007 Joint Conference on Empirical Methods in Natural Language Processing and Computational Natural Language Learning (EMNLP-CoNLL)*, pages 12–21, Prague, Czech Republic. Association for Computational Linguistics.

Noah A. Smith. 2011. *Linguistic Structure Prediction*. Synthesis Lectures on Human Language Technologies. Morgan and Claypool.

Swabha Swayamdipta, Sam Thomson, Chris Dyer, and Noah A. Smith. 2017. Frame-semantic parsing with softmax-margin segmental rnns and a syntactic scaffold.

Swabha Swayamdipta, Sam Thomson, Kenton Lee, Luke Zettlemoyer, Chris Dyer, and Noah A. Smith. 2018. Syntactic scaffolds for semantic structures. In *Proceedings of the 2018 Conference on Empirical Methods in Natural Language Processing*, pages 3772–3782, Brussels, Belgium. Association for Computational Linguistics.

Bishan Yang and Tom Mitchell. 2017. A joint sequential and relational model for frame-semantic parsing. In *Proceedings of the 2017 Conference on Empirical Methods in Natural Language Processing*, pages 1247–1256, Copenhagen, Denmark. Association for Computational Linguistics.

A Qualitative Examples

Table 2 provides lexicographic annotations with sister LUs and their corresponding empty LUs, the latter being populated by our approach.

Sister Lexical Units		Empty Lexical Units
He AGENT *stamped* his foot BODY_PART into his flying-boot PERIPHERAL .	→	He AGENT *bended* his foot BODY_PART into his flying-boot PERIPHERAL .
John-William , who knew that he would have been a Chartist himself had he remained a *poor* man PERSON , felt sorry about that death .	→	John-William , who knew that he would have been a Chartist himself had he remained a *rich* man PERSON , felt sorry about that death .
Because of the censorship , and the obvious need to avoid dangerously DEGREE *critical* comments EXPRESSOR about the regime and the war EVALUEE , the correspondence to and from the front provides no easy guide to political attitudes .	→	Because of the censorship , and the obvious need to avoid dangerously DEGREE *commendable* comments EXPRESSOR about the regime and the war EVALUEE , the correspondence to and from the front provides no easy guide to political attitudes .
When I did eventually tell her she EXPERIENCER was really DEGREE *embarrassed* , and tried telling me that I was making it up !	→	When I did eventually tell her she EXPERIENCER was really DEGREE *tormented* , and tried telling me that I was making it up !
This regulation prevented US banks THEME *located* in the US LOCATION , but not abroad, from paying interest on deposits above a given rate .	→	This regulation prevented US banks THEME *situated* in the US LOCATION , but not abroad, from paying interest on deposits above a given rate .

Table 2: Parallel lexicographic annotations of sister LUs (expert-annotated) and emtpy LUs (augmented by our approach). Frame Element (FE) names are in SMALL CAPS and their instantiations are color-coordinated; and LUs or targets are in *italics*.

A Corpus Study of Creating Rule-Based Enhanced Universal Dependencies for German

Teresa Bürkle[♦] **Stefan Grünewald**[♦★] **Annemarie Friedrich**[♦]
[♦]Bosch Center for Artificial Intelligence, Renningen, Germany
[★]Institut für Maschinelle Sprachverarbeitung, University of Stuttgart
teresa.buerkle|stefan.gruenewald|annemarie.friedrich
@de.bosch.com

Abstract

In this paper, we present a first attempt at enriching German Universal Dependencies (UD) treebanks with enhanced dependencies. Similarly to the converter for English (Schuster and Manning, 2016), we develop a rule-based system for deriving enhanced dependencies from the basic layer, covering three linguistic phenomena: relative clauses, coordination, and raising/control. For quality control, we manually correct or validate a set of 196 sentences, finding that around 90% of added relations are correct. Our data analysis reveals that difficulties arise mainly due to inconsistencies in the basic layer annotations. We show that the English system is in general applicable to German data, but that adapting to the particularities of the German treebanks and language increases precision and recall by up to 10%. Comparing the application of our converter on gold standard dependencies vs. automatic parses, we find that F1 drops by around 10% in the latter setting due to error propagation. Finally, an enhanced UD parser trained on a converted treebank performs poorly when evaluated against our annotations, indicating that more work remains to be done to create gold standard enhanced German treebanks.

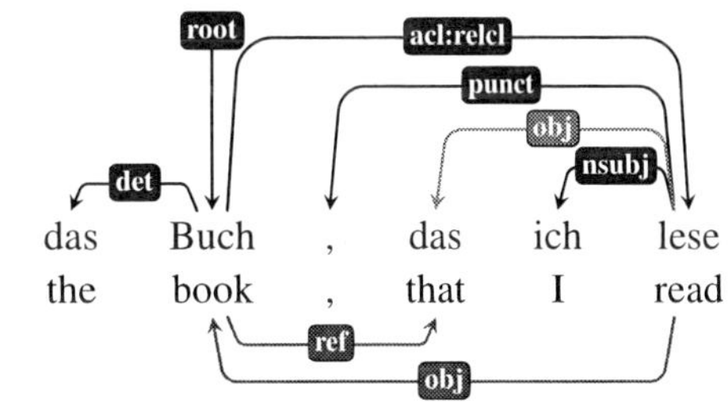

(a) Relative clause

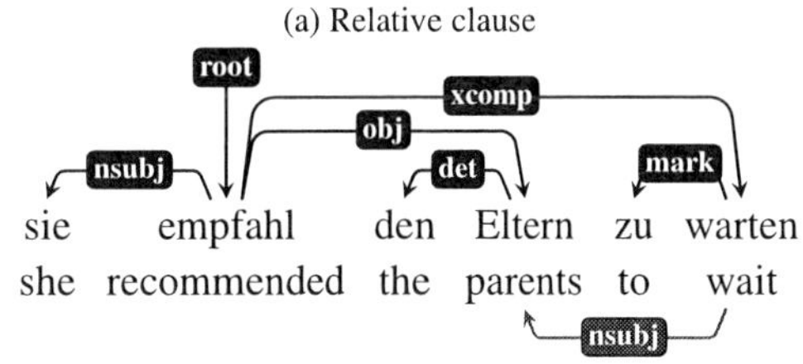

(b) Raising/control

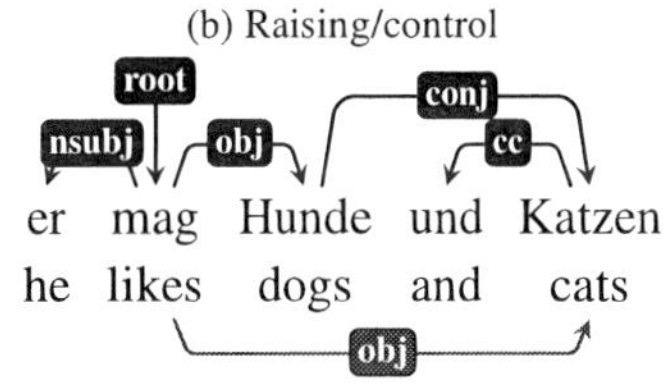

(c) Coordination

Figure 1: Linguistic structures in German enhanced UD.

1 Introduction

Universal Dependencies (UD; de Marneffe et al., 2014) are a widely used framework for syntactic dependency annotation. Aiming to provide a cross-lingual representation that focuses on relations between content words, nearly 200 UD treebanks for over 100 languages are currently available.[1] An extension of UD are *Enhanced* Universal Dependencies (Schuster and Manning, 2016), which have since become an official part of the UD guidelines (Nivre et al., 2020). Enhanced UD augments "basic" UD syntax trees by including additional dependency edges in the presence of linguistic phenomena such as coordination, relative clauses, and raising/control.

As a result, Enhanced UD structures are not necessarily trees, but more general syntax graphs. For example, in Figure 1b, the basic dependency tree (black edges on top) is augmented by an enhanced `nsubj` link (blue edge at bottom) in order to represent that the subject of "warten", "Eltern", has been raised to the object position of "empfahl."

Enhanced UD representations have been shown to be useful for downstream NLP tasks (Schuster et al., 2017), and parsing them has experienced a rise of attention in the scope of two recent shared tasks (Bouma et al., 2020, 2021). Yet, annota-

[1] https://universaldependencies.org

Proceedings of the Joint 15th Linguistic Annotation Workshop (LAW) and 3rd Designing Meaning Representations (DMR) Workshop, pages 85–95
November, 2021. ©2021 Association for Computational Linguistics

tions for this dependency representation are still only available for a small subset of UD treebanks.[2] Many of these existing annotations were created using rule-based systems operating on the basic layer with little to no human supervision/evaluation, or via conversion from other syntactic representations (Droganova and Zeman, 2019).

In this paper, we take a first step towards extending Enhanced UD coverage to German treebanks, for which no enhanced annotations exist to date. We give details on our findings when generating Enhanced UD representations from the basic layer of German UD treebanks in a rule-based way, similarly to the work of Schuster and Manning (2016) for English. We focus on three linguistic phenomena (relative clauses, raising/control, and coordination) and present rule-based algorithms for each phenomenon that take into account the peculiarities of the German language, which has less strict rules for word order compared to English.

We assess the accuracy of the extractions made by our system with the help of expert human annotators, evaluating system performance on both gold as well as automatically parsed basic dependencies. In the gold setting, we find that around 90 % of added relations are correct, outperforming the system by Schuster and Manning (2016). On automatically parsed text, performance drops by around 10 %, indicating a reliance on correct basic dependencies. A graph parser trained on automatically extracted enhanced dependencies achieves low accuracy, indicating that more work remains to be done to automatically create high-quality enhanced German treebanks.

To the best of our knowledge, our work presents the first investigation into creating Enhanced UD annotations for German treebanks. Our system achieves accuracies which we believe may already be useful in downstream applications (e.g., to increase recall in information extraction tasks). Furthermore, we hope that our findings may serve as a starting point for the creation of high-quality Enhanced UD corpora for the German language. To facilitate further research, our code and annotations will be made freely available.[3]

[2]The official UD website lists 41 treebanks as providing enhanced dependencies, however, manual inspection shows that in some of them the enhanced layer is identical to the basic layer. 29 treebanks for 17 languages were used for Enhanced UD parsing in the 2020 and 2021 IWPT Shared Tasks.

[3]https://github.com/boschresearch/german_enhanced_ud_converter_law_dmr_2021

2 Related Work

In this section, we briefly review work on extracting enhanced UD from the basic representation, as well as enhanced UD parsing and related graph-based meaning representations.

Extracting enhanced UD from basic UD. Much prior work has focused on automatically retrieving enhanced dependencies from the basic layer for various languages. Prior to the introduction of UD, Nyblom et al. (2013) used an SVM-based approach to retrieve enhanced Stanford dependencies for the Finnish-TDT treebank. They find that their approach works well for gold basic dependencies, but less so for automatic parses. A rule-based converter for English UD was first proposed by Schuster and Manning (2016) together with their initial formulation of the enhanced UD layer. Nivre et al. (2018) compare the above two approaches for enhancing Italian and Swedish, finding that both are adequate for creating enhanced treebanks. Candito et al. (2017) use graph-rewriting rules to create enhanced dependencies for two French treebanks, finding good accuracy in a manual evaluation.

More specific works on modeling certain phenomena within enhanced UD further include automatically reconstructing elided predicates in sentences with gapping constructions (Schuster et al., 2018) and the modeling of coordinate constructions (Grünewald et al., 2021b).

Parsing into Enhanced UD. Following a series of shared tasks focusing on basic UD (Zeman et al., 2017, 2018), the 2020 and 2021 IWPT shared tasks (Bouma et al., 2020, 2021) address the prediction of enhanced UD from raw text. While some participating systems directly parse enhanced dependency graphs using a graph-based parser (e.g. He and Choi, 2020; Wang et al., 2020; Grünewald and Friedrich, 2020), others parsed into standard UD before applying hand-written enhancement rules (e.g., Dehouck et al., 2020; Attardi et al., 2020). Heinecke (2020) employs a rule-based approach to convert from basic to enhanced UD and then optimize the result using a classifier.

Graph-based Meaning Representations. Aiming to move annotations closer to "meaning" on the meaning–form scale (Droganova and Zeman, 2019), Enhanced UD can be seen as part of a larger effort to annotate sentences with graph-based representations of their meaning. Other frameworks with the same goal include Abstract Meaning Representation (AMR; Banarescu et al., 2013), Universal Conceptual Cognitive Annotation (UCCA; Abend and Rappoport, 2013), Universal Decompositional Semantics (UDS; White et al., 2016) and broad-coverage Semantic Dependency Graphs (SDP; Oepen et al., 2016). Enhanced UD differs from these frameworks due to its very close integration with the syntactic annotation of a sentence.

3 Basic-to-Enhanced Converter

In this section, we describe the implementation of our basic-to-enhanced UD converter for German. Along the way, we discuss important differences w.r.t. the converter for English (Schuster and Manning, 2016).

3.1 Enhancing Relative Clauses

As shown in Figure 2, in basic UD, relative clauses are represented as sub-trees, with the root of this subtree being linked to the noun modified by the clause. The basic UD representation provides no direct link between a relative pronoun and its antecedent. As the relative pronoun and the antecedent can be interpreted as co-referring, the referent of the antecedent can also be considered as an argument of the relative pronoun's head (here: "kenne"). Enhanced UD marks this by means of a `ref` relation linking the antecedent and the relative pronouns, as well as adding an argument link (here: `obj`) from the relative clause's main verb to the antecedent.

Algorithm. If a relative clause is indicated by an `acl:relcl` relation, we add a `ref` relation from the clauses' antecedent (which is head of the `acl:relcl` relation) to the relative pronoun or relativizer. Because not all treebanks use the subtype `relcl` for this construction, an `acl` relation is also considered if the token that might be the relative pronoun has the UPOS `PRON` or the lemma "wo" ("where"). The relative pronoun is found by selecting the first child of the `acl` relation's dependent according to surface order which is linked to the relative clause's root via any relation except `punct`. The relation between the relative pronoun or relativizer and its head is deleted, and a relation from the relative pronoun's / relativizer's former head to the antecedent is added, using the relation type of the deleted relation, as in Figure 2.

The English converter (Schuster and Manning,

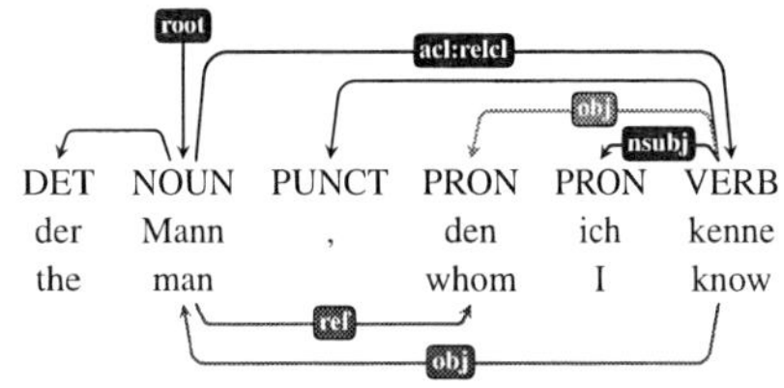

Figure 2: Basic and enhanced representation of a relative clause.

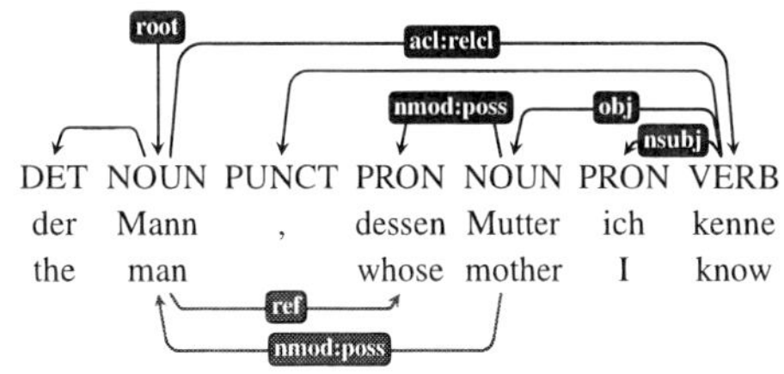

Figure 3: Relative clause with possessive relative pronoun.

2016) treats relative clauses the same way, but their way of identifying the relative pronoun is slightly different to ours. The leftmost word contained in a word list of possible relative pronouns is taken as the dependent of the ref relation if any child or grandchild of the `acl:relcl` relation depends on a possible relative pronoun. In addition, only the specific subtype `acl:relcl` is considered for the identification of relative clauses.

We treat the special case of possessive relative pronouns as follows. As shown in Figure 3, if the relative pronoun is possessive, it is not a direct child of the relative clause's root, but rather attaches to a child node thereof. In German, the only two possessive relative pronouns are "deren" or "dessen." These word forms can be detected easily and unambigously. In such constructions, the relative pronoun or relativizer (here: "dessen"), refers to "Mann." Accordingly, a `ref` relation is inserted between "Mann" and "dessen." In contrast to the case of Figure 2, the object of "kenne" is not the pronoun's antecedent "Mann," but "Mutter" within the relative clause. Hence, an `nmod:poss` relation is added between "Mutter" and "Mann" instead.

In English, this type of relative clause exists with the possessive pronoun "whose" functioning as a relativizer. When analysing the differences of our converter to the output of the converter of Schuster and Manning (2016), we noted the following. In English treebanks, the relevant relation is always nmod:poss, while in some German treebanks, the relative pronoun is linked via det or det:poss. Our converter hence covers these cases as well. Further, Schuster and Manning (2016) delete the nmod:poss relation between the possessive relative pronoun and its former governor in the enhanced layer, which our converter as used in Sec. 4 does not.[4]

3.2 Enhancing Raising and Control

The linguistic phenomena called raising and control describe sentences with embedded verbs whose subjects have been "raised" to some higher position in the syntactic structure (Polinsky, 2013). In the constructions "Susan decided to start" and "Susan seemed to start," the subject of the embedded clause is shared with that of matrix clause. In the control constructing "Susan told them to start," the object "them" is also the subject of the embedded clause. While raising verbs (e.g., "seem") do not select their arguments, control verbs such as "tell" or "decide" do. In enhanced UD, as shown in Figure 4 and Figure 5, the two phenomena are represented in the same way, i.e., by making the nsubj relation explicit. The embedded clause is linked to the matrix verb via xcomp ("open clausal complement"), hence, the construction can be detected easily in the basic layer. However, resolving is non-trivial, as we will discuss in Sec. 4.

Algorithm. We first identify xcomp relations whose head node is a verb or adjective and whose dependent is a verb, noun, or adjective node. For these, we add nsubj links starting at the xcomp relation's child node according to the following criteria. We check the outgoing links of the xcomp relation's head node (the embedding predicate) for the relations iobj, obj, and nsubj in this fixed order. For the first match, we assume that child node linked using this relation is the endpoint of the newly added nsubj relation.

Raising and control constructions where the controlling or raising predicate is a noun, such as "der Versuch, etwas zu tun" ("the attempt to do something") or "die Möglichkeit, etwas zu tun" ("the opportunity to do something") often lead to the insertion of wrong links. This is the reason for only addressing cases where the contolling or raising predicate is a verb or an adjective and the controlled or embedded predicate is a verb, an adjective or a noun.

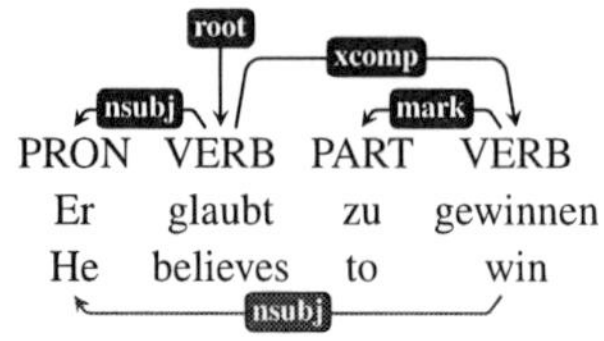

Figure 4: Raising construction example.

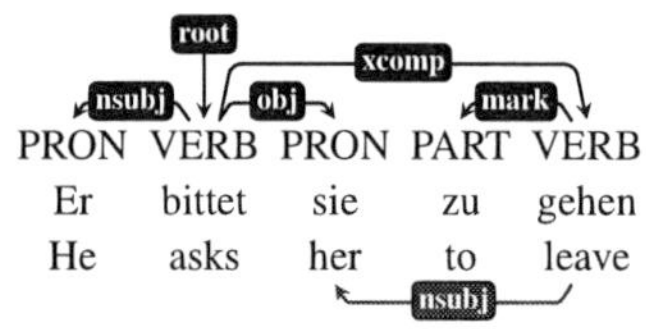

Figure 5: Object control example.

3.3 Enhancing Coordinate Constructions

In UD, coordinate constructions are represented by a conj relation between the coordinated tokens (see, e.g., Figure 9). Generally, the first conjunct of a coordinate construction according to surface order is the head, with all other conjuncts attached to it via conj relations. Other dependency relations that are semantically shared by all conjuncts (e. g., nsubj or obj relations) are also attached to the first one. Since the first conjunct can also have dependents that are **not** shared by the other conjunct(s), this means that the dependency structures do not capture the information whether a dependent of the first conjunct is also a dependent of the other conjuncts.

For enhancing conjunctions, we distinguish two cases: (a) conjoined verbs, and (b) other types of conjunctions.

Conjoined Verbs. When two verbs are conjoined, the basic UD representation lacks an explicit link between the second verb and complements that both verbs share semantically, such as subjects or objects.

Algorithm. If the second conjunct does not have an outgoing nsubj link, we add an nsubj link between the second conjunct and all nodes that are linked to the first conjunct via nsubj links.

Regarding shared objects, we distinguish three cases. If the second conjunct ("schreibt" ("writes")) comes after the first conjunct ("liest" ("reads")) and before the first conjunct's object ("Bücher" ("books")) according to surface order, as in Figure 6, we propagate an obj link between the sec-

[4]This oversight is fixed in the released version of our converter.

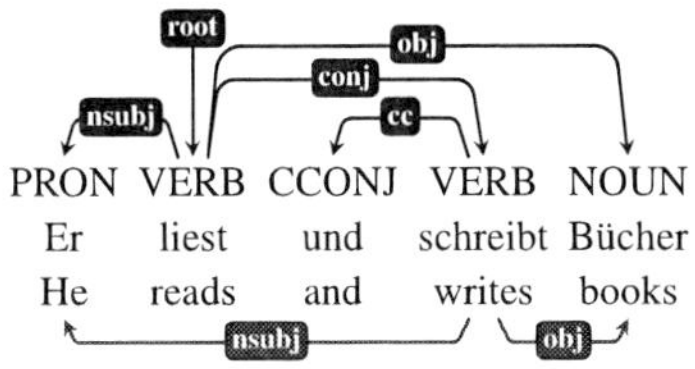

Figure 6: Conjoined verbs that unambiguously share a subject and an object

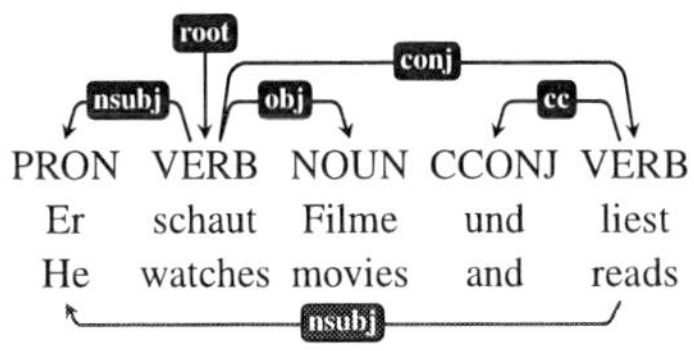

Figure 7: Conjoined verbs that unambiguously share a subject, but no object

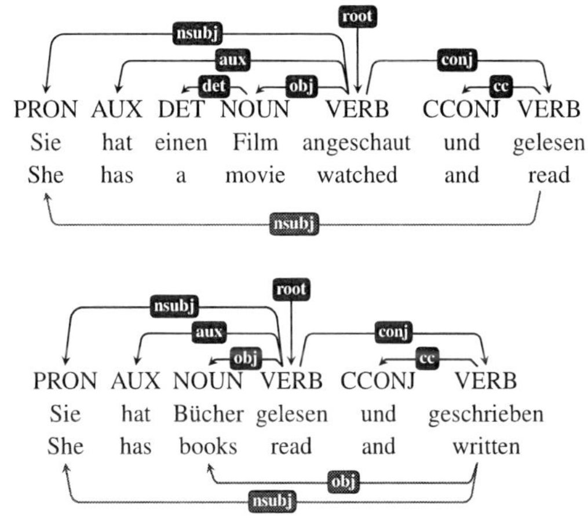

Figure 8: Conjoined verb constructions that are ambiguous regarding the question whether they semantically share the object or not

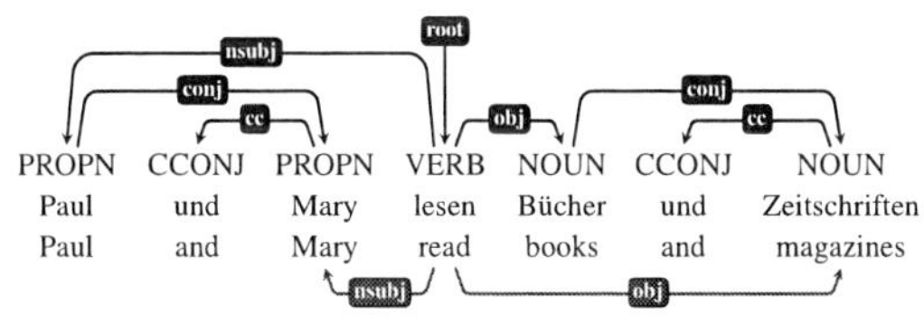

Figure 9: Conjunction of noun phrases and objects, whith both conjuncts sharing the verb

ond conjunct and this object. If the first conjunct's object comes after the first conjunct but before the second conjunct in surface order, as exemplified by Figure 7, no `obj` link is inserted. In these scenarios, it is possible to decide with certainty whether the first conjunct's object is semantically shared by both conjuncts, as it is always the case in English due to the strict surface order.

However, if the object comes before both conjuncts according to surface order, as in Figure 8, we face an ambiguity. In spite of both sentences in Figure 8 having the same dependency relations and POS tags, in the first sentence, the first conjunct's object ("Film") is semantically not shared with the second conjunct, while in the second sentence, both conjuncts share the object ("Bücher"). Therefore, in the second case, the enhanced UD representation should contain an additional `obj` link. However, we do not propagate in such cases in order to maximize precision rather than recall.

Other types of conjunctions. In case of coordinated noun phrases, adjectives, or modifiers, the token with an incoming `conj` relation (the "second conjunct"), is not explicitly linked to the governor or dependents of the first conjunct. That the two conjuncts fill the same roles in the sentence's argument structure is made explicit in the enhanced layer.

Algorithm. First, we identify the `conj` relation and the tokens it interlinks. We add a direct link between the second conjunct and the governor of the first conjunct. The type of the added relation is copied over from the relation linking the first conjunct to its governor.

4 Analysis and Evaluation

In this section, we first describe our manual corpus study to measure the performance of our converter. We compute precision, recall and F1 on enhanced links and draw comparisons to the English converter by Schuster and Manning (2016). In addition, we evaluate the performance of the converter in automatic parsing settings.

4.1 Manually Annotated Gold Standard

We create a test set containing sentences from the two German treebanks GSD and PUD, against which the converter is then evaluated. The test set consists of three subsets, one for each of the three phenomena we address. The subset for coordinate constructions contains 50 sentences containing at least one `conj` relation between two tokens, while the subsets for relative clauses and raising and control structures contain 80 sentences containing respectively an `acl` or subtype of it or an `xcomp` relation. The more specific relation subtype `acl:relcl` would have been more suitable for extracting relative clauses, however, the GSD treebank only uses the generic type `acl`.

These subsets were created by first collecting all sentences for each phenomenon from each treebank and then selecting every n/25th sentence for the coordination subset and every n/40th sentence for the relative clause and raising and control subsets, with n being the total number of sentences found for this phenomenon in this treebank. After removing duplicates and six sentences with severe errors in the basic layer, this results in 196 annotated sentences which are the basis for our evaluation.

Annotation. The test set was then converted to include enhanced UD representations by our system and manually corrected by three annotators, two computational linguists with extensive linguistic training, and one undergraduate student with basic linguistic training. Each annotator corrected a subset of the test set, discussing sentences they were unsure about with the other annotators.

Minor errors occuring in the basic layer (e.g., a wrong dependency type assigned or an inverted head and child node of a relation) were corrected, while more severe errors affecting multiple dependency relations or tokens lead to an exclusion of the sentence from the evaluation set. In total, 18 sentences were found to contain errors in the basic layer, and six were removed from the evaluation set due to severe errors.

4.2 Performance of Converter in Gold Setting

Rather than starting out with the original treebanks, we create the input for the converter by removing the enhanced layer from the manually corrected gold set. In other words, our evaluation takes into account the minor fixes we applied to the basic layer. Arguably, this procedure does not result in a completely realistic estimate how well our system would perform on the still somewhat noisy treebanks; however, we consider improving the consistency and quality of the current German treebanks to be future work and decided to abstract away from this problem in our study in order to make it less dependent on the idiosyncrasies of the current treebank versions.

We then run our converter on the basic trees for these sentences and compare the enhanced dependency relations in the converted set to the enhanced layer of the gold set. In order to make a fair comparison, we freeze the code of our converter before starting out with our annotation study. The results reported here are thus an estimate how far we can get with a rule-based approach (which, of course, was based on extensive data analysis, but not targeted to our evaluation set).

In Table 1, we report precision, recall, and F1 for all links in the enhanced layer, as well as for several relevant relations. In addition to the overall score, calculated by evaluating all sentences in our test set, we compute scores for each phenomenon by evaluating all sentences in which this phenomenon occurs. This results in the evaluation set for a phenomenon containing more sentences than the originally sampled test set for this phenomenon did, because sentences from the other phenomena's subsets can be included. For example, a sentence originally selected for the relative clause set is included in the evaluation set for conjunctions if it also contains a `conj` relation. This results in the evaluation for coordination constructions being based on 117 sentences, the evaluation for relative clauses being based on 105 sentences and the evaluation for raising and control being based on 98 sentences.

Considering all sentences and label types, we achieve a precision of 89.5%, recall of 89.1% and F1 of 89.3%. Comparing the scores for the three phenomena implies that the converter works best on relative clauses with F1 of 94.2%. Recall of 100% for the `ref` relation indicates that all relative clauses in the test set were detected as such. For sentences containing conjunctions, all scores were slightly lower with an F1 of 89.3%. Raising and control is the phenomenon for which we achieved the lowest scores, with an F1 of 82.1%. Here, `nsubj` is the only relation type that our converter automatically propagates, while we did not restrict propagation of relation types in our manual annotation. Precision and recall both around 77% indicate that for some cases, our converter selects the wrong token as subject of the embedded or controlled predicate. This decreases both precision and recall, because the actual subject is lacking an `nsubj` link to the controlled or embedded predicate and at the same time a spurious `nsubj` link to the wrong node is created. E.g., for the sentence "wir verwenden Zeit darauf, ein Konzept zu entwickeln" ("we spend time on developing a concept,") instead of "wir" ("we"), the converter would treat "Zeit" ("time"), the object of "verwenden" ("spend"), as a subject of the embedded verb "entwickeln" ("develop").

In our evaluation, we also noticed minor implementation errors.[5] These are fixed in the released version of our converter.

In the following, we compare our converter to the one created by Schuster and Manning (2016).[6] Our aim is to check whether implementing a targeted version for German was worth the effort compared to simply running the existing system developed for English. We made one adaptation to the English converter, which originally expects only `acl:relcl` to indicate relative clauses (see Sec. 3.1). We relax this constraint to looking for `acl`, as several German treebanks do not use the `relcl` subtype.

Since the English converter by Schuster and Manning (2016) uses some relation subtypes that we did not use in the gold set, only the generic relation type was considered in the evaluation. Overall, we found that the English converter performed worse on our test set, with an overall F1 score of 79.5% (about ten percent points lower than our targeted version for German). For `obj` and `obl` relations, the reported scores diverge from our scores by respectively 28.2 and 16.8 percentage points. The main reason for this is the different treatment of relative clauses in which the relative pronoun is governed by an `obj` relation. While we add an `obj` relation between the antecedent and the token governed by the `acl:relcl` or `acl` relation in this case, the converter by Schuster and Manning (2016) inserts an `obl:relobj` relation in this case, which is treated as an `obl` relation in the evaluation due to the evaluation algorithm ignoring subtypes. There is no meaningful difference in the handling of coordination except for the usage of more specific subtypes. Therefore, the difference in scores in Table 1 stems from the other phenomena that also occur in this evaluation subset.

Regarding raising and control constructions, in contrast to our converter (as explained in Sec. 3.2), the English converter propagates links when the head of the `xcomp` relation is a noun. Furthermore, while we used the general `nsubj` relation, they used the subtype `nsubj:xsubj` for links added while treating a raising or control construction. This is in fact an extension of the UD guidelines, which do not include the `nsubj:xsubj` subtype to date. Following the official guidelines, our system outputs only `nsubj`, but our final release includes an option for adding the `xsubj` subtype.

4.3 Performance of Converter in Automatic Parsing Setting and End-to-End Graph Parsing

To evaluate our converter's performance on automatically parsed basic dependencies, we use Grünewald et al.'s (2021a) STEPS parser (along with the provided pre-trained model for German) to parse our test set and then run our converter on the output. We find that performance of our rule-based system drops by about 10% compared to the results achieved when using gold basic dependencies. This is in line with findings reported by Grünewald et al. (2021b), who also find that a pipeline-based approach leads to considerable performance decreases. However, precision and recall exceed 75% in most cases, meaning that the resulting output may still be useful in practice.

We also investigated the alternative path of directly training an enhanced UD parser on a treebank created using our converter. Using the STEPS framework, we train an end-to-end graph parser on the converted GSD treebank, use it to parse our test set, and again evaluate against our manual annotations. As shown in Table 1, F1 for the enhanced layer drops by over 40%. By contrast, the parser achieves an F1 score of 85.1% on the same evaluation set for the prediction of the *basic* layer. These results indicate that the enhanced data produced by converting the existing German treebanks is, as of yet, of limited use for training machine learning systems.

5 Conclusion and Outlook

In this paper, we have described our approach of enriching German UD treebanks with enhanced dependencies by implementing a rule-based converter. Evaluating on a set of manually annotated sentences, our system achieves an F1 score of around 90% when operating on gold basic dependencies, outperforming the English-based system by Schuster and Manning (2016). In an automatic parsing setting, accuracy is lower with an F1 score of

[5]One such example is checking whether the second conjunct already has an outgoing `nsubj` link before propagating an addional link when enhancing conjunctions.

[6]To ensure the strongest possible baseline, we here use a slightly modified version of that converter, created by Grünewald et al. (2021b), which fixes dependency propagation in certain edge cases involving coordinate constructions. For more details, see their paper.

Phenomenon	Basic Layer	System	Score	all	advmod	amod	nmod	nsubj	obj	obl	ref
all			total	440	10	14	22	198	40	40	97
			P	89.5	100.0	100.0	95.0	82.7	97.4	95.2	95.1
	gold	ours	R	89.1	90.0	100.0	86.4	84.3	92.5	100.0	100.0
			F1	89.3	94.7	100.0	90.5	83.5	94.9	97.6	97.5
	gold	SM16	F1	79.5	57.1	100.0	90.5	82.4	66.7	80.8	89.3
	automatic	ours	F1	80.1	94.7	88.9	76.0	77.2	83.8	79.0	90.5
	end-to-end parser		F1	46.7	20.3	70.0	31.3	65.7	72.3	51.3	88.2
conjunctions			total	315	8	14	21	135	31	36	51
			P	90.0	100.0	100.0	94.7	85.2	96.7	94.7	91.1
	gold	ours	R	88.6	87.5	100.0	85.7	85.2	93.5	100.0	100.0
			F1	89.3	93.3	100.0	90.0	85.2	95.1	97.3	95.3
	gold	SM16	F1	80.8	66.7	100.0	90.0	84.9	78.4	86.7	87.3
	automatic	ours	F1	79.0	93.3	88.9	75.0	79.7	84.2	76.7	86.0
	end-to-end parser		F1	47.1	23.5	80.0	38.3	63.2	76.2	56.3	85.0
rel. clauses			total	316	7	7	11	127	31	29	97
			P	93.5	100.0	100.0	90.0	89.9	96.7	96.7	95.1
	gold	ours	R	94.9	85.7	100.0	81.8	91.3	93.5	100.0	100.0
			F1	94.2	92.3	100.0	85.7	90.6	95.1	98.3	97.5
	gold	SM16	F1	81.4	25.0	100.0	85.7	88.5	62.2	76.3	89.3
	automatic	ours	F1	83.6	92.3	84.2	70.6	80.9	88.5	80.6	90.5
	end-to-end parser		F1	51.6	26.7	76.2	31.0	68.4	73.5	53.5	88.2
raising +			total	221	2	7	13	131	14	9	33
control			P	84.6	100.0	100.0	100.0	77.3	100.0	100.0	97.1
	gold	ours	R	79.6	50.0	100.0	76.9	77.9	78.6	100.0	100.0
			F1	82.1	66.7	100.0	87.0	77.6	88.0	100.0	98.5
	gold	SM16	F1	76.2	66.7	100.0	87.0	77.2	44.4	72.0	97.1
	automatic	ours	F1	76.1	66.7	92.3	76.9	72.5	76.5	82.4	90.4
	end-to-end parser		F1	41.2	5.3	63.6	32.4	61.6	48.8	34.3	85.3

Table 1: **Annotation study: converter results**. Rows for phenomena report results for **all** links in enhanced layer for set of sentences that contain the phenomenon. **all** = all links in enhanced layer in the subset of sentences, **total** = total count of this label type in the evaluated gold sentences. Number of sentences in the evaluation subset: Coordination: 117, Relative Clause: 105, Raising and Control: 98. SM16 = Schuster and Manning (2016).

around 80 %, which may still be useful in practice. Training an enhanced parser on treebanks created using our converter yields poor results.

In our annotation study, we found that our system fails mainly due to errors in the basic layer, which have been derived semi-automatically from German treebanks annotated with different dependency frameworks. For example, an `xcomp` relation in the wrong direction leads to severe errors in the enhanced layer when following our rule-based approach. We further observed divergences in regards to the annotation schemes applied across German treebanks, for instance the usage of different relation types for the same sentence structures. We therefore conclude that measures to increase consistency across German treebanks are an important step to facilitate the conversion to enhanced dependencies.

Outlook. There remains a number of ambiguous cases for which we have not found a solution thus far, such as the propagation of objects in case of two conjoined verbs (see Sec. 3.2). Regarding raising and control structures, examples like "Wir lassen den Jungen gehen" ("We let the boy leave") vs. "Wir lassen den Reifen montieren" ("We have the tyre mounted") are identical regarding their basic dependency structure and POS tags, yet should be treated differently by the converter. In control structures such as "Wir entschieden, hier nicht zu schwimmen" ("We decided not to swim here,") the subject of the embedded verb "schwimmen" ("swim") is the same as that of "entschieden" ("decided"), while in the sentence "Wir empfehlen, hier nicht zu schwimmen" ("We recommend not to swim here,") the subject does not co-refer with the speaker. A possibility to improve here might be the usage of word lists containing control/raising verbs for which the subject of the controlled/embedded predicate can not co-refer with the speaker (as for "recommend").

To conclude, our work demonstrates that rule-based conversion is a suitable method for creating enhanced dependencies for German. However, our analysis also shows that taking language-specific phenomena into account is important to ensure correctness of the extractions. Hence, creating targeted enhanced UD converters for more languages is a promising avenue, but will likely require further manual work for each instance.

Acknowledgments

We thank the anonymous reviewers and Jannik Strötgen for their helpful comments regarding this work.

References

Omri Abend and Ari Rappoport. 2013. Universal Conceptual Cognitive Annotation (UCCA). In *Proceedings of the 51st Annual Meeting of the Association for Computational Linguistics (Volume 1: Long Papers)*, pages 228–238, Sofia, Bulgaria. Association for Computational Linguistics.

Giuseppe Attardi, Daniele Sartiano, and Maria Simi. 2020. Linear neural parsing and hybrid enhancement for enhanced Universal Dependencies. In *Proceedings of the 16th International Conference on Parsing Technologies and the IWPT 2020 Shared Task on Parsing into Enhanced Universal Dependencies*, pages 206–214, Online. Association for Computational Linguistics.

Laura Banarescu, Claire Bonial, Shu Cai, Madalina Georgescu, Kira Griffitt, Ulf Hermjakob, Kevin Knight, Philipp Koehn, Martha Palmer, and Nathan Schneider. 2013. Abstract Meaning Representation for sembanking. In *Proceedings of the 7th Linguistic Annotation Workshop and Interoperability with Discourse*, pages 178–186, Sofia, Bulgaria. Association for Computational Linguistics.

Gosse Bouma, Djamé Seddah, and Daniel Zeman. 2020. Overview of the IWPT 2020 shared task on parsing into enhanced Universal Dependencies. In *Proceedings of the 16th International Conference on Parsing Technologies and the IWPT 2020 Shared Task on Parsing into Enhanced Universal Dependencies*, pages 151–161, Online. Association for Computational Linguistics.

Gosse Bouma, Djamé Seddah, and Daniel Zeman. 2021. From raw text to enhanced Universal Dependencies: The parsing shared task at IWPT 2021. In *Proceedings of the 17th International Conference on Parsing Technologies and the IWPT 2021 Shared Task on Parsing into Enhanced Universal Dependencies (IWPT 2021)*, pages 146–157, Online. Association for Computational Linguistics.

Marie Candito, Bruno Guillaume, Guy Perrier, and Djamé Seddah. 2017. Enhanced UD dependencies with neutralized diathesis alternation. In *Proceedings of the Fourth International Conference on Dependency Linguistics (Depling 2017)*, pages 42–53, Pisa,Italy. Linköping University Electronic Press.

Mathieu Dehouck, Mark Anderson, and Carlos Gómez-Rodríguez. 2020. Efficient EUD parsing. In *Proceedings of the 16th International Conference on Parsing Technologies and the IWPT 2020 Shared Task on Parsing into Enhanced Universal Dependencies*, pages 192–205, Online. Association for Computational Linguistics.

Kira Droganova and Daniel Zeman. 2019. Towards deep Universal Dependencies. In *Proceedings of the Fifth International Conference on Dependency Linguistics (Depling, SyntaxFest 2019)*, pages 144–152, Paris, France. Association for Computational Linguistics.

Stefan Grünewald and Annemarie Friedrich. 2020. RobertNLP at the IWPT 2020 shared task: Surprisingly simple enhanced UD parsing for English. In *Proceedings of the 16th International Conference on Parsing Technologies and the IWPT 2020 Shared Task on Parsing into Enhanced Universal Dependencies*, pages 245–252, Online. Association for Computational Linguistics.

Stefan Grünewald, Annemarie Friedrich, and Jonas Kuhn. 2021a. Applying occam's razor to transformer-based dependency parsing: What works, what doesn't, and what is really necessary. In *Proceedings of the 17th International Conference on Parsing Technologies and the IWPT 2021 Shared Task on Parsing into Enhanced Universal Dependencies (IWPT 2021)*, pages 131–144, Online. Association for Computational Linguistics.

Stefan Grünewald, Prisca Piccirilli, and Annemarie Friedrich. 2021b. Coordinate constructions in English enhanced Universal Dependencies: Analysis and computational modeling. In *Proceedings of the 16th Conference of the European Chapter of the Association for Computational Linguistics: Main Volume*, pages 795–809, Online. Association for Computational Linguistics.

Han He and Jinho D. Choi. 2020. Adaptation of multilingual transformer encoder for robust enhanced Universal Dependency parsing. In *Proceedings of the 16th International Conference on Parsing Technologies and the IWPT 2020 Shared Task on Parsing into Enhanced Universal Dependencies*, pages 181–191, Online. Association for Computational Linguistics.

Johannes Heinecke. 2020. Hybrid enhanced Universal Dependencies parsing. In *Proceedings of the 16th International Conference on Parsing Technologies and the IWPT 2020 Shared Task on Parsing into Enhanced Universal Dependencies*, pages 174–180, Online. Association for Computational Linguistics.

Marie-Catherine de Marneffe, Timothy Dozat, Natalia Silveira, Katri Haverinen, Filip Ginter, Joakim Nivre, and Christopher D. Manning. 2014. Universal Stanford dependencies: A cross-linguistic typology. In *Proceedings of the Ninth International Conference on Language Resources and Evaluation (LREC'14)*, pages 4585–4592, Reykjavik, Iceland. European Language Resources Association (ELRA).

Joakim Nivre, Marie-Catherine de Marneffe, Filip Ginter, Jan Hajič, Christopher D. Manning, Sampo Pyysalo, Sebastian Schuster, Francis Tyers, and Daniel Zeman. 2020. Universal Dependencies v2: An evergrowing multilingual treebank collection. In *Proceedings of the 12th Language Resources and Evaluation Conference*, pages 4034–4043, Marseille, France. European Language Resources Association.

Joakim Nivre, Paola Marongiu, Filip Ginter, Jenna Kanerva, Simonetta Montemagni, Sebastian Schuster, and Maria Simi. 2018. Enhancing Universal Dependency treebanks: A case study. In *Proceedings of the Second Workshop on Universal Dependencies (UDW 2018)*, pages 102–107, Brussels, Belgium. Association for Computational Linguistics.

Jenna Nyblom, Samuel Kohonen, Katri Haverinen, Tapio Salakoski, and Filip Ginter. 2013. Predicting conjunct propagation and other extended Stanford dependencies. In *Proceedings of the Second International Conference on Dependency Linguistics (DepLing 2013)*, pages 252–261, Prague, Czech Republic. Charles University in Prague, Matfyzpress, Prague, Czech Republic.

Stephan Oepen, Marco Kuhlmann, Yusuke Miyao, Daniel Zeman, Silvie Cinková, Dan Flickinger, Jan Hajič, Angelina Ivanova, and Zdeňka Urešová. 2016. Towards comparability of linguistic graph Banks for semantic parsing. In *Proceedings of the Tenth International Conference on Language Resources and Evaluation (LREC'16)*, pages 3991–3995, Portorož, Slovenia. European Language Resources Association (ELRA).

Maria Polinsky. 2013. *Raising and control*. Cambridge University Press, Cambridge.

Sebastian Schuster, Éric Villemonte de La Clergerie, Marie D Candito, Benoît Sagot, Christopher D Manning, and Djamé Seddah. 2017. Paris and Stanford at EPE 2017: Downstream Evaluation of Graph-based Dependency Representations. In *EPE 2017 - The First Shared Task on Extrinsic Parser Evaluation*, Proceedings of the 2017 Shared Task on Extrinsic Parser Evaluation, pages 47–59, Pisa, Italy.

Sebastian Schuster and Christopher D. Manning. 2016. Enhanced English Universal Dependencies: An improved representation for natural language understanding tasks. In *Proceedings of the Tenth International Conference on Language Resources and Evaluation (LREC'16)*, pages 2371–2378, Portorož, Slovenia. European Language Resources Association (ELRA).

Sebastian Schuster, Joakim Nivre, and Christopher D. Manning. 2018. Sentences with gapping: Parsing and reconstructing elided predicates. In *Proceedings of the 2018 Conference of the North American Chapter of the Association for Computational Linguistics: Human Language Technologies, Volume 1 (Long Papers)*, pages 1156–1168, New Orleans, Louisiana. Association for Computational Linguistics.

Xinyu Wang, Yong Jiang, and Kewei Tu. 2020. Enhanced Universal Dependency parsing with second-order inference and mixture of training data. In *Proceedings of the 16th International Conference on Parsing Technologies and the IWPT 2020 Shared Task on Parsing into Enhanced Universal Dependencies*, pages 215–220, Online. Association for Computational Linguistics.

Aaron Steven White, Drew Reisinger, Keisuke Sakaguchi, Tim Vieira, Sheng Zhang, Rachel Rudinger, Kyle Rawlins, and Benjamin Van Durme. 2016. Universal decompositional semantics on Universal Dependencies. In *Proceedings of the 2016 Conference on Empirical Methods in Natural Language Processing*, pages 1713–1723, Austin, Texas. Association for Computational Linguistics.

Daniel Zeman, Jan Hajič, Martin Popel, Martin Potthast, Milan Straka, Filip Ginter, Joakim Nivre, and Slav Petrov. 2018. CoNLL 2018 shared task: Multilingual parsing from raw text to Universal Dependencies. In *Proceedings of the CoNLL 2018 Shared Task: Multilingual Parsing from Raw Text to Universal Dependencies*, pages 1–21, Brussels, Belgium. Association for Computational Linguistics.

Daniel Zeman, Martin Popel, Milan Straka, Jan Hajič, Joakim Nivre, Filip Ginter, Juhani Luotolahti, Sampo Pyysalo, Slav Petrov, Martin Potthast, Francis Tyers, Elena Badmaeva, Memduh Gokirmak, Anna Nedoluzhko, Silvie Cinková, Jan Hajič jr., Jaroslava Hlaváčová, Václava Kettnerová, Zdeňka Urešová, Jenna Kanerva, Stina Ojala, Anna Missilä, Christopher D. Manning, Sebastian Schuster, Siva Reddy, Dima Taji, Nizar Habash, Herman Leung, Marie-Catherine de Marneffe, Manuela Sanguinetti, Maria Simi, Hiroshi Kanayama, Valeria de Paiva, Kira Droganova, Héctor Martínez Alonso, Çağrı Çöltekin, Umut Sulubacak, Hans Uszkoreit,

Vivien Macketanz, Aljoscha Burchardt, Kim Harris, Katrin Marheinecke, Georg Rehm, Tolga Kayadelen, Mohammed Attia, Ali Elkahky, Zhuoran Yu, Emily Pitler, Saran Lertpradit, Michael Mandl, Jesse Kirchner, Hector Fernandez Alcalde, Jana Strnadová, Esha Banerjee, Ruli Manurung, Antonio Stella, Atsuko Shimada, Sookyoung Kwak, Gustavo Mendonça, Tatiana Lando, Rattima Nitisaroj, and Josie Li. 2017. CoNLL 2017 shared task: Multilingual parsing from raw text to Universal Dependencies. In *Proceedings of the CoNLL 2017 Shared Task: Multilingual Parsing from Raw Text to Universal Dependencies*, pages 1–19, Vancouver, Canada. Association for Computational Linguistics.

Subcategorizing Adverbials in Universal Conceptual Cognitive Annotation

Zhuxin Wang Jakob Prange Nathan Schneider
Georgetown University
{zw85, jp1724, nathan.schneider}@georgetown.edu

Abstract

Universal Conceptual Cognitive Annotation (UCCA) is a semantic annotation scheme that organizes texts into coarse predicate-argument structure, offering a broad coverage of semantic phenomena. At the same time, there is still need for a finer-grained treatment of many of the categories. The Adverbial category is of special interest, as it covers a wide range of fundamentally different meanings such as negation, causation, aspect, and event quantification. In this paper we introduce a refinement annotation scheme for UCCA's Adverbial category, showing that UCCA Adverbials can indeed be subcategorized into at least 7 semantic types, and doing so can help clarify and disambiguate the otherwise coarse-grained labels. We provide a preliminary set of annotation guidelines, as well as pilot annotation experiments with high inter-annotator agreement, confirming the validity of the scheme.

1 Introduction

The UCCA representation scheme is designed to be a multi-layered, cross-linguistically portable and stable semantic annotation scheme based on linguistic typology (Abend and Rappoport, 2013; Dixon, 2010). Among its 14 coarse-grained semantic categories, Adverbial serves as the label for modifiers to a scene's main predicate. Despite the syntactic-sounding name, Adverbial is a semantic category that cuts across a range of syntactic constructions that provide scene-modifying meanings. These meanings fall into drastically different semantic categories—negations, manner PPs, modals, adverbs are all candidates for the Adverbial category—that change the sentence's meaning in different ways.

This paper proposes to refine UCCA Adverbials, in order to better understand the semantic functions they encode. By distinguishing different Adverbial functions, we can disambiguate sentences that are otherwise annotated similarly (if not identically) in UCCA. For example:

(1) The chicken was [**deliciously** D] [cooked P]. DESCRIPTION

(2) The chicken was [**not** D] [cooked P]. NEGATION

(3) The chicken was [**more** D] [cooked P]. COMPARISON

(4) The chicken was [**already** D] [cooked P]. ASPECTUAL

We propose to add 7 refinement labels for the Adverbial (D) category in the UCCA scheme. The current work is in line with a series of other UCCA refinements (§2), and fills the gap of Adverbials, as subtyping Adverbials in particular can refine UCCA annotation to be more informative and precise (§3). After providing the motivation to study Adverbials, we propose a subcategorization scheme with explanations (§4).[1] Finally we present pilot results of annotation on UCCA data and IAA measures (§5),[2] followed by discussions of difficulties, complexities, and limitations (§6).

2 Background

Adverbs. It is important to differentiate the *semantic adverbial* category from the morpho-syntactic class of *adverbs* (Dixon, 2010). In UCCA, for example, the current Adverbial (D) material ranges from manner adverbs and expressions of negation to comparatives to semi-contentful light verbs (Hershcovich et al., 2019).

UCCA categories. The annotation of the UCCA scheme is organized into layers. In the foundational layer, each passage is broken down into scenes,

[1] A complete annotation manual is available at https://github.com/IvyWang13/ucca_adverbials_dmr/blob/master/UCCA_DMR_annotation_guidelines.pdf

[2] All data used for the pilot annotation can be found at https://github.com/IvyWang13/ucca_adverbials_dmr.

Proceedings of the Joint 15th Linguistic Annotation Workshop (LAW) and 3rd Designing Meaning Representations (DMR) Workshop, pages 96–105
November, 2021. ©2021 Association for Computational Linguistics

which in turn are made up of scene evokers labeled either State (S) or Process (P), core argument units called Participants (A), which may be either non-scenes (i.e., roughly, 'entities') or scenes themselves, and modifiers such as Time (T) or Adverbial (D) units (Abend et al., 2020). Adverbials can be understood as denoting secondary predications over a scene's main State or Process relation.

Other extensions to UCCA. Building upon the UCCA foundational layer, there have been several efforts and proposals to refine annotations of specific constructions such as implicit arguments (Cui and Hershcovich, 2020), numeric expressions (Cui and Hershcovich, 2021), coreference (Prange et al., 2019b), and adpositional phrases (Prange et al., 2019a; Shalev et al., 2019). The latter class in particular partially overlaps with the Adverbial category, as discussed in §6. This paper will accompany these annotation refinements, with a special focus on the Adverbials.

3 Motivation

Adverbial category is relatively broad. As mentioned briefly, Adverbials represent a wide range of semantic functions; this level of diversity is not shared by other foundational layer categories. Consider, for example, the category 'Time': it is also a scene-level category, but has a much more specific semantic purpose. The other categories like 'State,' 'Process,' and 'Participant,' also have better-delimited/dedicated functions, whereas Adverbials can target all general non-scene-evoking elements. Some Adverbials are manner adverbs describing an action, such as *He spoke* ***softly***; some are modal auxiliaries such as *should, might*; others involve constructions expressing aspectual information such as *continue to....* Not all Adverbials are syntactically adverbs, nor do they resemble one another in semantic contributions. This leads to challenges when disambiguating the actual semantic content in sentences in UCCA. Consider (1, 2), repeated here as (5, 6):

(5) The chicken was [**deliciously** D] [cooked P].

(6) The chicken was [**not** D] [cooked P].

Clearly, their meanings are drastically different, but without subcategorization of the D-instances, they receive the same semantic annotation in the UCCA foundational layer. Adverbials (negation, quantification, modality, manner, etc.) fulfill fundamentally different functions with respect to *how* the meaning of the rest of the sentence is interpreted. Because Adverbials (D) cover wide semantic ground, refining the semantic annotation can thus be more informative, along similar lines as refining Participants with semantic roles (Prange et al., 2019a; Shalev et al., 2019).

Foundational layer annotations are inconsistent. Beyond the domain of Adverbial-proper, another key motivation of D-refinements is to identify sources of disagreement or confusion among the foundational layer categories. While the detailed UCCA annotation guidelines serve as a point of reference when choosing between categories, many borderline cases remain. For example, the below D-instance *during the last week* was identified during our refinement annotation as a borderline case between D-Aspectual and T (Time), despite being annotated as D.

(7) Assets ... [grew P] by $1.5 billion [**during the latest week** D], to $352.7 billion.

With the proposed refinement, we hope to eliminate such confusion as much as possible, suggesting revisions to the current guidelines as a whole. The goal is to clarify differences between categories such as D-Aspectual vs. Time, D-Possibility vs. Ground, etc., the former being in the extension layer and the latter being in the foundational layer.

Another aspect of foundational layer inconsistency lies in whether or not to treat a unit as unanalyzable, i.e. omitting further internal structure in multiword instances, such as *one by one, have to, no longer, no matter how*, etc. In the current task, certain Adverbial multiword phrases are encountered with different internal structures. While the current refinement does not depend or bear on Adverbial internal structures, this is an opportunity for annotators to flag such inconsistencies. With our proposed refinements added, we thus expect the foundational layer consistency to increase.

4 Proposed Annotation Scheme

4.1 Semantic Types of Adverbials

We propose seven Adverbial refinement labels (Table 1). Below we provide a synopsis of all proposed categories with a few examples attached. The set of labels aims to subdivide the Adverbial category by semantic functions such that it has a comparable level of granularity as its peers. We strive to draw clear lines among the categories, with each category serving one distinct semantic function as a modifier in the sentence. The origin of this label set is empirical: we examined and refined the Adverbial instances in the UCCA *Twenty Thousand League Under the Sea* (English) corpus (Abend and Rappoport, 2013), the source of many of the enumerated examples throughout the paper. So far the current scheme is specific to English—we leave cross-linguistic generalizations to future research. The ultimate goal for these labels is to equip UCCA with a useful extension with which annotators can pinpoint a specific label rather than grouping distinct modifier items into a catch-all category.

We also add that, in the current proposal, we work with and conform to previous foundational layer categories and do not change the existing analyses, but we expect our annotated data to be useful for detecting and correcting foundational layer inconsistencies in future work (§3).

4.1.1 Aspectual

ASPECTUAL is a label for D-instances that indicate the start-/end-points of a state or event. It also includes an event's duration or repetition, whether it is temporary or habitual, and event quantification.

(8) Captain Baker [**at first** D] [thought P] he was in the presence of an unknown reef. <u>ASPECTUAL</u>

(9) I would not [go P] there [**again** D]. <u>ASPECTUAL</u>

4.1.2 Causal

CAUSAL is reserved for Adverbials conveying causes or conditions. Examples include words that mention cause or reason, and phrasal causatives like the verbs *make, cause, ensure, prevent.*

(10) There was good [**reason** D] to [stop and think P]. <u>CAUSAL</u>

(11) I [**let** D] it [wag P]. <u>CAUSAL</u>

(12) The material [**prevents** D] water from [leaking P] out of the bag. <u>CAUSAL</u>

Note that the word *prevent* is considered CAUSAL because it signifies 'causing-to-not-happen.'[3]

4.1.3 Comparison

COMPARISON includes explicit comparative and superlative markers, e.g., *more, most,* and *less.*

(13) ...for the world 's [**most** D] [emotionless S] man. <u>COMPARISON</u>

(14) That a private individual had such a mechanism at his disposal was [**less than** D] [probable S]. <u>COMPARISON</u>[4]

(15) This is [**tantamount** D] to [saying P]... <u>COMPARISON</u>

4.1.4 Degree

DEGREE is for words and phrases that convey the extent of an action or a state.

(16) That would [**profoundly** D] [affect P] public opinion. <u>DEGREE</u>

(17) You [get P] [**just** D] the collision we need to cause the specified catastrophe. <u>DEGREE</u>

4.1.5 Description

DESCRIPTION is used to label additional properties, features, attributes with which an action or state happens.

(18) ...those sheets of water had been [**violently** D] [churned P]. <u>DESCRIPTION</u>

(19) ...for [its P...] [**shrewd** D] [management ...P]. <u>DESCRIPTION</u>

Degree vs. Description. Ideally, the semantic functions of DEGREE and DESCRIPTION do not overlap. DEGREE is reserved for adverbials that convey the sheer extent (low or high) of the predicate, or in UCCA's terms, the State or Process. DESCRIPTION gives one (or more) additional, discrete property to the State or Process. It helps to formulate DEGREE in terms of reinforcing a scale dimension upon the property, as is often done in formal semantics literature (Kennedy and McNally, 2005). A DEGREE adverbial should explicitly give the information of 'where' on the scale of property P the target is. The scale of the property P must have already been provided by the context. On the other hand, DESCRIPTION *is* the material that provides the property, which is then used to modify the State or Process. For instance, in the phrase 'the big surprise,' it is more desirable to analyze 'big' as DEGREE, whereas in the phrase 'the big news'

[3]However it does not receive the NEGATION label because it does not include additional or explicit negation; see below.

[4]While the word 'probable' would qualify as D-POSSIBILITY if it were annotated as Adverbial in the foundational layer (emphasizing the 'availability of a mechanism' as the main scene), we conform to the existing annotation of 'probable' as the scene's main (stative) predicate in our pilot study.

Type	Description	Examples
Aspectual	Describing the start-/end-points, duration, or repetition of S/P	*later, still, three times, constantly*
Causal	Causatives and conditions	*had it not been, cause, let, make*
Comparison	Involves comparison upon the said S/P	*more, most, less*
Degree	Describing the extent of S/P	*extremely, colossal*
Description	Descriptives, bounding S/P to a certain property or dimension or evaluation, semantically contentful	*fast, feverishly, (was) busy (doing...)*
Negation	Involves uses of negation	*without, nothing, no longer*
Possibility	Conveys modality or possible events, thoughts, expectations	*want, will, actually, must, attempt (to do...)*

Table 1: Proposed semantic functions across UCCA Adverbials; S stands for State and P stands for Process

the word 'big' is analyzed as DESCRIPTION. In the former, the property of being a surprise is provided by the word 'surprise,' and the extent of surprise is given by the word 'big.' In the latter, the word 'big' is giving a new size attribute to the news, hence the label DESCRIPTION.

(20) In an instant the frigate's deck would become [**densely** D] [populated P]. DEGREE

'Densely' in (20) is annotated as DEGREE. With the predicate being 'populated,' one could roughly ask the question 'How much is this deck populated?', in which case 'densely' corresponds better to DEGREE than to DESCRIPTION. Meanwhile, DESCRIPTION labels are commonly found with adjectives and manner adverbs. DESCRIPTION can also be a partial verb phrase, when it adds additional information to the scene-evoking unit.

(21) Several people [**did me the honor of** D] [consulting P] me on the phenomenon in question. DESCRIPTION

A tricky case for English (arguably extensible to other languages as well) is the word 'well.' When used as an adverb, 'well' can either denote a high degree, or 'good' in terms of description—sometimes both. Annotators should read the context carefully to arrive at a decision.

(22) [**well** D] [received P] in scholarly circles. DESCRIPTION

(23) [**well** D] [versed P] in the theory of classification. DESCRIPTION

(24) The frigate [kept P...] [**well** D] [out ... P]. DEGREE

(25) I was [**well** D] [satisfied S] with my cabin. DEGREE

4.1.6 Negation

The NEGATION label is applied to D-instances with explicit negation morphology.

(26) [**No** D] business dealings have been [crowned P] with greater success. NEGATION

(27) It did [**n't** D] seem due for [resurrection P]. NEGATION

It might be argued that NEGATION is more dependent on morphological than semantic criteria, as least for English. But, we see NEGATION as a necessary category here that should not be subsumed under other labels, because its function indeed changes the meaning of a sentence or utterance, and gives the Adverbial instance a unique, irreplaceable flavor.

4.1.7 Possibility

POSSIBILITY not only includes modal auxiliaries (*would, could, should, must*, etc.), but also all D-instances that convey possible outcomes, attempts, thoughts, and expectations.

(28) ...the Moravian [**apparently** D] [undamaged P]. POSSIBILITY

(29) It [turned out to be S] [a foolish business A] [**after all** D]. POSSIBILITY

(30) In this event I [**would be inclined to** D] [accept P] the existence of a giant narwhale. POSSIBILITY

(31) Oh [**really** D]? POSSIBILITY

Some D-instances can be interpreted as including a certain level of speaker belief, but they are not annotated as POSSIBILITY in the current schema, if they serve a more salient contextual modification function that assigns them to another category.

(32) He [took a P...] [**definite** D] [liking ... P] to me. DEGREE

(33) Our server was [**quite** D] [attentive S] and the food was fantastic. DEGREE

(34) Some [saw P] it [**purely** D] as a scientific problem to be solved. DEGREE

In (32), *definite* conveys the extent of the liking, and from context the phrase *definite liking* is not immediately read as having strong speaker beliefs. Similarly, in (33) and (34), the most immediate interpretations are factual, rather than intensional or possible. In general, if there is a more "factual" meaning available, annotators are encouraged to avoid over-interpretation and choose the most apparent reading.

Empirically, one may encounter more ambiguous, borderline examples, such as (35),[5] and in those cases one should exercise their judgment to evaluate whether the element of POSSIBILITY overweighs that from another label.

(35) At the front door of his office, I [**nearly** D] [turned P] around.

4.2 Multiple labels

A particular feature of the current subcategorization scheme is the ability to add multiple labels to one Adverbial instance. The reason for a multi-label scheme is that there is not necessarily a one-to-one mapping of semantic function and linguistic construction. English shows frequent uses of one construction denoting multiple functions, and this might be even more common in other languages.

Some functions, such as NEGATION and COMPARISON, are easily layered on top of other functions such as DESCRIPTION or DEGREE by means of, e.g., morphology. Meanwhile there are also D-instances that cover both DESCRIPTION and DEGREE domains, for example. In order to accommodate all of these cases, the current scheme proposes that subtypes can be combined.

Co-occurrence with Negation. The label NEGATION can be added in parallel with other labels.

(36) I [**no longer** D] [left P] the ship's deck. NEGATION, ASPECTUAL

(37) ...[**nothing more than** D] to [go forth P]. NEGATION, COMPARISON

However, we only consider phrases with explicit phrasal negation, and do not include scene-evoking elements that have morphologically or semantically apparent antonyms.

(38) Master 's eyes would kindly [**stop** D] [bulging P]. ASPECTUAL

(39) They were [**unable** D] to [say P]. DESCRIPTION

Co-occurrence with Comparison. Like NEGATION, COMPARISON is often added upon another semantic function. Due to morphological properties of English, some comparatives take a form of suffixation on one word unit, some do not. Annotators should take care and add the label COMPARISON when appropriate.

(40) You'd be [squashed P] [**as flat** D]. COMPARISON, DESCRIPTION

(41) No whaling vessel could have been [**better** D] [armed S]. COMPARISON, DESCRIPTION

Other co-occurrences. As mentioned, there are also Adverbials, often phrasal, that combine other categories. For example:

(42) [Attitude D] of staff was [[**very** E] [**bad** C] D]. DESCRIPTION, DEGREE

(43) The store is clean, [run P] [[**very** E] [**professionally** C] D] and a pleasure to be in. DESCRIPTION, DEGREE

In (42) and (43), the labels DESRIPTION and DEGREE are combined because both examples include both labels, as exemplified by the degree modifier 'very' and the descriptive words that follow.

It is also worth noting that (42) and (43) both show Adverbial internal structure. Namely *very* is Elaborator, and *bad*, *professionally* are both Center of the Adverbial instances. For the current task, we treat the D-instances flatly, leaving to future research the possibility of potentially refining the internal categories in a similar fashion.

4.3 Verbs

Verbs that are not identified as main predicates form a substantial part of the Adverbial category. These are verbs that precede the main scene-evoking State or Process, or verbs of subevents at the scene level. Verbs constitute a syntactic category that is semantically diverse on its own, so they warrant further explication for ease of annotation. Currently, we have identified several groups of verbs that could be fit into our categories.

[5] In fact this sentence comes from one of our annotation studies, with one POSSIBILITY and two DEGREE labels.

First, verbs relating to event start or end points, or that situate the main action in a temporal dimension, should be labeled ASPECTUAL. Examples include *begin, start, finish, complete, continue*, etc.

(44) The day was [**beginning** D] to [break P].

(45) He [**postponed** D] our [meeting P] until next Monday.

Second, verbs of causes or preventions should be CAUSAL, such as *make, force, cause, tempt; let, permit, allow, prevent, avoid, spare*, etc.

(46) Those dogs are not [**allowed** D] to [enter P].

(47) Candy [**helped** D] Ann [bake P] a cake.

Third, verbs of wanting, needing, or trying should be POSSIBILITY.

(48) I never [**expected** D] to [win P] that prize.

(49) She [**pretended** D] to be [looking P] away from the disaster.

Lastly, verbs that do not clearly fit into one of the above categories are likely subevents that involve more concrete actions, and should belong with the DESCRIPTION category.

(50) "What about master's collections?" Conseil [**ventured** D] to [observe P].

(51) He [**received** D] a [call P].

(52) ...how many times I [**shared** D] the [excitement P] of general staff and crew.

5 Agreement Studies

As a pilot to verify the effectiveness of the subcategorization, three computational linguists familiar with UCCA independently annotated Adverbial subcategories. Two sets of annotation were conducted. The first set involved two annotators. Difficulties encountered were used to revise the annotation guidelines, and then a second data sample was annotated by all three annotators.

	# Annotators	# D-instances
Set 1	2	167
Set 2	3	122
Total	3	289

Table 2: Annotation set statistics.

	Annotator 1		Annotator 2		Ann. 3
Category	*Set 1*	*Set 2*	*Set 1*	*Set 2*	*Set 2*
Description	66	32	54	25	19
Negation	15	19	15	19	19
Possibility	26	17	22	18	17
Degree	20	24	25	25	23
Aspectual	27	18	29	20	21
Comparison	1	2	2	4	3
Causal	2	1	10	4	5
Comp.+Desc.	5	3	1	3	2
Neg.+Asp.	4	–	4	–	–
Desc.+Deg.	1	3	2	1	–
Poss.+Neg.	–	–	1	–	–
Comp.+Deg.	–	2	–	–	1
Asp.+Caus.	–	–	–	1	1
N/A	–	1	2	2	11
Total	167	122	167	122	122

Table 3: Subcategory counts for annotation sets 1 & 2. Annotator 3 did not participate in Set 1 annotation. N/A refers to a judgment that the unit should not have been considered an Adverbial in the foundational layer.

5.1 Data

For both annotation sets, we used unseen sentences from UCCA-annotated English Web Treebank and Wikipedia corpora (Abend and Rappoport, 2013). We randomly sampled 100 sentences for each round of annotation, and annotated 289 Adverbial instances out of the 200 sentences (Table 2).

5.2 Results

The count results for two annotation sets are shown in Table 3. In the first annotation set, the largest class by far was DESCRIPTION, which was partially due to the sampled sentences, but partially also due to lack of clarity in the guidelines for other categories. Annotators tended to default to DESCRIPTION when uncertain about a more distinct semantic function. This led to a revision to the guidelines, which then was used in the second round. Among the remaining categories, NEGATION, POSSIBILITY, DEGREE, and ASPECTUAL are all fairly frequent and balanced, whereas COMPARISON and CAUSAL are much rarer. The scheme should be examined on more unseen data in the future to determine how these cases (COMPARISON and CAUSAL) can be better handled as Adverbials or in UCCA more generally. We also add a row for "N/A" instances—D-instances which the annotator(s) deemed to be foundational layer misannotation, or for which the annotator(s) did not find a suitable fit in the current scheme (see §6).

The inter-annotator agreement results for each

Category	Set 1		Set 2
	κ	F1-score	α
Description	0.76	0.85	0.70
Negation	0.97	0.97	1.00
Possibility	0.78	0.82	0.87
Degree	0.81	0.83	0.79
Aspectual	0.85	0.88	0.84
Comparison	0.66	0.67	0.95
Causal	0.32	0.33	0.57
N/A	0.00	0.00	0.26
Avg. with N/A	0.64	0.84	0.74
Avg. without N/A	0.74	0.84	0.82

Table 4: Inter-annotator agreement results for Sets 1 & 2. Since Cohen's κ does not support multi-label input, we provide average across the categories for it (macro-average) whereas for F1 score we provide micro-average across the instances rather than the categories. For Krippendorff's α we provide macro-average.

	A1 & A2		A1 & A3		A2 & A3	
Exact Match	104	85.2%	93	76.2%	99	81.1%
+ Partial Match	108	88.5%	98	80.3%	102	83.6%
+ N/A	109	89.3%	99	81.1%	104	85.2%
Cohen's κ	0.85		0.77		0.82	

Table 5: Pairwise raw agreement for Set 2. **Row 1**: 'Exact Match' means two annotators agreed completely, regardless of multi-label or not. Percentage out of all 122 instances. **Row 2**: 'Partial Match' indicates the annotators did not disagree completely. This includes the scenario where one annotator assigned one label and the other assigned multi-label and one label overlaps. Percentages out of 122 instances. **Row 3**: We then add the scenario where both annotators assigned N/A to the instance. Percentages out of 122 instances. **Row 4**: Pairwise Cohen's κ by exact match.

category are shown in Table 4. For the first set with two annotators, we report Cohen's κ as well as F1 measure, and for the second set, with an additional annotator, we report Krippendorff's α as one metric for inter-annotator agreement. Table 5 reports more details on the second set, which involved three annotators. We report counts of different kinds of agreement/disagreement, as well as pairwise Cohen's κ.

Overall we observe good agreement among the annotators. NEGATION has the highest rate of agreement. This is likely due to the fact that, at least in English, negation morphology (*no, not, n't*) is easy to identify, even when it co-occurs with another category, such as ASPECTUAL, i.e. *never*. The categories with the next highest agreement are ASPECTUAL, POSSIBILITY, and DEGREE. The CAUSAL label suffers in agreement, which is likely due to its rarity, as well as annotators' varying willing to assign this label altogether. The revised guidelines used in Set 2 improve this somewhat.

6 Discussion

Based on the results, we turn to some specific challenges with D-refinement annotation, as well as discussing how our scheme relates to two similar representation frameworks.

6.1 Challenges

Non-applicable instances. In Table 3, some instances have not been annotated with any refinements ('N/A') by at least one annotator. Many such instances are either questionable as Adverbial to start with, or are exceptions that are not covered yet by our proposed guidelines, or both.

(53) [**Back** D] to my poor rating - I was excepted to medical school and went in to cancel my membership as I was told I could do so since I was moving away.

For example, (53) contains the word 'back,' but given the context, 'back' has a salient discourse function, arguably Ground in the foundational layer. (54) is another example: the proform 'one' construes an event instance (the event being 'being someone's favorite') as selecting an entity out of a set. This is a kind of 'atemporal' event quantification, and while our ASPECTUAL label perhaps comes closest, some annotators did not assign any label.

(54) Little Women was [**one** D] of Hepburn's personal [favorites P].

The current guidelines lack a clear direction on how to deal with such cases, as they become empirically discovered. We will keep updating and improving the guidelines in future work.

Verbs as Adverbials. While the guidelines strive to cover many verbs, during our pilot annotation there are still a number of verbs that have caused some disagreement.

(55) The only thing I [**found** D] [edible S] were the potato wedges, I finally gave up, he kept trying - he [**found** D] the fried wantons to be [OK S].

In (55), there are two occurrences of the verb 'found,' both of which are Adverbials. The annotators had difficulty classifying these verbs: Annotator 1 labeled the first 'found' as DESCRIPTION and the second as POSSIBILITY, annotator 2 labeled both as POSSIBILITY, while annotator 3 labeled N/A for both.

(56) The album's hard rock edge [**included** D] conspicuous guitar [contributions P] from Robert Fripp, ... and Tom Verlaine.

In (56), while annotators 1 and 2 labeled 'included' as DESCRIPTION, annotator 3 deemed it N/A.[6] Future annotators should especially take care with verbal Adverbials, try to paraphrase them if possible—if no categories seem to fit, one should flag the instance as an exception, which will be aggregated for future improvements of the refinement.

Multiple labels. Another source of disagreement is multiple annotation. Interestingly, when two annotators agree that an instance has multiple labels, they tend to also agree on *which* labels to choose (e.g., NEGATION+ASPECTUAL (57)). However, Adverbial instances that require more than one refinement are relatively rare to begin with, and annotators do not always agree on *when* this is the case. For example, consider (58).

(57) I would [**never** D] [sing P] in public. NEGATION, ASPECTUAL

(58) So don't get taken in, [**keep** D] your eyes [open S] if you choose to shop here.

For 'keep' in (58), annotator 1 only labeled ASPECTUAL, while annotators 2 and 3 labeled ASPECTUAL+CAUSAL, citing the reason that 'keep' is equivalent to 'causing to stay.' In general, annotators should semantically decompose each instance in this way before making a decision. As more of such potentially multi-labeled instances occur, further iterations of the guidelines will add more concrete directions on the extent of semantic decomposition with D-refinements.

Clarifying foundational layer decisions. We find two cases where other foundational layer categories and D are not reliably distinguished. First, we find that D-Aspectual and Time (T) overlap: both have been applied to instances of frequency and duration, e.g. (59, 60). Empirically, D-Aspectual also includes event quantification (61), change-of-state verbs (62), as well as temporally unspecific indicators of recency (or urgency, or lateness) (63).

(59) John will [come P] [**at around eight** T].

(60) John will [come P] [**regularly** T].

(61) John will [come P] [**for the second time** D]. ASPECTUAL

(62) Information [**becomes** D] more [abundant D]. ASPECTUAL

(63) You'd [**just** D] been [yanked P]. ASPECTUAL

Second, some foundational layer Adverbials serve similar functions as the GROUND category. According to the UCCA Foundational Layer guidelines, GROUND serves to "relate some unit to its speech event", i.e., a pragmatic element occurring with the scene. However, there are many edge cases that blur the the line between pragmatics and semantics and in those cases GROUND may overlap with certain (roughly, epistemic or deontic) modal usages of D-POSSIBILITY. For example, the units in (64) and (65) are annotated as GROUND and D-POSSIBILITY respectively.

(64) You can [go P], [**for all I care** G].

(65) He [**reportedly** D] [told P] Hepburn... POSSIBILITY

The similarities between D-ASPECTUAL and TIME, as well as D-POSSIBILITY and GROUND, respectively, invite future investigations into the boundaries between these categories.

6.2 Relation to Other Representations

AMR. In Abstract Meaning Representation (AMR) and its proposed extensions (Banarescu et al., 2013; Donatelli et al., 2018; Bonial et al., 2018), a sentence is labeled with relations and concepts in a rooted, directed, acyclic graph.[7] The current work has overlaps with AMR concepts—at different levels of the AMR graph—some of which can even be said to be close mappings, but overall our proposed scheme is designed to be compatible with UCCA's layered annotation structure rather than already-fine-grained AMR graphs. For example, in (66) and (67) we juxtapose the AMR and D-refined UCCA annotations of a sentence, respectively. While D-POSSIBILITY maps to the AMR concept `possible-01` and D-NEGATION maps to `:polarity -`, their structures remain distinct (the main predicate in AMR is `possible-01`, whereas

[6]Annotator 3 noted in a comment that DESCRIPTION is closest if "N/A" was not an option.

[7]Retrieved from `https://github.com/amrisi/amr-guidelines/blob/master/amr.md`

in UCCA it is [go P]). We leave more thorough comparison of the two schemes to future research.

(66) The boy can't go.

```
(p / possible-01
    :polarity -
    :ARG1  (g / go-02
             :ARG0 (b / boy)))
```

(67) [The boy A] [can D-POSSIBILITY] ['t D-NEGATION] [go P]

SNACS. SNACS is a token-based adpositional sense-disambiguation scheme that is known to integrate well with UCCA Foundational Layer annotation labels (Schneider et al., 2018; Prange et al., 2019a). As a refinement layer, the current scheme is also compatible with SNACS adpositional categories to a certain degree. The overlap is notably seen in adpositional phrases that as a whole are also labeled as D category. For instance, the MANNER category in SNACS would map onto D-DESCRIPTION instances where the instance is a prepositional manner modifier.

(68) Its paddle wheels were [churning P] the sea [**with perfect steadiness** D]. DESCRIPTION

7 Conclusion

Finding an appropriate level of abstraction is a central problem in meaning representation design. Motivated by the observation that UCCA's Adverbial category encompasses too wide a range of *heterogeneous* semantic functions as a scene-level category, we proposed a semantic refinement annotation scheme consisting of 7 subtypes, allowing multiple annotation to cover a limited amount of compositionality. Pilot annotation studies on corpora previously annotated with the UCCA foundational layer showed that this subcategorization scheme offers a good coverage of the existing Adverbial instances.

Some challenges remain. Though rare, some Adverbial instances were marked by annotators as non-applicable under the scheme. We also found that allowing multiple labels can cause annotator disagreement depending on annotators' extent or style of analysis. As more empirical data accrue, future work should aim to mitigate such sources of disagreement.

Acknowledgements

We sincerely thank Daniel Hershcovich as well as three anonymous reviewers for their constructive criticism and feedback on this paper.

References

Omri Abend and Ari Rappoport. 2013. Universal Conceptual Cognitive Annotation (UCCA). In *Proceedings of the 51st Annual Meeting of the Association for Computational Linguistics (Volume 1: Long Papers)*, pages 228–238, Sofia, Bulgaria. Association for Computational Linguistics.

Omri Abend, Nathan Schneider, Dotan Dvir, Jakob Prange, and Ari Rappoport. 2020. UCCA's foundational layer: Annotation guidelines v2.1. *arXiv preprint arXiv:2012.15810.*

Laura Banarescu, Claire Bonial, Shu Cai, Madalina Georgescu, Kira Griffitt, Ulf Hermjakob, Kevin Knight, Philipp Koehn, Martha Palmer, and Nathan Schneider. 2013. Abstract Meaning Representation for sembanking. In *Proceedings of the 7th Linguistic Annotation Workshop and Interoperability with Discourse*, pages 178–186, Sofia, Bulgaria. Association for Computational Linguistics.

Claire Bonial, Bianca Badarau, Kira Griffitt, Ulf Hermjakob, Kevin Knight, Tim O'Gorman, Martha Palmer, and Nathan Schneider. 2018. Abstract Meaning Representation of constructions: The more we include, the better the representation. In *Proceedings of the Eleventh International Conference on Language Resources and Evaluation (LREC 2018)*, Miyazaki, Japan. European Language Resources Association (ELRA).

Ruixiang Cui and Daniel Hershcovich. 2020. Refining implicit argument annotation for UCCA. In *Proceedings of the Second International Workshop on Designing Meaning Representations*, pages 41–52, Barcelona Spain (online). Association for Computational Linguistics.

Ruixiang Cui and Daniel Hershcovich. 2021. Meaning representation of numeric fused-heads in UCCA. *arXiv preprint arXiv:2106.07364.*

R. M. W. Dixon. 2010. *Basic Linguistic Theory.*

Lucia Donatelli, Michael Regan, William Croft, and Nathan Schneider. 2018. Annotation of tense and aspect semantics for sentential AMR. In *Proceedings of the Joint Workshop on Linguistic Annotation, Multiword Expressions and Constructions (LAW-MWE-CxG-2018)*, pages 96–108, Santa Fe, New Mexico, USA.

Daniel Hershcovich, Omri Abend, and Ari Rappoport. 2019. Content differences in syntactic and semantic representation. In *Proceedings of the 2019 Conference of the North American Chapter of the Association for Computational Linguistics: Human Language Technologies, Volume 1 (Long and Short Papers)*, pages 478–488, Minneapolis, Minnesota. Association for Computational Linguistics.

Christopher Kennedy and Christopher Louise McNally. 2005. Scale structure, degree modification, and the semantics of gradable predicates. *Language*, 81:345 – 381.

Jakob Prange, Nathan Schneider, and Omri Abend. 2019a. Made for each other: Broad-coverage semantic structures meet preposition supersenses. In *Proceedings of CoNLL*, pages 174–185, Hong Kong, China. Association for Computational Linguistics.

Jakob Prange, Nathan Schneider, and Omri Abend. 2019b. Semantically constrained multilayer annotation: the case of coreference. In *Proceedings of DMR*, pages 164–176, Florence, Italy.

Nathan Schneider, Jena D. Hwang, Vivek Srikumar, Jakob Prange, Austin Blodgett, Sarah R. Moeller, Aviram Stern, Adi Bitan, and Omri Abend. 2018. Comprehensive supersense disambiguation of English prepositions and possessives. In *Proceedings of the 56th Annual Meeting of the Association for Computational Linguistics (Volume 1: Long Papers)*, pages 185–196, Melbourne, Australia. Association for Computational Linguistics.

Adi Shalev, Jena D. Hwang, Nathan Schneider, Vivek Srikumar, Omri Abend, and Ari Rappoport. 2019. Preparing SNACS for subjects and objects. In *Proceedings of the First International Workshop on Designing Meaning Representations*, pages 141–147, Florence, Italy.

Simplifying annotation of intersections in time normalization annotation: exploring syntactic and semantic validation

Peiwen Su and **Steven Bethard**
University of Arizona
Tucson, AZ, USA
{peiwensu,bethard}@email.arizona.edu

Abstract

While annotating normalized times in food security documents, we found that the semantically compositional annotation for time normalization (SCATE) scheme required several near-duplicate annotations to get the correct semantics for expressions like *Nov. 7th to 11th 2021*. To reduce this problem, we explored replacing SCATE's SUB-INTERVAL property with a SUPER-INTERVAL property, that is, making the smallest units (e.g., *7th* and *11th*) rather than the largest units (e.g., *2021*) the heads of the intersection chains. To ensure that the semantics of annotated time intervals remained unaltered despite our changes to the syntax of the annotation scheme, we applied several different techniques to validate our changes. These validation techniques detected and allowed us to resolve several important bugs in our automated translation from SUB-INTERVAL to SUPER-INTERVAL syntax.

1 Introduction

Time normalization is the task of translating natural language expressions of time, e.g., *three days ago*, to computer-readable forms, e.g., 2021-11-04. Time normalization is an important component of applications like monitoring patient symptoms (Lin et al., 2015), matching news events across languages (Vossen et al., 2016), and studying date-based literature trends (Fischer and Strötgen, 2015). As part of a larger project studying the causes and effects of food insecurity, we were interested in annotating normalized times in this highly time-sensitive domain.

Several schemes have been proposed for annotating normalized times. TimeML (Pustejovsky et al., 2003; ISO, 2012) primarily focuses on times that can be described as a prefix of YYYY-MM-DDTHH:MM:SS, including relative time expressions like *next Monday*, but excluding time expressions like *the past three summers* that refer to more than one time interval. The semantically compositional annotation for time normalization (SCATE; Bethard and Parker, 2016) scheme breaks time expressions down into individual temporal operators like NEXT or BETWEEN, and can therefore cover a wider variety of time expressions than TimeML. The Time Event Ontology (TEO; Li et al., 2020) draws ideas from both TimeML and SCATE, to provide a simplified annotation scheme specifically targeted at clinical notes.

Because the SCATE scheme covered the widest variety of time expressions, we selected this scheme for annotating normalized times in food security documents. We annotated 17 documents (22K words), producing 2305 time annotations, and achieved an acceptable inter-annotator agreement of 0.808 F1. However, during the process we noticed that to get the correct temporal semantics of expressions like *Nov. 7th to 11th 2021*, we had to add many near-duplicate annotations. Under the SCATE scheme, to get this expression interpreted correctly as [2021-11-07 00:00:00, 2021-11-12 00:00:00), two MONTH-OF-YEAR annotations are needed on *Nov.* and two YEAR annotations are needed on *2021*, as shown in fig. 1 (top). These duplicate annotations are necessary because the BETWEEN needs two intervals, one for 2021-11-07 and one for 2021-11-11, and a YEAR with a chain of SUB-INTERVAL links can represent only a single interval. For example, the top-most YEAR in the figure, based on its chain of SUB-INTERVAL links, is interpreted as 2021-11-11.

Because these types of time expressions were common in our food security documents, we explored a possible change to the SCATE scheme which would replace SUB-INTERVAL links with SUPER-INTERVAL links. In essence, we would reverse the links in the chains, removing the need for the additional annotations, as shown in Figure 1 (bottom). This works because while in the SUB-INTERVAL version each MONTH-OF-YEAR

Proceedings of the Joint 15th Linguistic Annotation Workshop (LAW) and 3rd Designing Meaning Representations (DMR) Workshop, pages 106–111
November, 2021.

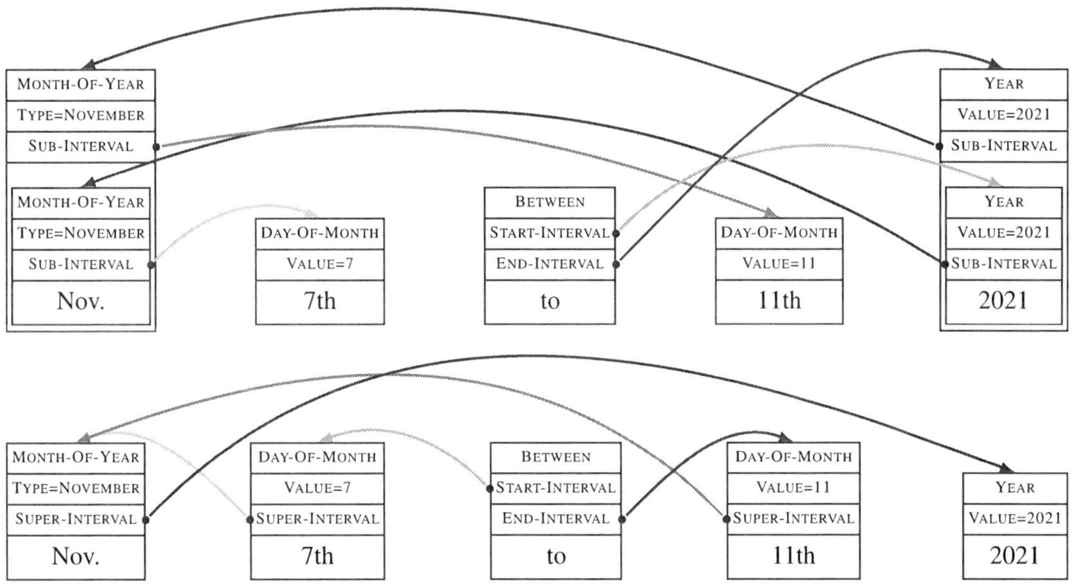

Figure 1: SCATE representation of *Nov. 7th to 11th 2021* using standard SUB-INTERVAL (top) and proposed SUPER-INTERVAL (bottom). Arrows of the same color are performing similar functions.

is linked to a different day and therefore cannot be shared, in the SUPER-INTERVAL version the MONTH-OF-YEAR can be shared because it is linked only to the YEAR, which is also shared.

Our proposed change to SCATE is purely syntactic; if implemented correctly, it should not change the semantics of any complete time expression. But SUB-INTERVAL is extremely common in SCATE-annotated documents, such as the SemEval 2018 Task 6 annotated corpus Laparra et al. (2018), so the conversion from SUB-INTERVAL to SUPER-INTERVAL would have to be automatic, not manual. We thus designed an automatic conversion tool, and a series of validations to ensure that our conversions behaved as expected.

Because SCATE, in addition to defining a set of annotations syntactically, also defines a formal semantics for each annotation, we were able to validate our tool in two different ways: syntactically, ensuring that the XML annotations were valid SCATE annotations and lost no information, and semantically, ensuring that the time intervals inferrable from the SCATE annotations were identical before and after the conversion.

2 Anafora XML to LabelStudio JSON

SCATE was originally implemented in the XML format of the Anafora annotation tool (Chen and Styler, 2013), but that tool has not been actively maintained since 2018. To allow easy visualization of our annotations, we translated the SCATE scheme into a LabelStudio[1] config, and a corresponding LabelStudio JSON format.

To convert between Anafora XML and LabelStudio JSON, we created an XML-to-JSON script that translated each `<entity>` into a JSON object for its `<type>` and a JSON object for each of its `<properties>`. The structure of these JSON objects follows the LabelStudio requirements. The objects for type and text-based properties have an `id` field, give the name via `from_name`, and give the span and value in the `value` sub-object. The objects for link-based properties have `from_id` and `to_id` fields and give the name via `labels`. Figure 2 shows a sample of the original Anafora XML and the corresponding LabelStudio JSON, as well as a screenshot of LabelStudio visualizing the SCATE annotations.

3 Validating XML-to-JSON

Before implementing the proposed SUB-INTERVAL to SUPER-INTERVAL conversion in the JSON files, we tested our Anafora XML to LabelStudio JSON conversion. We first implemented a JSON-to-XML script designed to be an inverse of the XML-to-JSON script described in section 2, which collected all JSON objects for each `id` and merged them into a single `<entity>`. We then tested that the composition of the two scripts (i.e., XML-to-JSON-to-

[1] `https://labelstud.io/`

```
<entity>
  <id>51@e@ABC19980114.1830.0611@gold</id>
  <span>29,31</span>
  <type>Month-Of-Year</type>
  <parentsType>Repeating-Interval</parentsType>
  <properties>
    <Type>January</Type>
    <Sub-Interval>50@e@ABC19980114.1830.0611@gold
      </Sub-Interval>
  </properties>
</entity>
```

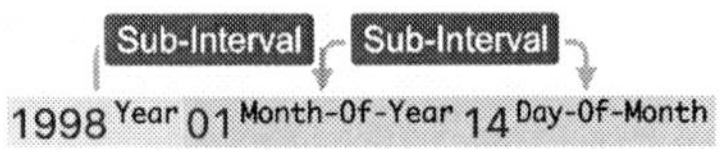


```
{
  "value": {
    "start": 29, "end": 31,
    "labels": ["Month-Of-Year"]},
  "id": "51@e@ABC19980114.1830.0611@gold",
  "from_name": "type",
},
{
  "value": {
    "start": 29, "end": 31,
    "choices": ["January"]},
  "id": "51@e@ABC19980114.1830.0611@gold",
  "from_name": "Month-Of-Year-type",
},
{
  "from_id": "51@e@ABC19980114.1830.0611@gold",
  "to_id": "50@e@ABC19980114.1830.0611@gold",
  "type": "relation",
  "labels": ["Sub-Interval"]
},
```

Figure 2: Abbreviated example of Anafora XML format (top left), LabelStudio JSON format (right), and LabelStudio visualization (bottom left). See fig. A1 in appendix A for the complete SUB-INTERVAL chain.

```
<entity>
  <id>571@e@ID159_clinic_470@gold</id>
  <span>6491,6495</span>
  <type>After</type>
  <parentsType>Operator</parentsType>
  <properties>
    <Semantics>Interval-Not-Included</Semantics>
    <Interval-Type>Link</Interval-Type>
    <Interval>326@e@ID159_clinic_470@gold</Interval>
  </properties>
</entity>
```

Figure 3: An annotation error. No `<entity>` in the document has id `326@e@ID159_clinic_470@gold`. The phrase *Post* spans the offsets 6491 to 6495 within the phrase *Postoperative*. It is likely that an annotation over the *operative* was lost in the original annotations.

```
<entity>
  <id>130@e@APW19980213.1320@gold</id>
  <span>934,937</span>
  <type>Union</type>
  <parentsType>Operator</parentsType>
  <properties>
    <Repeating-Intervals>111@e@APW19980213.1320@gold
      </Repeating-Intervals>
    <Repeating-Intervals>112@e@APW19980213.1320@gold
      </Repeating-Intervals>
  </properties>
</entity>
```

Figure 4: A `<Repeating-Intervals>` property with multiple values. The phrase *and* spans the offsets 934 to 937 in the phrase *Mondays and Tuesdays*. The first `<Repeating-Intervals>` is an annotation over *Mondays* and the second is an annotation over *Tuesdays*.

XML) produced Anafora XML that was equivalent to the original Anafora XML. Performing this type of syntactic validation revealed a number of errors.

Annotation errors We found 43 cases in the SemEval 2018 Task 6 annotated corpus where there were errors in the original Anafora XML. For example, fig. 3 shows an `<entity>` whose `<Interval>` appears to link to another entity, but the document contains no entity with id `326@e@ID159_clinic_470@gold`. These were revealed as exceptions in the XML-to-JSON script when it attempted to look up the non-existing entity.

Properties with multiple values Almost all SCATE annotations allow only a single value for each property. However, our XML-to-JSON-to-XML validation revealed that a small number of annotations in the SemEval 2018 Task 6 corpus had properties with multiple values. For example, as shown in fig. 4, *and* in the phrase *Mondays and Tuesdays* was annotated as a UNION with two `<Repeating-Intervals>` arguments, *Mondays* and *Tuesdays*. Our original code assumed one value per property, resulting in missing links in the generated XML. We resolved the issue by ensuring that properties with multiple values resulted in multiple JSON objects instead of just one.

Annotations with multiple spans Almost all SCATE annotations are over just a single, continuous span of text. However, our XML-to-JSON-to-XML validation revealed that a small number of annotations in the SemEval 2018 Task 6 corpus had multiple spans. For example, in fig. 5, the event *status, stable* (an event from a clinical note that describes the state of the patient) was annotated to exclude the comma and space characters. Similar problems arise in our food security data, where expressions like *Kiremt 2016 rainy season* needs a discontinuous span for the season *Kiremt . . . rainy season*. We resolved this issue by creating an extra JSON object for each additional span, where the ID is suffixed with `continued` to allow for easy reconstruction of the multi-span annotation.

```
<entity>
  <id>66@e@ID017_clinic_049@gold</id>
  <span>748,754;756,762</span>
  <type>Event</type>
  <parentsType>Other</parentsType>
</entity>
```

Figure 5: An annotation with multiple spans. The phrase *status, stable* spans the offsets 748 to 762, but the comma and space are excluded from the annotation.

4 Validating Sub-to-Super-Interval

Having validated our XML-to-JSON conversion, we implemented our SUB-INTERVAL to SUPER-INTERVAL conversion. Our initial implementation simply changed the `labels` from `Sub-Interval` to `Super-Interval` and swapped the `from_id` and `to_id` fields.

To perform semantic validation of this conversion, we took advantage of the interpretation API provided by Bethard and Parker (2016)[2], which takes annotations as input and produces time intervals as output. For example, the BETWEEN annotation in fig. 1 would be interpreted as the interval [2021-11-07 00:00:00, 2021-11-12 00:00:00). Since the API requires Anafora XML, we used our JSON-to-XML script to convert our SUPER-INTERVAL JSON into SUPER-INTERVAL XML. To check if our syntactic changes to the annotation scheme maintained the intended semantics, we paired up each annotation in the original SUB-INTERVAL XML files with the corresponding annotation in the newly generated SUPER-INTERVAL XML files, and tested that the paired annotations both resulted in the same time intervals. Performing this type of semantic validation revealed a number of errors.

Mid-chain entities The validation showed that the interpretation of entities in the middle of a SUB-INTERVAL chain changed with the SUPER-INTERVAL conversion. For example, the *Nov.* of fig. 1 (top) is intersected with *7th* via its SUB-INTERVAL link, and is therefore interpreted as all November 7th intervals on the timeline. On the other hand, the *Nov.* of fig. 1 (bottom) is intersected with *2021* via its SUPER-INTERVAL link, and is therefore interpreted as the single interval November 2021. This was a desirable consequence of the conversion, since these partial interpretations are necessary to allow re-use of expressions like *Nov.* in *Nov. 7th to 11th.* We therefore changed our semantic validation code to allow mismatches between mid-chain entities.

Entities with chain arguments Our simple swapping of `from_id` and `to_id` turned out to be insufficent for entities that are not part of a SUB-INTERVAL chain, but take one as an argument. For example, the BETWEEN in fig. 1 (top) has chains as its START-INTERVAL and END-INTERVAL arguments. In the SUB-INTERVAL encoding, these chains are represented by YEARs, but in the SUPER-INTERVAL encoding, these chains are represented by DAY-OF-MONTHs. We resolved this issue by finding entities with chain arguments, and replacing the root of the SUB-INTERVAL chain (i.e., the largest time unit) with the root of the SUPER-INTERVAL chain (i.e., the smallest time unit).

5 Discussion

The change from SUB-INTERVAL to SUPER-INTERVAL achieved our primary goal, successfully removing 69 near-duplicate annotations in our food security corpus, without changing the semantics of any time expression. There was only one place where the switch caused a new near-duplicate annotation to be added: *Meher 2016/17.* The *Meher* here refers to two different seasons, May to September 2016 and May to September 2017. With SUB-INTERVALs, both *2016* and *17* could link to the same *Meher* SEASON-OF-YEAR, but with SUPER-INTERVALs, there must be two SEASON-OF-YEARs annotated, each pointing their SUPER-INTERVAL to exactly one of *2016* or *17.* We nonetheless consider the experiment a success: 69 near-duplicates removed, at the cost of just 1 near-duplicate added.

In terms of validation strategies, we found it helpful to be working with an annotation scheme that had both a syntactic specification of how annotations should be applied to words in the text, and a formal semantic interpretation that converted the annotations to explicit intervals on the timeline. This allowed us to change the syntax of the annotation scheme, while making sure that we did not unintentionally change the semantics of the annotations. Having both a syntactic specification and a formal semantic interpretation is uncommon in annotation schemes. At one end of the spectrum are purely syntactic annotation schemes, like Universal Dependencies (UD; Nivre et al., 2020), with no formal semantic interpretation at all. At the other end of the spectrum are purely semantic annota-

[2] https://github.com/clulab/timenorm/

tion schemes, like abstract meaning representation (AMR; Banarescu et al., 2013) where only the formal logic-like interpretation is annotated, with no explicit links to individual words of the original text. Our experience was that having both a syntactic and semantic specification made it easier to apply and validate improvements to the annotation scheme.

All code produced during this work can be found at `https://github.com/clulab/timenorm/`.

Acknowledgements

Research reported in this publication was supported by the National Library of Medicine of the National Institutes of Health under Award Number R01LM010090. The content is solely the responsibility of the authors and does not necessarily represent the official views of the National Institutes of Health.

References

Laura Banarescu, Claire Bonial, Shu Cai, Madalina Georgescu, Kira Griffitt, Ulf Hermjakob, Kevin Knight, Philipp Koehn, Martha Palmer, and Nathan Schneider. 2013. Abstract Meaning Representation for sembanking. In *Proceedings of the 7th Linguistic Annotation Workshop and Interoperability with Discourse*, pages 178–186, Sofia, Bulgaria. Association for Computational Linguistics.

Steven Bethard and Jonathan Parker. 2016. A semantically compositional annotation scheme for time normalization. In *Proceedings of the Tenth International Conference on Language Resources and Evaluation (LREC'16)*, pages 3779–3786, Portorož, Slovenia. European Language Resources Association (ELRA).

Wei-Te Chen and Will Styler. 2013. Anafora: A web-based general purpose annotation tool. In *Proceedings of the 2013 NAACL HLT Demonstration Session*, pages 14–19, Atlanta, Georgia. Association for Computational Linguistics.

Frank Fischer and Jannik Strötgen. 2015. When Does (German) Literature Take Place? On the Analysis of Temporal Expressions in Large Corpora. In *Proceedings of DH 2015: Annual Conference of the Alliance of Digital Humanities Organizations*, volume 6, Sydney, Australia.

ISO. 2012. Language resource management – semantic annotation framework (semaf) – part 1: Time and events (semaf-time, iso-timeml). Technical report, ISO. 24617-1:2012.

Egoitz Laparra, Dongfang Xu, Ahmed Elsayed, Steven Bethard, and Martha Palmer. 2018. SemEval 2018 task 6: Parsing time normalizations. In *Proceedings of The 12th International Workshop on Semantic Evaluation*, pages 88–96, New Orleans, Louisiana. Association for Computational Linguistics.

Fang Li, Jingcheng Du, Yongqun He, Hsing-Yi Song, Mohcine Madkour, Guozheng Rao, Yang Xiang, Yi Luo, Henry W Chen, Sijia Liu, Liwei Wang, Hongfang Liu, Hua Xu, and Cui Tao. 2020. Time event ontology (TEO): to support semantic representation and reasoning of complex temporal relations of clinical events. *Journal of the American Medical Informatics Association*, 27(7):1046–1056.

Chen Lin, Elizabeth W. Karlson, Dmitriy Dligach, Monica P. Ramirez, Timothy A. Miller, Huan Mo, Natalie S. Braggs, Andrew Cagan, Vivian S. Gainer, Joshua C. Denny, and Guergana K. Savova. 2015. Automatic identification of methotrexate-induced liver toxicity in patients with rheumatoid arthritis from the electronic medical record. *Journal of the American Medical Informatics Association*, 22(e1):e151–e161.

Joakim Nivre, Marie-Catherine de Marneffe, Filip Ginter, Jan Hajič, Christopher D. Manning, Sampo Pyysalo, Sebastian Schuster, Francis Tyers, and Daniel Zeman. 2020. Universal Dependencies v2: An evergrowing multilingual treebank collection. In *Proceedings of the 12th Language Resources and Evaluation Conference*, pages 4034–4043, Marseille, France. European Language Resources Association.

James Pustejovsky, José M. Castaño, Robert Ingria, Roser Saurí, Robert J. Gaizauskas, Andrea Setzer, Graham Katz, and Dragomir R. Radev. 2003. Timeml: Robust specification of event and temporal expressions in text. In *New Directions in Question Answering, Papers from 2003 AAAI Spring Symposium, Stanford University, Stanford, CA, USA*, pages 28–34. AAAI Press.

Piek Vossen, Rodrigo Agerri, Itziar Aldabe, Agata Cybulska, Marieke van Erp, Antske Fokkens, Egoitz Laparra, Anne-Lyse Minard, Alessio Palmero Aprosio, German Rigau, Marco Rospocher, and Roxane Segers. 2016. NewsReader: Using knowledge resources in a cross-lingual reading machine to generate more knowledge from massive streams of news. *Special Issue Knowledge-Based Systems, Elsevier*.

A Appendix

Figure A1 shows an extended example of what SUB-INTERVAL chains look like in both Anafora XML and LabelStudio JSON.

```
<entity>
  <id>50@e@ABC19980114.1830.0611@gold</id>
  <span>31,33</span>
  <type>Day-Of-Month</type>
  <parentsType>Repeating-Interval</parentsType>
  <properties>
  <Value>14</Value>
  <Sub-Interval></Sub-Interval>
  <Number></Number>
  <Modifier></Modifier>
  </properties>
</entity>
<entity>
  <id>51@e@ABC19980114.1830.0611@gold</id>
  <span>29,31</span>
  <type>Month-Of-Year</type>
  <parentsType>Repeating-Interval</parentsType>
  <properties>
  <Type>January</Type>
  <Sub-Interval>50@e@ABC19980114.1830.0611@gold
    </Sub-Interval>
  <Number></Number>
  <Modifier></Modifier>
  </properties>
</entity>
<entity>
  <id>52@e@ABC19980114.1830.0611@gold</id>
  <span>25,29</span>
  <type>Year</type>
  <parentsType>Interval</parentsType>
  <properties>
  <Value>1998</Value>
  <Sub-Interval>51@e@ABC19980114.1830.0611@gold
    </Sub-Interval>
  <Modifier></Modifier>
  </properties>
</entity>
```



```
{
  "value": {
    "start": 31,
    "end": 33,
    "labels": ["Day-Of-Month"]
  },
  "id": "50@e@ABC19980114.1830.0611@gold",
  "from_name": "type",
  "to_name": "text",
  "type": "labels"
},
{
  "value": {
    "start": 31,
    "end": 33,
    "text": ["14"]
  },
  "id": "50@e@ABC19980114.1830.0611@gold",
  "from_name": "Day-Of-Month-value",
  "to_name": "text",
  "type": "textarea"
},
{
  "value": {
    "start": 29,
    "end": 31,
    "labels": ["Month-Of-Year"]
  },
  "id": "51@e@ABC19980114.1830.0611@gold",
  "from_name": "type",
  "to_name": "text",
  "type": "labels"
},
{
  "value": {
    "start": 29,
    "end": 31,
    "choices": ["January"]
  },
  "id": "51@e@ABC19980114.1830.0611@gold",
  "from_name": "Month-Of-Year-type",
  "to_name": "text",
  "type": "choices"
},
{
  "from_id": "51@e@ABC19980114.1830.0611@gold",
  "to_id": "50@e@ABC19980114.1830.0611@gold",
  "type": "relation",
  "labels": ["Sub-Interval"]
},
{
  "value": {
    "start": 25,
    "end": 29,
    "labels": ["Year"]
  },
  "id": "52@e@ABC19980114.1830.0611@gold",
  "from_name": "type",
  "to_name": "text",
  "type": "labels"
},
{
  "value": {
    "start": 25,
    "end": 29,
    "text": ["1998"]
  },
  "id": "52@e@ABC19980114.1830.0611@gold",
  "from_name": "Year-value",
  "to_name": "text",
  "type": "textarea"
},
{
  "from_id": "52@e@ABC19980114.1830.0611@gold",
  "to_id": "51@e@ABC19980114.1830.0611@gold",
  "type": "relation",
  "labels": ["Sub-Interval"]
}
```


Figure A1: Example Anafora XML format (left) and LabelStudio JSON format (right).

Overcoming the challenges in morphological annotation of Turkish in universal dependencies framework

Seyyit Talha Bedir
Dept. of Linguistics
Bogazici University, Turkey
talha.bedir@boun.edu.tr

Karahan Şahin
Dept. of Linguistics
Bogazici University, Turkey
karahan.sahin@boun.edu.tr

Onur Güngör
Computer Engineering
Bogazici University, Turkey
onurgu@boun.edu.tr

Suzan Üsküdarlı
Computer Engineering
Bogazici University, Turkey
suzan.uskudarli@boun.edu.tr

Arzucan Özgür
Computer Engineering
Bogazici University, Turkey
arzucan.ozgur@boun.edu.tr

Tunga Güngör
Computer Engineering
Bogazici University, Turkey
gungort@boun.edu.tr

Balkız Öztürk
Dept. of Linguistics
Bogazici University, Turkey
balkiz.ozturk@boun.edu.tr

Abstract

This paper presents several challenges faced when annotating Turkish treebanks in accordance with the Universal Dependencies (UD) guidelines and proposes solutions to address them. Most of these challenges stem from the lack of adequate support in the UD framework to accurately represent null morphemes and complex derivations, which results in significant loss of information for Turkish. This loss negatively impacts the tools that are developed based on these treebanks. We raised and discussed these issues within the community on the official UD portal. This paper presents these issues and our proposals to more accurately represent morphosyntactic information for Turkish while adhering to guidelines of UD. This work aims to contribute to the representation of Turkish and other agglutinative languages in UD-based treebanks, which in turn aids to develop more accurately annotated datasets for such languages.

1 Introduction

Universal Dependencies[1] (henceforth, UD) is an international cooperative project for annotating treebanks with a standardized format to facilitate the development of automated support for natural language processing (NLP). At present (version 2.8) it includes 202 treebanks from 114 different languages. In this paper, we outline and propose solutions to two main challenges for the UD based annotation of Turkish, which is a highly inflectional agglutinative language. These challenges stem from the inadequate representation of derivations and null morphemes. In addition, we also propose a thorough annotation scheme for a commonly used Turkish verb, *ol-* (to be), which has a very rich scope of usage.

The first challenge that we address is the lack of representation of derivations in UD, which causes annotators to take derived forms of nouns, verbs, adjectives, and adverbs as lemmas. Turkish has a morphology that uses very rich and productive derivational suffixes. Kapan (2019) states that a Turkish word may have up to six derivational suffixes at the same time. Without any tool for derivation, for example, a word like *okuldakilerden* (from the ones in school) would have the lemma *okuldaki*, losing the annotation for the morphemes *okul* (school), and *-da* (locative case suffix) that comes before the derivation. Since the English translation of the same word consists of five different words, *from the ones in school*, it is represented with five dependencies in the UD framework. It annotates much more information than the current annotation scheme of Turkish does. This unparallelism may harm future cross-linguistic analyses. Properly locating the roots of such derived nouns in the system might be also useful in lemmatization processes. In this paper, we aim to contribute to the representation of derivation in UD, which will be helpful for the annotations of agglutinative languages like Turkish.

The second challenge is the lack of official rep-

[1]The official website is https://universaldependencies.org/.

Proceedings of the Joint 15th Linguistic Annotation Workshop (LAW) and 3rd Designing Meaning Representations (DMR) Workshop, pages 112–122
November, 2021.

resentation for null morphemes. Accounting for this type of morphemes is also considered vital by our team, since the Turkish copula is frequently encountered as a null morpheme. Except for present tense copula, most Turkic treebanks split copulas which alleviates the problem. However, we did not find any account for the present tense copula which is always null. Here, we also propose an annotation for the Turkish present tense copular paradigm.

Besides these two challenges, we also target the presentation of a more complete annotation scheme for the commonly used yet ambiguous Turkish verb *ol-* (to be), for which no clear annotation scheme exists in the Turkish UD treebanks such as BOUN (Türk et al., 2020) and IMST-UD (Sulubacak et al., 2016b). We detected that different usages of *ol-* were usually being used interchangeably with each other. In this paper, we introduce a list of all the *ol-* types and propose an annotation scheme for each.

According to our proposed solutions for the outlined challenges, we started re-annotating the recently introduced BOUN Treebank (2,000 sentences have been annotated so far), which is one of the largest UD-based Turkish treebanks (Türk et al., 2020). Our re-annotation of BOUN Treebank entails all of the morphological and syntactic annotations in the UD framework. That is, we add, remove or change lemmas, parts-of-speech (POS) tags, features and their values, dependency relations and other miscellaneous information as per the decisions taken by the annotation team. Our team is comprised of three linguists and four computer scientists who are all native speakers of Turkish.

In the morphological part of the 2,000 sentences that we have annotated, we changed 5,418 parts-of-speech tags, added 12,654 features, and removed 9,513 features. In the syntactic part, we segmented 701 words into multiple words as well as altered 5,456 dependency relations and 7,333 heads. We also annotated 2,895 slots in the miscellaneous information tab.

While taking decisions for the annotation scheme, the main objective is to represent the Turkish morphosyntax as accurately as possible in accordance with the UD guidelines.[2] We believe, the proposed annotation solutions will contribute to more precise representation not only for Turkish, but also for other agglutinative languages in the UD framework as well.

[2]https://universaldependencies.org/guidelines.html

The remainder of the paper is organized as follows. Section 2 includes a brief survey about Turkish treebanks. Section 3 deals with the problem of derivation in UD. We touch on the difficulties of representing Turkish in a derivation-free framework such as UD. In Section 4, we comment on the representation of the null present tense copula in UD which discourages the representation of any type of null elements in a sentence. In Section 5, we explain how we resolve the multilayered ambiguity problem the verb *ol-* (to be) - a polysemous multi-functional verb - creates for UD. Section 6 concludes the paper.

2 Related Work

As stated in the UD website UD started as a joint result of Stanford dependencies (De Marneffe et al., 2006; De Marneffe and Manning, 2008; De Marneffe et al., 2014), Google universal parts-of-speech tags (Petrov et al., 2011) and the Interset interlingua for morphosyntactic tagsets (Zeman, 2008).

Treebank efforts date back much earlier. With Leech and Garside (1991) and Marcus et al. (1993), we see the earliest treebanks in English. About a decade later Turkish treebanks started to emerge when Atalay et al. (2003) and Oflazer et al. (2003) introduced the METU-Sabancı Treebank (MST) which consists of 5,635 sentences. This treebank was then revisited by Sulubacak et al. (2016a) to alleviate some issues attributed to the corpus like excessive parsing difficulty and cross-parser instability. As a result, they proposed the ITU-METU-Sabancı Treebank (IMST). In Sulubacak et al. (2016b) they converted IMST into UD framework via a semi-automated process and mapping, naming it as IMST-UD which is one of the first Turkish UD treebanks. This treebank was later re-annotated by Türk et al. (2019b), improving the annotation of embedded structures and core versus non-core dependents.

The first Turkish treebank that adopts the UD framework is Grammar Book Treebank (GB) by Çöltekin (2015). GB treebank draws 2,803 sentences or sentence fragments from the grammar book of Göksel and Kerslake (2005) and uses TRMorph (Çöltekin, 2010) to provide morphological annotation. One downside of this treebank is that it mainly consists of textbook examples rather than naturally occurring language.

Another important treebank effort was Turkish-PUD Treebank which was published as a part of the

CoNLL 2017 Shared Task on Multilingual Parsing from Raw Text to Universal Dependencies (Zeman et al., 2017). Turkish-PUD Treebank consists of 1000 sentences which are first annotated as per the annotation guidelines of Google and then converted into the UD framework. This treebank is especially noteworthy, since it has parallel annotations for 18 different languages, making it a useful resource for cross-linguistic analyses. This treebank was later re-annotated by Türk et al. (2019a) to make it more linguistically consistent.

One of the largest Turkish UD based treebanks, BOUN Treebank[3], has been presented recently by Türk et al. (2020) with 9,761 manually annotated sentences. These sentences are a subset of Turkish National Corpus (TNC), a corpus first presented by Aksan et al. (2012) that consists of more than 50 million words. The BOUN Treebank sampled a great variety of text types, which are essays, broadsheet national newspapers, instructional texts, popular culture articles, and biographical texts. Before the manual annotation, they used an end-to-end pipeline (Kanerva et al., 2018) to parse raw texts to UD dependencies in CoNLL-U format. The output was then re-annotated by Turkish linguists. This is also the treebank our team is currently working on.

3 Problems in derivation

One of the UD's main pitfalls when it comes to annotating a language like Turkish is the lack of derivation in the system. Being mostly a syntax-based project, UD only prefers to mark syntactically relevant morphological distinctions, namely the inflectional morphology. The UD website gives the example of the word *organizations* in English whose lemma is marked as *organization* as opposed to *organize*. The suffix *-tion* is not annotated. In a way, the suffixes till the last derivation are ignored by the system. We can show the general idea as follows. Say, `Infl1`, `Infl2`,... are inflectional suffixes and `Der1`, `Der2`,... are derivational suffixes. For a word like `Root + Infl1 + Der1 + Infl2 + Infl3 + Der2 + Infl4`, the entirety of `Root + Infl1 + Der1 + Infl2 + Infl3 + Der2` is a fixed, unprocessed, single lemma according to the UD guidelines. `Der2`, the last derivative suffix here, *blocks access* to the annotation of the previous part (i.e. `Infl1 + Der1 + Infl2 + Infl3`), making all of them invisible to the system – examples are provided in Section 3.1 to illustrate this phenomenon. This is because derivation is not annotated and it is included as a part of the lemma under the UD framework.

The current solutions for the languages that use derivation are not unified. For example, Quechua, a language with an extremely agglutinative morphology (Rios et al., 2012), devised a derivation annotation strategy explained in a UD thread.[4] They use word split immensely and annotate verbs using expressions like `Root_VDeriv_VDeriv` instead of features. They also add the functions of those derivations like `VRoot|+Dir|+Inch` where `+Dir` and `+Inch` represent functions of each individual derivative suffix. Since this method annotates each derivative suffix precisely, it provides a more fine-grained approach for derivation annotation than our approach. However, one downside for this approach is that it has a very distinct annotation style than those we see on other treebanks. A different system than classical feature and value system proposed by the UD guidelines is utilized in this treebank. One other derivation scheme we examined was that of Finnish. In the Finnish TDT treebank, they annotate derivations under the `Features` tab using an additional feature called `Derivation`. The value of this feature is the derivative suffix itself, e.g. `Derivation=Minnen`. This approach is useful since it marks the derivative suffix itself. However, with this scheme, it is hard to annotate a derived item when it has more than one derivative suffix.

Turkish sometimes uses derivation so productively, even to the point that it becomes syntactically significant. In the following, we will introduce the derivation related problems Turkish presents and how we handled them via the tools permitted under the UD guidelines.

3.1 Utilizing MISC tab

In many languages, derivation is expected to occur closer to the root, i.e. inflections usually follow the derivation. In Turkish, albeit this is the general tendency, there are a lot of instances in which a derivational affix modifies an inflected item:[5]

[3]https://github.com/UniversalDependencies/UD_Turkish-BOUN/

[4]https://github.com/UniversalDependencies/docs/issues/660

[5]The morphological features used in the examples throughout the paper are as follows 1 = first person, 2 = second person, 3 = third person, ACC = accusative, AOR = aorist, ATTR = attributive, COP = copula, DAT = dative, DEPR = deprivative, DET = determiner, FUT = future, GEN = genitive, IMPF = imperfective, INS = instrumental, LOC = locative, PL = plural, POSS = possessive, PROF = profession, PRS = present,

(1) anne-m-siz
mother-1SG.POSS-DEPR
'without my mother'

-sIz[6] is a derivational deprivative suffix that adds the meaning of "without". In (1) it comes after the first person possessive suffix which is an inflection. This word will appear as a lemma with its full form *(annemsiz)* in UD. There are even instances in which a derivational affix modifies a phrase or a full clause as shown by the derivational suffix *-CI* in (2).

(2) nasılsa sabah erken
anyways morning early
kalk-ar-ım-cı
get.up-AOR-1SG-PROF
'a person who lives by the motto: "I can get up early anyways"'

nasılsa sabah erken kalkarım (I can get up early anyways) is a finite sentence, *nasılsa sabah erken kalkarımcı* is a person who would say this a lot, procrastinating till midnight and still believing that he/she would get up early anyways. Although this type of usage is rare, in UD we have absolutely no way to deal with the syntax of this sort of expressions. For example, *kalkarımcı*, the last word in the phrase, would have the lemma *kalkarımcı*, since the derivation blocks access to the interior inflectional suffixes, hence *-(A)r* (the aorist TAM (Tense-Aspect-Modality) marker) and *-(I)m* (first person singular agreement marker) will be invisible to the UD.

Although examples like (2) are rare, there are other very common situations like (3) where a derivational affix modifies an entire phrase and it is impossible to annotate it justly with the tools of UD.

(3) [uzun boy]-lu bir insan
[long height]-ATTR DET person
'lit: a person with long height'

-lI suffix is modifying the entire phrase in brackets. For *uzun boylu bir insan*, the current UD tree representation[7] is shown in (4).

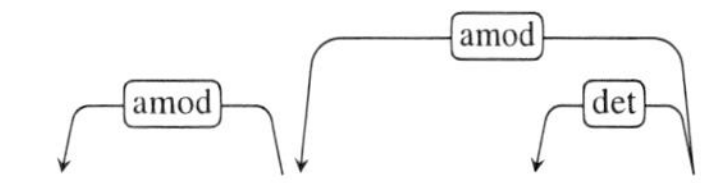

(4)

ADJ	ADJ	DET	NOUN
uzun	boy-lu	bir	insan
long	height-ATTR	DET	person

'a person with long height'

This annotation is problematic for two reasons:[8]

- Because *-lI* is a derivational suffix, we cannot represent it in the UD framework. Should we represent it in some way, in UD framework *-lI* would only modify *boy* whereas the correct syntactic explanation is that the suffix *-lI* modifies the whole noun phrase (NP) *uzun boy* rather than just *boy*.[9]
- In Turkish, like many languages, adjectives are modified by adverbs rather than adjectives. However, in the current annotation shown in (4); an adjective, *uzun*, modifies another adjective, *boylu*, via the dependency `amod` (short for "adjectival modifier").

To solve the problem, the first thing we did was to indicate the root of the derived item utilizing the miscellaneous slot[10] as UD lacks traditional ways of parsing derivation. We use our made up function called `df`, which is an abbreviation of "derived from". For instance, considering the word *organization* in English its `MISC` slot will read `df=organize`. For us to annotate the roots of

PST = past, PTCP = participle, SG = singular.

[6]The capital letters in the suffixes throughout the paper indicate vowel harmony. In Turkish, like many other Turkic languages, high vowels are subject to a phonological harmonization process with regard to frontness and roundness. That means a suffix like *-sIz* might come in four ways depending on the vowel in the syllable before it: *-sız*, *-siz*, *-suz* and *-süz*. Suffixes with lower vowels such as *-(y)A* only vary as per frontness: *-(y)a* and *-(y)e*. In some suffixes, there are also consonants that are written in capital such as *-DA*. This is because the consonant /d/ may change to /t/ if a voiceless consonant comes immediately before it.

[7]In this format the arrows above represent dependencies. The first line gives POS tags, second line is the text, third line provides glosses for the text and the fourth line is the translation of the text.

[8]This example and the potential problems listed here have also been presented by one of the authors of this paper on https://github.com/UniversalDependencies/docs/issues/787. Although great ideas were exchanged by fellow linguists that participated in the discussion, the issue remains unresolved at the time of this writing.

[9]Note that this type of phrasal suffixation (a suffix modifying the entire phrase rather than a single word) can be inflectional as well. However, since inflectional suffixes are fully annotated in the UD framework, they do not cause any information loss. But, the derived elements are taken as whole units in UD causing information loss. Our goal in this paper is minimizing this information loss without leaving the boundaries of official UD guidelines.

[10]The miscellaneous slot or `MISC` is an additional slot that is placed on the rightmost tab in CONLL-U format that represents additional information. This field is usually looser than other fields in that it does not have any format restriction and it is up to the annotator team how to utilize it.

a derived word via the use of `df` under the `MISC` field, the derivational suffix(es) attached to the root have to be very productive. For example, the word *boylu* in (3) above would have `df=boy` on the `MISC` field, since the affix *-lI* is judged to be productive and the root *boy* is deemed accessible to any native Turkish speaker.

There are many unproductive derivative suffixes in Turkish as well. The derivations in (5) are excluded from the root annotation process explained above as they are not judged to be parsable by native Turkish speakers.

(5) a. yağ-mur
rain(v)-MUR
'rain(n)'

b. bas-amak
step.on(v)-AMAK
'step(n)'

The suffixes in (5) generally are unproductive and selected by very few verbal roots. Others are a little bit more productive. The full list of the productive derivative affixes that we deemed accessible by native speakers is given in Appendix A. This list was determined by our linguistic team. Other derivations were not annotated.

By annotating the roots of the derived nouns, verbs, adjectives and adverbs by using the MISC tab, we are providing a simple input for derived items. This makes the information regarding the productive derivation accessible, which we believe to be an important step towards introducing derivation to UD.

3.2 The *-ki* derivation

Another case of productive derivation which introduces a challenge for UD is the derivative suffix *-ki*, which is so productive that we had to split it off even though it is discouraged in the UD framework.

It has been established in Turkish syntactic literature that Turkish mainly has two types of *-ki* suffixes: adjectivizer *-ki* and pronominal *-ki* (Hankamer, 2004, 2005). We separate both of them.

3.2.1 Adjectivizer *-ki*

The adjectivizer suffix *-ki* is generally preceded by a temporal noun as in (6a) or a noun in the locative case which is an inflectional suffix as in (6b):

(6) a. geçen sene-ki program
last year-KI program
'the program in the last year'

b. okul-da-ki öğrenci-ler-in
school-LOC-KI student-PL-GEN
'of the students at school'

Since there is currently no dependency relation in UD to mark any derivation, we had to make our own: `dep:der`. `dep` is a canonical dependency in the UD framework which is advised to be used when no other dependency fits as noted in the official UD website. `dep:der` is our subtype of `dep` which stands for "derivation".

The use of `dep:der` relation is exemplified in Figure 1b which shows the annotated form of (6a). The reason why it is chosen over the old annotation (Figure 1a) is that in the old annotation the features of the word *sene* are lost, and in the revised version the adjective *geçen* is correctly modifying the noun *sene*, rather than the adjective *seneki*.

By introducing the `dep:der` relation, we are able to account for all of the inflection before and after *-ki*. For instance, if the *-ki* suffix in *okuldaki* in (6b) is not separated, then the entirety of the word will be regarded as a single lemma and there will be no way to annotate the locative case suffix *-da* since it is situated before the derivative suffix *-ki*.

3.2.2 The pronominal *-ki*

This *-ki* is a substitute for the possessive noun in Turkish classical genitive-possessive noun phrases (Hankamer, 2004; Öztürk and Taylan, 2018). This *-ki* is also split and its annotation is completely parallel to the item it substitutes.

Example (7) shows a genitive-possessive construction in Turkish and (8) illustrates how *-ki* substitutes the possessive noun *arabası* (his/her car):

(7) Ahmet-in araba-sı-yla
Ahmet-GEN car-3SG.POSS-INS
'by Ahmet's car'

(8) Ahmet-in-ki-yle
Ahmet-GEN-KI-INS
'by that of Ahmet's'

The "that" in the translation of (8) is obviously a fill-in-the-blank item whose content is to be derived by the context. In our case, it refers to *arabası* (his car). Therefore, we kept the dependency construction parallel to that of (7), except for the possessive suffix which goes away during the substitution by *-ki*. That is, the *-ki* is regarded as a pronoun that substitutes the possessive noun in the phrase rather than as a suffix.

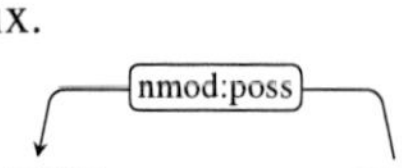

NOUN NOUN
Ahmet'in araba-sı-yla
Ahmet-GEN car-1SG.POSS-INS
(9) 'by Ahmet's car'

Token	Form	Lemma	UPOS	XPOS	Features	Head	Deprel	MISC
1	geçen	geçen	ADJ	Adj	_	2	amod	_
2	seneki	seneki	ADJ	Adj	_	3	amod	_
3	program	program	NOUN	Noun	Case=Nom|Number=Sing|Person=3	0	root	_

(a) The original annotation of *geçen seneki program* in CONLL-U format

Token	Form	Lemma	UPOS	XPOS	Features	Head	Deprel	MISC
1	geçen	geçen	ADJ	Adj	_	2	amod	_
2-3	seneki	_	_	_	_	_	_	_
2	sene	sene	NOUN	Noun	Case=Nom|Number=Sing|Person=3	4	nmod	_
3	ki	ki	PART	Attr	_	2	dep:der	_
4	program	program	NOUN	Noun	Case=Nom|Number=Sing|Person=3	0	root	_

(b) The revised annotation of *geçen seneki program* in CONLL-U format

Figure 1: Comparison of the previous and the proposed annotations for *geçen seneki program*

Token	Form	Lemma	UPOS	XPOS	Features	Head	Deprel	MISC
1	Ahmet'inkiyle	Ahmet'inki	NOUN	Noun	Case=Ins|Number=Sing|Person=3	0	root	_

(a) The original annotation of *Ahmet'inkiyle* in CONLL-U format

Token	Form	Lemma	UPOS	XPOS	Features	Head	Deprel	MISC
1-2	Ahmet'inkiyle	_	_	_	_	_	_	_
1	Ahmet'in	Ahmet	PROPN	Prop	Case=Gen|Number=Sing|Person=3	2	nmod:poss	_
2	kiyle	ki	PRON	Partic	Case=Ins|Number=Sing|Person=3	0	root	_

(b) The revised annotation of *Ahmet'inkiyle* in CONLL-U format

Figure 2: Comparison of the previous and the proposed annotations for *Ahmet'inkiyle*

(10)
nmod:poss
NOUN PRON
Ahmet'in ki-yle
Ahmet-GEN KI-INS
'by that of Ahmet's'

If we did not separate *-ki* like in Figure 2a, the entirety of *Ahmet'inki* would be taken as the root that only bears the instrumental case suffix *-yle*. In that case, we would lose the annotation of the genitive case suffix *-in* that is situated before *-ki* and be unaware of the fact that *-ki* acts as a pronoun that substitutes a noun phrase. The dependency tree in (10) and its CONLL-U form in Figure 2b exhibit our new annotation which correctly marks this *-ki* as a pronoun and annotates the features of *Ahmet'in* which were lost in Figure 2a.

4 Lack of null morphemes

In UD, there is no official way to represent null items. This presents a challenge for Turkish since one of the allomorphs of Turkish copula is a null morpheme. This section presents potential annotation problems in UD stemming from the lack of null morphemes, and proposes a solution without imposing radical changes such as introducing null morphemes to the UD framework.

Turkish copula has three allomorphs: *-y-*, *i-* and ∅ (Göksel and Kerslake, 2005; Kornfilt, 1996; Kelepir, 2001). *i-* only surfaces when the copula is written separately. When it is connected to the predicate it can appear as *-y-* or ∅ depending on the last sound of the predicate, respectively, being a vowel or a consonant. Examples in (11) show the separated variation of the Turkish copula for the past tense. Examples in (12) show the same sentences but with the attached form of the copula. The only difference might be the slightly less formal register in the sentences in (12).

(11) a. Ben öğretmen i-di-m.
I teacher COP-PST-1SG
'I was a teacher.'

b. O öğrenci i-di-∅.
S/he student COP-PST-3SG
'S/he was a student.'

(12) a. Ben öğretmen-∅-di-m.
I teacher-COP-PST-1SG
'I was a teacher.'

b. O öğrenci-y-di-∅.
S/he student-COP-PST-3SG
'S/he was a student.'

The sentences in (11) and (12) have the identical meaning. The only difference is that in (12) copulas are in affix form. Except for the present tense copula, all other affixed copulas are already segmented in previous Turkish treebanks.

We added segmentation of the present tense copula which is always null as shown in (13). The previous annotation of this sentence is shown in Figure 3a. We consider this annotation problematic since the `Features` slot contains only the features of the first person copular suffix *-(y)Im*, that is `Number=Sing|Person=1`. In order to represent the features of the nominal predicate, like *öğrenci* (student), we decided to split the present tense copula as shown in Figure 3b – not a common practice in Turkic UD treebanks.[11]

(13) Ben bir öğrenci-∅-yim.
I DET student-COP.PRS-1SG
'I am a student.'

In Turkish, the 3rd person paradigm almost always bears a null suffix. This means that we are unable to split it as there is nothing to split. Table 1 shows the present tense copular forms in Turkish. In the 3rd person singular form, we end up with two successive null suffixes. The only case when an overt morpheme may be 3rd person is the optional *-lAr* after the third person plural copula and only if the subject is human. If *-lAr* shows up in such a case, we separate it just like in Figure 3.

Person	Singular	Plural
1	öğrenci-∅-yim 'I am a student'	öğrenci-∅-yiz 'we are students'
2	öğrenci-∅-sin 'you are a student'	öğrenci-∅-siniz 'you are students'
3	öğrenci-∅-∅ 'he/she is a student'	öğrenci-∅-(ler) 'they are students'

Table 1: Turkish present tense copular paradigm

One solution to solve this issue might be introducing empty nodes and categories into our UD representation. However, our team judged that it would be too unorthodox for the current form of the UD framework. Instead we decided to introduce a compromised solution which includes utilizing the `MISC` slot.

We introduce two new features, `nullcop=3s` and `nullcop=3p` which stand for, respectively, 3rd person singular null copula and 3rd person plural null copula. These are written under the `MISC` slot of the nominal or adjectival predicate that is in agreement with a third person subject. An example is shown below, and its CONLL-U annotation is given in Figure 4:

(14) İşçi-ler grev-de-∅-∅.
worker-PL strike-LOC-COP-3PL
'Workers are on strike.'

5 Turkish *ol-* verb and its many faces

Turkish *ol-* (to be) is an extremely common verb which has many usages. Unfortunately, to this day, not all of its uses are dealt with properly in Turkish treebanks. Since this verb can act as a copula, auxiliary verb, light verb and as a verb in itself, it is extremely important to have a system that clearly differentiates among them. Since in UD it is not possible to input more than one entry for the same item, it is crucial to make that difference visible via part-of-speech tags `UPOS` and `XPOS`, as well as via features and dependency relations within the framework of UD. Six ol- variants (Table 2) are detailed in the following sections.

ol- type	UPOS (XPOS)	dependency relation
ol- the intransitive verb	`VERB`	regular verb
ol- 'to become'	`VERB`	regular verb, where an `xcomp` interior argument is expected
ol- the embedded copula	`AUX`	connected to its dependent with `cop` like a regular copula
ol- the embedded *var/yok*	`VERB` (`Exist`)	dependencies of regular verb
ol- the auxiliary	`AUX`	connected to its host with `aux`
ol- the light verb	`VERB`	connected to its dependent with `compound:lvc`

Table 2: The *ol-* types that we classified

5.1 *ol-* as intransitive verb

As an intransitive verb, the verb *ol-* can have a variety of meanings such as 'to be fit' or 'to be ripe'. In these cases, it is annotated just like a regular intransitive verb as seen in (15).

[11] This decision emerged based on discussions initiated by an author of this paper on https://github.com/UniversalDependencies/docs/issues/774. The issue is closed and idea of splitting copulas is favored.

Token	Form	Lemma	UPOS	XPOS	Features	Head	Deprel	MISC
1	Ben	ben	PRON	Pers	Case=Nom|Number=Sing|Person=1|PronType=Prs	3	nsubj	_
2	bir	bir	DET	Det	_	3	det	_
3	öğrenciyim	öğrenci	NOUN	Noun	Case=Nom|Number=Sing|Person=1	0	root	_

(a) The original annotation of *Ben bir öğrenciyim* in CONLL-U format

Token	Form	Lemma	UPOS	XPOS	Features	Head	Deprel	MISC
1	Ben	ben	PRON	Pers	Case=Nom|Number=Sing|Person=1|PronType=Prs	3	nsubj	_
2	bir	bir	DET	Det	_	3	det	_
3-4	öğrenciyim	_	_	_	_	_	_	_
3	öğrenci	öğrenci	NOUN	Noun	Case=Nom|Number=Sing|Person=3	0	root	_
4	yim	N/A	AUX	Zero	Number=Sing|Person=1|Polarity=Pos|Tense=Pres	3	cop	_

(b) The revised annotation of *Ben bir öğrenciyim* in CONLL-U format

Figure 3: Comparison of the previous and the proposed annotations for *Ben bir öğrenciyim*

Token	Form	Lemma	UPOS	XPOS	Features	Head	Deprel	MISC
1	İşçiler	işçi	NOUN	Noun	Case=Nom|Number=Plur|Person-3	2	nsubj	df=iş
2	grevde	grev	NOUN	Noun	Case=Dat|Number=Sing|Person-3	0	root	nullcop=3p

Figure 4: UD Annotation of *İşçiler grevde*

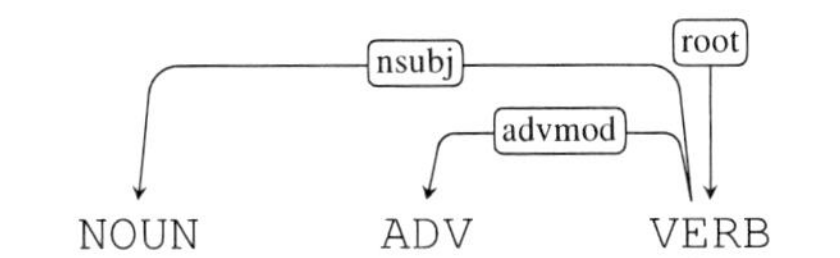

(15) Nektarin-ler yazın ol-ur
nectarine-PL in.summer be.ripe-AOR
'The nectarines will be ripe in summer.'

5.2 *ol-* that means 'to become'

ol- that means 'to become' is annotated just like a regular verb except that its internal argument is a small clause and this type of clauses is annotated with the dependency `xcomp`. An example is shown in (16) and its dependency tree[12] in (17).

(16) Ahmet lise-ye öğretmen
Ahmet high.school-DAT teacher
ol-du.
become-PST
'Ahmet became a teacher at the high school.'

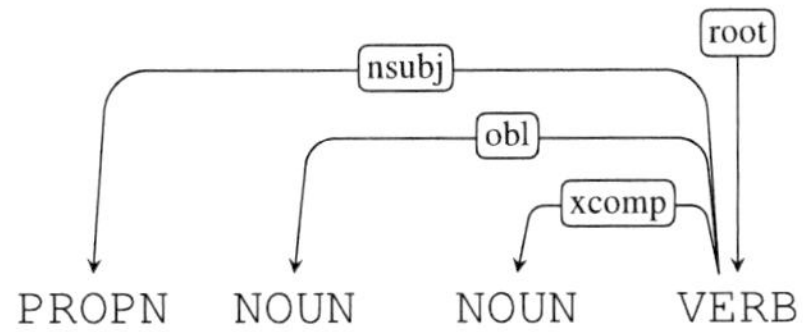

(17) Ahmet liseye öğretmen oldu
'Ahmet became a teacher at the high school.'

[12]In longer sentences such as (17), the glosses are given as a separate example like in (16) in order not to exceed the column.

5.3 *ol-* used as a Turkish copula in the embedded structures

In Turkish, copula is represented via the verb *ol-* in genitive-possessive type nominalized embedded clauses (Göksel, 2001). In that regard, it could be considered as the fourth allomorph among other three Turkish copulas mentioned above: *i-*, *-y-* and ∅. Take the sentence in (18) whose embedded form is given in (19) in brackets (copulas are in bold):

(18) İşçi-ler grev-de-**∅**-∅.
worker-PL strike-LOC-**COP**-3PL
'Workers are on strike.'

(19) [İşçi-ler-in grev-de
worker-PL-GEN strike-LOC
ol-duğ-un]-u bil-iyor-um.
COP-PTCP-3SG.POSS-ACC know-IMPF-1SG
'I know [that workers are on strike].'

The way we annotate (19) is parallel to our annotation for the copulas as shown in (20).

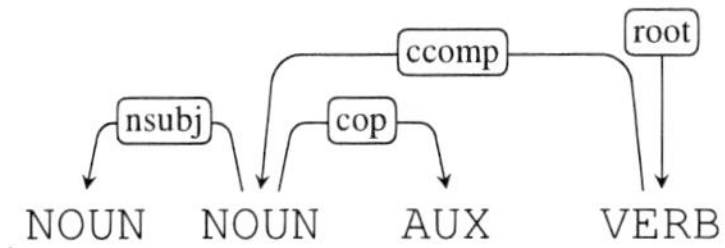

(20) İşçilerin grevde olduğunu biliyorum
'I know that workers are on strike.'

The copular element *olduğunu* in (20) is connected to the embedded nominal predicate *grevde* (on strike) with the `cop` dependency and its UPOS is `AUX` as in a regular copula. Notice that in (15) and (17) the UPOS tags of the verb *ol-* were `VERB`.

5.4 *ol-* which is the embedded form of Turkish existential predicates *var* and *yok*

Turkish utilizes two existential predicates: *var* (there is) and *yok* (there is not), as in:

(21) Kabin-de oksijen yok.
cabin-LOC oxygen YOK
'There is no oxygen in the cabin.'

Possession is expressed with these existential predicates as:

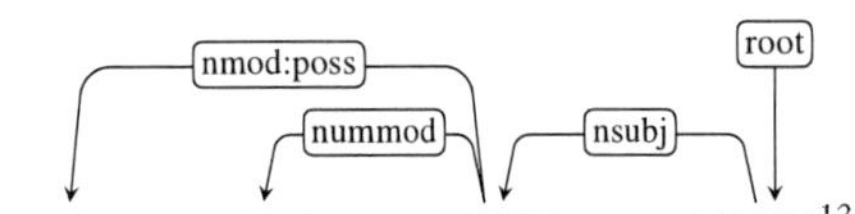

PRON NUM NOUN NOUN[13]
Sen-in üç araba-n var
you-GEN three car-2SG.POSS VAR

(22) 'You have three cars.'

where *senin* modifies *araban* with the `nmod:poss` dependency just like in a regular genitive-possessive NP. This is due to the syntactic structure of Turkish; which literally translates to 'Your three cars exist.'

Hence, we decided that its embedded form (within the brackets) should be parallel to (22) even though the predicate changes its form as shown in (23) and (24).

(23) [Sen-in üç araba-n
[you-GEN three car-2SG.POSS
ol-duğ-un]-u bil-iyor-um.
OL-PTCP-2SG.POSS]-ACC know-IMPF-1SG
'I know [that you have three cars].'

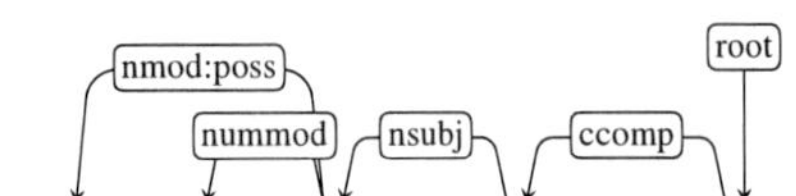

PRON NUM NOUN VERB[13] VERB
Senin üç araban olduğunu biliyorum

(24) 'I know that you have three cars.'

Note that although the forms of *olduğunu* in (24) and (20) are identical, their UPOS and XPOS values and dependency structures differ.

5.5 *ol-* as auxiliary verb

Turkish also utilizes *ol-* as an auxiliary verb in order to give extra information about the aspect and tense of a verb. We annotate its POS tag as `AUX` and its dependency as `aux`. These cases are more easily recognizable since they are most often observed after a participle (e.g. *bitirmiş* in the example (25)).

[13] *var* in (22) and *olduğunu* in (24) also have a significant XPOS that we name `Exist` which stands for *existential*. We annotate this tag to existential predicates.

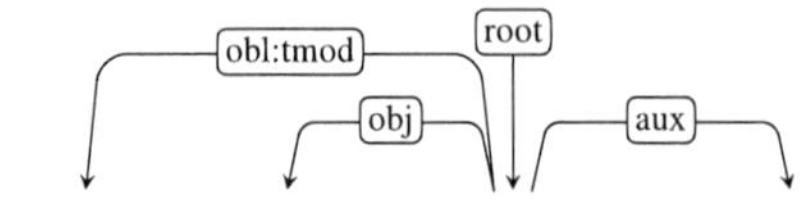

NOUN NOUN VERB AUX
Sene-ye tez-i bitir-miş ol-acağ-ım
year-DAT tez-ACC finish-PTCP OL-FUT-1SG

(25) 'I will have finished the thesis by next year.'

5.6 *ol-* as light verb

Finally, Turkish employs *ol-* in light verb constructions. In verbs like *tatmin ol-* (to be satisfied), *rahatsız ol-* (to be bothered), *ol-* is considered as a light verb. Such verbs usually have an active counterpart with *et-*: *tatmin et-* (to satisfy) and *rahatsız et-* (to bother). Just like its *et-* counterpart it is annotated via the dependency `compound:lvc` (`lvc` stands for light verb construction) and UPOS `VERB`. We should inform that this particular variant of *ol-* has already been differentiated in previous Turkish treebanks and is included here for the sake of completeness.

6 Conclusion

Having a highly rich morphology, Turkish poses a great deal of challenges for linguists regarding representation in a dependency syntax framework. Some of these challenges come from the rich morphology and some from the unexpected behavior of derivation in Turkish. In this paper, we laid out some problems with respect to derivation and lexical ambiguities in the language and their adaptation to the UD framework. Especially in the derivation part, we feel that some significant amount of work awaits us and other linguists who aim to enhance annotation of Turkish in a syntactic framework based on dependency relations. We expect this study to contribute towards a more precise annotation scheme for Turkish and other agglutinative languages, which in turn may also lead to the training of more accurate NLP tools including lemmatizers and dependency parsers.

7 Acknowledgement

This work was supported by Boğaziçi University Research Fund Grant Number 16909. TUBA-GEBIP Award of the Turkish Science Academy (to A.O.) is gratefully acknowledged. We would also like to thank Utku Türk for his valuable counsel and review for this paper.

References

Yesim Aksan, Mustafa Aksan, Ahmet Koltuksuz, Taner Sezer, Ümit Mersinli, Umut Ufuk Demirhan, Hakan Yilmazer, Gülsüm Atasoy, Seda Öz, Ipek Yildiz, et al. 2012. Construction of the Turkish national corpus (tnc). In *LREC*, pages 3223–3227.

Nart B Atalay, Kemal Oflazer, and Bilge Say. 2003. The annotation process in the Turkish treebank. In *Proceedings of 4th International Workshop on Linguistically Interpreted Corpora (LINC-03) at EACL 2003*.

Çağrı Çöltekin. 2010. A freely available morphological analyzer for Turkish. In Proceedings of the Seventh International Conference on Language Resources and Evaluation (LREC'10), Valletta, Malta. European Language Resources Association (ELRA).

Çağrı Çöltekin. 2015. A grammar-book treebank of Turkish. In *Proceedings of the 14th Workshop on Treebanks and Linguistic Theories (TLT 14)*, pages 35–49.

Marie-Catherine De Marneffe, Timothy Dozat, Natalia Silveira, Katri Haverinen, Filip Ginter, Joakim Nivre, and Christopher D Manning. 2014. Universal Stanford dependencies: A cross-linguistic typology. In *LREC*, volume 14, pages 4585–4592.

Marie-Catherine De Marneffe, Bill MacCartney, Christopher D Manning, et al. 2006. Generating typed dependency parses from phrase structure parses. In *Lrec*, volume 6, pages 449–454.

Marie-Catherine De Marneffe and Christopher D Manning. 2008. The Stanford typed dependencies representation. In *Coling 2008: proceedings of the workshop on cross-framework and cross-domain parser evaluation*, pages 1–8.

Aslı Göksel. 2001. The auxiliary verb ol at the morphology-syntax interface. *The Verb in Turkish. Amsterdam: John Benjamins*, pages 151–181.

Aslı Göksel and Celia Kerslake. 2005. Turkish: A Comprehensive Grammar. Comprehensive grammars. Routledge.

Jorge Hankamer. 2004. An ad-phrasal affix in Turkish. *MIT Working Papers in Linguistics*, 46:289–299.

Jorge Hankamer. 2005. Why there are two –ki's in Turkish. *Ms., USC.*

Jenna Kanerva, Filip Ginter, Niko Miekka, Akseli Leino, and Tapio Salakoski. 2018. Turku neural parser pipeline: An end-to-end system for the CoNLL 2018 shared task. In *Proceedings of the CoNLL 2018 Shared Task: Multilingual parsing from raw text to universal dependencies*, pages 133–142.

Aysel Kapan. 2019. *Derivational networks of nouns and adjectives in Turkish*. Master's thesis, Boğaziçi University, İstanbul, Turkey.

Meltem Kelepir. 2001. *Topics in Turkish syntax: Clausal structure and scope*. Ph.D. thesis, Massachusetts Institute of Technology.

Jaklin Kornfilt. 1996. On copular clitic forms in Turkish. *ZAS Working Papers*.

Geoffrey Leech and Roger Garside. 1991. Running a grammar factory: The production of syntactically analysed corpora or treebanks. English Computer Corpora: Selected Papers and Research Guide, pages 15–32.

Mitchell Marcus, Beatrice Santorini, and Mary Ann Marcinkiewicz. 1993. Building a large annotated corpus of english: The penn treebank.

Kemal Oflazer, Bilge Say, Dilek Zeynep Hakkani-Tür, and Gökhan Tür. 2003. Building a Turkish treebank. In *Treebanks*, pages 261–277. Springer.

Balkız Öztürk and Eser Erguvanlı Taylan. 2018. Türkçede iyelik yapıları ve geçişli adlar. In *Dilbilimde Güncel Tartışmalar*. Ankara: Dilbilim Dernegi Yayınları.

Slav Petrov, Dipanjan Das, and Ryan McDonald. 2011. A universal part-of-speech tagset. *arXiv preprint arXiv:1104.2086*.

Annette Rios, Anne Göhring, and Martin Volk. 2012. Parallel treebanking spanish-quechua: how and how well do they align? *Linguistic Issues in Language Technology*, (7/13):online.

Umut Sulubacak, Gülşen Eryiğit, Tuğba Pamay, et al. 2016a. Imst: A revisited Turkish dependency treebank. In *Proceedings of TurCLing 2016, the 1st International Conference on Turkic Computational Linguistics*. Ege University Press.

Umut Sulubacak, Memduh Gökırmak, Francis Tyers, Çağrı Çöltekin, Joakim Nivre, and Gülşen Eryiğit. 2016b. Universal dependencies for Turkish. In *Proceedings of COLING 2016, the 26th International Conference on Computational Linguistics: Technical Papers*, pages 3444–3454.

Utku Türk, Furkan Atmaca, Şaziye Betül Özateş, Gözde Berk, Seyyit Talha Bedir, Abdullatif Köksal, Balkız Öztürk, Tunga Güngör, and Arzucan Özgür. 2020. Resources for Turkish dependency parsing: Introducing the boun treebank and the boat annotation tool. *arXiv preprint arXiv:2002.10416*.

Utku Türk, Furkan Atmaca, Şaziye Betül Özateş, Abdullatif Köksal, Balkiz Öztürk, Tunga Güngör, and Arzucan Özgür. 2019a. Turkish treebanking: Unifying and constructing efforts. In Proceedings of the 13th Linguistic Annotation Workshop, pages 166–177, Florence, Italy. Association for Computational Linguistics.

Utku Türk, Furkan Atmaca, Şaziye Betül Özateş, Balkız Öztürk, Tunga Güngör, and Arzucan Özgür. 2019b. Improving the annotations in the Turkish universal dependency treebank. In *Proceedings of the Third Workshop on Universal Dependencies (UDW, SyntaxFest 2019)*, pages 108–115.

Daniel Zeman. 2008. Reusable tagset conversion using tagset drivers. In *LREC*, volume 2008, pages 28–30.

Daniel Zeman, Martin Popel, Milan Straka, Jan Hajic, Joakim Nivre, Filip Ginter, Juhani Luotolahti, Sampo Pyysalo, and Slav Petrov. 2017. CoNLL 2017 shared task: Multilingual parsing from raw text to Universal Dependencies. In Proceedings of the CoNLL 2017 Shared Task: Multilingual Parsing from Raw Text to Universal Dependencies, pages 1–19, Vancouver, Canada. Association for Computational Linguistics.

8 Appendix

A The derivative suffixes that are annotated using MISC column

Derivative suffixes	**examples**	**on MISC slot**
-lI	*tatlı* (sweet)	`df=tat` (taste)
-sIz	*hissiz* (emotionless, indifferent)	`df=his` (emotion)
-lA	*pencerele-* (to window)	`df=pencere` (window)
-lAn (1)	*hızlan-* (to accelerate)	`df=hız` (speed)
-lAn (2)	*gizlen-* (to disguise, to lie low)	`df=gizle` (to hide stg)
-lAş	*aptallaş-* (to be stupified)	`df=aptal` (stupid)
-CA	*aptalca* (foolish), bence (to me, in my opinion)	`df=aptal` (stupid), `df=ben` (I)
-CI	*simitçi* (bagel seller)	`df=simit` (bagel)
-(y)IcI	*koşucu* (runner)	`df=koş` (to run)
-sAl	*dönemsel* (periodical)	`df=dönem` (period)
-CIk	*gemicik* (ship *diminutive*)	`df=gemi` (ship)
-mA	*araştırma* (research)	`df=araştır` (to research)
-(y)Iş	*çıkış* (exit)	`df=çık` (to exit)
-lIk	*özellik* (attribute, specialty)	`df=özel` (special)
the enforcement prefix	*masmavi* (deep blue, rich blue)	`df=mavi` (blue)

Automatic Entity State Annotation using the VerbNet Semantic Parser

Ghazaleh Kazeminejad[1] **Martha Palmer**[1] **Tao Li**[2] **Vivek Srikumar**[2]

[1] University of Colorado Boulder
[2] University of Utah

{ghazaleh.kazeminejad,martha.palmer}@colorado.edu
{tli,svivek}@cs.utah.edu

Abstract

Tracking entity states is a natural language processing task assumed to require human annotation. In order to reduce the time and expenses associated with annotation, we introduce a new method to automatically extract entity states, including location and existence state of entities, following Dalvi et al. (2018) and Tandon et al. (2020). For this purpose, we rely primarily on the semantic representations generated by the state of the art VerbNet parser (Gung, 2020), and extract the entities (event participants) and their states, based on the semantic predicates of the generated VerbNet semantic representation, which is in propositional logic format. For evaluation, we used ProPara (Dalvi et al., 2018), a reading comprehension dataset which is annotated with entity states in each sentence, and tracks those states in paragraphs of natural human-authored procedural texts. Given the presented limitations of the method, the peculiarities of the ProPara dataset annotations, and that our system, Lexis, makes no use of task-specific training data and relies solely on VerbNet, the results are promising, showcasing the value of lexical resources.

1 Introduction

Question answering in reading comprehension tasks focusing on procedural texts (i.e. texts describing processes) is particularly challenging in natural language processing (NLP), because this type of text describes a changing world state (Clark et al. 2018, Dalvi et al. 2018, Tandon et al. 2018, Du et al. 2019, Gupta and Durrett 2019). Tracking the state of entities in such texts is an important task to enable proper question answering in reading comprehension tasks. The challenging part in such question answering tasks is not where answers are explicitly mentioned in a sentence (Clark et al., 2018). For example, in Figure 1, the sentence with bold elements tells us explicitly that urea and carbon dioxide are located in kidneys by the end of

> ***Paragraph:***
> *Blood delivers oxygen in the body.*
> *Proteins and acids are broken down in the liver.*
> *The liver releases waste in the form of urea.*
> *The* ***blood carries*** *the urea and carbon dioxide* ***to the kidneys****.*
> *The kidneys strain the urea and salts needed from the blood.*
> *The carbon dioxide by product is transported back to the lungs.*
> ***Q:*** *Does blood enter the kidney?*
> ***A:*** *Yes.*

Figure 1: A paragraph from *ProPara* about blood, showing one kind of inference needed to answer a question. Knowing that blood (as well as the urea and carbon dioxide) will end up in the kidney requires lexical semantics knowledge.

this sentence. However, the fact that the blood itself will also be located at the kidneys is implicit in the semantics of the verb "carry", in which the agent of the action (mover) moves along with the theme (thing moved). Therefore, answering the question in Figure 1 requires knowledge of the particular semantics of this verb. This is the kind of inference our system, Lexis, is able to model using VerbNet.

This type of reasoning requires event extraction as a first step, and event participant state extraction as a second step. Our method covers both steps, but is at this point limited to sentence-level inference.

In section 2, we provide an overview of the work related to this research. Section 3 introduces the dataset used to evaluate Lexis, as well as the details of the methods we have used. Section 4 presents our experimental settings, followed by section 5 which illustrates the results of each setting. Section 6 discusses the advantages of Lexis, and provides an error analysis to illuminate the sources of weakness. In section 7, we conclude and briefly discuss our future work.

Proceedings of the Joint 15th Linguistic Annotation Workshop (LAW) and 3rd Designing Meaning Representations (DMR) Workshop, pages 123–132
November, 2021.

Sentence:
The water forms a stream.

VNSP VerbNet semantic predicates output:
[{'polarity': False, 'predicateType': 'Has State', 'args': [{'type': 'Material', 'value': ''}, {'type': 'Verbspecific', 'value': 'V_Final_State'}]}, {'polarity': True, 'predicateType': 'Do', 'args': [{'type': 'Agent', 'value': 'The water'}]}, {'polarity': True, 'predicateType': 'Be', 'args': [{'type': 'Result', 'value': 'a stream'}]}]

A more readable format:
¬HAS_STATE(?$_{\text{Material}}$, V_Final_State$_{\text{VerbSpecific}}$)
¬BE(a stream$_{\text{Result}}$)
DO(The water$_{\text{Agent}}$)
BE(a stream$_{\text{Result}}$)
HAS_STATE(?$_{\text{Material}}$, V_Final_State$_{\text{VerbSpecific}}$)

Extracting a CREATE entity state:

In this case, based on the predicateType 'Be' along with a 'Result' argument type, we can conclude that the value 'a stream' is the *created* entity. This is then fed into spaCy to extract the head noun 'stream' as the entity.

Figure 2: VerbNet semantic predicate output of VNSP on the input sentence above, and how it is used to predict a CREATE type change of state for the entity 'stream'

2 Related Work

Our method is similar to Clark et al. (2018) in the sense that we both rely on VerbNet semantic representations to make inferences. However, our point of departure is that previously, VerbNet did not have a neural semantic parser, and Clark et al. (2018) did not disambiguate verb senses, and used the most frequently used verb sense instead. Also, they had to develop a huge rulebase to encode commonsense knowledge about the states that events produce, using a STRIPS-style list of before (preconditions) and after (effects) expressed as possibly negated literals. In order to extract arguments (i.e. event participants), they relied on the syntactic patterns provided in the VerbNet, and used them to instantiate the arguments in the before/after literals. They also performed a manual annotation effort to check and correct the rulebase entries, and added entries for other verbs that affect existence and location. In addition, they added new entries for verbs not existing in VerbNet. In contrast, our method is fully automatic (see section 3.2).

Most work on tracking entity states uses neural methods (Henaff et al. 2016, Ji et al. 2017, Tandon et al. 2018, Tang et al. 2020). However, these models rely on large amounts of annotated data, which is expensive and labor-intensive to provide (Sun et al., 2020). One of the commonly used solutions to the data scarcity problem in NLP tasks is data augmentation. According to Feng et al. (2021), the goal of data augmentation is increasing training data diversity without directly collecting more data. Most strategies for data augmentation consist of creating synthetic data based on the main data. On the same note, automatic training data generation attempts show promise in various NLP tasks, such as event extraction (Chen et al. 2017, Zeng et al. 2018), and named entity recognition (Tchoua et al., 2019).

As explained below, Lexis uses a state-of-the-art semantic parser to automatically generate entity states for each sentence. These entity states are the same as the entity state labels provided by human annotators in the dataset on which we evaluate Lexis. The generated inferences can be used, in future work, to augment the existing training data.

3 Data and Methodology

The main contribution of this work is bringing to the forefront the advantages of using lexical resource based methods. In particular, in this work, these methods are used for automatic annotation of text with labels regarding the location and existence states of entities in a given sentence.

3.1 Data

The ProPara (Process Paragraphs) dataset (Dalvi et al., 2018), developed by the Allen Institute for AI (AI2), contains 183 prompts (with 152 topics) and 488 human authored paragraphs of procedural text in response to these prompts (each paragraph having 10 or less sentences), along with 81k annotations about the changing states (existence and location) of entities in those paragraphs. The training set contains 391 paragraphs (80% of the data). The end-task of the dataset is predicting and tracking location and existence changes for the entities. ProPara is the first dataset of annotated, natural text for real-world processes, which also contains a simple representation of entity states during those processes.

3.2 Methodology

We used the recently developed BERT-based VerbNet semantic parser (Gung 2020, Gung and Palmer 2021), which is located at the GitHub SemParse site [1], to parse every single sentence in each paragraph. The VerbNet semantic parser (VNSP) returns a json file containing the verb sense disambiguated VerbNet class, the complete logical predicates for that class instantiated with arguments extracted from the sentence, as well as the text spans (phrases) labeled with both VerbNet thematic roles (Schuler, 2005) (if applicable) and PropBank argument role labels (Kingsbury and Palmer 2002, Palmer et al. 2005).

The main idea of using VNSP, and in general what gives VNSP an edge over other semantic parsers, is the logical predicates it generates (for a list of some of the VerbNet predicates used in this work, see Table 1). These predicates are utilized here to infer/predict an entity's change of location and change of existence state (i.e. whether it has been created or destroyed during the course of the sentence). Some of these predicates uncover implicit information about entity states, so our method covers explicit and implicit information, as long as the information is implicit in the semantics of the verb, rather than requiring world knowledge. Figure 2 illustrates the utility of the semantic predicate part of the VNSP output and how it is used to predict that the entity 'stream' is CREATED in the input sentence 'The water forms a stream'. The VNSP output is close to our desired form, but does not match exactly. Certain inferences first need to be drawn, and we have implemented blocks of Python code for this purpose. Figure x gives the block of Python code for 'Results' that extracts "a stream" as the created entity. VNSP also gives us syntactic phrases, and we still have to extract head nouns and objects of prepositions, etc, to get specific entities, as well as before-after states. We use spaCy (Honnibal et al., 2020) to do this.

We represent the inferred entity states as a triple for change of location cases (entity, AtLoc, location), and a tuple for change of existence cases (entity, Created) or (entity, Destroyed). These generated states can, in future work, be used for data augmentation, to improve the performance of machine learning models on this task.

[1]https://github.com/jgung/verbnet-parser

Location	Existence
Has Location	Appear
Take In	Becomes
Admit	Create Image
Apply Material	Degradation Material Integrity
Contain	Destroyed
Free	Develop
Contact	Emit

Table 1: Some of the VerbNet predicates used in our method to infer state changes.

Sentence:
The roots absorb water and minerals from the soil.

VNSP VerbNet semantic predicates output:
[{'polarity': True, 'predicateType': 'Take In', 'args': [{'type': 'Goal', 'value': ''}, {'type': 'Theme', 'value': 'water and minerals'}]}]

VNSP PropBank parse output:
[{'text': 'The roots', 'pb': 'A0'},
{'text': 'absorb', 'pb': 'V'},
{'text': 'water and minerals',
'pb': 'A1'}, {'text': 'from the soil', 'pb': 'A2'}}]

Extracting a MOVE entity state:
In this case, based on the predicateType 'Take In' along with a 'Theme' and a 'Goal' argument type, we can conclude that the value 'water and minerals' is an entity that moves to the value for 'Goal'. However, the value for 'Goal' has remained uninstantiated, so we resort to the PropBank parse. Knowing that the 'Goal' argument for the 'Take In' predicate is the same as A0 numbered argument, we extract 'The roots' as the destination for the extracted entity. This is then fed into spaCy to extract 'water' and 'minerals' as two entities, both moving to the destination 'root'. A separate block of Python code draws Take In inferences

Figure 3: VerbNet semantic predicate and PropBank output of VNSP on the input sentence above, and how it is used to predict a MOVE type change of state for the entities 'water' and 'minerals'

This completes the process used for Setting 1 in Section 4.1. In the second setting for our experiments, 4.2, we added information from the PropBank argument roles generated by VNSP to cover cases where there are uninstantiated arguments in the VerbNet semantic parse that PropBank can supply. This should, in theory, increase recall, but may decrease precision, because VerbNet thematic roles are more fine grained compared to PropBank, and are therefore more accurate in predicting semantic roles. Figure 3 illustrates the utility of the PropBank parse part of the VNSP output and how it is used to predict that the entity 'water' and the entity 'minerals' is MOVED to 'root' in the input sentence 'The roots absorb water and minerals from the soil'. This example illustrates a case in which the VerbNet semantic predicate generated by the VNSP fails to generate a value for the 'Goal' argument, while looking at the PropBank A0 argument supplies us with it. It also illustrates another example of lexically encoded implicit semantic information, since for the *Take In* predicate that is provided in the VNSP output, the 'Goal' argument is the same as 'Agent' argument. For that reason, we can confidently extract the value for A0 from the PropBank parse as the value for the Goal, and therefore the destination of the MOVE event.

In addition, we have also introduced a relaxed setting in which the predicted false positive labels are evaluated by a human judge to be true false positives or correctly predicted labels that are missed in the gold labels in ProPara.

4 Experiments

The text spans that represent arguments are either noun phrases (for entities, e.g. *sediment from the ocean* in the sentence *The waves contain sediment from the ocean.*) or prepositional phrases (for location state tracking, e.g. *in sediment* in the sentence *They are buried in sediment.*). A human annotator labels *sediment* as the destination of *they*, but the parser labels the whole phrase *in sediment* as the destination. On the other hand, there are cases of conjunction, where several entities are conjoined and one predicate is stated about them. In that case, we should be able to separate the conjoined entities and generate a triple or tuple for each. For example, in the sentence *Algae and plankton die*, two change of existence tuples should be generated: (algae, Destroyed), and (plankton, Destroyed).

Such syntactic problems were solved using the spaCy (Honnibal et al., 2020) dependency parser. Nouns were lemmatized, the nominal heads of the noun phrases in prepositional phrases were extracted, the conjoined noun phrases were disjoined.

4.1 Setting 1

In setting 1, we only relied on the predicates from the VerbNet semantic representations part of the output of the VNSP. Given the definition of each predicate and the types of arguments it can take across the VerbNet, we categorized the predicates into those indicating a change of location and those indicating a change of existence (in particular, creation and destruction). We also used the VerbNet thematic role hierarchy to collect all thematic roles that could point to an event participant (e.g. Agent, Co-Agent, Pivot, Patient, etc.), a location (e.g. Destination, Location, Goal, Source, etc.), an Undergoer (e.g. Patient, Theme, Pivot, etc.), as well as those particularly indicating a Destination-type location and a Source-type location. For example, in the sentence *Water from oceans, lakes, swamps, rivers, and plants turns into water vapor.*, the semantic predicate output of the VNSP is summarized (by our algorithm) into the following:

```
[(True, 'Has State', [('Patient', 'Water from oceans , lakes , swamps , rivers , and plants'), ('Initial State', '')]),
(True, 'Has State', [('Patient', 'Water from oceans , lakes , swamps , rivers , and plants'), ('Result', 'into water vapor')])]
```

From this logical statement, since the final sub-predicate is a 'Has State' predicate and it has a 'Result' argument, our algorithm extracts the value for the 'Result', i.e. into water vapor, as the entity created.

Another example of the semantic predicate output that explains the inference in Figure 1 follows:

```
[ (True, 'Has Location', [('Theme', 'the urea and carbon dioxide'), ('Initial Location', '')]), (True, 'Has Location', [('Agent', 'The blood'), ('Initial Location', '')]), (True, 'Do', [('Agent', 'The blood')]), (True, 'Motion', [('Theme', 'the urea and carbon dioxide'), ('Verbspecific', 'Trajectory')]), (True, 'Motion', [('Agent', 'The blood'), ('Verbspecific', 'Trajectory')]), (True, 'Has Location', [('Theme', 'the urea and carbon dioxide'), ('Destination', 'to the kidneys')]), (True, 'Has Location', [('Agent', 'The blood'), ('Destination', 'to the kidneys')])]
```

The last two lines show that both the Theme (the urea and carbon dioxide) and the Agent (The blood) will end up in the Destination (to the kidneys), uncovering the implicit information in the semantics of the verb carry.

Some predicates required special handling. For example, the *Take In* predicate (representing verbs such as inject, drink, eat, smoke) is fairly opaque, and does not explicitly indicate a change of location in VerbNet. However, we know that as a result of

Block of Python Code:

```
elif 'Take In' in preds:
    for p in predlist:
        if p['predicateType'] == 'Location' and p['polarity']:
            for a in p['args']:
                if a['type'] == 'Theme' and a['value']:
                    sp = SpacyObject(a['value'])
                    motion_dict['entity'] = sp.treatNP()
                    motion_dict['before'] = []
                elif a['type'] in all_srl('goal') or \
                a['type'] in all_srl('agent') and a['value']:
                    sp = SpacyObject(a['value'])
                    motion_dict['after'] = sp.PP2NP()
```

Figure 4: Python code for extracting a MOVED entity, along with its location states, from the VerbNet semantic predicate `Take In`.

Pseudo Code:

If `Take In` is in the list of generated VNSP semantic predicates for this sentence:
    loop over the generated predicates
        If there is a `Take In` predicate with positive polarity:
            loop over the arguments of that predicate:
                If the type of an argument is `Theme`:
                    extract the head noun of the value as an entity which has MOVED.
                If the type of an argument is `Goal` or `Agent`:
                    extract the noun head of the prepositional object as the *after* state.

this type of event, an undergoer (such as a Theme) would move to the Goal, Agent, or Recipient of the event, whichever is specified in the predicates. The block of Python code for Take In (Figure 4) includes an explicit expansion of Take In to indicate the Goal is now At The Agent. Such semantic expansions needed to be assumed in the semantics of such predicates in the entity extraction algorithm, as VerbNet fails to do its normal expansion of the predicates. These expansions will be added to the next VerbNet release.

4.2 Setting 2

In setting 2, we used the PropBank argument roles included in the VNSP output in addition to the VerbNet predicates. This covered cases of verbs that exist in VerbNet, but VNSP fails to instantiate the entity or location. This is most likely due to the small size of the VerbNet labeled training data compared to PropBank labeled training data. For example, in the sentence *The stream becomes a river.* from the training data, here is the output of the VNSP:

```
[(False, 'Has State', [('Patient', 'The stream'), ('Result', '')]),
(True, 'Has State', [('Patient', 'The stream'), ('Result', '')])]
```

Here, the value for the 'Result' semantic role has remained uninstantiated, which means that setting 1 yields no output (i.e. does not extract 'river' as a created entity). Therefore, we look at the A2 argument in the PropBank parse output of the VNSP, summarized below:

```
['text': 'The stream', 'pb': 'A1', 'vn': 'Patient',
'text': 'becomes', 'pb': 'V', 'vn': 'Verb',
'text': 'a river', 'pb': 'A2', 'vn': '']
```

Linguistically, the A2 argument for this verb is described as 'new state', which is exactly what we need. Since the numbered arguments in PropBank are too coarse-grained, we use SemLink (Palmer 2009, Bonial et al. 2013, Stowe et al. 2021) to find their mapping into VerbNet thematic roles and find those that suit our purposes in this task.

In general, we assumed that A1 (proto-patient, which is typically the undergoer) is the entity moved or created. This assumption should be accurate in theory at least for verbs indicating creation or motion, because an entity in motion is theoretically a "theme", and an entity created could be a "result", a "product", or "theme", which are all labeled A1 in PropBank. However, there are also change of state verbs such as become, for which the 'Result' (new state) is not the entity undergoing change or created, so it is marked as A2 rather than

A1. It should also be noted that since the PropBank numbered arguments A2 and above are very coarse-grained and overloaded. That is the reason we consult SemLink to find the correct mapping.

4.3 Relaxed Setting

Since Lexis generates more states than gold standard annotations in ProPara. For example, for the sentence 'Magma rises from deep in the earth.' in the training data, no motion has been predicted for *magma*, while as a human judge, we know that magma moves in this sentence. Lexis predicts this movement of magma in this sentence, and this is counted as a false positive in evaluation, reducing the precision and F1 score. Therefore, we examined a third setting in which we do not count the extra annotations as false positives, if they are correct. Knowledge of whether these extra predicted entities are correct or wrong requires human judgment.

For that matter, we set up a judgment task on the system output (i.e. the predicted created/destroyed/moved entities) on the test data, and asked two unbiased human annotators to make judgments. The results were then examined by the authors to identify the sources of false negatives. These will be discussed in section 6.2, and illustrated in Table 6.

5 Results

Tables 2, 3, and 4 illustrate the evaluation results. In addition to the cumulative/general state tracking results, we have evaluated location tracking and existence tracking separately in order to monitor the sources of error. We have also provided the results for the relaxed setting in Table 4 (see 4.3).

As expected, the inclusion of PropBank argument roles (in setting 2) increases recall from 0.29 (Table 2) to 0.39 (Table 3). Interestingly, this is achieved through existence tracking, not location tracking. Within location tracking, not much change is observed between the two settings, as discussed in section 6.2.

While performing the human judgment task for the relaxed setting, we also came across cases of gold label errors (see 'GLE' in Table 6), as well as useless gold labels in location tracking, labeling the location of an entity as *unk* (i.e. unknown). Both the GLE and superfluous labels were considered unlabeled in the gold data for evaluation purposes. Therefore, the results in the top section of Table 4 are different from the results in setting 2 (VerbNet + PropBank, see Table 3), because here we removed the gold label errors. These will be discussed further in section 6. Within Table 4, it is notable that the precision significantly increases (by 20%) in the relaxed setting (compared to the strict setting in the same table).

Within the Allen AI leaderboard for the ProPara task (see Table 5), our general recall in setting 2 (VerbNet + PropBank) beats Facebook AI Research EntNet, University of Washington QRN, and AI2 ProLocal. The recall increases from 0.39 to 0.48 in the relaxed setting (Table 4). There are 6 teams that have a higher recall, and Lexis Relaxed would stand on the 7th place with respect to recall. For the general F1 score, too, Lexis Relaxed would take the 7th place on the leaderboard.

6 Discussion

6.1 Advantages

First and foremost, it should be noted that in this work, we have relied solely on a lexical resource, and no task-specific learning-based methods have been utilized. Also, our method generates more entity states than human annotators generated. That increases our system's false positives, which in turn decreases the precision and F1 scores. For this reason, we decided to create a relaxed setting (cf. section 4.3) and judge which one of the false positives are true false positives and which ones are correct labels which are missing from the train set. In the judgment task to find true false positives, out of 235 false positives (in 42% of the train set), 129 were in fact judged as correct labels missed in the gold data. Therefore, the count of false positives in the relaxed settings was reduced from 235 to 106 (i.e. 45% of the false positives were not true false positives).

Another advantage of Lexis is that it predicts states for all possible entities in a sentence, and is not limited to the set of entities labeled in ProPara. However, for evaluation purposes, we only compared our results against the gold labeled entities.

What makes our method valuable is the fact that, unlike learning models which need annotated data, Lexis does not require training. As such, this method can be used for automatic generation of entity states, potentially with higher recall than human annotation. In addition, this is not limited to the ProPara dataset, or even procedural texts. Since VerbNet is a general semantic lexicon for

	Precision	Recall	F1 Score
Lexis			
General	0.38	0.29	0.33
Location	0.41	0.21	0.28
Existence	0.85	0.40	0.55

Table 2: Evaluation Results for Setting 1 - using only VerbNet semantic predicates and semantic representations provided in the VNSP output.

	Precision	Recall	F1 Score
Lexis			
General	0.36	0.39	0.38
Location	0.41	0.22	0.29
Existence	0.64	0.65	0.64

Table 3: Evaluation Results for Setting 2 - using the VerbNet predicates, and utilizing PropBank argument roles (numbered arguments) when an argument is uninstantiated in the semantic representations. Both the VerbNet semantic representations and PropBank argument labels are provided by the VNSP.

	Precision	Recall	F1 Score
Lexis (Gold Label Errors Removed)			
General	0.44	0.48	0.46
Location	0.54	0.44	0.49
Existence	0.37	0.53	0.44
Lexis (Relaxed: True False Positives Filtered)			
General	0.64	0.48	0.55
Location	0.79	0.44	0.57
Existence	0.53	0.53	0.53

Table 4: Evaluation Results for the Relaxed Setting. At the top, we have the predicted labels from Table 3, except that we have removed the gold label errors. At the bottom, in addition to removing gold label errors, we have also filtered the false positives and kept only the true false positives (not counting the correct labels that are only missing from the gold data).

English verbs, the VNSP output can be utilized to predict entity states in any domain. However, we should also acknowledge the sources of error and weaknesses of this method, which are discussed in section 6.2 below.

6.2 Error Analysis

In this section, we discuss and analyze the sources of error and weakness of our method and results, illuminating the limitations.

The first noticeable source of weakness is the limited coverage of the VerbNet lexicon itself. There are currently 4588 unique verbs in VerbNet. For the verbs that are absent from the VerbNet, the VNSP output is empty. Out of 2639 sentences in the train set, 158 remained unparsed (6%). This increases false negative counts and therefore decreases our recall and F1 score.

Another source of weakness of VNSP, and therefore our method, is the relatively small size of VerbNet-labeled data for training the VNSP. This is in comparison to the size of the PropBank-labeled data.

One of the most important sources of error was use of world knowledge in the gold standard human annotation in addition to the explicit linguistic knowledge – something that is beyond the scope of VerbNet. For a complete picture of the false negative underlying reasons, see Table 6. An illustrative example follows. Given the paragraph

> *Get some seeds. Pick a spot to plant them. Dig a hole in the dirt. Put the seed in the hole. Pour some water on the seed and hold.* ***Cover up the hole.*** *Press down on it. Spray some plant food on it.*

The annotator has annotated the highlighted step with a 'Move' state change of the 'seed' entity to 'dirt'. This knowledge requires recovering of information from step 4 to know that the seed is in the hole, from step 3 to know that the hole is dug in the dirt, and from world knowledge to know that covering up the seed in the hole which is in the dirt normally happens with the dirt that has been dug. Another example of the same type is in the paragraph below.

> *Water from the surface seeps below the soil. The water comes into contact with the rock below.* ***The water over the years carves through the rock.*** *The space in the rock becomes larger and forms into a cave. As more rather rushes through the cave becomes a cavern.*

One of the annotations is that in the highlighted sentence, the entity 'space' has been 'Created', whereas, space is not even mentioned in this sentence (or before that). The annotator infers, from the following sentence, that a space must have been created at this point. These types of inference require real world knowledge that goes way beyond lexical semantics.

Finally, true entity state tracking requires entity-reference tracking in a given paragraph. For this, we need to go beyond sentence-level semantic analysis (i.e. what we have achieved in this work) and

ProPara Leaderboard			
	Precision	**Recall**	**F1 Score**
KOALA	0.777	0.644	0.704
TSLM	0.684	0.689	0.686
DynaPro	0.752	0.579	0.655
NCET	0.671	0.585	0.625
KG-MRC	0.693	0.493	0.576
LACE	0.753	0.454	0.566
Lexis Relaxed	0.64	0.48	0.55
ProStruct	0.743	0.430	0.545
AQA	0.620	0.451	0.523
ProGlobal	0.488	0.617	0.519
ProLocal	0.817	0.368	0.507
QRN	0.609	0.311	0.411
EntNet	0.547	0.307	0.394
Lexis (VN+PB)	0.36	0.39	0.38
Lexis (VN)	0.38	0.29	0.33

Table 5: ProPara Leaderboard and where different settings of Lexis would be placed.

analyze the whole paragraph as one unit of discourse. This is mandatory to uncover anaphora (or even cataphora) cases in the text, which is required to track the state of entities in a paragraph. For example, in the sentence *"Spray some plant food on it."*, our system predicts that the location of 'plant food' at the end of this sentence will be 'it', without finding the reference to 'seed'. State-of-the-art reference resolution is clearly indicated to improve results.

7 Conclusion and Future Work

The goal of this work was demonstrating how lexical resource-based methods using existing NLP resources could be utilized in automatic annotation of text for tracking entity states. The results were quite encouraging and demonstrated the potential of leveraging pre-existing rich lexical resources for challenging inference tasks. The limitations of our approach were examined, including VerbNet's lack of coverage compared to PropBank, another semantic role labeling lexical resource. We also found certain VerbNet predicates that were particularly opaque and benefited from expansion. In addition, and as expected, using the VerbNet semantic parser does not always yield a 100% accurate parse, resulting in downstream errors. In addition, there is a clear need for document-level entity state tracking, which requires automatic reference resolution.

Given the limitations of the VerbNet semantic parser discussed in section 6.2, we can expect to increase the recall by backing-off to a PropBank semantic parser (e.g. Li et al. 2020), that has been trained on much larger training data. This is the next step we plan to undertake. However, it is important to note that the reason we chose VNSP for this task is that it is the only semantic parser that generates the rich semantic representations in the predicate logic format that we employed in our method. Therefore, another possibility that looks more promising (but is a much longer-term solution) is continuing to update the VerbNet lexical resource based on the error analysis introduced in this work, annotating new data to cover examples from these updates, and re-training the VerbNet semantic parser.

Another area for planned future work is to use the generated entity states to augment the ProPara data and feed it into a machine learning model to assess performance improvement. Finally, as proposed in section 6.2, we will be adding a state-of-the-art reference resolution system to achieve document-level entity state tracking. All of these additions will be evaluated and reported on.

False Negative Type	**Frequency**
RT	34
WK	30
GLE	22
REF	7
UP	3
ONT	2
Other	100
Total	198

Table 6: Underlying reasons for predicted labels judged as false negative. **RT** (*Reverse Tracing*): the annotator has assumed the existence or motion of an entity in a prior state for it to have an effect later. **WK** (*World Knowledge*): the annotator has used world knowledge to generate this label. **GLE** (*Gold Label Error*): This was judged as erroneous – something that is not true even given the world knowledge or reverse tracing. In the judgment task, this was considered an empty gold label. **REF** (*Reference Resolution*): the gold label is achievable given a reliable reference resolution system. **UP**: (*Unparsed*): state extraction failure due to parsing failure. **ONT** (*Ontology*): the gold label is achievable given a reliable entity ontology. **Other**: failure in predicting the state due to none of the above reasons.

Acknowledgements

We thank the reviewers for their helpful feedback. We gratefully acknowledge the support of NSF under grants #1801446 (SATC) and #1822877 (Cyberlearning), and of DARPA CwC (subcontracts from UIUC and SIFT), DARPA AIDA Award FA8750-18-2-0016 (RAMFIS), DARPA KAIROS FA8750-19-2-1004-A20-0047-S005 (RESIN, sub to RPI, PI: Heng Ji), as well as DTRA HDTRA1-16-1-0002/Project 1553695 (eTASC - Empirical Evidence for a Theoretical Approach to Semantic Components). Any opinions, findings, and conclusions or recommendations expressed in this material are those of the authors and do not necessarily reflect the views of any government agency.

References

Claire Bonial, Kevin Stowe, and Martha Palmer. 2013. Renewing and revising semlink. In *Proceedings of the 2nd Workshop on Linked Data in Linguistics (LDL-2013): Representing and linking lexicons, terminologies and other language data*, pages 9–17.

Yubo Chen, Shulin Liu, Xiang Zhang, Kang Liu, and Jun Zhao. 2017. Automatically labeled data generation for large scale event extraction. In *Proceedings of the 55th Annual Meeting of the Association for Computational Linguistics (Volume 1: Long Papers)*, pages 409–419.

Peter Clark, Bhavana Dalvi, and Niket Tandon. 2018. What happened? leveraging verbnet to predict the effects of actions in procedural text. *arXiv preprint arXiv:1804.05435*.

Bhavana Dalvi, Lifu Huang, Niket Tandon, Wen-tau Yih, and Peter Clark. 2018. Tracking state changes in procedural text: a challenge dataset and models for process paragraph comprehension. In *Proceedings of the 2018 Conference of the North American Chapter of the Association for Computational Linguistics: Human Language Technologies, Volume 1 (Long Papers)*, pages 1595–1604.

Xinya Du, Bhavana Dalvi, Niket Tandon, Antoine Bosselut, Wen-tau Yih, Peter Clark, and Claire Cardie. 2019. Be consistent! improving procedural text comprehension using label consistency. In *Proceedings of the 2019 Conference of the North American Chapter of the Association for Computational Linguistics: Human Language Technologies, Volume 1 (Long and Short Papers)*, pages 2347–2356.

Steven Y Feng, Varun Gangal, Jason Wei, Sarath Chandar, Soroush Vosoughi, Teruko Mitamura, and Eduard Hovy. 2021. A survey of data augmentation approaches for nlp. *arXiv preprint arXiv:2105.03075*.

James Gung. 2020. *Abstraction, Sense Distinctions and Syntax in Neural Semantic Role Labeling*. Ph.D. thesis, University of Colorado at Boulder.

James Gung and Martha Palmer. 2021. Predicate representations and polysemy in verbnet semantic parsing. In *Proceedings of the 14th International Conference on Computational Semantics (IWCS)*, pages 51–62, Groningen, The Netherlands (online). Association for Computational Linguistics.

Aditya Gupta and Greg Durrett. 2019. Tracking discrete and continuous entity state for process understanding. In *Proceedings of the Third Workshop on Structured Prediction for NLP*, pages 7–12.

Mikael Henaff, Jason Weston, Arthur Szlam, Antoine Bordes, and Yann LeCun. 2016. Tracking the world state with recurrent entity networks. *arXiv preprint arXiv:1612.03969*.

Matthew Honnibal, Ines Montani, Sofie Van Landeghem, and Adriane Boyd. 2020. spaCy: Industrial-strength Natural Language Processing in Python.

Yangfeng Ji, Chenhao Tan, Sebastian Martschat, Yejin Choi, and Noah A Smith. 2017. Dynamic entity representations in neural language models. In *Proceedings of the 2017 Conference on Empirical Methods in Natural Language Processing*, pages 1830–1839.

Paul R Kingsbury and Martha Palmer. 2002. From treebank to propbank. In *LREC*, pages 1989–1993. Citeseer.

Tao Li, Parth Anand Jawale, Martha Palmer, and Vivek Srikumar. 2020. Structured tuning for semantic role labeling. In *Proceedings of the 58th Annual Meeting of the Association for Computational Linguistics*, pages 8402–8412, Online. Association for Computational Linguistics.

Martha Palmer. 2009. Semlink: Linking propbank, verbnet and framenet. In *Proceedings of the generative lexicon conference*, pages 9–15. GenLex-09, Pisa, Italy.

Martha Palmer, Daniel Gildea, and Paul Kingsbury. 2005. The proposition bank: An annotated corpus of semantic roles. *Computational linguistics*, 31(1):71–106.

Karin Kipper Schuler. 2005. *VerbNet: A broad-coverage, comprehensive verb lexicon*. University of Pennsylvania.

Kevin Stowe, Jenette Preciado, Kathryn Conger, Susan Windisch Brown, Ghazaleh Kazeminejad, and Martha Palmer. 2021. Semlink 2.0: Chasing lexical resources. In *30th Annual Meeting of the Association for Computational Linguistics*, pages 222–227, Gronigen, Netherlands. Association for Computational Linguistics.

Lichao Sun, Congying Xia, Wenpeng Yin, Tingting Liang, Philip Yu, and Lifang He. 2020. Mixup-transformer: Dynamic data augmentation for NLP tasks. In *Proceedings of the 28th International Conference on Computational Linguistics*, pages 3436–3440, Barcelona, Spain (Online). International Committee on Computational Linguistics.

Niket Tandon, Bhavana Dalvi, Joel Grus, Wen-tau Yih, Antoine Bosselut, and Peter Clark. 2018. Reasoning about actions and state changes by injecting commonsense knowledge. In *Proceedings of the 2018 Conference on Empirical Methods in Natural Language Processing*, pages 57–66.

Niket Tandon, Keisuke Sakaguchi, Bhavana Dalvi Mishra, Dheeraj Rajagopal, Peter Clark, Michal Guerquin, Kyle Richardson, and Eduard Hovy. 2020. A dataset for tracking entities in open domain procedural text. *arXiv preprint arXiv:2011.08092*.

Jizhi Tang, Yansong Feng, and Dongyan Zhao. 2020. Understanding procedural text using interactive entity networks. In *Proceedings of the 2020 Conference on Empirical Methods in Natural Language Processing (EMNLP)*, pages 7281–7290, Online. Association for Computational Linguistics.

Roselyne B Tchoua, Aswathy Ajith, Zhi Hong, Logan T Ward, Kyle Chard, Alexander Belikov, Debra J Audus, Shrayesh Patel, Juan J de Pablo, and Ian T Foster. 2019. Creating training data for scientific named entity recognition with minimal human effort. In *International Conference on Computational Science*, pages 398–411. Springer.

Ying Zeng, Yansong Feng, Rong Ma, Zheng Wang, Rui Yan, Chongde Shi, and Dongyan Zhao. 2018. Scale up event extraction learning via automatic training data generation. In *Thirty-Second AAAI Conference on Artificial Intelligence*.

On Releasing Annotator-Level Labels and Information in Datasets

Vinodkumar Prabhakaran[*]
Google Research
vinodkpg@google.com

Aida Mostafazadeh Davani[*†]
University of Southern California
mostafaz@usc.edu

Mark Díaz
Google Research
markdiaz@google.com

Abstract

A common practice in building NLP datasets, especially using crowd-sourced annotations, involves obtaining multiple annotator judgements on the same data instances, which are then flattened to produce a single "ground truth" label or score, through majority voting, averaging, or adjudication. While these approaches may be appropriate in certain annotation tasks, such aggregations overlook the socially constructed nature of human perceptions that annotations for relatively more subjective tasks are meant to capture. In particular, systematic disagreements between annotators owing to their socio-cultural backgrounds and/or lived experiences are often obfuscated through such aggregations. In this paper, we empirically demonstrate that label aggregation may introduce representational biases of individual and group perspectives. Based on this finding, we propose a set of recommendations for increased utility and transparency of datasets for downstream use cases.

1 Introduction

Obtaining multiple annotator judgements on the same data instances is a common practice in NLP in order to improve the quality of final labels (Snow et al., 2008; Nowak and Rüger, 2010). Cases of disagreement between annotations are often resolved through majority voting, averaging, or adjudication in order to derive a single "ground truth", often with the aim of training supervised machine learning models. However, in relatively subjective tasks such as sentiment analysis or offensiveness detection, there often exists no single "right" answer (Alm, 2011). Enforcing such a single ground truth in such tasks will sacrifice valuable nuances about the task that are embedded in annotators' assessments of the stimuli, especially their disagreements (Aroyo and Welty, 2013).

Annotators' socio-demographic factors, moral values, and lived experiences often influence their interpretations of language, especially in subjective tasks such as identifying political stances (Luo et al., 2020), sentiment (Díaz et al., 2018), and online abuse (Waseem, 2016; Patton et al., 2019). For instance, feminist and anti-racist activists systematically disagree with crowd workers in their hate speech annotations (Waseem, 2016). Similarly, annotators' political affiliation is shown to correlate with how they annotate the neutrality of political stances (Luo et al., 2020). A potential adverse effect of majority voting in such cases is that it may sideline minority perspectives in data.

In this paper, we analyze annotated data for eight different tasks across three different datasets to study the impact of majority voting as an aggregation approach. We answer two questions:

- **Q1**: Does aggregated data uniformly capture all annotators' perspectives, when available?
- **Q2**: Does aggregated data reflect certain socio-demographic groups' perspectives more so than others?

Our analysis demonstrates that in the annotations for many tasks, the aggregated majority vote does not uniformly reflect the perspectives of all annotators in the annotator pool. For many tasks in our analysis, a significant proportion of the annotators had very low agreement scores (0 to 0.4) with the majority vote label. While certain individual annotator's labels may have low agreement with the majority label due to valid/expected reasons (e.g., if they produced noisy labels), we further show that these agreement scores may vary significantly across different socio-demographic groups that annotators identify with. This finding has important fairness implications, as it demonstrates how the aggregation step can sometimes cause the final dataset to under-represent certain groups' perspectives.

[*]Authors contributed equally
[†]Work done while at Google Research

Proceedings of the Joint 15th Linguistic Annotation Workshop (LAW) and 3rd Designing Meaning Representations (DMR) Workshop, pages 133–138
November, 2021.

Meaningfully addressing such issues in multiply-annotated datasets requires understanding and accounting for systematic disagreements between annotators. However, most annotated datasets often only release the aggregated labels, without any annotator-level information. We argue that dataset developers should consider including annotator-level labels as well as annotators' socio-demographic information (when viable to do so responsibly) when releasing datasets, especially those capturing relatively subjective tasks. Inclusion of this information will enable more research on how to account for systematic disagreements between annotators in training tasks.

2 Background

NLP has a long history of developing techniques to interpret subjective language (Wiebe et al., 2004; Alm, 2011). While all human judgments embed some degree of subjectivity, some tasks such as sentiment analysis (Liu et al., 2010), affect modeling (Alm, 2008; Liu et al., 2003), emotion detection (Hirschberg et al., 2003), and hate speech detection (Warner and Hirschberg, 2012) are agreed upon as relatively more subjective in nature. As Alm (2011) points out, achieving a single *real 'ground truth'* is not possible, nor essential in case of such subjective tasks. Instead, we should investigate how to model the subjective interpretations of the annotators, and how to account for them in application scenarios.

However, the current practice in the NLP community continues to be applying different aggregation strategies to arrive at a single score or label that makes it amenable to train and evaluate supervised machine learning models. Oftentimes, datasets are released with only the final scores/labels, essentially obfuscating important nuances in the task. The information released about the annotations can be at one of the following four levels of information-richness.

Firstly, the most common approach is one in which multiple annotations obtained for a data instance are aggregated to derive a single "ground truth" label, and these labels are the only annotations included in the released dataset (e.g., Founta et al. (2018)). The aggregation strategy most commonly used, especially in large datasets, is *majority voting*, although smaller datasets sometimes use *adjudication* by an 'expert' (often one of the study authors themselves) to arrive at a single label (e.g., in Waseem and Hovy (2016)) when there are substantial disagreements between annotators. These aggregation approaches rely on the assumption that there always exist a single correct label, and that either the majority label or the 'expert' label is more likely to be that correct label. What it fails to account for is the fact that in many subjective tasks, e.g., detecting hate speech, the perceptions of individual annotators may be as valuable as an 'expert' perspective.

Secondly, some datasets (e.g., Jigsaw (2018); Davidson et al. (2017)) release the distribution across labels rather than a single aggregated label. In binary classification tasks, this corresponds to the percentage of annotators who chose one of the labels. In multi-class classification, this may be the distribution across labels obtained for an instance. While this provides more information than a single aggregated label does (e.g., identifies the instances with high disagreement), it fails to capture annotator-level systematic differences.

Thirdly, some datasets release annotations made by each individual annotators in an anonymous fashion (e.g., Kennedy et al. (2020); Jigsaw (2019)). Such annotator-level labels allow downstream dataset users to investigate and account for systematic differences between individual annotators' perspectives on the tasks, although they do not contain any information about each annotators' socio-cultural backgrounds. Finally, some recent datasets (e.g., Díaz et al. (2018)) also release such socio-demographic information about the annotators in addition to annotator-level labels. This information may include various identity subgroups the annotators self-identify with (e.g., gender, race, age range, etc.), or survey responses from the annotators that capture their value systems, lived experiences, or expertise, as they relate to the specific task at hand. Such information, while tricky to share responsibly, would help enable analysis around representation of marginalized perspectives in datasets, as we demonstrate in the next section.

3 Impacts of Aggregation

In this section, we investigate how the aggregation of multiple annotations to a single label impact representations of individual and group perspectives in the resulting datasets. We analyze annotations for eight binary classification tasks, across three different datasets: hate-speech (Kennedy et al., 2020), sentiment (Díaz et al., 2018), and emotion (Demszky et al., 2020). Table 1 shows the number of

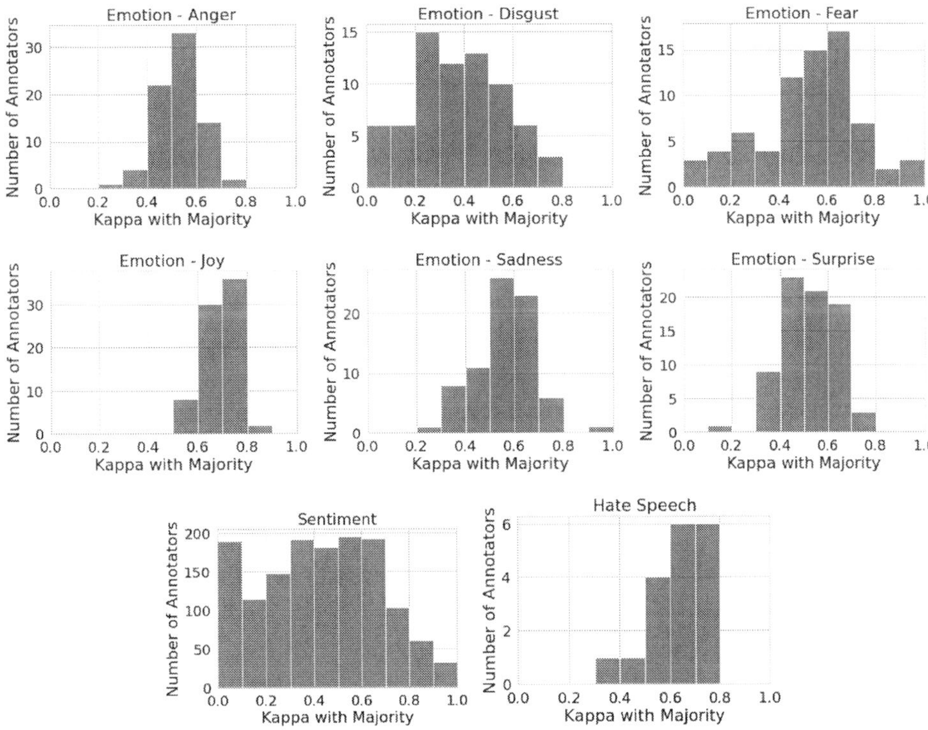

Figure 1: Histograms represent the frequency distribution of annotator agreement with the aggregated label for eight tasks under three datasets for Emotions, Sentiment and Hate Speech datasets. The lack of uniformity in the distributions means that annotator perspectives are not equally captured in the majority labels.

instances, annotators and individual annotations present in the datasets. For hate-speech and emotion datasets, we use the binary label in the raw annotations, whereas for the sentiment dataset, we map the 5-point ordinal labels (-2, -1, 0, +1, +2) in the raw data to a binary distinction denoting whether the text was deemed positive or negative.[1] While the emotion dataset contains annotations for 28 different emotions, in this work, for brevity, we focused on the annotations for only the six standard Ekman emotions (Ekman, 1992) — *anger*, *disgust*, *fear*, *joy*, *sadness*, and *surprise*. In particular, we use the raw annotations for these six emotions, rather than the mapping of all 28 emotions onto these six emotions that Demszky et al. (2020) use in some of their experiments.

3.1 Q1: Do Aggregated Labels Represent Individual Annotators Uniformly?

First, we investigate whether the aggregated labels obtained through majority labels provide a more or less equal representation for all annotator perspectives. For this analysis, we calculate the majority label for each instance as the label that half or more annotators who annotated that instance agreed on. We then measure Cohen's Kappa agreement score for each individual annotator's labels and the majority labels on the subset of instances they annotated. While lower agreement scores between some individual annotators and the majority vote is expected (e.g., if the annotator produced noisy labels, or they misunderstood the task), the assumption is that the majority label captures the perspective of the 'average human annotator' within the annotator pool.

Dataset	#instances	#annotators	#annotations
Hate-speech	27,665	18	86,529
Sentiment	14,071	1,481	59,240
Emotion	58,011	82	211,225

Table 1: Statistics on the three datasets we analyze: Hate-speech (Kennedy et al., 2020), Sentiment (Díaz et al., 2018), and Emotions (Demszky et al., 2020)

Figure 1 represents the histogram of annotators' agreement scores with majority votes for all eight tasks. While the majority vote in some tasks such as *joy* and *sadness* (to some extent) do represent

[1]We do this mapping for the purposes of this analysis, where we are focusing on binary tasks. Ideally, a more nuanced 5-point labeling schema will be more useful.

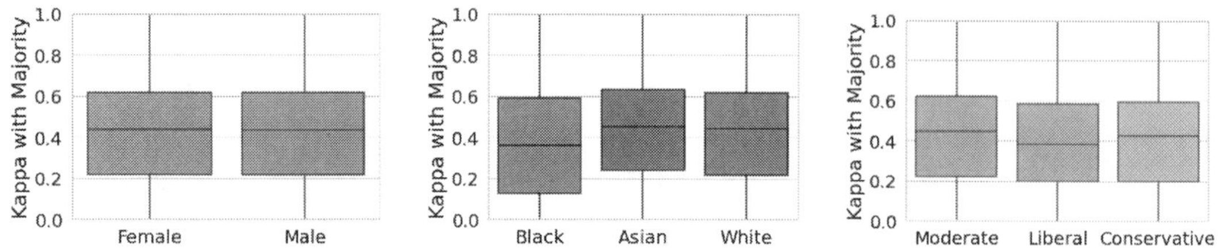

Figure 2: Average and standard deviation of annotator agreement with aggregated labels, calculated for annotators grouped by their socio-demographics under gender, race, and political affiliation.

most of the annotator pool more or less uniformly (i.e., majority vote agrees with most annotators at around the same rate), in most cases, the majority vote under-represents or outright ignores the perspectives of a substantial number of annotators. For instance, majority vote for *disgust* has very low agreement ($\kappa < 0.3$) with almost one-third (27 out of 82) of the annotator pool. Similarly, majority vote for *sentiment* has very low agreement with around one-third (450+) of their annotator pool.

3.2 Q2: Do Aggregated Labels Represent All Social Groups Uniformly?

While the analysis on **Q1** reveals that certain annotator perspectives are more likely to be ignored in the majority vote, it is especially problematic from a fairness perspective, if these differences vary across different social groups. Here, we investigate whether specific socio-demographic groups and their perspectives are unevenly disregarded through annotation aggregation. To this end, we analyze the sentiment analysis dataset (Díaz et al., 2018) since it includes raw annotations as well as annotators' self-identified socio-demographic information. Furthermore, as observed in Figure 1, a large subset of annotators in this dataset are in low agreement with the aggregated labels.

We study three demographic attributes, namely race, gender, and political affiliation and compare the agreement scores between the aggregated labels and the individual annotators' labels within each group. Figure 2 shows the average and standard deviation of annotators' agreement scores with aggregated labels for each demographic group: race (*Asian*, *Black*, and *White*), gender (*Male*, and *Female*), and political affiliation (*Conservative*, *Moderate*, and *Liberal*).[2]

We perform three one-way ANOVA tests to test whether annotators belonging to different demographic groups have significantly different agreement scores with the aggregated labels, on average. The results show significant differences among racial groups ($F(2, 2387)$=3.77, p=0.02); in particular, White annotators show an average agreement of 0.42 (SD=0.26), significantly higher (p=0.03 according to a post-hoc Tukey test) than Black annotators with average of 0.37 (SD=0.27). The difference between average agreement scores across different political groups are not statistically significant, although moderate annotators on average have higher agreement (0.42) compared to conservative and liberal annotators (0.40 and 0.38, respectively). Similarly, annotation agreements of male and female annotators are not significantly different.

4 Utility of Annotator-level Labels

Another argument in favor of retaining annotator-level labels is their utility in modeling disagreement during training and evaluation. Prabhakaran et al. (2012) and Plank et al. (2014) incorporated annotator disagreement in the loss functions used during training to improve predictive performance. Cohn and Specia (2013) and Fornaciari et al. (2021) use a multi-task approach to incorporate annotator disagreements to improve machine translation and part-of-speech tagging performance, respectively. Chou and Lee (2019) and Guan et al. (2018) developed learning architectures that model individual annotators as a way to improved performance. Wich et al. (2020) show the utility of detecting clusters of annotators in hate-speech detection based on how often they agree with each other. Finally, Davani et al. (2021) introduce a multi-annotator architecture that models each annotators' perspectives separately using a multi-task approach. They demonstrate that this architecture helps to model

[2]We removed social groups with fewer than 50 annotators from this analysis for lack of sufficient data points. These include other racial groups such as 'Middle Eastern' with 2 annotators, 'Native Hawaiian or Pacific Islander' with 4 annotators, and non-binary gender identity with one annotator).

uncertainty in predictions, without any significant loss of accuracy or efficiency. This array of recent work further demonstrates the utility of retaining annotator-level information in the datasets for downstream modeling steps.

5 Discussion and Conclusion

Building models to predict or measure subjective phenomena based on human annotations should involve explicit consideration for the unique perspectives each annotator brings forth in their annotations. Annotators are not interchangeable– that is, they draw from their socially-embedded experiences and knowledge when making annotation judgments. As a result, retaining their perspectives separately in the datasets will enable dataset users to account for these differences according to their needs. We demonstrated that annotation aggregation may unfairly disregard perspectives of certain annotators, and sometimes certain socio-demographic groups. Based on our analysis, we propose three recommendations aimed to avoid these issues:

Annotator-level labels: We urge dataset developers to release the annotator-level labels, preferably in an anonymous fashion, and leave open the choice of whether and how to utilize or aggregate these labels for the dataset users.

Socio-demographic information: Sociodemographic identity of the annotators is crucial to ascertain that the datasets (and the models trained on them) equitably represent perspectives of various social groups. We urge dataset developers to include socio-demographic information of annotators, when viable to do so responsibly.

Documentation about recruitment, selection, and assignment of annotators: Finally, we urge dataset developers to document how the annotators were recruited, the criteria used to select them and assign data to them, and any efforts to ensure representational diversity, through transparency artefacts such datasheets (Gebru et al., 2018) or data statements (Bender and Friedman, 2018).

Acknowledgements

We thank Ben Hutchinson for valuable feedback on the manuscript. We also thank the anonymous reviewers for their feedback.

References

Cecilia Ovesdotter Alm. 2011. Subjective natural language problems: Motivations, applications, characterizations, and implications. In *Proceedings of the 49th Annual Meeting of the Association for Computational Linguistics: Human Language Technologies*, pages 107–112.

Ebba Cecilia Ovesdotter Alm. 2008. *Affect in* Text and Speech*. Ph.D. thesis, University of Illinois at Urbana-Champaign.

Lora Aroyo and Chris Welty. 2013. Crowd truth: Harnessing disagreement in crowdsourcing a relation extraction gold standard. *WebSci2013. ACM*, 2013.

Emily M Bender and Batya Friedman. 2018. Data statements for natural language processing: Toward mitigating system bias and enabling better science. *Transactions of the Association for Computational Linguistics*, 6:587–604.

Huang-Cheng Chou and Chi-Chun Lee. 2019. Every rating matters: Joint learning of subjective labels and individual annotators for speech emotion classification. In *ICASSP 2019-2019 IEEE International Conference on Acoustics, Speech and Signal Processing (ICASSP)*, pages 5886–5890. IEEE.

Trevor Cohn and Lucia Specia. 2013. Modelling annotator bias with multi-task gaussian processes: An application to machine translation quality estimation. In *Proceedings of the 51st Annual Meeting of the Association for Computational Linguistics (Volume 1: Long Papers)*, pages 32–42.

Aida Mostafazadeh Davani, Mark Diaz, and Vinodkumar Prabhakaran. 2021. Dealing with disagreements: Looking beyond the majority vote in subjective annotations. *Transactions of the Association for Computational Linguistics*.

Thomas Davidson, Dana Warmsley, Michael Macy, and Ingmar Weber. 2017. Automated hate speech detection and the problem of offensive language. *Proceedings of the International AAAI Conference on Web and Social Media*, 11(1).

Dorottya Demszky, Dana Movshovitz-Attias, Jeongwoo Ko, Alan Cowen, Gaurav Nemade, and Sujith Ravi. 2020. GoEmotions: A dataset of fine-grained emotions. In *Proceedings of the 58th Annual Meeting of the Association for Computational Linguistics*, Online. Association for Computational Linguistics.

Mark Díaz, Isaac Johnson, Amanda Lazar, Anne Marie Piper, and Darren Gergle. 2018. Addressing age-related bias in sentiment analysis. In *Proceedings of the 2018 CHI Conference on Human Factors in Computing Systems*, pages 1–14.

Paul Ekman. 1992. An argument for basic emotions. *Cognition & emotion*, 6(3-4):169–200.

Tommaso Fornaciari, Alexandra Uma, Silviu Paun, Barbara Plank, Dirk Hovy, and Massimo Poesio. 2021. Beyond black & white: Leveraging annotator disagreement via soft-label multi-task learning. In *Proceedings of the 2021 Conference of the North American Chapter of the Association for Computational Linguistics: Human Language Technologies*, pages 2591–2597, Online. Association for Computational Linguistics.

Antigoni Maria Founta, Constantinos Djouvas, Despoina Chatzakou, Ilias Leontiadis, Jeremy Blackburn, Gianluca Stringhini, Athena Vakali, Michael Sirivianos, and Nicolas Kourtellis. 2018. Large scale crowdsourcing and characterization of twitter abusive behavior. In *Twelfth International AAAI Conference on Web and Social Media*.

Timnit Gebru, Jamie Morgenstern, Briana Vecchione, Jennifer Wortman Vaughan, Hanna Wallach, Hal Daumé III, and Kate Crawford. 2018. Datasheets for datasets. *arXiv preprint arXiv:1803.09010*.

Melody Guan, Varun Gulshan, Andrew Dai, and Geoffrey Hinton. 2018. Who said what: Modeling individual labelers improves classification. *Proceedings of the AAAI Conference on Artificial Intelligence*, 32(1).

Julia Hirschberg, Jackson Liscombe, and Jennifer Venditti. 2003. Experiments in emotional speech. In *ISCA & IEEE Workshop on Spontaneous Speech Processing and Recognition*.

Jigsaw. 2018. Toxic comment classification challenge. Accessed: 2021-05-01.

Jigsaw. 2019. Unintended bias in toxicity classification. Accessed: 2021-05-01.

Brendan Kennedy, Mohammad Atari, Aida Mostafazadeh Davani, Leigh Yeh, Ali Omrani, Yehsong Kim, Kris Coombs Jr., Shreya Havaldar, Gwenyth Portillo-Wightman, Elaine Gonzalez, Joe Hoover, Aida Azatian, Gabriel Cardenas, Alyzeh Hussain, Austin Lara, Adam Omary, Christina Park, Xin Wang, Clarisa Wijaya, Yong Zhang, Beth Meyerowitz, and Morteza Dehghani. 2020. The gab hate corpus: A collection of 27k posts annotated for hate speech.

Bing Liu et al. 2010. Sentiment analysis and subjectivity. *Handbook of natural language processing*, 2(2010):627–666.

Hugo Liu, Henry Lieberman, and Ted Selker. 2003. A model of textual affect sensing using real-world knowledge. In *Proceedings of the 8th international conference on Intelligent user interfaces*, pages 125–132.

Yiwei Luo, Dallas Card, and Dan Jurafsky. 2020. Detecting stance in media on global warming. In *Findings of the Association for Computational Linguistics: EMNLP 2020*, pages 3296–3315, Online. Association for Computational Linguistics.

Stefanie Nowak and Stefan Rüger. 2010. How reliable are annotations via crowdsourcing: a study about inter-annotator agreement for multi-label image annotation. In *Proceedings of the international conference on Multimedia information retrieval*, pages 557–566.

Desmond Patton, Philipp Blandfort, William Frey, Michael Gaskell, and Svebor Karaman. 2019. Annotating social media data from vulnerable populations: Evaluating disagreement between domain experts and graduate student annotators. In *Proceedings of the 52nd Hawaii International Conference on System Sciences*.

Barbara Plank, Dirk Hovy, and Anders Søgaard. 2014. Learning part-of-speech taggers with inter-annotator agreement loss. In *Proceedings of the 14th Conference of the European Chapter of the Association for Computational Linguistics*, pages 742–751.

Vinodkumar Prabhakaran, Michael Bloodgood, Mona Diab, Bonnie Dorr, Lori Levin, Christine Piatko, Owen Rambow, and Benjamin Van Durme. 2012. Statistical modality tagging from rule-based annotations and crowdsourcing. In *Proceedings of the Workshop on Extra-Propositional Aspects of Meaning in Computational Linguistics*, pages 57–64.

Rion Snow, Brendan O'connor, Dan Jurafsky, and Andrew Y Ng. 2008. Cheap and fast–but is it good? evaluating non-expert annotations for natural language tasks. In *Proceedings of the 2008 conference on empirical methods in natural language processing*, pages 254–263.

William Warner and Julia Hirschberg. 2012. Detecting hate speech on the world wide web. In *Proceedings of the second workshop on language in social media*, pages 19–26.

Zeerak Waseem. 2016. Are you a racist or am i seeing things? annotator influence on hate speech detection on twitter. In *Proceedings of the first workshop on NLP and computational social science*, pages 138–142.

Zeerak Waseem and Dirk Hovy. 2016. Hateful symbols or hateful people? predictive features for hate speech detection on twitter. In *Proceedings of the NAACL student research workshop*, pages 88–93.

Maximilian Wich, Hala Al Kuwatly, and Georg Groh. 2020. Investigating annotator bias with a graph-based approach. In *Proceedings of the Fourth Workshop on Online Abuse and Harms*, pages 191–199.

Janyce Wiebe, Theresa Wilson, Rebecca Bruce, Matthew Bell, and Melanie Martin. 2004. Learning subjective language. *Computational linguistics*, 30(3):277–308.

Increasing Sentence-Level Comprehension Through Text Classification of Epistemic Functions

Maria Berger
Ruhr University Bochum
maria.berger-a21@rub.de

Elizabeth J. Goldstein
Carlisle, PA, USA
lizgoldstein15@gmail.com

Abstract

Word embeddings capture semantic meaning of individual words. How to bridge word-level linguistic knowledge with sentence-level language representation is an open problem. This paper examines whether sentence-level representations can be achieved by building a custom sentence database focusing on one aspect of a sentence's meaning. Our three separate semantic aspects are whether the sentence: (1) communicates a causal relationship, (2) indicates that two things are correlated with each other, and (3) expresses information or knowledge. The three classifiers provide epistemic information about a sentence's content.

1 Introduction

In reading comprehension, the sum is greater than the parts. A strong reader combines the reader's prior knowledge, reasoning ability, and the text's substance to reason about the events, entities, and their relations across a full document (Kočiský et al., 2018). In essence, reading comprehension requires the reader to develop high levels of abstraction. (Kočiský et al., 2018)

Each classification task introduced in the paper, if mastered by a computer model, allow a model to comprehend a sentence's meaning at greater level of abstraction than comparing word meaning similarity between sentences. With this new ability, the model should be able to master more complex downstream tasks than a model limited to word-level comprehension (Kim et al., 2019).

1.1 Causal and Correlating Relations

Causality: Causal relationships are a key to critical reasoning (Magliano and Pillow, 2021; Asghar, 2016). Causal relationship knowledge allows people to control their environment and make predictions about the future (Magliano and Pillow, 2021). It links one's actions with their probable consequences. Text causality recognition is crucial for natural language information retrieval, event prediction, question answering, generating future scenarios, decision processing, medical text mining, and behavior prediction (Li et al., 2021).

For purposes of this paper, a sentence containing a causal relationship expresses a cause and effect relationship. Following (Li et al., 2021), the expression can be explicit such as, "Financial stress is one of the main causes of divorce." This paper also recognizes cause and effect relationships, which are implicit such as, "He could choose to go on a diet, but this would bring significant muscle loss."

Correlation: Correlations are patterns where changes in one variable are associated with changes in a second variable. In other words, one variable's changes are statistically dependent on the other variable. For purposes of this paper, causal relationships are not considered correlations because we have developed a separate model for causal relationships. Examples of sentences containing correlations are, "Roosters always crow before the sun rises." and "Chocolate sales were 30% higher in communities with a high number of Covid-cases". Since there is no causal link, correlative relationship identification allows one to anticipate the future, but not to control one's surroundings. (Meehan, 1988) For example, prohibiting chocolate sales cannot reduce a community's Covid-19 rates.

1.2 Knowledge and Information

Knowledge: Humans are master pattern recognizers. Humans automatically and mostly without conscious effort turn experiences into simple patterns that they use to anticipate what will happen, to make things happen, and to choose among options. Spence (Spence, 2005; Meehan, 1988) writes that these simple patterns are generalized, meaning that they are assumed to transcend time. These patterns are what the authors define as knowledge.

Information: Information is knowledge's building

Proceedings of the Joint 15th Linguistic Annotation Workshop (LAW) and 3rd Designing Meaning Representations (DMR) Workshop, pages 139–150
November, 2021.

blocks. It consists of specific instances (Spence, 2005; Meehan, 1988) of, say, descriptions of events, objects, and relations among things. (Spence, 2005; Meehan, 1988) Facts, when used to mean an actual occurrence at a specific time and place, fit within information's scope. Data, on the other hand, is a smaller unit contained within facts. Bouthillier and Sheare define information as data in context. They identify "-10 degrees" as data and "it is -10 degrees outside" as information. (Bouthillier and Shearer, 2002)

John Dewey explains the concept of knowledge as follows: *To run against a hard painful stone is not of itself, I should say, an act of knowing; but if running into a hard and painful thing is an outcome predicted after inspection of data and elaboration of a hypothesis, then the hardness and the painful bruise which define the thing as a stone also constitute it emphatically an object of knowledge. (Ratner et al., 1939, p. 932)*

In other words, data about past individual experiences with the pain caused by the skin's contacts with particular stones at a particular instance is information. One can aggregate these individual data points into a hypothesis, which is referred to in this paper as knowledge.

2 Related Work

2.1 Epistemic Classification

(Marco and Navarro, 1993) define epistemology as, "the study of the process of human knowledge, its logic, origins and basis" and recognize that its study is essential to "the design and implementation of better cognitive strategies for guiding the process of documentary analysis". (Marco and Navarro, 1993, p. 126–132) The authors, following Meehan's applied, tactical approach to epistemology, define epistemic as describing the patterns used by humans to organize their experience thereby allowing them to generate future expectations. (Meehan, 1988) Humans create patterns by aggregating specific experiences into general rules to address the future. These patterns include: causation, correlation, and knowledge. Causal and correlative relationships divined from aggregating individual experiences allow humans to anticipate future events. Both causal and correlative relationships which are generalized from individual events fit within the scope of knowledge. Knowledge encompasses all generalized patterns, which humans use to create future expectations. Text classification relating to epistemic distinctions apply universally. (Meehan, 1988) Thus, epistemic text classifications can be utilized by models across disciplines to solve problems presented by downstream tasks.

(Meehan, 1988) introduces an epistemic framework for computational knowledge generation. Humans construct knowledge to serve as a tool to accomplish three basic purposes: anticipating the future, causing change, and choosing among options. (Meehan, 1988) Others refer to computational knowledge engineering as computational epistemology. (i Segura, 2009) This paper's classification tasks fit within (Meehan, 1988)'s epistemic framework.

2.2 Comprehension Functions

Following (Petukhova and Bunt, 2011), language can be divided into two main components: the communication's functions and its semantic content. While we have not found earlier research on classifying text based upon whether the text contains a correlative relationship or encodes knowledge, these tasks can be viewed as examining the sentence's function through an epistemic lens. Researchers have examined various algorithms' ability to detect communicative functions such as identifying whether a speaker has posed a question (Zhang et al., 2015) or a sentence serves a certain rhetorical purpose in an academic paper. (Iwatsuki et al., 2020).

2.3 Causal Relation Extraction

(Asghar, 2016) divides cause-effect extraction techniques into two main categories: (i) non-statistical, pattern-matching techniques (Khoo et al. (1998), Girju et al. (2002)) and (ii) machine learning techniques Girju (2003), Girju et al. (2010), Sil et al. (2010), Rink et al. (2010), (Zhao et al., 2016)). Each approach has its limitations. The non-statistical rule based technique cannot succeed across domains, produces significantly skewed precision and recall scores, and requires subject-matter experts to craft the pattern-recognition rules. In contrast, statistical and machine learning approaches require a significant amount of time for feature engineering through experimentation (Li et al., 2021), and large, manually created, domain-specifically labeled data sets.

Most research models approach causality extraction as a two-step classification problem requiring the model to first identify cause-effect pair candidates and then to remove those candidates that do not share a causal link. (Li et al., 2021) However, in recent work, (Li et al., 2021) represent causality extraction as a sequence labeling problem and utiliz a BiLSTM-CRF model with Flair contextual embeddings to extract cause–effect pairs directly (Flair embeddings (Akbik et al., 2018))

Work by (Mirza and Tonelli, 2016) also fits into this group. The authors present CATENA, a sieve-based system for extracting temporal and causal relations. The authors evaluating their system on TempEval-3 and TimeBank-Dense data and show that each of the sieves, the rule-based, the machine-learned and the reasoning-based one contribute to achieving state-of-the-art performance. An analysis of the interaction between the temporal and the causal components show a tight connection between the temporal and the causal dimension of texts.

2.4 Limited Data Sets and Data Augmentation Technique Guidance

Current annotated data sets are relatively limited. For cause and effect pair extraction, the largest data set is EventStoryLine (Caselli and Vossen, 2017). (Zuo et al., 2021) It only contains 258 documents, 4,316 sentences, and 1,770 causal event pairs.

It is an open question on what are the optimal data augmentation techniques. One part of our work is to experiment with data enrichment of training data by generating noisy labels based on labeling functions.

3 Study Overview

3.1 Research Question

In this paper, we examine whether machine and deep learning techniques can identify sentences which communicate causal or correlative relationships and distinguish between sentences that contain knowledge and information.

Our models do not seek to identify candidate pairs (e.g., prior candidate extraction). Pair selection can be difficult when a sentence contains a cause with multiple effects or implicit relationships. Instead we use a gold-labeled data set and test a diverse set of classifiers including a weakly supervised that enriches training data with noisy labels form generated functions. For causality relationships, our technique has the potential to identify sentences that do not utilize traditional, causal function words (e.g., "because") or impact verbs (e.g., "to poison"). An example of a sentence implicitly indicating a causal relationship, but not utilizing such words is, "Other countries in Southeast Asia—Thailand in particular—wanted to take advantage of these expanding urban markets and jumped into the hot economic fray."

3.2 Contribution

Following, our contributions are listed:

1. a new approximately 8,300 sentence data set (referred to as the Gold data set) derived from internet articles covering diverse subject-matter, manually labeled for the following three categories: causation, correlation, and knowledge;
2. a new 500 sentence data set (referred to as WikiGold data) derived from Wiki News, manually labeled for the same three categories;
3. experiments assessing the ability of traditional classifiers and neural networks powered by a pre-trained language model to accomplish sentence-level classification for the three classification categories; and
4. experiments evaluating whether a famous data augmentation approach (aka Snorkel, c.f., Sec. 6) can improve model training for discerning the three classification categories.

3.3 Classification Tasks

Our classification tasks are defined as follows:

1. Does the sentence communicate a causal relationship or is none communicated?
2. Does the sentence communicate either a causal or correlative relationship or is neither communicated?
3. Does the sentence communicate a causal relationship or a correlative relationship?
4. Does the sentence contain information or knowledge?

To run the experiments, we use established statistical-based algorithms and neural classifiers (c.f., Sec. 5). We also utilize Snorkel's weakly supervised data augmentation approach (c.f., Sec. 6).

4 Text Data Used

4.1 Gold Data

To accomplish each of the classification tasks, we created a Gold data set by manually annotating articles from the internet (e.g., Reuters, The Guardian, etc. See Appendix A for details) written for general readership on a wide range of topics, including artificial intelligence, books, finance, and Covid-19 (see Tab. 1). Fig.1 shows the topic-wise distribution of the Gold data by sentences, articles, and classification tasks. We can see that the topics are distributed similarly in all the tasks and that—for most of the topics—the balancing in both classes is comparable too. The data set contains 8,327 labeled sentences.

Each article's sentences were manually labeled for the three classification categories, causality, correlation, and knowledge. No pattern recognition rules were used to label the data. Thus, the labeling method captured a diverse range of sentences which met the labeling criteria.

We create task-specific balanced data sets.

4.2 Gold Data Labeling Conventions

For the first two aspects, causality and correlation, sentences expressing that one such relationship existed between two things were labeled as positively fitting within the respective class. For example, "Eating a cup of blueberries a day does not reduce your risk of cancer" was labeled a causal sentence. The reason for this labeling rule is sentences such as the foregoing one allow the reader to extract causation information from the sentence.

If a sentence contained both a causal and correlative relationship, the sentence was labeled as causal. One such sentence is, "And a study we looked at in 2012 suggested people who owned cats had a higher risk of suicide, as their pets could make them vulnerable to a Toxoplasma gondii (T. gondii) infection." If a correlation solely related to time, a trend, it was not labeled as a correlation. An example of such a database sentence is, "By the late 1990s, countries such as Indonesia and Brazil were increasing their commercial production by about 10 percent a year." We chose not to label trends as we sought to identify correlations that are time invariant. If a sentence contained both information and knowledge, it was labeled as fitting within the smaller class, knowledge.

4.3 Wikinews Big Data Set

Snorkel works well in increasing the classification accuracy based on a big data set of noisily labeled data together with a small gold labeled data set. As a big data set, we downloaded a recent version of the English Wikinews data from the web.[1] We filter out articles with titles that contain the prefixes "Template:", "Portal:", "Wikinews:", "Category:" or "Comments:", because we are not interested in those. "Templates" because they are empty placeholders. "Portal" indicates specific information on the Wikinews portal and its usage. Articles containing the "Wikinews" prefix often simply list short headlines of independent news which are too short for our use cases. "Categories" also indicate some templates that allocate space for news articles with a certain function such as future articles or single dates. Finally, "Comments" are articles that only indicate legacy comments that are now moved to a newly created comments namespace. We also filter out articles that start with a "Redirect" in their text bodies. From a total of 100,277 articles originally culled from Wikinews, 28,460 remained after the filtering-out process. Using NLTK's sentence parser, we derived 327,366 sentences from these articles. For our experiments we use a subset of this data holding 10,000 sentences. We refer to this data set by "Wiki" data.

4.4 Wikinews Gold Data Set

From the Wiki data, we sampled 500 sentences that we annotated manually for causal and correlating relations. The task-specific, balanced data sets (Sec. 3.3) have sample sizes: 296 (causal versus none), 332 (causal-correlating versus neither), and 36 (causal versus correlating). We refer to this data set as the "WikiGold" data.

5 Supervised Classification

5.1 Classifier Set Up

Data Pre-processing: We perform sentence preprocessing by removing punctuation and lower casing the text. We also enrich the text with part-of-speech (POS) tags using the NLTK library version 3.5. We did not remove stop words because such words include key function words such as "because" which often indicate causal relationships.[2]

For the traditional classifiers, we compute the tf-idf matrix using TfidfVectorizer of Python's scikit-learn module, and for the bag of words matrix, we use CountVectorizer (c.f., Tab. 2 showing classifiers used).

[1] "enwikinews-latest-pages-articles_2020_10_09.xml" `https://dumps.wikimedia.org/enwikinews/`

[2] We performed experiments with lemmatizing and stemming the text, but this did not increase performance.

topic	#articles	#sentences	causal vs. corr		caus/corr vs. neither		causal vs. none	
			causal	correlating	causal/corr.	neither	causal	none
ai	4	390	19	3	89	122	86	96
animal	2	65	6	3	18	18	15	18
art protest	3	147	13	3	68	30	65	24
blm	3	483	25	18	115	142	97	111
books	6	251	7	4	54	91	121	62
china	1	176	21	8	74	49	66	46
covid	19	1398	82	82	398	424	316	313
creativity	8	617	41	61	232	171	171	154
culture	12	715	20	3	107	241	153	195
depression	10	724	57	77	319	164	242	153
economy	12	868	34	37	191	368	154	203
education	1	136	10	15	61	34	46	32
entertainment	2	180	6	0	29	69	29	51
farming	1	42	5	2	18	4	16	8
food	8	416	17	13	95	118	82	92
gender	1	105	6	2	23	37	21	26
health	1	74	6	24	45	14	21	13
history	2	78	3	2	20	21	18	18
home	1	33	3	0	8	16	8	13
math	3	268	27	3	79	80	76	57
music	1	45	0	3	10	12	7	15
politics	4	237	8	2	52	76	50	66
poverty	10	240	9	62	108	56	46	66
psychology	4	213	16	16	109	47	93	35
science	3	142	10	15	108	59	92	39
sports	1	15	1	0	2	6	2	5
technology	3	268	11	5	59	83	54	50
total	126	8326	463	463	2424	2424	1961	1961

(The columns "causal vs. corr" through "causal vs. none" fall under the spanning header "task-wise topic distributions in #sentences".)

Table 1: left: The Gold data's topic-wise distribution by articles and sentences; right: topic-wise distribution by number of sentences for each of our three classification categories

BERT Model: We choose a BERT pre-trained model using the implementation for TensorFlow (bert-for-tf2). Specifically, we use the model known as "BERT-base". For the hyper parameters, we choose the maximum token as 150, a batch size of 32, a learning rate of 1e-5, and a maximum of 5 epochs with a patience of 1. We utilize an Adam optimizer and a sparse categorical cross-entropy loss function. The BERT model's sentence representation vector is the hidden state of the representation of the first token (CLS) in the final BERT layer. (Devlin et al., 2018)

Our model feeds this CLS token vector into a drop out layer (set to .8) to prevent overfitting. Then, the model utilizes a dense layer to output the probabilities for the binary classes.

5.2 Results & Discussion

For the BERT model, there was a strong positive relationship between the training data size and accuracy. The BERT model was the most successful model for all classification tasks except correlation versus causation. This is not surprising since this task had significantly less training data than the other three tasks. The BERT model on average did 5.9% better than the next most successful model for the three classification tasks where there was a significant amount of training data.

On average, the BERT models had a wider dispersion between the precision and recall scores (9.3%) than the best simple models for each classification task (2.5%). There was an even split for both the BERT and simple models on whether they did better on accuracy or recall.

In examining the true positives generated by the BERT causal versus none model, we saw that four of the ten sentences BERT was most confident about (with 99.9% confidence level) all contained the word "lead". The remaining six sentences all contained verbs that indicate causation.[3] For some sentences, BERT was confident but wrong when a word associated with causal relationships (such as *worst*) was used without introducing any cause-effect pair such as, "one of the worst behaviors sometimes exhibited by owl observers is feeding the bird". BERT was most confident and correct in identifying sentences that were not causal when

[3]These are: *affect, contribute, encourage, foster, produce, improve*, and *modify*

task	train	test	classifier	vector.	r	p	f1	a
causal vs none	3136	785	Bayes G	tf-idf	.60	.62	.61	.61
	3136	785	Bayes G	bow	.63	.61	.62	.62
	3136	785	Log Reg	tf-idf	.71	.68	.70	.70
	3136	785	Log Reg	bow	.69	.73	.71	.71
	3136	785	Naive B	tf-idf	.73	.62	.67	.65
	3136	785	Naive B	bow	.73	.60	.66	.64
	3136	785	RF	tf-idf	.68	.69	.68	.68
	3136	785	RF	bow	.65	.74	.69	.68
	3374	844	BERT	context	.75	.79	.77	.78
causal/co vs neither	3877	970	Bayes G	tf-idf	.58	.60	.59	.60
	3877	970	Bayes G	bow	.74	.63	.68	.60
	3877	970	Log Reg	tf-idf	.77	.68	.72	.70
	3877	970	Log Reg	bow	.72	.72	.72	.72
	3877	970	Naïve B	tf-idf	.86	.61	.71	.66
	3877	970	Naïve B	bow	.86	.60	.70	.64
	3877	970	RF	tf-idf	.68	.70	.69	.70
	3877	970	RF	bow	.62	.75	.68	.71
	3877	970	BERT	context	.77	.80	.79	.79
causal vs correlating	740	186	Bayes G	tf-idf	.76	.71	.73	.73
	740	186	Bayes G	bow	.75	.68	.72	.70
	740	186	Log Reg	tf-odf	.70	.78	.74	.75
	740	186	Log Reg	bow	.66	.74	.70	.72
	740	186	Naïve B	tf-idf	.82	.77	.79	.78
	740	186	Naïve B	bow	.79	.73	.76	.75
	740	186	RF	tf-idf	.67	.74	.70	.72
	740	186	RF	bow	.59	.86	.70	.75
	740	186	BERT	context	.77	.51	.62	.52
knowledge vs info	4251	1063	Bayes G	tf-idf	.79	.63	.70	.67
	4251	1063	Bayes G	bow	.78	.67	.72	.70
	4251	1063	Log Reg	tf-idf	.79	.78	.79	.79
	4251	1063	Log Reg	bow	.76	.79	.77	.78
	4251	1063	Naïve B	tf-idf	.86	.74	.80	.78
	4251	1063	Naïve B	bow	.82	.74	.78	.78
	4251	1063	RF	tf-idf	.75	.73	.74	.74
	4251	1063	RF	bow	.72	.76	.74	.75
	4251	1063	BERT	context	.86	.80	.82	.83

Table 2: Results of comparing experiment showing (p)recision, (r)ecall, (f1)-score, and (a)ccuracy; Experiments run using (Bayes G)aussian, BERT, (Log)istic (Reg)ression, (Naïve B)ayes and (R)andom (F)orest classifiers and model; Classes are causal, (co)rrelating and none/neither, and knowledge and (info)rmation; For BERT, training data set sizes include validation data (80-20-split)

the sentence had a proper name in it.

For the cause-correlation versus neither task, BERT was most confident and correct when a verb strongly associated with causation or correlation appeared in the sentence.[4] The sentences which correctly classified neither causative nor correlative and for which the model had the highest confidence were ones which were either short or contained proper nouns.

For the correlation versus causal task, we found that the three sentences that Naive Bayes, the most successful algorithm, most confidently labeled as causal (91% confidence level) all contained "percent" in them.[5] 30% of the top 10 sentences that the Naïve Bayes algorithm correctly identified as causal and for which Naïve Bayes was most confident contained function words associated with causation.[6]

For the knowledge versus information task, the 20 sentences the BERT model was most confident and correct classifying as knowledge mostly related to depression or other health issues and reflects the database's subject matter. For the 20 sentences the model was most confident and correct in identifying as informational sentences, the sentences contained either a pronoun or a proper noun and a majority contained both of these parts of speech. [7]

6 Weakly Supervised Classification

To determine the effectiveness of data augmentation, we now compare neural classification through supervised learning to a mixed approach of weak supervision and neural classification. The experiments are performed on our three main tasks.

6.1 Snorkel Library

We use the recently released programming library Snorkel (Ratner et al., 2020)[8], which was developed to improve utilizing handcrafted rules to build training data. It works by detecting unidentified correlations and other dependencies among these rules (called "labeling functions"). Snorkel's learning approach is twofold: First, the LabelModel learns the parameters for accuracy and correlation structure based on weak supervision represented by the labeling functions. The LabelModel generates noisy labels for the training data by weighting the labeling functions. In addition, a final classification model (an LSTM in this work) is applied, which generalizes the information learned from the weighted labeling functions by using the noisy labeled data as training data (Ratner et al., 2020).

[4]The verbs strongly associated with causation-correlation showing the highest confidence levels are: *associated, bring, cause, contribute, lead, make, and relieve.*

[5]An example sentence is, "four in ten hispanics are members of the working class compared to 28 percent of blacks 25 percent of whites but just 16 percent of asians"

[6]These functions words were: *because, by* and *so*.

[7]These sentences contained a pronoun and referred to a specific individual's experience, thus contained information. One of the informational sentences the BERT model correctly and most confidently labeled was, "when she was 17 in 2013 mary climbed out of her bedroom window and ran across a field".

[8]`https://github.com/snorkel-team/snorkel`

6.2 Train-Test Data Splits

We use the Wiki data (Sec. 4.3) for training Snorkel's LabelModel[9] and the Gold data (comprising our Gold (Sec. 4.1) and WikiGold (Sec. 4.4) data) for testing it. The neural model then uses the predicted labels from the LabelModel as training data, and, again, the Gold data for testing. Note that we combine 80% of our Gold/WikiGold data with the noisy labeled data to train the neural classifier model and 20% of the Gold/WikiGold data for testing. Fig. 1 illustrates this procedure.

6.3 Baseline on Gold Data

First, we run a baseline experiment using GloVe embeddings (Pennington et al., 2014).[10] Our LSTM uses GloVe embeddings from the 100-dimensions file as features for the neural network. We choose 1000 as the vocabulary length, 100 as output dimension and 100 as input length. Following an Embedding layer, we add the LSTM layer (followed by a 256-dimensions Dense layer with RELU Activation and 0.5 Dropout). For the output, another 1-dimensional Dense layer with Sigmoid Activation is added. While fitting the model, we choose a batch size of 128, 10 epochs and a min_delta of 1e-4.[11]

6.4 Train on Wiki Data using Function Rules

The LSTM (same parameters as above) is trained using noisily labeled Wiki data plus 80% of Gold/WikiGold, and tested on 20% of the Gold/WikiGold (see Tab. 4).

Our labeling functions are generated by a script that uses **keywords** typically appearing in causal and correlating sentences. For causal sentences we collected keywords *affect, alter, ameliorate, aggravate, because, cause, consequence, contribute, decrease, due, effect, exacerbate, help, impact, improve, increase, lead, reason, reduce, relate, result, so, spur, trigger* and *worsen*. As keywords for correlating sentences we use *accompany, associate, correlate, indicate, link, predict, and tend.* We collected these terms while preparing the Gold data. This approach is comparable with work by (Girju, 2003) who uses specific verbs placed between two noun phrases to indicate causal relations. Depending on the task, we label a sentence 0 when none of the causal or causal and correlating words appear in the sentences. For causal versus correlating, we label -1 when neither appear.

6.5 Part-of-Speech Features on Top

We also add labeling functions generated from **POS tags.**[12] Tab. 5 lists the POS tags used. Specifically, the rules applied are: (1) if either of the following POS tags is contained in the sentence's POS tag sequence: *IN, WDT, RB, MD*, then the sentence fits in the causal category; and (2) if the *CC* tag is found within the sentence, then the sentence fits in the correlating sentences category.

After experimenting with a simple entropy measure to find POS tag signals, we expand the POS tags list for identifying causal rules. We add: *PRP, RP,* and *TO*.

6.6 Results & Discussion

For the baseline experiment, the accuracy, recall, precision and f1-score values are listed in Tab. 3. The cause versus correlation task performs significantly worse than the other two tasks. However, the training data we have available for this task is only about one fifth of the training data available for the other two tasks. Comparing these results to those in Tab. 2, one finds that the baseline accuracy scores align with the BERT accuracy scores. This means the baseline models and the BERT model perform best on the task with the most data; the cause-correlation versus neither task, and the poorest on the one with the least data: the cause versus correlation task.

Utilizing POS tags and keywords for creating the labeling rules, we reach the baseline in the **causal-correlation versus neither task** (see Tab. 4). The recall score is better than the baseline. Thus, the training data generated from the POS tags must provide the model with more diverse data; consequently, the classification model is able to recognize more nuanced patterns indicative of causation and correlation. This ability might help the model to perform well in finding true positives (causal and correlative sentences). However, many false positives also show that the rules (key words and

[9] Snorkel's LabelModel class (Ratner et al., 2019) uses the covariances of the junction tree representation of the dependency tree built by applying the learning functions to all data points. After matrix completion, the resulting conditional probabilities of the functions serve as parameters to re-weight and combine the label output.

[10] Using GloVe gives us a comprehensive view on the problem. Being more straightforward, it better applies for testing against weak supervision and keeps computational costs low.

[11] Presenting a comparable problem, we follow `https://www.kaggle.com/kredy10/simple-lstm-for-text-classification`

[12] The Wiki and WikiGold data were POS-tagged using the NLTK library version 3.4.5. The Gold data was POS-tagged using NLTK 3.5.

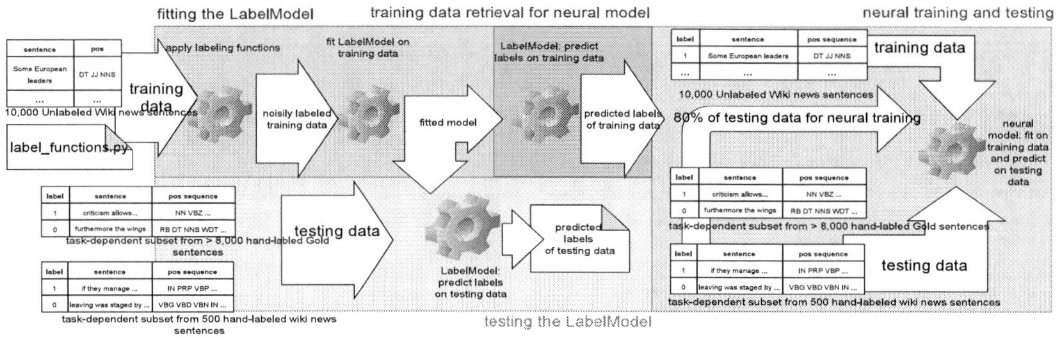

Figure 1: Snorkel workflow: Training and testing data splits in Snorkel's LabelModel and the neural model

	—				LSTM (on textual representations)						
task					train (validate) on	test on	r	p	f1	a	loss
ca vs none					WikiGold+Gold	WikiGold+Gold	.93	.57	.71	.62	.70
sample size					2699 (675)	844					
ca/co vs neither					WikiGold+Gold	WikiGold+Gold	.45	.77	.57	.64	.66
sample size					3315 (829)	1036					
ca vs co					WikiGold+Gold	WikiGold+Gold	.75	.53	.62	.55	.74
sample size					616 (154)	192					

Table 3: Results of baseline experiment

	LabelModel (on keywords and POS tags)						LSTM (on textual representations)						
task	train on	test on	r	p	f1	a	train (validate) on	test on	r	p	f1	a	loss
ca vs none	Wiki	WikiGold+Gold	.87	.60	.71	.64	Wiki+WikiGold+Gold	WikiGold+Gold	.92	.57	.70	.62	.79
sample size	9929	4218					10642 (2661)	844					
ca/co vs neither	Wiki	WikiGold+Gold	.85	.59	.70	.63	Wiki+WikiGold+Gold	WikiGold+Gold	.88	.61	.72	.64	.77
sample size	9929	5180					11258 (2815)	1036					
ca vs co	Wiki	WikiGold+Gold	.00	1.0	.00	.50	Wiki+WikiGold+Gold	WikiGold+Gold	.46	.62	.53	.60	.72
sample size	9929	962					7908 (1977)	192					

Table 4: Results of mixed approach: Validation data on top of training data. Tables show (r)ecall, (p)recision, (f1)-score, and (a)ccuracy

POS tags) are not specific enough, since they also appear in "neither" sentences.

The **causal versus none task** performs comparable to the baseline, showing a slightly lower recall and f1-score.

The results of the LabelModel show an accuracy of 50% for the **causal versus correlation task**. Only having one POS feature to identify correlating sentences causes this dismal performance. The LabelModel appears to ignore the correlative POS rule, and instead predicts almost only causal sentences. Since the majority of model rules points to each sentence falling within the causal category, the model only reaches 50% accuracy. Moreover, in the causal versus correlation task, because we arbitrarily assigned the correlative sentences to the positive polarity and the causal sentences to the negative polarity, the model created with the POS feature rules leads to almost no true positives.

However, the LSTM reaches a much higher precision (at the cost of low recall) and higher accuracy compared to the baseline. Looking at samples, one can conclude that the "CC" pattern is a weak one as most true negatives (causal sentence votes) do contain the "CC" pattern too. One also finds that many of false negatives (predicted causal (0), actual correlating (1))—which negatively impacts the recall—do also contain a "CC" pattern. These samples also tend to be relatively short, which often is indicative for being a causal sentence rather than a correlating one.

6.7 Fisher Score for POS Tag Features

Inspired by (Cheng et al., 2007), we perform a Fischer Score test (Duda et al., 1973; Fisher, 1934) to verify suitable POS features. The Fisher Score is defined as follows:

$$FS = \frac{\sum_{i=1}^{c} n_i(\mu_i - \mu)^2}{\sum_{i=1}^{c} n_i \sigma_i^2} \quad (1)$$

where c is the number of classes (2 in our case), n_i is the number of data samples in class i, μ_i and μ are the average appearance of the given feature in class i and the whole dataset respectively. σ_i is the standard deviation of the feature's appearance in class i. Our features have a boolean character, which means that they either appear in a sample or they don't. Hence, our μ's cannot be greater than 1. The higher the FS, the more important is the given feature.

feature	part-of-speech	ca vs n	ca vs co	ca/co vs n
IN	preposition	**.03**	.00	**.04**
WDT	Wh-determiner	.02	.02	.01
RB	adverb	.01	.00	.02
MD	modal	**.04**	**.03**	**.03**
PRP	personal pronoun	.01	**.03**	.00
RP	particle	.00	.00	.00
TO	*to*	**.04**	.02	**.03**
CC	coordinating conjunc.	.02	.00	.02

Table 5: Fisher Score for our POS-tag[13] features calculated on our Gold dataset

The POS-tags *IN, MD,* and *TO* are outstanding for each of the three tasks, all of which we use to find causal sentences. It confirms that modals and subordinating conjunctions play a special role for classifying causal sentences.

6.8 Summary

Summarizing, Snorkel works moderately well in the sentence classifying epistemic tasks. The causal versus none task works comparable to the baseline, the causal versus correlating task reaches a higher f1-score with lower accuracy, and the causal-correlating versus neither task reaches a 15%-higher f1-score while accuracy is on par with the baseline. The overall aim to improve classification accuracy using a big corpus of noisily labeled data worked partly for our problem. Note that even though we ran some basic clean-up steps on our Wiki data, we are aware that special characters, prefixes or re-codings of them can corrupt a significant portion of the data set's sentences, hence leading to affecting noise.

7 Conclusion

To classify sentences based upon their epistemic functions, we created a new data set[14] containing 8,327 sentences that we annotated for whether a sentence communicates a causal or correlating relationship, and whether it expresses information or knowledge. Utilizing BERT, the three epistemic function models achieved sufficient accuracy that future work should include determining the models' abilities to solve real world problems. In that vein, we plan to utilize our models for a range of downstream tasks such as event detection, question answering, and discourse parsing. Our approach may be able to improve upon these tasks by providing the underlying model additional features through which to comprehend the text in a more nuanced fashion. In addition, as the Snorkel approach appears promising, we plan in future work to determine if there is a systematic method, which can be utilized to determine the underlying functions needed to gather the weakly-supervised data. If this can be accomplished, then a lesser amount of gold data may be needed. As gold data is generally the biggest bottleneck that NLP practitioners face, a systematic approach to Snorkel may allow for a significant time reduction for building future NLP models.

[14]available at: `https://github.com/Goldstein-Berger/law-dmr21-sentence-meaning-annotation`

References

Alan Akbik, Duncan Blythe, and Roland Vollgraf. 2018. Contextual string embeddings for sequence labeling. In *Proceedings of the 27th international conference on computational linguistics*, pages 1638–1649.

Nabiha Asghar. 2016. Automatic extraction of causal relations from natural language texts: a comprehensive survey. *arXiv preprint arXiv:1605.07895*.

France Bouthillier and Kathleen Shearer. 2002. Understanding knowledge management and information management: the need for an empirical perspective. *Information research*, 8(1):8–1.

Tommaso Caselli and Piek Vossen. 2017. The event storyline corpus: A new benchmark for causal and temporal relation extraction. In *Proceedings of the Events and Stories in the News Workshop*, pages 77–86.

Hong Cheng, Xifeng Yan, Jiawei Han, and Chih-Wei Hsu. 2007. Discriminative frequent pattern analysis for effective classification. In *2007 IEEE 23rd international conference on data engineering*, pages 716–725. IEEE.

Jacob Devlin, Ming-Wei Chang, Kenton Lee, and Kristina Toutanova. 2018. Bert: Pre-training of deep bidirectional transformers for language understanding. *arXiv preprint arXiv:1810.04805*.

Richard O Duda, Peter E Hart, et al. 1973. *Pattern classification and scene analysis*, volume 3. Wiley New York.

Ronald Aylmer Fisher. 1934. Two new properties of mathematical likelihood. *Proceedings of the Royal Society of London. Series A, Containing Papers of a Mathematical and Physical Character*, 144(852):285–307.

Roxana Girju. 2003. Automatic detection of causal relations for question answering. In *Proceedings of the ACL 2003 workshop on Multilingual summarization and question answering*, pages 76–83.

Roxana Girju, Brandon Beamer, Alla Rozovskaya, Andrew Fister, and Suma Bhat. 2010. A knowledge-rich approach to identifying semantic relations between nominals. *Information processing & management*, 46(5):589–610.

Roxana Girju, Dan I Moldovan, et al. 2002. Text mining for causal relations. In *FLAIRS conference*, pages 360–364.

Kenichi Iwatsuki, Florian Boudin, and Akiko Aizawa. 2020. An evaluation dataset for identifying communicative functions of sentences in english scholarly papers. In *Proceedings of the 12th Language Resources and Evaluation Conference*, pages 1712–1720.

Christopher SG Khoo, Jaklin Kornfilt, Robert N Oddy, and Sung Hyon Myaeng. 1998. Automatic extraction of cause-effect information from newspaper text without knowledge-based inferencing. *Literary and Linguistic Computing*, 13(4):177–186.

Jihyeok Kim, Reinald Kim Amplayo, Kyungjae Lee, Sua Sung, Minji Seo, and Seung-won Hwang. 2019. Categorical metadata representation for customized text classification. *Transactions of the Association for Computational Linguistics*, 7:201–215.

Tomáš Kočiský, Jonathan Schwarz, Phil Blunsom, Chris Dyer, Karl Moritz Hermann, Gábor Melis, and Edward Grefenstette. 2018. The narrativeqa reading comprehension challenge. *Transactions of the Association for Computational Linguistics*, 6:317–328.

Zhaoning Li, Qi Li, Xiaotian Zou, and Jiangtao Ren. 2021. Causality extraction based on self-attentive bilstm-crf with transferred embeddings. *Neurocomputing*, 423:207–219.

Joseph P. Magliano and Bradford H. Pillow. 2021. Learning - causal reasoning - events, event, students, and effect. `https://education.stateuniversity.com/pages/2163/Learning-CAUSAL-REASONING.html#ixzz6vc5QYKKa`. Accessed: May 2021.

Francisco Javier Garcia Marco and Miguel Angel Esteban Navarro. 1993. On some contributions of the cognitive sciences and epistemology to a theory of classification. *KO KNOWLEDGE ORGANIZATION*, 20(3):126–132.

Egene J. Meehan. 1988. *The Thinking Game: A Guide to Effective Study*. Chatham House Publishers, Inc.

Paramita Mirza and Sara Tonelli. 2016. Catena: Causal and temporal relation extraction from natural language texts. In *Proceedings of COLING 2016, the 26th International Conference on Computational Linguistics: Technical Papers*, pages 64–75.

Jeffrey Pennington, Richard Socher, and Christopher D Manning. 2014. Glove: Global vectors for word representation. In *Proceedings of the 2014 conference on empirical methods in natural language processing (EMNLP)*, pages 1532–1543.

Volha Petukhova and Harry Bunt. 2011. Incremental dialogue act understanding. In *Proceedings of the Ninth International Conference on Computational Semantics (IWCS 2011)*.

Alexander Ratner, Stephen H Bach, Henry Ehrenberg, Jason Fries, Sen Wu, and Christopher Ré. 2020. Snorkel: Rapid training data creation with weak supervision. *The VLDB Journal*, 29:709–730.

Alexander Ratner, Braden Hancock, Jared Dunnmon, Frederic Sala, Shreyash Pandey, and Christopher Ré. 2019. Training complex models with multi-task weak supervision. In *Proceedings of the AAAI Conference on Artificial Intelligence*, volume 33, pages 4763–4771.

Joseph Ratner et al. 1939. Intelligence in the modern world. john dewey's philosophy. *Journal of Philosophy*, 36(21).

Bryan Rink, Cosmin Adrian Bejan, and Sanda Harabagiu. 2010. Learning textual graph patterns to detect causal event relations. In *Twenty-Third International FLAIRS Conference*.

Jordi Vallverdú i Segura. 2009. Computational epistemology and e-science: A new way of thinking. *Minds and Machines*, 19(4):557–567.

Avirup Sil, Fei Huang, and Alexander Yates. 2010. Extracting action and event semantics from web text. In *AAAI Fall Symposium: Commonsense Knowledge*. Citeseer.

Larry Spence. 2005. Knowledge versus information. Unpublished, on file with authors.

Yun Zhang, David Lo, Xin Xia, and Jian-Ling Sun. 2015. Multi-factor duplicate question detection in stack overflow. *Journal of Computer Science and Technology*, 30(5):981–997.

Sendong Zhao, Ting Liu, Sicheng Zhao, Yiheng Chen, and Jian-Yun Nie. 2016. Event causality extraction based on connectives analysis. *Neurocomputing*, 173:1943–1950.

Xinyu Zuo, Pengfei Cao, Yubo Chen, Kang Liu, Jun Zhao, Weihua Peng, and Yuguang Chen. 2021. Learnda: Learnable knowledge-guided data augmentation for event causality identification. *arXiv preprint arXiv:2106.01649*.

A Appendix: Sources of Web Articles

Article Title	Website	Date Accesse	Who	Why selected	How Selected
Causes of Depression	https://www.webmd.com/depression/guide/causes-depression#1	12/27/2019	EJG	causes of depression	Google search
Causes and Risk Factors of Dep	https://www.verywellmind.com/common-causes-of-depression-1066772	12/31/2019	EJG	causes of depression	Google search
Depression in Women	https://www.psycom.net/depression.central.women.html	1/2/2020	EJG	causes of depression	Google search
What is depression and what c	https://www.medicalnewstoday.com/articles/8933.php	1/6/2020	EJG	causes of depression	Google search
Could depression be the result	https://www.nhs.uk/news/mental-health/could-depression-be-the-result-of-a-brain-infection/	2/22/20	EJG	causes of depression	Google search
Cannabis Lightens Mood, but N	https://www.psychcongress.com/article/cannabis-lightens-mood-may-worsen-depression-over-time	2/22/20	EJG	causes of depression	Google search
Online mindfulness-based cogn	https://www.medicalnewstoday.com/articles/online-mindfulness-based-cognitive-therapy-to-improve-lingering-depression	2/22/20	EJG	causes of depression	Google search
The Link Between Migraine, De	https://americanmigrainefoundation.org/resource-library/link-between-migraine-depression-anxiety/	2/22/20	EJG	causes of depression	Google search
Can Artificial Intelligence Help	https://www.verywellmind.com/can-artificial-intelligence-help-depression-4158330	2/22/20	EJG	causes of depression	Google search
How Artificial Intelligence Can	https://time.com/5786081/depression-medication-treatment-artificial-intelligence/	2/22/20	EJG	causes of depression	Google search
Lifelong poverty increases hea	https://www.reuters.com/article/us-lifelong-poverty/lifelong-poverty-increases-heart-disease-risks-idUSTRE52Q35520090327	3/21/2020	EJG	poverty & heart disease	Google search
Higher heart disease risk persis	https://www.modernhealthcare.com/article/20170607/NEWS/170609924/higher-heart-disease-risk-persists-for-low-income-populations	3/21/2020	EJG	poverty & heart disease	Google search
Understanding the	https://www.heart.org/en/news/2019/08/27/understanding-the-connection-between-poverty-childhood-trauma-and-heart-disease	3/21/2020	EJG	poverty & heart disease	Google search
Shining a light on poverty and	https://blog.providence.org/archive/shining-a-light-on-poverty-and-heart-disease	3/22/2020	EJG	poverty & heart disease	Google search
Poverty is the main predictor o	https://www.thelancet.com/pdfs/journals/lancet/PIIS0140673602086117.pdf	3/22/2020	EJG	poverty & heart disease	Google search
Lower socioeconomic status	https://health.ucdavis.edu/health-news/newsroom/lower-socioeconomic-status-linked-with-heart-disease-despite-improvements-in-other-	3/26/2020	EJG	poverty & heart disease	Google search
Poverty Makes Heart Failure Ev	https://www.usnews.com/news/health-news/articles/2019-09-04/poverty-makes-heart-failure-even-more-lethal-study-shows	3/27/2020	EJG	poverty & heart disease	Google search
Reports on impact of poverty	https://medicalxpress.com/news/2012-03-impact-poverty-social-class-myocardial.html	4/5/2020	EJG	poverty & heart disease	Google search
Data Analysis Finds Hospitals	https://www.aimc.com/conferences/acc15/data-analysis-finds-hospitals-in-low-income-areas-scored-high-in-mi-care-even-if-patients-had-	4/5/2020	EJG	poverty & heart disease	Google search
Economic issues drive dispariti	https://www.heart.org/en/news/2018/05/10/economic-issues-drive-disparities-in-heart-disease-stroke	4/8/2020	EJG	poverty & heart disease	Google search
Is It OK to Take a Walk?	https://www.nytimes.com/2020/03/17/style/self-care/is-it-ok-to-go-for-a-walk-coronavirus.html?	3/21/2020	EJG	covid	EJG Nuzzel Feed 3/22/20
Keeping the Coronavirus from	https://www.newyorker.com/news/news-desk/keeping-the-coronavirus-from-infecting-health-care-workers	3/22/2020	EJG	covid	EJG Nuzzel Feed 3/22/20
How the Coronavirus Became a	https://www.theatlantic.com/health/archive/2020/03/how-many-americans-are-sick-lost-february/608521/	3/22/2020	EJG	covid	EJG Nuzzel Feed 3/22/20
Mark Cuban says how	https://www.cnbc.com/2020/03/25/coronavirus-mark-cuban-warns-against-rushing-employees-back-to-work.html	3/27/2020	EJG	covid	EJG Nuzzel Feed 3/26/20
Lessons from Italy's Response t	https://hbr.org/2020/03/lessons-from-italys-response-to-coronavirus	3/29/2020	EJG	covid	EJG Nuzzel Feed 3/29/20
What Everyone's Getting Wron	https://marker.medium.com/what-everyones-getting-wrong-about-the-toilet-paper-shortage-c812e1358fe0	4/4/2020	EJG	covid	EJG Pocket Feed 4/4/20
How science finally caught up	https://www.theguardian.com/us-news/2020/apr/04/trump-coronavirus-science-analysis	4/5/2020	EJG	covid	EJG Nuzzel Feed 4/5/20
Coronavirus: low antibody leve	https://www.scmp.com/news/china/science/article/3078840/coronavirus-low-antibody-levels-raise-questions-about	4/9/2020	EJG	covid	EJG Nuzzel Feed 4/8/20
THE STAGGERING ECONOMIC	http://filesforprogress.org/memos/the-staggering-economic-impact-coronavirus.pdf	4/10/2020	EJG	covid	EJG Nuzzel Feed 4/10/20
The Real Reason Every Fashion	https://marker.medium.com/the-real-reason-every-fashion-company-is-now-making-face-masks-939c2055a3b3	4/10/2020	EJG	covid	EJG Medium Feed 4/10/20
Follow the Science	https://www.lrb.co.uk/the-paper/v42/n08/james-butler/follow-the-science	4/11/2020	EJG	covid	EJG hand-selected
Deaths in New York City Are M	https://www.nytimes.com/interactive/2020/04/10/upshot/coronavirus-deaths-new-york-city.html	4/11/2020	EJG	covid	EJG Nuzzel Feed 4/11/20
Why Companies Need Creative	https://www.forbes.com/sites/jasonwingard/2020/05/29/why-companies-need-creative-leaders-in-the-future-of-work/#4145a142482a	5/31/2020	EJG	creativity	Google search
Groupthink	https://www.newyorker.com/magazine/2012/01/30/groupthink	6/5/2020	EJG	creativity	EJG hand-selected
Racial Essentialism Reduces Cr	https://www.psychologicalscience.org/news/releases/racial-essentialism-reduces-creative-thinking-by-making-people-more-closed-	6/5/2020	EJG	creativity	Google search
For a More Creative Brain Follc	https://jamesclear.com/five-step-creative-process#:~:text=The%20Creative%20Process%20in%20Short,it%20is%20a%20good%	6/5/2020	EJG	creativity	Google search
Stories About the Art of Makin	https://humanparts.medium.com/stories-about-the-art-of-making-art-b4e248cf993a	6/5/2020	EJG	creativity	Google search
How to Declutter Your Studio f	https://www.artsy.net/article/artsy-editorial-declutter-studio-maximum-creativity-marie-kondo	6/6/2020	EJG	creativity	Google search
What is Design Thinking?	https://www.ideou.com/blogs/inspiration/what-is-design-thinking#:~:text=Design%20thinking%20is%20a%20process,%2C%20services%2C%2	6/6/2020	EJG	creativity	Google search
Race, Gender, and the Creative	https://www.citylab.com/life/2012/06/race-gender-and-creative-class/2225/	6/6/2020	EJG	creativity	Google search
'Creativity out of tragedy:' Milw	https://fox6now.com/2020/06/05/creativity-out-of-tragedy-milwaukee-artists-complete-mural-in-memory-of-george-floyd/	6/7/2020	EJG	art protest	Google search
Our creativity is such a powerfu	https://theundefeated.com/galleries/street-art-of-george-floyd-reflects-our-pain-suffering-and-the-potential-for-healing/?view=list	6/7/2020	EJG	art protest	Google search
Creative Resistance: Why We N	https://www.alternet.org/2014/03/we-need-art-our-activism/	6/7/2020	EJG	art protest	Google search
A Breakthrough for A.I. Techno	https://www.nytimes.com/2019/09/04/technology/artificial-intelligence-aristo-passed-test.html	5/31/2020	EJG	AI	EJG hand-selected
Anthony Davis's Revolutionary	https://www.newyorker.com/culture/cultural-comment/anthony-daviss-revolutionary-opera-x	5/31/2020	EJG	black lives matter	EJG hand-selected
Reading J. M. Coetzee's "Disgra	https://www.newyorker.com/culture/cultural-comment/reading-j-m-coetzees-disgrace-during-the-harvey-weinstein-trial	5/31/2020	EJG	gender	EJG hand-selected
Frederick Douglass, Seen Up Cl	https://www.nytimes.com/2020/07/03/arts/frederick-douglass-yale.html	7/4/2020	EJG	black lives matter	EJG 7/4/20 nuzzle feed
Steve Jobs Said 1 Thing	https://getpocket.com/explore/item/steve-jobs-said-1-thing-separates-successful-people-from-everyone-else-and-will-make-all-the	7/4/2020	EJG	success	EJG 7/4/20 pocket feed
While Statues Sleep	https://www.lrb.co.uk/the-paper/v42/n12/thomas-laqueur/while-statues-sleep	7/4/2020	EJG	black lives matter	EJG hand-selected
China cuts Uighur births with I	https://apnews.com/269b3de1af34e17c1941a514f78d764c	7/4/2020	EJG	china	EJG Nuzzel Feed 6/30/20
A Warning from the Chickens c	https://thewalrus.ca/a-warning-from-the-chickens-of-the-world/	7/14/2020	EJG	coronavirus	EJG pocket feed 7/11/20

Figure 2: Information of manually collected and annotated articles, page 1

January's Book Club Pick: 'Hea	https://www.nytimes.com/2018/01/30/books/review-heart-berries-terese-marie-mailhot.html	7/14/2020	EJG	native american	EJG hand-selected
How To Make Indoor Air Safer	https://fivethirtyeight.com/features/how-to-make-indoor-air-safer/?utm_source=pocket&utm_medium=email&utm_campaign=pockethits	7/23/2020	EJG	covid	EJG pocket feed 7/21/20
What is Essential? And Who?	https://lithub.com/what-is-essential-and-who/	7/23/2020	EJG	covid	EJG literary hub feed 7/22/2
Apple Seems To Predict COVID	https://www.mediapost.com/publications/article/353387/apple-seems-to-predict-covid-19-hot-spots.html	7/24/2020	EJG	covid	EJG hand-selected
Jim Chanos pockets $100m fro	https://www.ft.com/content/4f72e8bc-fafd-4ede-a418-22904e6d5b5f	7/25/2020	EJG	finance	EJG hand-selected
The Worst for U.S. Renters and	https://www.bloomberg.com/news/articles/2020-07-24/the-worst-for-u-s-renters-and-apartment-owners-is-yet-to-come	7/25/2020	EJG	economy	EJG 7/25/20 Nuzzel Feed
Could Consciousness All Come	https://getpocket.com/explore/item/could-consciousness-all-come-down-to-the-way-things-vibrate	7/25/2020	EJG	science	EJG pocket feed 7/23/20
How You Feel Depends on Whe	https://www.wsj.com/articles/how-you-feel-depends-on-where-you-are-11594311622?	7/25/2020	EJG	psychology	EJG pocket feed 7/18/20
The Message Behind Gold's Ra	https://www.bloomberg.com/news/articles/2020-07-25/the-message-behind-gold-s-rally-the-world-economy-is-in-trouble	7/26/2020	EJG	economy	EJG pocket feed 7/26/20
SuperGLUE: The Slippery Bencl	https://medium.com/pat-inc/super-glue-the-slippery-benchmark-with-no-language-understanding-eb92680bfb14	8/3/2020	EJG	AI	EJG hand-selected
Stevie Smith: "Not Waving but	https://www.poetryfoundation.org/poems/46479/not-waving-but-drowning	8/10/2020	EJG	poetry	EJG hand-selected
Manhattan Apartment Rents P	https://www.bloomberg.com/news/articles/2020-08-13/manhattan-apartment-rents-plunge-10-in-pandemic-fueled-exodus#:~:	8/13/2010	EJG	covid	EJG hand-selected
Obsession and Desire in an Anc	https://lithub.com/obsession-and-desire-in-an-ancient-assyrian-library/	9/2/2020	EJG	history	EJG hand-selected
Pop diva Dana International tu	https://www.israelhayom.com/2020/09/01/pop-diva-dana-international-turns-literary-agent/	9/2/2020	EJG	literature	EJG hand-selected
Helen Cullen on Jane Austen, N	https://bookmarks.reviews/helen-cullen-on-jane-austen-michael-cunningham-and-donna-tartt/	9/3/2020	EJG	literature	EJG hand-selected
How to Read Aloud	https://www.lrb.co.uk/the-paper/v42/n17/irina-dumitrescu/how-to-read-aloud	9/3/2020	EJG	literature	EJG hand-selected
Maestro Bogomolny	https://medium.com/incerto/maestro-bogomolny-8498f08c0f0c	11/22/2020	EJG	math	EJG hand-selected
No Revenue Is No Problem in t	https://www.bloomberg.com/opinion/articles/2020-09-18/spac-deals-no-revenue-is-no-problem-in-the-2020-stock-market	11/22/2020	EJG	economy	EJG hand-selected
Evolution Made Really Smart P	https://www.inverse.com/article/24819-intelligent-people-friendships-satisfaction-savanna-theory	11/22/2020	EJG	economy	EJG hand-selected
Reading Comprehension - Elep	https://www.myenglishpages.com/site_php_files/reading-elephants-ivory-trade.php	9/19/2020	EJG	psychology	EJG hand-selected
People's words and actions car	https://ideas.ted.com/peoples-words-and-actions-can-actually-shape-your-brain-a-neuroscientist-explains-how/?utm_source=pocket&utm_n	11/22/2020	EJG	psychology	EJG hand-selected
Heirloom corn harvests	https://www.inquirer.com/food/craig-laban/philadelphia-restaurants-corn-harvest-lancaster-farms-20201106.html	11/8/2020	EJG	farming	EJG hand-selected
Motorists warned not to let mo	https://www.msn.com/en-us/news/technology/motorists-warned-not-to-let-moose-lick-their-cars/ar-BB1bfLI1?ocid=msedgdhp	11/22/2020	EJG	animal	EJG hand-selected
UFC fighter accidentally gets	https://www.msn.com/en-us/sports/mma-ufc/ufc-fighter-accidentally-gets-beyonc%C3%A9-halo-as-walk-up-music-hilariously-starts-	11/22/2020	EJG	sports	EJG hand-selected
Five Reasons Vinyl Is Making a	https://hub.yamaha.com/five-reasons-vinyl-is-making-a-comeback/	11/28/2020	EJG	music	EJG hand-selected
GIFTS THEY MIGHT ACTUALLY W	https://nymag.com/strategist/article/best-cozy-gifts.html	11/28/2020	EJG	christmas	EJG hand-selected
How to Make Baked Potatoes F	https://getpocket.com/explore/item/the-secret-to-better-baked-potatoes-cook-them-like-the-british-do	11/29/2020	EJG	food	EJG pocket feed 11/28/20
Raccoon Was Once a Thanksgiv	https://getpocket.com/explore/item/raccoon-was-once-a-thanksgiving-feast-fit-for-a-president	11/29/2020	EJG	food	EJG pocket feed 11/26/20
Neutrinos Lead to Unexpected	https://www.quantamagazine.org/neutrinos-lead-to-unexpected-discovery-in-basic-math-20191113/	11/29/2020	EJG	math	EJG hand-selected
The Ten Best Books About Foo	https://www.smithsonianmag.com/arts-culture/ten-best-books-about-food-2020-180976406/?	11/30/2020	EJG	food	EJG hand-selected
L.A.'s dance crisis: Studios fight	https://www.latimes.com/entertainment-arts/story/2020-09-02/la-dance-studio-classes-covid-closures	12/2/2020	EJG	covid	EJG hand-selected
How to Finally Organize Your K	https://getpocket.com/explore/item/how-to-finally-organize-your-kitchen-cabinets-for-good-this-time	12/2/2020	EJG	home	EJG pocket feed 12/1/20
Archaeologists uncover ancien	https://www.reuters.com/article/italy-pompeii-idUSKBN2900D3	12/27/2020	EJG	history	EJG Nuzzel feed 12/27/20
Some notes on funniness	https://www.newyorker.com/magazine/2020/12/28/some-notes-on-funniness?utm_source=pocket&utm_medium=email&utm_campaign=pc	12/27/2020	EJG	entertainment	EJG pocket feed 12/26/20
Gitanjali Rao Is Time Magazine	https://www.dogonews.com/2020/12/14/gitanjali-rao-is-time-magazines-first-kid-of-the-year	12/27/2020	EJG	science	EJG hand-selected

Figure 3: Information of manually collected and annotated articles, page 2

Towards a Methodology Supporting Semiautomatic Annotation of Head Movements in Video-recorded Conversations

Patrizia Paggio
University of Copenhagen
University of Malta
paggio@hum.ku.dk

Costanza Navarretta
University of Copenhagen
costanza@hum.ku.dk

Bart Jongejan
University of Copenhagen
bartj@hum.ku.dk

Manex Agirrezabal
University of Copenhagen
manex.aguirrezabal@hum.ku.dk

Abstract

We present a method to support the annotation of head movements in video-recorded conversations. Head movement segments from annotated multimodal data are used to train a model to detect head movements in unseen data. The resulting predicted movement sequences are uploaded to the ANVIL tool for post-annotation editing. The automatically identified head movements and the original annotations are compared to assess the overlap between the two. This analysis showed that movement onsets were more easily detected than offsets, and pointed at a number of patterns in the mismatches between original annotations and model predictions that could be dealt with in general terms in post-annotation guidelines.

1 Introduction

Communicative gestures, such as head movements, gaze and hand gestures, are important in face-to-face communication, where they provide relevant and non redundant information that must be processed together with speech (Kendon, 2004). The automatic annotation of gestures is still problematic while their manual annotation is challenging and resource intensive.

Head movements are the most frequent gesture type and their importance as feedback and turn management signals has been recognised in numerous studies (Duncan, 1972; Hadar et al., 1983; McClave, 2000; Heylen et al., 2007; Allwood et al., 2007). For this reason, the automatic identification of the most frequent types of head movement has often been addressed as a component in multimodal systems where humans communicate with software agents or robots (Morency, 2009; Germesin and Wilson, 2009; Türker et al., 2018).

Many factors influence the frequency and type of gestures produced by speakers, e.g. the language (Navarretta et al., 2011) and the communicative setting. Therefore, it is important to have reliably annotated data of conversations in different languages and contexts. There are a wealth of video-recorded monologues and conversation on the internet that could be used for multimodal analysis. However, although several projects have developed multimodal data annotated with gestural information (for a discussion, see Wagner et al., 2014), few of these efforts have yet resulted in freely available annotated corpora for multiple languages such as in Koutsombogera and Vogel (2018). In parallel with this work, the linguistics community interested in co-speech gesture has created and annotated many multimodal data collections, but typically for experimental purposes and thus in very specific contexts (Holler, 2013).

In the NLP community there is a growing interest for multimodal sentiment analysis, in which visual and acoustic features are used to analyse sentiment and emotion in video data (Zadeh et al., 2017; Soleymani et al., 2017). The data collections used for this task are consequently annotated with sentiment and emotion labels, not with gestural information. A recent example is the CMU-MOSEI corpus (Zadeh et al., 2018).

This paper describes work aimed to support the annotation of head movements in video-recorded spontaneous conversations. More specifically, we propose a method in which automatically identified head movement segments from dyadic conversations are uploaded to the ANVIL multimodal annotation tool (Kipp, 2004), from which human annotators will be able to correct them. To assess how demanding it would be for human annotators to work with the system's suggestions, we compare the automatically identified head movements with manually annotated ones from the same corpus, and present both quantitative and qualitative analyses of this comparison. Finally we discuss possible improvements of the system and future work.

Proceedings of the Joint 15th Linguistic Annotation Workshop (LAW) and 3rd Designing Meaning Representations (DMR) Workshop, pages 151–159
November, 2021.

In section 2 we present background and related studies; in section 3 we describe the corpus, particularly the head movement annotations; in section 4 we give a succinct account of the method used to train models that predict head movements; in section 5 we analyse the results in terms of how well they match what the human annotators did; finally, in section 6 we summarise our results and suggest some feature perspectives.

2 Related Studies

The automatic identification of head movements can be based on the use of different tracking systems, e.g. looking at the coordinates provided by Kinect (Wei et al., 2013) or by various eye-tracking systems (Al-Rahayfeh and Faezipour, 2013). A number of researchers have worked with automatic detection of head movements in video-recordings of human-human and human-robot conversations, and the results of these studies have been evaluated using the manual annotations of the relevant movements. Two main approaches have been used. In the first one, computer vision techniques have been applied (Murphy-Chutorian and Trivedi, 2009; Gavrila, 1999), but most of these attempts have posed certain requirements to the quality, light and settings of the videos. The second approach concerns training various classifiers on automatically extracted visual and, possibly, audio features. For the visual features the two freely available systems OpenCV[1] and OpenPose[2] have been used, while audio features have been extracted via different systems. The focus of the majority of these studies has been that of determining the best visual and auditory features and the most effective classifiers for the task (Morency et al., 2005, 2007; Morency, 2009; Germesin and Wilson, 2009; Jongejan et al., 2017; Frid et al., 2017; Ambrazaitis and House, 2017; Paggio et al., 2020).

Only a couple of studies have addressed the integration of automatically identified head movements in annotation tools. Jongejan (2012) integrated the OpenCV facetracker into ANVIL to support head movement annotation for users of that system. The Max Planck Institute for Psycholinguistics and the Fraunhofer institutes HHI and IAIS developed AVAtech (Lenkiewicz et al., 2012), a gesture recogniser which is integrated into the ELAN multimodal annotation system (Wittenburg et al., 2006). The recogniser identifies head movements and hand gestures in videos. The system is based on skin recognition and other computer vision techniques, and therefore only works when videos follow specific requirements with respect to video quality, background colour, position of the speaker(s) and light. The system works best in cases when only one speaker is recorded and both face and hands can clearly been seen. When successful, AVAtech generates a video where the gestures are marked, and ELAN tracks with the head and gesture annotations given certain specifications. The system is not being further-developed, but it is still an integrated part of ELAN. We tested the recogniser on our data, but it failed to process the videos because of their quality, and in some cases, their format.

Given this background, additional efforts are needed to provide the research community with more and better automatic support for the creation of gestural annotation of conversational data.

3 The corpus

The corpus used in our study is the Danish NOMCO corpus of first encounter dialogues (Paggio and Navarretta, 2016), which consists of twelve spontaneous conversations between young people (six males and six females) of about five minutes each, for a total recording time of approximately one hour. Each participant took part in two dialogues with persons of different genders. During the encounters, the participants were standing facing each other and were recorded by three cameras. For this study we used recordings in which two frontal views of the participants are joined as shown in Figure 1.

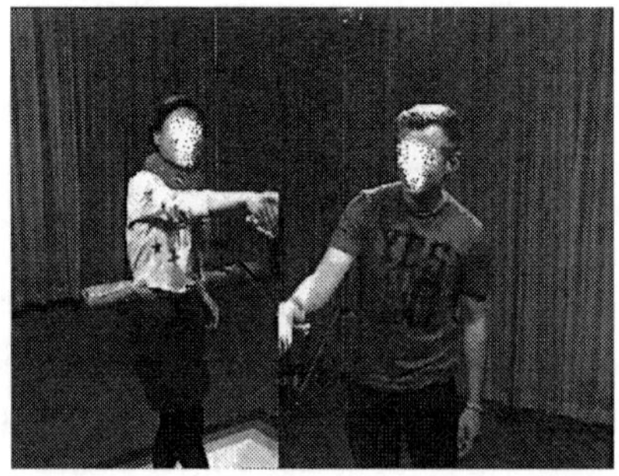

Figure 1: Screenshot from one of the NOMCO dialogues: split view

The videos were transcribed and annotated in many different ways using the ANVIL tool, and following the guidelines provided by the MUMIN

[1] https://opencv.org/

[2] https://github.com/CMU-Perceptual-Computing-Lab/openpose

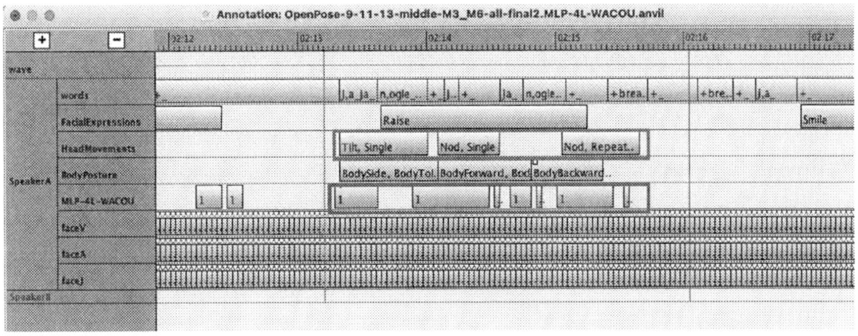

Figure 2: Screenshot of the ANVIL annotation board with manually and automatically annotated head movement sequences outlined in red and green, respectively

coding scheme for formal and functional annotation of gestural behaviour (Allwood et al., 2007). This study is concerned with the formal annotation of the speakers' head movements, for which the coding scheme provides the following labels: *Nod, Up-nod, Shake, HeadBackward, HeadForward, SideTurn, Tilt, Waggle* and *HeadOther*. A head movement is annotated by defining start and end point of the movement on the tool's annotation board, and by picking one of the labels.

The linguistic context was taken into account in order to select and annotate only those head movements that were judged to have a communicative function. To familiarise themselves with the annotation scheme and guidelines, the three annotators involved went through an initial training exercise in which they annotated the gestures in one video together, and discussed all disagreements with one another and with two expert researchers. After that, they annotated a second video independently and their mutual agreement was measured.

The inter-coder agreement for identification and classification of head movements reached a Cohen's *kappa* score in the range 0.72-0.8 (Navarretta et al., 2011). To produce the final version of the annotations, all disagreements were adjudicated by involving an expert annotator.

The annotations have been used in numerous studies addressing aspects such as the identification of feedback and turn-taking signals given through head movements and facial expressions (Paggio and Navarretta, 2011; Navarretta and Paggio, 2013). The manual annotations of head movements, as well as of other gesture types, are available for research[3].

[3]https://cst.ku.dk/projekter/the-danish-nomco-corpus/

4 Automatic detection of head movement

In this section we summarise the method we use for the automatic detection of head movements. A more detailed explanation and discussion is provided in Paggio et al. (2020).

The manual annotations of head movements were used as a basis for training a classifier to detect the presence of head movement in a frame-wise fashion. To create a speaker-independent model, the classifier had to detect movement for each speaker after having being trained on the data from the other eleven participants following a leave-one-out cross validation strategy.

The training data consisted of visual, acoustic and textual features. OpenPose (Cao et al., 2018) was used to extract nose tip positions from the data. For each of these positions we include both the cartesian (x and y) and polar (radius and angle) coordinates, thus, four different scalar values. We then calculate velocity, acceleration and jerk of these positions by computing the first, second and third order derivatives, using the previous 9, 11 and 13 frames, respectively. We include these three orders of derivatives, resulting in a total of twelve visual features.

Intensity and pitch measurements were extracted from the audio files using PRAAT (Boersma and Weenink, 2009). Finally, head movement labels, as well as word information, were extracted from the annotations.

As a result, for each frame in each video a vector was created with labels expressing presence/absence of movement and the head movement class; velocity, acceleration and jerk features; pitch and intensity values referring to the gesturer; and finally a binary feature expressing whether the same gesturer is speaking or not.

Several classifiers were tested on the data. The

best performing one was a Multilayer Perceptron (MLP) with 4 layers, which achieved an average accuracy across the twelve speakers of 0.730 and an F1 score of 0.684 (macro average).

The frame-wise head movement predictions were combined into sequences by conjoining directly adjacent frames for which a positive movement value had been assigned by the predictor and mapped onto the XML format necessary to read them into the ANVIL tool as independent tracks. In this way, a comparison could be carried out between the manual and the automatic annotations.

Figure 2 is a screenshot of the ANVIL annotation board visualising an excerpt of the annotation with tracks for one of the speakers (Speaker A). There are eight tracks corresponding to i) the speech transcription, ii-iv) the manual annotations of facial expressions, head movements and body posture, v) the head movement annotations detected by the MLP classifier, and vi-viii) the values for movement velocity, acceleration and jerk. The two tracks of interest here are the ones containing the manually annotated head movements, a sequence of which has been highlighted in red, and the corresponding automatically derived head movement elements, marked in green. In this example, we see that three head movements in the former track roughly correspond to three larger and two smaller elements in the latter. There are also, however, two additional predictions in the middle of the sequence which do not overlap with any annotated movement. In a scenario in which a new annotation task has to be produced, only the elements suggested by the model would be available, making it possible for an annotator to revise these suggestions as needed.

To get an impression of how much and what type of revision may become necessary, in the next section we look more closely at how well the two annotation tracks correspond to one other.

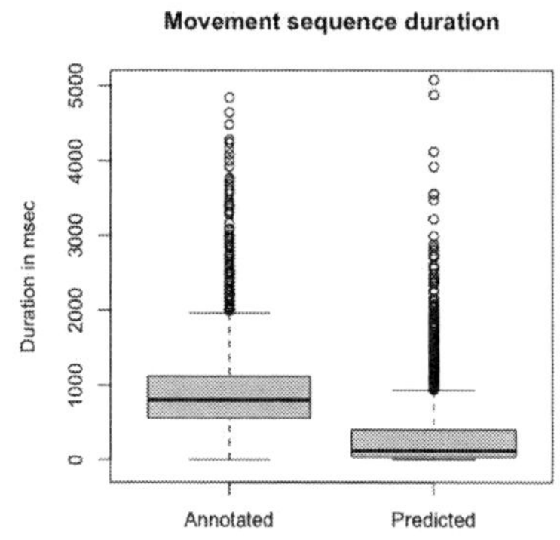

Figure 3: Distribution of the duration of head movements in the manual annotations vs model predictions

movements compared to the movement sequences identified by the human annotators. The duration distribution of annotated vs predicted movement is visualised in a combined boxplot in Figure 3. It is evident that the predicted movements are much shorter on average, however there are also large numbers of outliers in the upper end of both plots.

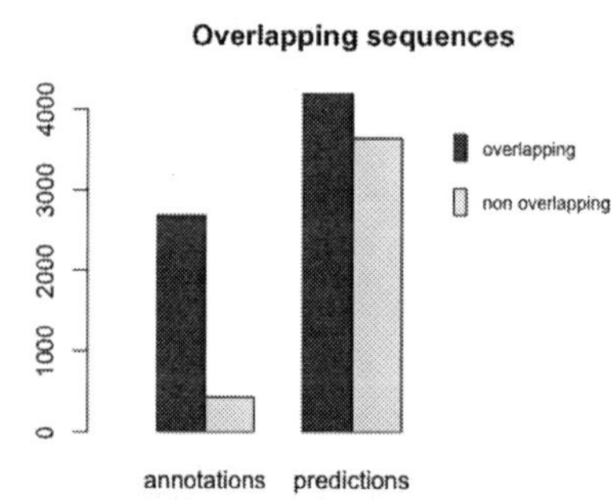

Figure 4: Number of overlaps in annotated and predicted head movements

5 Analysis of results

5.1 Overlaps between manual and automatic annotations

The total number of annotated head movements in the Danish NOMCO corpus is 3117. The number of movement sequences predicted by the MLP binary classifier, however, is 7827.

The mean duration of an annotated movement sequence is 935 ms (sd: 579) while the mean duration of a predicted movement is 286 ms (sd: 370). Thus the model predicts a much higher number of shorter

To reach a general understanding of the way the two sets of movements relate to one another in terms of alignment, overlaps between annotated and predicted movement sequences were extracted. There are multiple overlaps between the annotated and the predicted movement sequences, such that 2685 of the annotated sequences (86%) overlap with one or more predicted ones. Conversely, 4191 of the predicted sequences (53%) overlap with an annotated movement. In other words, the model has quite good recall, but also generates a relatively high number of false positives (predictions that do

Overlaps per annotation	Annotated elements #	%	Total predicted elements
One	1234	46	1234
Two	751	28	1502
Three	385	14	836
Four	209	8	285
Five	57	2	126
Six-Nine	49	2	208
Total	2685	100	4191

Table 1: Breakdown of number of overlaps per movement annotation

not overlap with manual annotation). A visualisation is provided in Figure 4.

Table 1 shows a breakdown of the overlaps. The table summarises how many annotated movements overlap with one predicted movement, two of them, three and so on. As can be seen, in the vast majority of cases (88%), an annotated movement overlaps with 1-3 predicted movement sequences. The example displayed in Figure 2 shows one such situation, in which three annotated elements correspond to five predicted ones. In 12% of the cases one annotation corresponds to more than three predictions, and marginally (only two cases in fact) to as many as nine different predicted elements.

For each annotated head movement that overlapped with some predicted movement, the longest overlap of at least 0.01 ms was then extracted. This generated a list of 2661 overlaps. The average duration of the longest overlaps is 445.83 ms (sd: 317.06).

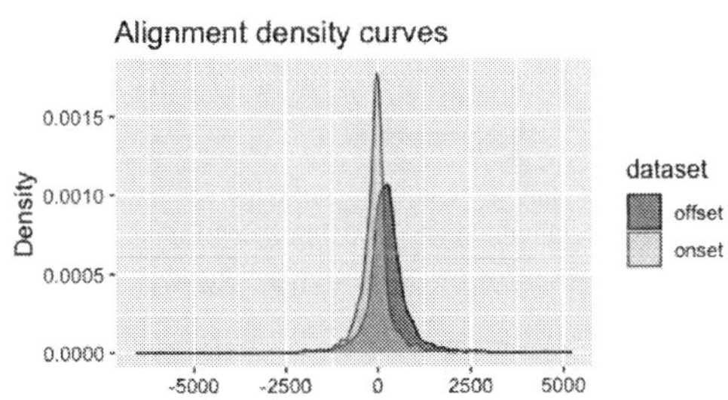

Figure 5: Overlap alignment at onset and offset points

None of these overlaps are complete. In other words, in no case does an annotated movement align completely both at onset and offset with a predicted one. To investigate whether the longest overlaps predicted by the model align better at onset or offset, we calculated the differences at start and end points between the annotated and the predicted movement for each overlap. The result is two lists of misalignments, which are visualised by means of a combined density plot in Figure 5.

The onset misalignment is -68 ms on average (sd: 500), indicating that the overlapping predicted sequence tends to start slightly after the annotated one (start of annotated – start of predicted). In comparison, the mean offset misalignment is 232 ms (sd: 613), indicating that the offset of the overlapping predicted sequence tends to occur earlier than the offset of the corresponding annotated movement (end of annotated – end of predicted). In other words, annotated and predicted movements align better at onset than at offset, albeit with considerable variation. The difference is significant on a Wilcoxon rank sum test (W = 2019582, p-value < 2.2e-16).

Here we advance some conjectures for why onsets may be easier for the model to detect. Predicting the offset of a movement may be more difficult due to inherent characteristics of head movements, and perhaps gestural movements in general, with movements petering out in a way that makes it difficult to distinguish the exact end point. An additional difficulty may also be due to movements containing holds, where the human annotators would consider such a hold part of a movement which has not yet come to an end, whereas automatic detection would probably divide such a movement up in several sequences. In fact in a number of cases, the offset misalignment is due to the fact that multiple sequences overlap with the tail of the annotated movements.

5.2 Comparing manual and automatic annotations: a qualitative analysis

In this section, we present a qualitative comparison of the manual and automatic annotations in ANVIL, focusing on the annotations of the head movements of one participant in a randomly chosen video. We distinguish four different situations in which there are differences between an annotated movement sequence and what should be the corresponding predicted one.

We start with cases in which head movements identified by the model were not annotated by the coders. There are several explanations for this difference between the two types of annotations:

a. The participant moves the head, but the gesture has not been annotated because it does not have a clear communicative function, e.g. the participant moves the head to look at the other speaker immediately before they shake hands at the beginning of the interaction.

b. The participant moves the whole body or her shoulders and the head moves with the rest of the body/upper body. In such cases, the annotators were instructed to code the movement as a body posture shift.

c. A non-movement is identified as a movement by the system (true error).

The discrepancy explained under (a) is due to the annotation guidelines adopted in the NOMCO project (op. cit.), in which a basic distinction between communicative and non-communicative gestures was adopted. An automatic annotator could not be expected to make such a distinction, and in fact other annotation projects may take a different approach to this issue. Cases subsumed under (b), in contrast, could perhaps be avoided with a more careful use of visual features in which head and body movement are handled separately. At the moment, in fact, we are not using any visual body markers from OpenPose. As for false positives due to true errors as in (c), they can probably not be entirely avoided. More analysis would be necessary to know exactly how many of these cases we have.

There are then a number of cases in which one manually annotated head movement overlaps with several automatically identified ones, again due to several reasons:

d. The manually identified head movement is a repeated gesture, e.g. a repeated nod was coded as one uninterrupted gesture whereas the system found a sequence of smaller independent movements. However, it must be noted that in some cases a manually coded repeated head movement is also identified as a single head movement by the system.

e. A movement of the upper body partially overlaps with a head movement in the manual annotations, whereas the model found two separate head movements.

f. The annotated movement contains one or several holds, or subsequences in which the movement slows down to then pick up in velocity again. The model typically identifies a number of separate movement sequences in such cases.

Cases such as described under (d) are relatively well-defined and could be handled in future annotations by instructing the coders to conflate the automatically generated components of a repeated gesture into one uninterrupted element. Cases under (e) are similar to (b) above. The same comments therefore hold. The situation described under (f), which was also discussed in the preceding section, requires some consideration. An annotator would have to judge whether the distinct elements should be considered part of an uninterrupted gesture and therefore joined, or not. A typical example of this are tilts of the head. Quite often, the speaker who performs a head tilt will keep the tilt for a few seconds – sometimes longer than that – before bringing the head back to normal position. In NOMCO a decision was made always to annotate such cases as uninterrupted gestures, however the hold may sometimes be so long as to warrant a different solution.

The third mismatch type considered consists of cases in which one automatically identified head movement corresponds to several manually annotated head movements. All of these seem in fact explainable in the same way:

g. The manually identified head movements are different but consecutive ones, e.g. a manually identified head forward movement followed by a repeated shake overlap with a single predicted movement.

Since the model is a binary classifier, no other solutions would have been possible for the (g) cases. Two scenarios can be envisaged here. In the first one, an annotator can be instructed to split a movement element into a sequence of separate ones if it corresponds to several different gestures. In the second one, a more complex model must be trained to detect not just presence of head movement but different movement classes.

Finally, there are cases in which the annotators coded a head movement that is clearly visible in the video, but which the system failed to identify. No explanation could be provided for such cases, which are, however, relatively rare. Recall in fact that 86% of the annotated head movements overlap with at least one predicted one.

6 Conclusion and future work

In this paper we have presented work aimed at creating support for the annotation of head movements in video-recorded data, an annotation which is a necessary first step in any analysis of the role played by head movements in the semantics and pragmatics of face-to-face conversations.

The first step in our methodology is to train machine learning models to detect head movements based on visual and acoustic features that are obtained from video-recorded materials without specific demands on the audio-visual quality. The second step is to make the automatically derived movement sequences available in the ANVIL multimodal annotation tool. The evaluation of the results showed a good coverage in that 86% of annotated movements were predicted with various degrees of overlap. However, a high number of non-existing movements were also incorrectly predicted.

Subsequent analysis showed that movement onsets were more easily detected than offsets, and pointed at a number of patterns in the mismatches between original annotations and model predictions that could be dealt with in general terms in post-annotation guidelines.

More work is needed to understand and possibly reduce the impact of false positives. The sequence-generation process may also be a source of errors, thus alternative methods to combine frames into sequences should be explored. Another obvious extension of this work concerns the automatic classification of head movement in different types. Moreover, we plan to work on adapting our results to make the predicted movement sequences compatible with the ELAN tool.

Finally, we need to determine how useful the automatic prediction is in a concrete annotation exercise. It is important to evaluate not only whether the annotators would save time post-editing the predicted movements rather than creating new ones from scratch, but also whether the same accuracy can be reached and what kinds of error the annotators would make in the post-editing scenario compared to the traditional one. We plan to conduct such a study in connection with the development of a new corpus of online group discussions that is being collected by the international network on GEstures and Head Movements in language (GEHM)[4]

Acknowledgements

This work was supported by the Independent Research Fund Denmark (grant 9055-00004B). We would also like to thank the anonymous reviewers for their useful comments.

[4]https://cst.ku.dk/english/projects/gestures-and-head-movements-in-language-gehm/

References

Amer Al-Rahayfeh and Miad Faezipour. 2013. Eye tracking and head movement detection: A state-of-art survey. *IEEE Journal of Translational Engineering in Health and Medicine*, 1:2100212 -2100212.

Jens Allwood, Loredana Cerrato, Kristiina Jokinen, Costanza Navarretta, and Patrizia Paggio. 2007. The MUMIN coding scheme for the annotation of feedback, turn management and sequencing phenomena. In Jean-Claude Martin, Patrizia Paggio, Peter Kuehnlein, Rainer Stiefelhagen, and Fabio Pianesi, editors, *Multimodal Corpora for Modelling Human Multimodal Behaviour*, volume 41 of *Special issue of the International Journal of Language Resources and Evaluation*, pages 273–287. Springer.

Gilbert Ambrazaitis and David House. 2017. Acoustic features of multimodal prominences: Do visual beat gestures affect verbal pitch accent realization? In *Proceedings of The 14th International Conference on Auditory-Visual Speech Processing (AVSP2017)*, pages 89–94. KTH.

Paul Boersma and David Weenink. 2009. Praat: doing phonetics by computer (version 5.1.05) [computer program]. Retrieved May 1, 2009, from http://www.praat.org/.

Zhe Cao, Gines Hidalgo, Tomas Simon, Shih-En Wei, and Yaser Sheikh. 2018. OpenPose: realtime multi-person 2D pose estimation using Part Affinity Fields. In *arXiv preprint arXiv:1812.08008*.

Starkey Duncan. 1972. Some signals and rules for taking speaking turns in conversations. *Journal of Personality and Social Psychology*, 23:283–292.

Johan Frid, Gilbert Ambrazaitis, Malin Svensson-Lundmark, and David House. 2017. Towards classification of head movements in audiovisual recordings of read news. In *Proceedings of the 4th European and 7th Nordic Symposium on Multimodal Communication (MMSYM 2016)*, 141, pages 4–9, Copenhagen. Linköping University Electronic Press, Linköpings universitet.

Dariu M Gavrila. 1999. The visual analysis of human movement: A survey. *Computer Vision and Image Understanding*, 73(1):82 – 98.

Sebastian Germesin and Theresa Wilson. 2009. Agreement detection in multiparty conversation. In *Proceedings of ICMI-MLMI 2009*, pages 7–14.

Uri Hadar, Timothy J Steiner, Ewan C Grant, and Frank Clifford Rose. 1983. Head Movement Correlates of Juncture and Stress at Sentence Level. *Language and Speech*, 26(2):117–129.

Dirk Heylen, Elisabetta Bevacqua, Marion Tellier, and Catherine Pelachaud. 2007. Searching for prototypical facial feedback signals. In *Proceedings of 7th International Conference on Intelligent Virtual Agents*, pages 147–153.

Judith Holler. 2013. *52. Experimental methods in co-speech gesture research*, pages 837–857. De Gruyter Mouton.

Bart Jongejan. 2012. Automatic annotation of head velocity and acceleration in anvil. In *Proceedings of the Eighth International Conference on Language Resources and Evaluation (LREC'12)*, pages 201–208.

Bart Jongejan, Patrizia Paggio, and Costanza Navarretta. 2017. Classifying head movements in video-recorded conversations based on movement velocity, acceleration and jerk. In *Proceedings of the 4th European and 7th Nordic Symposium on Multimodal Communication (MMSYM 2016), Copenhagen, 29-30 September 2016*, 141, pages 10–17. Linköping University Electronic Press, Linköpings universitet.

Adam Kendon. 2004. *Gesture*. Cambridge University Press.

Michael Kipp. 2004. *Gesture Generation by Imitation – From Human Behavior to Computer Character Animation*. Boca Raton, Florida: Dissertation.com.

Maria Koutsombogera and Carl Vogel. 2018. Modeling collaborative multimodal behavior in group dialogues: The multisimo corpus. In *Proceedings of the Eleventh International Conference on Language Resources and Evaluation (LREC 2018)*, Paris, France. European Language Resources Association (ELRA).

Przemyslaw Lenkiewicz, Binyam Gebrekidan Gebre, Oliver Schreer, Stefano Masneri, Daniel Schneider, and Sebastian Tschöpel. 2012. Avatech — automated annotation through audio and video analysis. In *Proceedings of the Eight International Conference on Language Resources and Evaluation (LREC'12)*, Istanbul, Turkey. European Language Resources Association (ELRA).

Evelyn McClave. 2000. Linguistic functions of head movements in the context of speech. *Journal of Pragmatics*, 32:855–878.

Louis-Philippe Morency. 2009. Co-occurrence graphs: contextual representation for head gesture recognition during multi-party interactions. In *Proceedings of the Workshop on Use of Context in Vision Processing*, pages 1–6.

Louis-Philippe Morency, Ariadna Quattoni, and Trevor Darrell. 2007. Latent-dynamic discriminative models for continuous gesture recognition. In *2007 IEEE conference on computer vision and pattern recognition*, pages 1–8. IEEE.

Louis-Philippe Morency, Candace Sidner, Christopher Lee, and Trevor Darrell. 2005. Contextual recognition of head gestures. In *Proceedings of the 7th international conference on Multimodal interfaces*, pages 18–24.

Erik Murphy-Chutorian and Mohan Manubhai Trivedi. 2009. Head pose estimation in computer vision: A survey. *IEEE Transactions on Pattern Analysis and Machine Intelligence*, 31(4):607–626.

Costanza Navarretta, Elisabeth Ahlsén, Jens Allwood, Kristiina Jokinen, and Patrizia Paggio. 2011. Creating Comparable Multimodal Corpora for Nordic Languages. In *Proceedings of the 18th Conference Nordic Conference of Computational Linguistics*, pages 153–160, Riga, Latvia.

Costanza Navarretta and Patrizia Paggio. 2013. Classifying Multimodal Turn Management in Danish Dyadic First Encounters. In *Proceedings of the 19th Nordic Conference of Computational Linguistics (Nodalida 2013)*, pages 133–146, Oslo, Norway. NEALT.

Patrizia Paggio, Manex Agirrezabal, Bart Jongejan, and Costanza Navarretta. 2020. Automatic detection and classification of head movements in face-to-face conversations. In *Proceedings of LREC2020 Workshop "People in language, vision and the mind" (ONION2020)*, pages 15–21, Marseille, France. European Language Resources Association (ELRA).

Patrizia Paggio and Costanza Navarretta. 2011. Head movements, facial expressions and feedback in Danish first encounters interactions: A culture-specific analysis. In *Universal Access in Human-Computer Interaction - Users Diversity. 6th International Conference. UAHCI 2011, Held as Part of HCI International 2011*, number 6766 in LNCS, pages 583–690, Orlando Florida. Springer Verlag.

Patrizia Paggio and Costanza Navarretta. 2016. The Danish NOMCO corpus: Multimodal interaction in first acquaintance conversations. *Language Resources and Evaluation*, pages 1–32.

Mohammad Soleymani, David Garcia, Brendan Jou, Björn Schuller, Shih-Fu Chang, and Maja Pantic. 2017. A survey of multimodal sentiment analysis. *Image and Vision Computing*, 65:3–14.

Bekir Berker Türker, E. Erzin, Y. Yemez, and T. M. Sezgin. 2018. Audio-visual prediction of head-nod and turn-taking events in dyadic interactions. In *INTERSPEECH*, pages 1741–1745.

Petra Wagner, Zofia Malisz, and Stefan Kopp. 2014. Gesture and speech in interaction: An overview. *Speech Communication*, 57:209 – 232.

Haolin Wei, Patricia Scanlon, Yingbo Li, David S Monaghan, and Noel E O'Connor. 2013. Real-time head nod and shake detection for continuous human affect recognition. In *14th International Workshop on Image Analysis for Multimedia Interactive Services (WIAMIS)*, pages 1–4. IEEE.

Peter Wittenburg, Hennie Brugman, Albert Russel, Alex Klassmann, and Han Sloetjes. 2006. ELAN: a Professional Framework for Multimodality Research. In *Proceedings of LREC 2006, Fifth International Conference on Language Resources and Evaluation*, pages 1556–1559.

Amir Zadeh, Minghai Chen, Soujanya Poria, Erik Cambria, and Louis-Philippe Morency. 2017. Tensor fusion network for multimodal sentiment analysis. *arXiv preprint arXiv:1707.07250*.

Amir Zadeh, Paul Pu Liang, Soujanya Poria, Prateek Vij, Erik Cambria, and Louis-Philippe Morency. 2018. Multi-attention recurrent network for human communication comprehension. In *Thirty-Second AAAI Conference on Artificial Intelligence*.

Intensionalizing Abstract Meaning Representations: Non-Veridicality and Scope

Gregor Williamson
Department of Computer Science
Emory University
Atlanta, GA 30322, USA
gregor.jude.williamson@emory.edu

Patrick Elliott
Department of Linguistics and Philosophy
Massachusetts Institute of Technology
Cambridge, MA 02139, USA
pdell@mit.edu

Yuxin Ji
Department of Quantitative Theory and Methods
Emory University
Atlanta, GA 30322, USA
jessica.ji@emory.edu

Abstract

Abstract Meaning Representation (AMR) is a graphical meaning representation language designed to represent propositional information about argument structure. However, at present it is unable to satisfyingly represent non-veridical intensional contexts, often licensing inappropriate inferences. In this paper, we show how to resolve the problem of non-veridicality without appealing to layered graphs through a mapping from AMRs into Simply-Typed Lambda Calculus (STLC). At least for some cases, this requires the introduction of a new role `:content` which functions as an intensional operator. The translation proposed is inspired by the formal linguistics literature on the event semantics of attitude reports. Next, we address the interaction of quantifier scope and intensional operators in so-called de re/de dicto ambiguities. We adopt a scope node from the literature and provide an explicit multidimensional semantics utilizing Cooper storage which allows us to derive the de re and de dicto scope readings as well as intermediate scope readings which prove difficult for accounts without a scope node.

1 Introduction

Abstract Meaning Representation (AMR) is a graphical meaning representation in which graphs are rooted, directed, and acyclic (Banarescu et al., 2013). Non-terminal nodes are assigned variable IDs, terminal nodes are sense concepts (e.g., `believe-01`, `boy`, etc.) or constants (e.g., the polarity attribute `-`, cardinals, names, etc.), and labelled edges represent semantic relations between nodes. The inventory of AMR disambiguated predicate senses (e.g., `believe-01`) are based on PropBank argument structure frames (Bonial et al., 2015; Palmer et al., 2005; Bonial et al., 2014). The graph in (1-b) is an AMR for the sentence in (1-a). More commonly, however, AMRs are represented in Penman notation (Matthiessen and Bateman, 1991) as in (1-c) or occasionally as a conjunction of logical triples (1-d).

(1) a. *The boy hugged the dog.*

b. 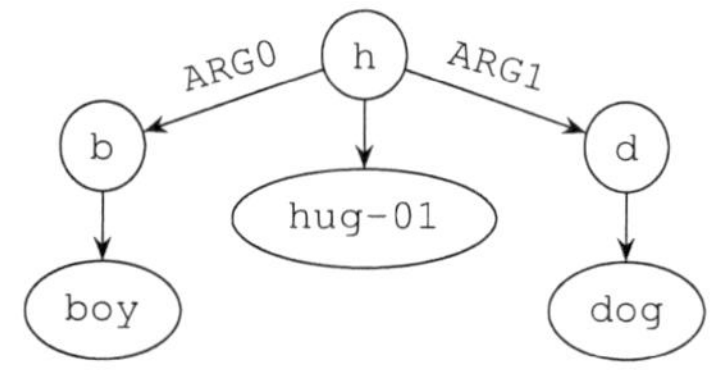

c.
```
(h / hug-01
   :ARG0 (b / boy)
   :ARG1 (d / dog))
```

d. $\text{INSTANCE}(\texttt{h}, \texttt{hug-01}) \wedge \text{INSTANCE}(\texttt{b}, \texttt{boy}) \wedge \texttt{ARG0}(\texttt{h}, \texttt{b}) \wedge \text{INSTANCE}(\texttt{d}, \texttt{dog}) \wedge \texttt{ARG1}(\texttt{h}, \texttt{d})$

The main strength of AMR is its ability to represent argument structure, as these logical triples translate naturally into a rudimentary neo-Davidsonian event semantics (Davidson, 1967; Parsons, 1990), with every INSTANCE relation split into an existential quantifier and a one-place predicate.

(2) $\exists x(\textbf{hug-01}(x) \wedge \exists y(\textbf{boy}(y) \wedge ARG0(x)(y) \wedge \exists z(\textbf{dog}(z) \wedge ARG1(x)(z))))$

Recent developments have seen the expressive power of AMR improved both in terms of its

Proceedings of the Joint 15th Linguistic Annotation Workshop (LAW) and 3rd Designing Meaning Representations (DMR) Workshop, pages 160–169

graphic representation as well as its translation into logical forms. For instance, AMR graphical representations have been enriched to represent Tense and Aspect (Donatelli et al., 2018, 2019; Van Gysel et al., 2021), quantifier scope (Pustejovsky et al., 2019; Van Gysel et al., 2021), semantic number (Stabler, 2017), and speech acts (Bonial et al., 2020), while translations into first and higher-order logics have been proposed as a means of capturing coreference (Artzi et al., 2015) and quantifier scope (Bos, 2016, 2020; Stabler, 2017; Lai et al., 2020).

Despite these advances in theoretical work, AMR encounters issues when it comes to the semantics of intensional contexts. For instance, Crouch and Kalouli (2018) note that an AMR like (3-b), represented as a conjunction of logical triples, would permit an inference to *'The girl is sick'* by conjunction elimination.

(3) a. *The boy believes that the girl is sick.*

b.
```
(b / believe-01
   :ARG0 (b2 / boy)
   :ARG1 (s / sick-05
      :ARG1 (g / girl)))
```

An even more striking consequence of this non-veridical problem is demonstrated by the following examples.[1]

(4) a. *The boy believes he is sick.*

b.
```
(b / believe-01
   :ARG0 (b2 / boy)
   :ARG1 (s / sick-05
      :ARG1 b2))
```

c.
```
(b / believe-01
   :ARG0 (b2 / boy
      :ARG1-of (s / sick-05))
   :ARG1 s))
```

At first glance, it might appear that the predicate `sick-05` is in a non-veridical context in (4-b) and a veridical context in (4-c). This is because the grammatical subject position of the verb *believe* is a veridical environment, while its sentential complement is not. However, these graphs are in fact logically equivalent because for any AMR relation R, $\mathrm{R}(x)(y) \Leftrightarrow \mathrm{R\text{-}of}(y)(x)$. Consequently, (4-b) and (4-c) depict the same conjunction of logical triples once inverse relations are normalized.

[1]These examples are based on examples in the *freakshow* section of the AMR guidelines, available at: `https://github.com/amrisi/amr-guidelines/blob/master/amr.md#amr-freak-show`

Crouch and Kalouli (2018) provide a solution to the problem of non-veridicality in a graph-based representation by making use of a Graphic Knowledge Representation (GKR) (Kalouli and Crouch, 2018), a layered graph in which identifiers, or names, are assigned to sub-graphs (Carroll et al., 2005). A GKR separates conceptual structure (i.e., predicate-argument structure) and contextual structure into two sub-graphs. The graph in (5) is a simplified GKR of (3-a). The lower context `bel` represents the intensional context of the boy's belief and is non-veridical (or averidical) with respect to the upper context `top`. Consequently, the GKR does not permit the inference from *'The boy believes the girl is sick'* to *'The girl is sick.'*

(5)

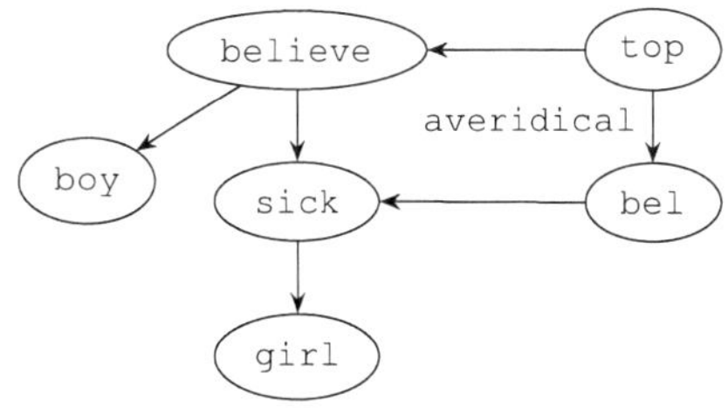

Another problem for AMR's representation of attitude reports such as those containing the verb *'believe'* is that PropBank argument structures often do not distinguish between propositional and non-propositional arguments. For instance, the PropBank argument structure for `believe-01` assigns both nominal and clausal arguments the same argument role, `:ARG1`.[2] Despite this, the PropBank frame includes a note that *'believe'* can have both a theme and a propositional argument simultaneously (e.g., *'Mary believed John that he didn't eat the last piece of pie'*).[3]

Given this lack of distinction between different types of arguments, it is not sufficient to lexically specify that the `:ARG1` of `believe-01` is always a non-veridical environment. While this might work for (3-b), it would also mean that we could not infer the existence of a girl from (6).

(6) a. *The boy believed the girl.*

b.
```
(b / believe-01
   :ARG0 (b2 / boy)
   :ARG1 (g / girl))
```

[2]PropBank frames are available at: `https://github.com/propbank/propbank-frames/`

[3]The annotator concludes "we could add an `:ARG2` [...] and use it only when `:ARG1` is already present, but that makes me sad, so let's just not mess with it until we actually see such an instance."

In what follows, we propose the introduction of an intensional relation `:content` responsible for introducing propositional arguments. Replacing the `:ARG1` of `believe-01` in (4) with the new `:content` role ensures firstly that (4-b) contains a non-veridical environment and secondly that (4-c) is not a representation for a coherent natural language sentence. Crucially, the addition of `:content` and the translation function proposed for AMRs into logical forms offers a satisfying representation for intensional contexts without the need for additional graph structure. Finally, we show how our logical forms interact with scope taking elements to derive attested interpretations of attitude reports with quantifier phrases (QPs).

2 Extensional Semantics for AMRs

We start by defining a simple translation for basic AMRs (without intensional operators or quantifiers) into the Simply-Typed Lambda Calculus (STLC). Following Bos (2016) we define the syntax of AMRs recursively. A simplex AMR is a constant `c`, variable `x`, or an instance assignment `(x / P)`. Complex graphs are defined recursively as one or more subgraphs $\{\mathtt{A}_1, \ldots, \mathtt{A}_n\}$ connected to an instance assignment by n relations.

(7) $\mathtt{A} :=$

a. `c`

b. `x`

c. `(x / P)`

d. $\mathtt{(x\ /\ P\ :R_1\ A_1 \ldots :R_n\ A_n)}$

Our semantics for AMRs is a departure from that of Bos (2016) and Lai et al. (2020). For now, we assume that the interpretation function $[\![.]\!]$ compositionally maps AMRs to a simple first-order calculus embedded in the STLC.[4] AMR constants and variables are mapped to STLC constants of type e, AMR predicates are mapped to STLC constants of type $e \to t$, and AMR roles are mapped to STLC constants of type $e \to e \to t$.[5]

(8) a. $[\![\mathtt{c}]\!] = \mathbf{c}$ $\qquad e$

b. $[\![\mathtt{x}]\!] = x$ $\qquad e$

Simple instance assignments are mapped to functional applications:

(9) **Instance assignment**

$[\![\mathtt{(x\ /\ P)}]\!] = P(x)$ $\qquad t$

To state a semantics for complex AMRs, we first state a semantics for a *role assignment* in (10), consisting of a role and an embedded AMR, via pattern matching on the embedded AMR. A sequence of role assignments $\rho_1 \ldots \rho_n$ is interpreted via iterated conjunction (11), and finally a complex AMR is interpreted by saturating a role sequence with the main variable of the AMR (12).

(10) **Role assignment**

a. $[\![\mathtt{:R\ y}]\!] = \lambda x \,.\, R(x)(y)$

b. $[\![\mathtt{:R\ (y\ /\ \ldots\ )}]\!]$
$= \lambda x \,.\, R(x)(y) \wedge [\![\mathtt{(y\ /\ \ldots\ )}]\!]$

(11) **Role sequence**

$[\![\rho_1 \ldots \rho_n]\!] = \lambda x \,.\, [\![\rho_1]\!]\,(x) \wedge \ldots \wedge [\![\rho_n]\!]\,(x)$

(12) **Complex AMR**

$[\![\mathtt{(x\ /\ P}\ \rho_1 \ldots \rho_n\mathtt{)}]\!]$
$= P(x) \wedge [\![\rho_1 \ldots \rho_n]\!]\,(x)$

Basic AMRs are thereby translated into simple conjunctive first-order formulae.

(13) *The boy admires himself.*

a.
```
(a / admire-01
    :ARG0 (b / boy)
    :ARG1 b))
```

b. $\mathbf{admire\text{-}01}(a) \wedge ARG0(a)(b)$
$\wedge\, \mathbf{boy}(b) \wedge ARG1(a)(b)$

Finally, we declare an operation `close` (version 1) which, applied to a STLC expression φ, introduces an existential quantifier which unselectively binds variables in the set $\mathbf{Free}(\varphi)$.

(14) **Close (version 1)**

$\mathtt{close}(\varphi) = \exists x_1 \ldots x_n(\varphi)$
where $\{x_1, \ldots, x_n\} = \mathbf{Free}(\varphi)$

Crucially for what follows, $\mathbf{Free}(\varphi)$ does not correspond to the classical notion of free variables in φ, but rather should be defined to ensure that recurrent variables are not bound by `close` prior to instance assignment. We define **Free** as follows:[6]

(15) a. $\mathbf{Free}\,(\mathtt{c}) = \emptyset$

b. $\mathbf{Free}\,(\mathtt{x}) = \emptyset$

c. $\mathbf{Free}\,(\mathtt{(x\ /\ P)}) = \{x\}$

d. $\mathbf{Free}\,(\mathtt{(x\ /\ P\ :R_1 A_1 \ldots R_n A_n)})$
$= \{x\} \cup \mathbf{Free}\,(\mathtt{A}_1) \cup \ldots \cup \mathbf{Free}\,(\mathtt{A}_n)$

[4] The STLC is widely used in analytical work on natural language semantics, and has a well-understood proof-theory and model-theory (Carpenter, 1998).

[5] e is the basic type of *individuals*, and t is the basic type of *truth-values*. The constructor for functional types $a \to b$ is right-associative.

[6] We are grateful to an anonymous reviewer for pressing us on this point.

Applying `close` to the example above returns an existential statement.

(16) $\exists a, b.\textbf{admire-01}(a) \wedge ARG0(a)(b)$
$\wedge\, \textbf{boy}(b) \wedge ARG1(a)(b)$

Putting re-entrant nodes to one side, it is harmless to defer existential binding of free variables, since $\psi \wedge \exists x(\varphi) \Leftrightarrow \exists x(\psi \wedge \varphi)$ (if $x \notin \textbf{Free}(\psi)$). This does away with the need to use continuation-passing style (c.f., Bos 2016; Lai et al. 2020). Cases involving re-entrant nodes such as *the dog scratched itself* are handled straightforwardly via matching variables.

3 An Intensional Semantics

Next, we systematically intensionalize the interpretation in a standard way by replacing the propositional type t with $s \rightarrow t$ (the type of a function from *worlds* to truth values; Gallin 1975). Our existing interpretation procedure for basic AMRs remains largely intact, although we tweak the definitions of conjunction and existential quantification in order to accommodate the presence of additional world arguments.

(17) a. $\varphi \wedge_w \psi := \lambda w.\, \varphi(w) \wedge \psi(w)$
b. $\exists_w x(\varphi) := \lambda w.\, \exists x(\varphi(w))$

To provide a semantics for intensional operators such as attitude predicates in AMR, we adopt a variant of Kratzer's (2006) Davidsonian event semantics for attitude verbs which has undergone a number of refinements (e.g., Moulton, 2009; Elliott, 2016, 2020). More specifically, we propose a translation of AMRs of attitude reports into logical forms in which attitude events are associated with propositional content via a dedicated modal operator **cont**. In order to achieve this, we increase the AMR inventory of semantic roles with a `:content` role which is interpreted as a relation of type $e \rightarrow (s \rightarrow t) \rightarrow (s \rightarrow t)$.

(18) $[\![$`:content A`$]\!]$
$= \lambda x\,.\,\textbf{cont}(x)(\texttt{close}([\![\texttt{A}]\!]))$

To see how this resolves the problem of non-veridicality consider again the two AMRs in (4), the first of which is repeated in (19-a) with the `:ARG1` role changed to `:content`. The underlined argument shows that the world of evaluation for the translation of the `:content` argument is shifted to w_2, and thus we cannot infer that the boy is sick in w as desired.

(19) a.
```
(b / believe-01
   :ARG0 (b2 / boy)
   :content (s / sick-05
      :ARG1 b2))
```
b. $\texttt{close}([\![\text{(19-a)}]\!])$
$= \lambda w\,.\,\exists b, b_2(\textbf{believe-01}(b)(w)$
$\wedge\, \textbf{boy}(b_2)(w)$
$\wedge\, ARG0(b)(b_2)(w)$
$\wedge\, \textbf{cont}(b)(\underline{\lambda w_2\,.\,\exists s(\textbf{sick-01}(s)(w_2)}$
$\underline{\wedge ARG1(s)(b_2)(w_2)))}(w))$

Next, consider the same modification for (4-c) repeated in (20), modulo `:ARG1`$\Rightarrow$`:content`.

(20)
```
(b / believe-01
   :ARG0 (b2 / boy
      :ARG1-of (s / sick-05))
   :content s))
```

The semantic rule for `:content` is only well-defined if the embedded AMR is an *instance assignment*, due to the type of **cont**. It follows that the interpretation of (20), in which `:content` embeds a recurrent variable, is undefined. For this reason, AMRs in which `:content` embeds a constant or variable should be avoided by annotators. The issue here is that reentrant nodes are used to model a diverse range of linguistic phenomena (Szubert et al., 2020), but are inappropriate for modelling anaphora to a proposition, such as *'The boy who is sick believes it'*.[7]

4 Content and Quantifier Scope: de re and de dicto Readings

Another property of intensional operators is their ability to interact scopally with other operators such as quantifier phrases (QPs) (see Keshet and Schwarz 2019 for a recent overview). For example, the sentence in (21) could be paraphrased as in (21-a) which can be analyzed as an existential QP *'a violin'* taking scope over the attitude predicate *'hope'*, in which case the restrictor argument of the QP is evaluated in the actual world (i.e., there is an actual violin that the boy wants). In contrast, the reading in (21-b) can be analyzed as the existential being within the scope of the attitude (i.e., the boy hopes to be a violin-owner, but is not necessarily concerned about owning any particular violin).

[7]It should be noted that the AMR in (4-c) in which `:ARG1` is not replaced with `:content` does have an interpretation which can be paraphrased as: *'the boy who is in a state s of being sick, believes the state s'*. However, it is not clear that this corresponds to any coherent natural language sentence.

(21) *The boy hopes to buy a violin.*

a. There is a violin the boy hopes to buy. *De re*

b. The boy hopes to be a violin-owner. *De dicto*

To capture these readings, we develop a semantics for AMRs enriched with additional graph structure for modelling scope (Pustejovsky et al., 2019) based on the mechanism of Cooper storage (Cooper, 1983; Kobele, 2018).

4.1 Scope Semantics

Before discussing the scope interaction of quantifiers and **cont**, let us first develop a semantics for scope in non-intensional contexts. Following Pustejovsky et al. (2019) and Van Gysel et al. (2021) we make use of a `scope` node, which has a predicative argument representing the core argument structure and reentrant variables to represent the order of quantifier scope. For example, in (22-b), the QP of `:ARG0` scopes over that of `:ARG1`.

(22) a. A computer is on every desk.

b.
```
(s / scope
   :pred (b / be-located-at-91
      :ARG0 (c / computer)
      :ARG1 (d / desk
         :quant every))
   :ARG0 d
   :ARG1 c)
```

Next, we define an explicit interpretation of scope nodes using Cooper storage (Cooper, 1983; Kobele, 2018). A *store* is an *assignment* of variables to STLC expressions of type $(e \to t) \to t$.[8]

(23) $\{(x, \mathbf{every}(\mathbf{boy})), (y, \mathbf{some}(\mathbf{girl})\}$

Instead of simply mapping AMRs to expressions of STLC, we map them to a pair consisting of a store s and an ordinary semantic value (i.e., an STLC expression). We assume the following notational conventions.

(24) a. $[\![\mathrm{A}]\!] = s \cdot \varphi$

b. $[\![\mathrm{A}]\!]_s = s$

c. $[\![\mathrm{A}]\!]_o = \varphi$

In this system, AMRs like those we have considered so far update the store vacuously (25-a) while retaining their ordinary semantic value (25-b).

[8]We leave world variables implicit in section 4.1 for the sake of readability.

(25) **Instance assignment (revised)**

a. $[\![\texttt{(d / dance-01)}]\!]_s = \emptyset$

b. $[\![\texttt{(d / dance-01)}]\!]_o = \mathbf{dance\text{-}01}(d)$

In order to illustrate how `:quant` is interpreted, we begin by stating a semantics for an instance assignment decorated with a single `:quant` role.[9] We assume that AMR determiner constants such as `every` are mapped to STLC constants of type $(e \to t) \to (e \to t) \to t$, such as the quantificational determiner **every** (e.g., Barwise and Cooper, 1981). The store is updated with a generalized quantifier constructed from the determiner and the property in the instance assignment (26-a). The ordinary semantic value, on the other hand, is the truth constant $\top$, the addition of which is redundant in a string of conjunctions (26-b).

(26) **Quantifier storage**

a. $[\![\texttt{(x / P :quant D)}]\!]_s = \{(x, \mathbf{D}(P))\}$

b. $[\![\texttt{(x / P :quant D)}]\!]_o = \top$

On this semantics, basic AMRs have a non-trivial ordinary value but perform a vacuous store update. Conversely, QPs perform a non-trivial store update but have a redundant ordinary semantic value. Crucially, however, QPs still contribute one or more variables to the ordinary value of a role assignment via pattern matching, as in (27) below.

We revise our translation function to ensure that the store gets passed up during the derivation.

(27) **Role assignment (revised)**

$[\![\texttt{:R (y / ...)}]\!] = [\![\texttt{(y / ...)}]\!]_s \cdot \lambda x\,.\,R(x)(y) \wedge [\![\texttt{(y / ...)}]\!]_o$

(28) **Role sequences (revised)**

$[\![\rho_1 \ldots \rho_n]\!] = [\![\rho_1]\!]_s \cup \ldots \cup [\![\rho_n]\!]_s \cdot \lambda x\,.\,[\![\rho_1]\!]_o(x) \wedge \ldots \wedge [\![\rho_n]\!]_o(x)$

(29) **Complex AMR (revised)**

$[\![\texttt{(x / P }\rho_1 \ldots \rho_n\texttt{)}]\!] = [\![\rho_1 \ldots \rho_n]\!]_s \cdot P(x) \wedge [\![\rho_1 \ldots \rho_n]\!]_o(x)$

In combination with (26-a), this ensures that the store of a complex AMR will contain the index-quantifier pairs added to the store by its subgraphs, as shown in the following example.

[9]We generalize this rule to the more complex case involving `:quant` and a sequence of role assignments, as well as cases of nested quantification in appendix A.

(30) *Every boy danced.*

a.
```
(d / dance
    :ARG0 (b / boy
        :quant every))
```

b. $[\![\text{(30-a)}]\!] =$
$$\{(b, \mathbf{every}(\mathbf{boy}))\} \cdot \mathbf{dance}(d) \wedge ARG0(d)(b)$$

In order to retrieve the quantifier from the store, we declare an operation $\texttt{pop}_x$ which, given a variable x, store s, and logical form φ retrieves the expression in s paired with x, and applies it to $\lambda x \,.\, \varphi$. We write s_x for the expression in s paired with x.

(31) **Pop**
$$\texttt{pop}_x(s, \varphi) = s - \{(x, s_x)\} \cdot s_x(\lambda x \,.\, \varphi)$$

We also restate our `close` operation which now existentially binds any free variables which are not associated with an index in the store.

(32) **Close (version 2)**
$$\texttt{close}(s, \varphi) = s \cdot \exists x_1 \ldots x_n(\varphi)$$
$$\{x_1, \ldots, x_n\} = \mathbf{Free}(\varphi) - \{v \mid (v, *) \in s\}$$

As mentioned above, scope nodes are decorated with roles embedding reentrant nodes indicating scope-takers (`:ARGn`), and a role to indicate the scope site (`:pred`). We state the semantics for a complex AMR headed by a scope node syncategorematically: a scope node with arguments $x_1, \ldots, x_n$ induces evaluation of the quantifiers stored at $x_1, \ldots, x_n$.[10,11]

(33) **Interpreting scope nodes**

$$\left[\!\!\left[\begin{array}{l} \texttt{(s / scope} \\ \quad \texttt{:ARG0 } \texttt{x}_1 \ \ldots \ \texttt{:ARG}n_{-1} \ \texttt{x}_n \\ \quad \texttt{:pred A)} \end{array} \right]\!\!\right]$$
$$= \texttt{pop}(x_1)\,(\ldots(\texttt{pop}(x_n))\,(\texttt{close}([\![\texttt{A}]\!])))\ldots)$$

Consider again the example *'every boy danced'*, but now with a scope node.

(34) a.
```
(s / scope
    :ARG0 b
    :pred (d / dance-01
        :ARG0 (b / boy
            :quant every)))
```

b. $[\![\text{(34-a)}]\!] =$
$$\emptyset \cdot \mathbf{every}(\mathbf{boy})\,(\lambda b \,.\, \exists d(\mathbf{dance\text{-}01}(d) \wedge ARG0(d)(b)))$$

[10] $\texttt{x}_n$ is associated with `:ARG`n_{-1} because the indexing of `:ARG`s starts at zero.

[11] Note that this property of scope nodes ensures that event quantification takes narrow scope with respect to other operators in the sentence (Champollion, 2015).

4.2 Deriving the de re and de dicto readings

Now we reintroduce world variables to see how this interpretation function can translate both the de re and de dicto readings of (21) above, starting with the de re reading. In (35-a), the variable `v` is the `:ARG0` of the scope node and consequently the QP *a violin* takes scope over the attitude verb.

(35) a.
```
(s / scope
    :ARG0 v
    :pred (h / hope-01
        :ARG0 (b / boy)
        :content (b2 / buy-01
            :ARG0 b
            :ARG1 (v / violin
                :quant a)))))
```

b. $[\![\text{(35-a)}]\!] = \emptyset \cdot$
$$\lambda w \,.\, \exists v, b, h(\mathbf{violin}(v)(w) \wedge \mathbf{hope\text{-}01}(h)(w) \wedge \mathbf{boy}(b)(w) \wedge ARG0(h)(b)(w) \wedge \mathbf{cont}(h)\,(\lambda w_2 \,.\, \exists b_2(\mathbf{buy\text{-}01}(b_2)(w_2) \wedge ARG0(b_2)(b)(w_2) \wedge ARG1(b_2)(v)(w_2)))(w))$$

Here, there is a specific violin in the world of evaluation w which the boy hopes to buy.

For the de dicto reading, we do not need to do anything special. However, to close off the interpretation we can either embed the entire AMR under a scope node or use the **close** operation to bind any free variables.

(36) a.
```
(h / hope-01
    :ARG0 (b / boy)
    :content (b2 / buy-01
        :ARG0 b
        :ARG1 (v / violin))))
```

b. $\mathbf{close}([\![\text{(36-a)}]\!]) = \emptyset \cdot$
$$\lambda w \,.\, \exists h, b(\mathbf{hope\text{-}01}(h)(w) \wedge \mathbf{boy}(b)(w) \wedge ARG0(h)(b)(w) \wedge \mathbf{cont}(h)\,(\lambda w_2 \,.\, \exists b_2, v(\mathbf{buy\text{-}01}(b_2)(w_2) \wedge \mathbf{violin}(v)(w_2) \wedge ARG0(b_2)(b)(w_2) \wedge ARG1(b_2)(v)(w_2)))(w))$$

Here, the existential is within the scope of the lambda operator λw_2 and the restrictor argument $\mathbf{violin}$ is evaluated in the boy's hope worlds w_2.

4.3 Intermediate de dicto reading

Although Pustejovsky et al. (2019) frame their proposal as "embed[ding an AMR] under a scope graph", our implementation also permits the embedding of a scope node within an AMR. Doing so allows us to derive intermediate scope readings. Consider the following example.

(37) *The boy thinks the girl hopes to buy a violin.*

a. The boy thinks there is a violin that the girl hopes to buy.

In this intermediate reading, the intensional object might not be a violin in the actual world, nor in the girl's desire worlds, rather it is a violin in the boys belief worlds. Stabler (2017) notes that accounts such as Bos (2016), and later Lai et al. (2020), cannot capture these sorts of intermediate scope readings since their projective semantics always derives widest scope of QPs. However, this reading can be captured on the present account straightforwardly from the following structure.[12]

(38)
```
(t / think-01
    :ARG0 (b / boy)
    :content (s / scope
        :ARG0 v
        :pred (h / hope-01
            :ARG0 (g / girl)
            :content (b / buy-01
                :ARG0 g
                :ARG1 (v / violin
                    :quant a)))))
```

4.4 Problematic Scope

Besides the de re and de dicto readings, Fodor (1970) considers two further readings in which the restrictor argument of the QP is interpreted separately from the scopal position of the quantifier.

(39) *The boy hopes to buy a violin.*

a. There are things which are violins and the boy hopes to buy one of them. *Non-specific de re*

b. #There is a thing the boy hopes to buy which he believes is a violin. *Specific de dicto*

[12] Van Gysel et al. (2021) adopt the scope node approach in combination with a variant of Lai et al.'s semantics. Such an approach should also derive intermediate scope readings.

Although there is a general consensus in the literature that (39-b) is not a possible reading of (39), the reading in (39-a) is possible. At present, we cannot derive the reading in (39-a). While it is possible to enrich AMRs further to accommodate such interpretations, it remains to be seen whether such an effort is worthwhile. Although such interpretations are attested and theoretically significant, they are not common, and accounting for such interpretations would likely involve enriching the graphical representation of AMRs in ways which would make them far less tractable for annotators and parsers. We leave it to future research to determine whether we can accommodate this third reading without unintentionally complicating the AMRs in undesirable ways.

5 Discussion

We have proposed to extend the expressive power of AMR in two respects. Firstly, we have enriched the graphical form of AMRs by increasing the inventory of AMR roles with the role `:content`. We did so in order to distinguish between intensional and non-intensional arguments of modal operators such as attitude predicates. Secondly, we provided a translation of AMRs into logical forms which allowed us to solve the problem of non-veridicality as well as complex scope interactions between quantifiers and intenstional operators.

The addition of `:content` has ramifications for AMR annotation as well as backwards compatibility. We opted to avoid proposing the addition of new numbered argument roles for predicate like `believe-01` since this would involve a wide-scale revision of AMR's frameset as well as complicating any effort to convert between existing corpora and an enriched corpus, as this would involve a many-to-many mapping. Instead, we proposed a semantically motivated intensional relation `:content` which will reduce the complexity of any conversion effort, requiring only a many-to-one mapping.

When designing meaning representations, there is inevitably a trade-off between how adequate the representation is (e.g., how much semantic information is present) and how tractable the representations are for large scale annotation projects. Although we believe that `:content` should not be any more difficult to annotate than non-core roles in AMR, it is likely that annotators may struggle to resolve and represent quantifier scope and de re/de dicto ambiguities. Thankfully, in addition to being representationally adequate, the scope node approach adopted from Pustejovsky et al. (2019) and Van Gysel et al. (2021) is both intuitive and transparent. Future research could aim to gauge the level inter-annotator agreement when representing such phenomena in a small scale annotation task.

Beyond AMR, the enriched graphical language Uniform Meaning Representation (UMR) (Van Gysel et al., 2021) also utilizes scope nodes to capture quantifier scope relations. The `:content` role and translation function proposed here can be adopted wholesale for UMR, and thus will prove useful in future annotation projects for this more expressive annotation scheme.

Finally, the `:content` role and its intensional translation may also facilitate downstream NLP tasks. Specifically, different attitude predicates trigger different lexical inferences regarding the truth of their complement depending on whether they are factive (e.g., `know-01`), counterfactive (e.g., `pretend-01`) or non-veridical (e.g., `believe-01`). A number of rich resources exist in this domain including the MegaVeridicality data sets (White and Rawlins, 2018; White et al., 2018) which contain factuality judgments for a comprehensive list of English verbs that embed finite clauses as well as a variety of predicates which embed non-finite clauses. Resources such as these may be deployed alongside AMR for NLI, since the logical forms which our interpretation function produces represent the scope of the attitude verb, unlike in a flat list of logical triples.

A python script for translating AMR into STLC is available at `https://github.com/emorynlp/Intensionalizing-AMR`, and we are currently working on developing a script to convert intensional uses of numbered arguments into the new `:content` role which we also plan to make publicly available.

6 Conclusion

Abstract Meaning Representations (AMRs) are unable to represent non-veridical environments in a semantically satisfying way. When an AMR is translated into a conjunctions of logical triples, it permits spurious inferences to the truth of any of its subgraphs via conjunction elimination. We proposed to rectify this through the introduction of a novel AMR role `:content`, before providing an intensional interpretation for AMRs which correctly invalidates such inferences. We then showed how such a semantics can be combined with a means of modelling scope to derive de re and de dicto readings of natural language sentences with intensional operators and quantifiers. We concluded that the inclusion of a scope node (Pustejovsky et al., 2019; Van Gysel et al., 2021) is necessary in order to capture intermediate scope readings, and we provided a translation function from AMRs into STLC permitting the derivation of complex interactions of natural language quantifiers with intensional operators. This work is part of the concerted effort to increase the expressive power of AMRs while also maintaining tractable representations ensuring that large scale annotation projects can be performed with minimal instruction.

References

Yoav Artzi, Kenton Lee, and Luke Zettlemoyer. 2015. Broad-coverage CCG semantic parsing with AMR. In *Proceedings of the 2015 Conference on Empirical Methods in Natural Language Processing*, pages 1699–1710, Lisbon, Portugal. Association for Computational Linguistics.

Laura Banarescu, Claire Bonial, Shu Cai, Madalina Georgescu, Kira Griffitt, Ulf Hermjakob, Kevin Knight, Philipp Koehn, Martha Palmer, and Nathan Schneider. 2013. Abstract Meaning Representation for sembanking. In *Proceedings of the 7th Linguistic Annotation Workshop and Interoperability with Discourse*, pages 178–186, Sofia, Bulgaria. Association for Computational Linguistics.

John Barwise and Robin Cooper. 1981. Generalized quantifiers and natural language. *Linguistics and Philosophy*, 4(2):159–219.

Claire Bonial, Julia Bonn, Kathryn Conger, Jena D. Hwang, and Martha Palmer. 2014. PropBank: Semantics of new predicate types. In *Proceedings of the Ninth International Conference on Language Resources and Evaluation (LREC'14)*, pages 3013–3019, Reykjavik, Iceland. European Language Resources Association (ELRA).

Claire Bonial, Julia Bonn, Kathryn Conger, Jena D. Hwang, Martha Palmer, and Nicholas Reese. 2015. English PropBank Annotation Guidelines.

Claire Bonial, Lucia Donatelli, Mitchell Abrams, Stephanie M. Lukin, Stephen Tratz, Matthew Marge, Ron Artstein, David Traum, and Clare Voss. 2020. Dialogue-AMR: Abstract Meaning Representation for dialogue. In *Proceedings of the 12th Language Resources and Evaluation Conference*, pages 684–695, Marseille, France. European Language Resources Association.

Johan Bos. 2016. Squib: Expressive power of Abstract Meaning Representations. *Computational Linguistics*, 42(3):527–535.

Johan Bos. 2020. Separating argument structure from logical structure in AMR. In *Proceedings of the Second International Workshop on Designing Meaning Representations*, pages 13–20, Barcelona Spain (online). Association for Computational Linguistics.

Bob Carpenter. 1998. *Type-Logical Semantics*. Language, Speech, and Communication. MIT Press, Cambridge, Mass.

Jeremy J Carroll, Christian Bizer, Pat Hayes, and Patrick Stickler. 2005. Named graphs, provenance and trust. In *Proceedings of the 14th international conference on World Wide Web*, pages 613–622.

Lucas Champollion. 2015. The interaction of compositional semantics and event semantics. *Linguistics and Philosophy*, 38(1):31–66.

Robin Cooper. 1983. *Quantification and Syntactic Theory*. Studies in Linguistics and Philosophy. Springer Netherlands.

Richard Crouch and Aikaterini-Lida Kalouli. 2018. Named graphs for semantic representation. In *Proceedings of the Seventh Joint Conference on Lexical and Computational Semantics*, pages 113–118, New Orleans, Louisiana. Association for Computational Linguistics.

Donald Davidson. 1967. The logical form of action sentences. In Nicholas Rescher, editor, *The Logic of Decision and Action*, pages 81–95. University of Pittsburgh Press.

Lucia Donatelli, Michael Regan, William Croft, and Nathan Schneider. 2018. Annotation of tense and aspect semantics for sentential AMR. In *Proceedings of the Joint Workshop on Linguistic Annotation, Multiword Expressions and Constructions (LAW-MWE-CxG-2018)*, pages 96–108, Santa Fe, New Mexico, USA. Association for Computational Linguistics.

Lucia Donatelli, Nathan Schneider, William Croft, and Michael Regan. 2019. Tense and aspect semantics for sentential AMR. *Proceedings of the Society for Computation in Linguistics*, 2(1):346–348.

Patrick D Elliott. 2016. Explaining dps vs. cps without syntax. *Proceedings of CLS*, 52:171–185.

Patrick D. Elliott. 2020. A plea for equality: Remarks on Moltmann's semantics for clausal embedding. *Theoretical Linguistics*, 46(3-4):241–251.

Janet Fodor. 1970. *The linguistic description of opaque contexts*. MIT.

Daniel Gallin. 1975. *Intensional and Higher-Order Modal Logic*. Number 19 in North-Holland Mathematics Studies. North-Holland Publ. Co. [u.a.], Amsterdam.

Aikaterini-Lida Kalouli and Richard Crouch. 2018. Gkr: the graphical knowledge representation for semantic parsing. In *Workshop on Computational Semantics beyond Events and Roles (SemBEaR 2018)*, pages 27–37.

William R. Keller. 1988. Nested Cooper Storage: The Proper Treatment of Quantification in Ordinary Noun Phrases. In U. Reyle and C. Rohrer, editors, *Natural Language Parsing and Linguistic Theories*, Studies in Linguistics and Philosophy, pages 432–447. Springer Netherlands, Dordrecht.

Ezra Keshet and Florian Schwarz. 2019. *De Re/De Dicto*. In Jeanette Gundel and Barbara Abbott, editors, *The Oxford Handbook of Reference*. Oxford University Press.

Gregory M Kobele. 2018. The cooper storage idiom. *Journal of Logic, Language and Information*, 27(2):95–131.

Angelika Kratzer. 2006. Decomposing attitude verbs. *Talk given at the Hebrew University of Jerusalem*.

Kenneth Lai, Lucia Donatelli, and James Pustejovsky. 2020. A continuation semantics for Abstract Meaning Representation. In *Proceedings of the Second International Workshop on Designing Meaning Representations*, pages 1–12, Barcelona Spain (online). Association for Computational Linguistics.

Christian M. I. M. Matthiessen and John A Bateman. 1991. *Text generation and systemic-functional linguistics: experiences from English and Japanese*. Pinter.

Keir Moulton. 2009. *Natural selection and the syntax of clausal complementation*. University of Massachusetts Amherst.

Martha Palmer, Daniel Gildea, and Paul Kingsbury. 2005. The Proposition Bank: An annotated corpus of semantic roles. *Computational Linguistics*, 31(1):71–106.

Terence Parsons. 1990. *Events in the Semantics of English: A Study in Subatomic Semantics*. MIT Press.

James Pustejovsky, Ken Lai, and Nianwen Xue. 2019. Modeling quantification and scope in Abstract Meaning Representations. In *Proceedings of the First International Workshop on Designing Meaning Representations*, pages 28–33, Florence, Italy. Association for Computational Linguistics.

Edward Stabler. 2017. Reforming AMR. *International Conference on Formal Grammar*, pages 72–87.

Ida Szubert, Marco Damonte, Shay B. Cohen, and Mark Steedman. 2020. The Role of Reentrancies in Abstract Meaning Representation Parsing. In *Findings of the Association for Computational Linguistics: EMNLP 2020*, pages 2198–2207, Online. Association for Computational Linguistics.

Jens EL Van Gysel, Meagan Vigus, Jayeol Chun, Kenneth Lai, Sarah Moeller, Jiarui Yao, Tim O'Gorman, Andrew Cowell, William Croft, Chu-Ren Huang, et al. 2021. Designing a uniform meaning representation for natural language processing. *KI-Künstliche Intelligenz*, pages 1–18.

Aaron Steven White and Kyle Rawlins. 2018. The role of veridicality and factivity in clause selection. In *Proceedings of the 48th Annual Meeting of the North East Linguistic Society*, pages 221–234.

Aaron Steven White, Rachel Rudinger, Kyle Rawlins, and Benjamin Van Durme. 2018. Lexicosyntactic inference in neural models. In *Proceedings of the 2018 Conference on Empirical Methods in Natural Language Processing*, pages 4717–4724, Brussels, Belgium. Association for Computational Linguistics.

A Cooper storage and nested quantification

In the main body, we state a semantics for instance assignments decorated with `:quant`. Here, we state a more general rule for interpreting an instance assignment decorated with `:quant` and an additional sequence of role assignments $\rho_1 \ldots \rho_2$. This is necessary for interpreting AMRs arising from sentences involving nested quantifiers, such as (40-a), which may correpond to a `scope`-enriched AMR such as (40-b), in which a `:quant` role co-occurs with an embedded AMR, itself decorated with a `:quant` role.

(40) a. *Every class with a certain two professors is difficult.*

b.
```
(s / scope
   :ARG0 p
   :ARG1 c
   :pred (d / difficult
      :domain (c / class
         :quant every
         :prep-with (p / prof.
            :quant 2))))
```

The rule for interpreting complex AMRs with a `:quant` role and an additional role sequence is given below. The idea is that stores associated with embedded AMRs are passed up, and the determiner introduce by `:quant` takes scope over the role sequence.

(41) $[\![\texttt{(x / P :quant D } \rho_1 \ldots \rho_n \texttt{)}]\!]_s = [\![\rho_1 \ldots \rho_n]\!]_s \cup \{(x, \mathbf{D}(\lambda x \,.\, P(x) \wedge [\![\rho_1 \ldots \rho_n]\!]_o (x))\}$

(42) $[\![\texttt{(x / P :quant D } \rho_1 \ldots \rho_n \texttt{)}]\!]_o = \top$

This more sophisticated interpretation rule allows us to interpret AMRs such as that in (40-b). The derivation involves storing a quantificational expression containing a free variable, which comes to be bound once the scope node is resolved. In (43) we provide the interpretation of the AMR embedded under `:pred` in (40-b). A full derivation is left as an exercise to the reader.

(43) $\left\{ \begin{matrix} (p, \mathbf{two}(\mathbf{professor}), \\ (c, \mathbf{every}(\lambda x.\, \mathbf{class}(x) \wedge \mathbf{with}(x)(p))) \end{matrix} \right\} \cdot \mathbf{difficult}(d) \wedge \mathbf{domain}(d)(c)$

As a final note, care has to be taken to ensure that the quantifiers are evaluated in a certain order in cases involving nested quantification. Concretely, if the values of `:ARG0` and `:ARG1` are flipped, in the AMR in (40-b), then the free variable in the stored universal quantifier will remain free post-evaluation, which does not correspond to an attested interpretation of (40-a). Besides placing an implausible cognitive load on annotators, this is a known deficiency of the rudimentary Cooper storage system adopted here (Keller, 1988). More sophisticated approaches to Cooper storage which avoid this issue (Kobele, 2018) could be adapted for the purpose of interpreting AMRs; we leave this to future work.

WikiGUM: Exhaustive Entity Linking for Wikification in 12 Genres

Jessica Lin
Department of Linguistics
Georgetown University
yl1290@georgetown.edu

Amir Zeldes
Department of Linguistics
Georgetown University
amir.zeldes@georgetown.edu

Abstract

Previous work on Entity Linking has focused on resources targeting non-nested proper named entity mentions, often in data from Wikipedia, i.e. Wikification. In this paper, we present and evaluate WikiGUM, a fully wikified dataset, covering all mentions of named entities, including their non-named and pronominal mentions, as well as mentions nested within other mentions. The dataset covers a broad range of 12 written and spoken genres, most of which have not been included in Entity Linking efforts to date, leading to poor performance by a pretrained SOTA system in our evaluation. The availability of a variety of other annotations for the same data also enables further research on entities in context.

1 Introduction

Entity linking (EL) involves identifying entities within a text and subsequently linking their mentions to a knowledge base or table of authorities. The former step is often referred to as Named Entity Recognition (NER) and the latter may also be referred to as entity disambiguation. In this study, we will focus on the latter task by following the popular approach of mapping named entities to Wikipedia entities (Milne and Witten, 2008; Shnayderman et al., 2019), i.e. Wikification.

Wikification is the task of adding links to Wikipedia pages to mentions of named entities in a written or spoken text. This task supports Natural Language Understanding in downstream tasks such as question answering, summarization, and relation extraction. However the scope and structure of EL depends heavily on datasets which are either automatically derived from hyperlinked text and thus suffer some limitations, or are created via human annotation, a time-consuming and expensive task. Despite numerous existing EL datasets (Cucerzan, 2007; Ji et al., 2015; Kulkarni et al., 2009; Milne and Witten, 2008; Ratinov et al., 2011), few have attempted to capture *nested* entity structure, as in Figure 1, which never occurs in hyperlinks, which cannot be nested.

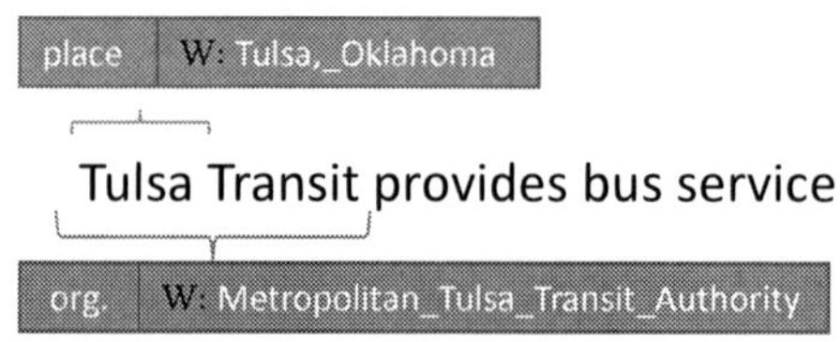

Figure 1: Nested entity linking.

Instead, annotations have focused on flat mention structure from popular online sources, leaving out important information in nested entities that can be useful for downstream tasks. Closest to the resource presented here is the Nested Named Entities (NNE) dataset (Ringland et al., 2019), which is a large, manually-annotated, nested named entity dataset over English newswire, however, it does not include entity linking. Although NNE includes fine-grained semantic information in nested entity types, it is not linked to any identifiers (e.g. a Wikipedia page). Furthermore, even if used for mention recognition, the data is not ideal for testing on diverse genres, as NNE solely covers news text. We also note other datasets capturing some nested entity structure, such as the Abstract Meaning Representation (AMR) corpus (Banarescu et al., 2013), which includes compositional nesting e.g. in possessives such as *Toronto's international airport*, composed of a city and an airport. However, since AMR is not word-aligned to text, even those nested entities that are covered are not aligned to their textual position.

In this paper, we present and evaluate a gold standard wikified dataset, called WikiGUM, in which named and non-named entities have been annotated manually. WikiGUM is based on the existing GUM dataset (Georgetown University Multilayer corpus,

Proceedings of the Joint 15th Linguistic Annotation Workshop (LAW) and 3rd Designing Meaning Representations (DMR) Workshop, pages 170–175
November, 2021.

Zeldes 2017), and goes beyond other EL corpora, in covering *all* mentions of named entities (NEs), including non-named and pronominal mentions, as well as nested mentions, for 12 genres of English text. WikiGUM also enables assessment of EL annotations by highlighting challenges that are common in our dataset, and reveals the relatively poor coverage of state-of-the-art NLP systems for EL in diverse genres (Section 4). Taken together, we aim to facilitate new research on nested NER and EL, to promote recognition of all NE mentions and a deeper understanding of the hierarchical structure of entities in text.

2 WikiGUM

The underying GUM (Zeldes, 2017) corpus is a manually annotated dataset with multiple layers, including POS tagging (Penn tags, CLAWS5, Universal POS), sentence types (e.g. declarative, imperative, yes/no question), UD dependency trees (Nivre et al., 2016), coreference resolution (including bridging anaphora and split antecedents), and RST discourse parses (Mann and Thompson, 1988). Data covers 12 genres: academic, biographies, conversation, fiction, forums, how-to, interviews, news, speeches, textbooks, travel and vlogs.

WikiGUM adds a layer of Wikipedia identifiers to all NEs in GUM, which are identified automatically by having the gold PTB POS tag NNP(S) for their syntactic head, based on gold syntax trees (for some resulting issues, see below), as well as non-named mentions coreferring to them based on coreference annotations. Since GUM is expanded by students in classroom annotation every year, and we plan to continue adding Wikification in the future, no closed or pre-prepared ontology is applied to the Wiki identifiers, making the task simpler for student annotators who only need to find a corresponding Wikipedia article.

That said, the existing 10 entity types in GUM[1] mean that our EL benefits from the same categorization scheme as a rough ontology, and the availability of semantic information from WikiData means that many relationships between entities can be explored. All referential NPs, including pronouns and even clauses (if they co-refer with a named entity based on GUM's coreference annotations, for example movie titles), were selected as markables for annotation. Note that nested markables are always included, for example:

(1) [*the airport in* [*Cuba*]$_{\text{place}}$]$_{\text{place}}$

Our general guideline for entity linking is that NEs, including pronominal and non-named mentions, were manually linked to the corresponding Wikipedia article whenever one exists, using the version controlled online editor GitDox (Zhang and Zeldes, 2017). For example:

(2) *Kim likes* [*The Terminator*]$_{\text{abstract}}$. [*This movie*]$_{\text{abstract}}$ *is her favorite.*

In this example, the span *This movie* should also be linked to the Wikipedia page that refers to *The Terminator (the movie)*. Statistics on WikiGUM, which is freely available under the same Creative Commons license as GUM, are shown in Table 1.

Although the basic Wikification task is fairly straightforward, some ambiguous/tricky cases during annotation included:

- **Generic terms**: some capitalized common nouns that have Wikipedia links appear within NEs, and are tagged NNP(S), but do not correspond to named entities. For example, *Oil* is incorrectly proposed as a NE due to capitalization within the NE *the Oil Capital of the World* (referring to Tulsa, OK) and due to the POS tag NNP. It can be tempting to link 'oil' as a NE candidate to the Wikipedia article 'Petroleum'. However in context, 'oil' is a generic, non-named modifier to 'Capital', and should not be linked as a NE. Annotators should be mindful of context of terms tagged NNP(S) within NEs, rather than linking any NNP span.

- **Subset of entity with the same type**: a common type of ambiguity for PLACE entities arises when names are reused in different countries, regions, cities or villages. For example, terms like 'North', 'South', 'East', and 'West' as a subset of a region are hard to disambiguate, and they are common in street names in North America. In this case, annotators must look at the broader context and carefully check whether the entity refers to a subset or not, for example cities and their metropolitan areas, streets with and without cardinal directions, or other parts of cities which sometimes have separate Wikipedia entries.

[1]Types: PERSON, PLACE, ORG, ANIMAL, PLANT, EVENT, TIME, SUBSTANCE, ABSTRACT and inanimate OBJECT.

Text Types	Source	Documents	# of NE Mentions	# of Nested Wikified Mentions	Total Mentions	Tokens
Interviews	Wikinews	19	1,146	107	5,204	18,037
News stories	Wikinews	21	1,221	217	4,130	14,094
Travel guides	Wikivoyage	17	1,327	174	4,087	14,955
How-to guides	WikiHow	19	94	8	4,469	16,920
Academic writing	various	16	329	48	4,486	15,110
Biographies	Wikipedia	20	2,450	413	5,763	17,951
Fiction	various	18	195	9	4,737	16,307
Forum discussions	Reddit	18	196	2	4,530	16,286
Conversations	UCSB corpus	5	31	0	1,477	5,698
Political speeches	various	5	316	32	1,423	4,831
CC Vlogs	YouTube	5	39	1	1,355	5,180
Textbooks	OpenStax	5	188	21	1,507	5,376
Total		168	7,352	1,032	43,168	150,745

Table 1: Statistics on WikiGUM

- **Distinct links for identical mentions**: It is sometimes hard for annotators to realize that an entity string has several EL variants. This happens often in abbreviations, which may be labelled with the wrong entity type. For example, 'JFK' can be a person's name (the 35th US President) or a place name (JFK Airport in New York), depending on context. We instructed annotators to prioritize the existing entity type annotation: if JFK is tagged as a place, it is linked to the article about the airport. Another common issue affects ancient place names which do not exist nowadays, resulting in difficulty for EL. For instance, *Jorvik* is the viking name of York, and was therefore linked to the closest equivalent article, 'Scandinavian York' rather than 'York'. In other cases, we relied on the coreference annotations to establish equivalence: for example *England's City of Festivals* was labeled as coreferring with *York*, and was therefore considered equivalent to York for EL purposes.

- **Lack of background knowledge**: In some cases context alone cannot help annotators decide on the right sense of an entity, especially in academic texts, but also in discussion forums. Academic articles often assume readers have detailed knowledge of the topic and thus provide little context for the target entity. For example, 'Su' in 'Su et al. 2016' is a named entity, but it may be difficult to know whether there is a corresponding Wikipedia article based solely on the author's name.

3 Related work

Table 2 compares WikiGUM to other EL corpora. Most current EL datasets are based on newswire text, overlooking the impact of genre on EL – for example, Dai (2018) notes that the biomedical domain involves complex and unique entity mentions. As EL datasets are developed for evaluation of EL systems, out-of-domain data could create challenges for conventional tools. Furthermore, most previous work (Cucerzan, 2007; Ji et al., 2015; Kulkarni et al., 2009; Milne and Witten, 2008; Ratinov et al., 2011) has focused on identifying and classifying atomic, flat mention structures, leaving out the semantic information available in nested mentions.

As shown in Table 2, most datasets do not contain nested entity linking annotations, with ACE2004 being the exception (Ratinov et al., 2011). Unfortunately, no dataset covers all mentions of named entities, including their non-named mentions ('the same airport', or 'it'). As mentioned above, we do see some research on nested entity structure (Glavaš and Šnajder, 2014; Hong et al., 2016), for example the NNE corpus (Ringland et al., 2019) contains fine-grained semantic information including e.g. the category CITY nesting a STATE, which could easily be used for EL. However they are not disambiguated or linked to a table of authorities, in addition to excluding non-named mentions of the same entities. WikiGUM thus differs from previous EL datasets and is rich in terms of both genre and entity structure, as well as being among the larger available datasets as shown in the Table.

4 Evaluation

In this section we evaluate inter-annotator agreement, as well as the extent to which existing Wikification technology already captures the information in WikiGUM.

Dataset	Paper	# of documents	# of NEs	# of genres	NE/N	Pronouns	Nested Entities
WikiGUM	–	168	7,352	12	NE&N	✓	✓
ACE2004	(Ratinov et al., 2011)	36	256	1	NE		✓
AIDA-A	(Hoffart et al., 2011)	216	5,917	1	NE		
AIDA-B	(Hoffart et al., 2011)	231	5,616	1	NE		
AQUAINT	(Milne and Witten, 2008)	50	727	1	NE&N		
Derczynski	(Derczynski et al., 2015)	182	210	1	NE		
IITB	(Kulkarni et al., 2009)	107	17,200	1	NE		
KORE50	(Hoffart et al., 2012)	50	148	1	NE		
MSNBC	(Cucerzan, 2007)	20	656	1	NE		
n3-RSS-500	(Röder et al., 2014)	500	1,000	1	NE		
n3-Reuters-128	(Röder et al., 2014)	128	880	1	NE		
OKE2015	(Nuzzolese et al., 2015)	not specified	718	1	NE&Roles		
OKE2016	(Nuzzolese et al., 2016)	not specified	940	1	NE&Roles		

Table 2: English EL datasets. NE/N indicates whether only named entities (NE) or also common nouns (N) are included. Note that ACE 2004 is a subset of the documents used in the ACE 2004 coreference documents.

Inter-annotator agreement Measuring agreement for Wikification involves two main complementary aspects: span detection and Wikification (including the decision whether to link an entity and to what). Since GUM already contains mention boundaries and named/non-named status, we focus on the latter task, measuring linking agreement. To calculate agreement, we carried out an inter-annotator agreement experiment by double annotating 3,103 tokens of corpus data containing 237 entities after adjudication, about 3% of the data. We compute both Cohen's Kappa and simple percent agreement (percentage of exact match), shown in Table 3. Note that computing Cohen's Kappa here is somewhat artificial, as in the real world there is an (almost) unlimited space of possible Wikipedia identifiers. For simplicity, we define the space of possible links as the union of any values annotators used in this subset, meaning that any link chosen at any point by any annotator is considered a possible value for the annotation, and any disagreement is penalized by the metric.[2]

Metric	Score
Agreement	0.8903
Cohen's κ	0.8782

Table 3: Results of the inter-annotator agreement experiment

[2]An anonymous reviewer has asked whether this means that search ambiguity and an overwhelming number of options impacted our process: this is certainly true, and somewhat inevitable given that annotators were unrestricted in the identifiers they could choose from Wikipedia. However the high level of absolute agreement suggests that in practice annotators were surprisingly internally consistent.

Results in Table 3 show that agreement is far beyond chance, with Kappa=.87 and simple agreement of .89. While this indicates very good agreement, raters did disagree on ambiguous cases, which is worth discussing. A major source of disagreement involves linking the same entity string to distinct but related identifiers, i.e. the **name variants** issue highlighted in Section 2. This is often due to lack of context information: for example, in the sentence "*CC makes things more complex*", the mention *CC* could be linked to *Creative Commons license* (public copyright license) or *Creative Commons* (organization that produced the Creative Commons license). In this case, broader context and reasoning are required to make consistent decisions. Another example is the sentence "*According to the Arts and Humanities Citation Index Professor Chomsky is the eighth most cited scholar of all time.*", the mention *Arts* is not a NE and should not be linked, but was linked by one annotator to "*The arts*", which has a linkable article and can easily be confused with a named concept of sorts.

NLP coverage To evaluate the usefulness of WikiGUM beyond existing resources, we test a recent SOTA pretrained end-to-end neural system (*e2e*, Kolitsas et al. 2018) on the test set and compare it to a baseline strategy. Our baseline system uses a neural constituent parser (Mrini et al., 2020) to identify predicted noun phrases and simply checks the exact string of every phrase headed by a proper noun to see if it has a Wikipedia article (using the Python library `wikipedia`). Since the SOTA system cannot identify nested mentions, but we do not know which one of two nested mentions it might identify (the bigger or smaller one), we evaluate in multiple scenarios: counting all mentions, only unnested mentions, and, since the system cannot identify pronouns, with and without them.

	data	P	R	F1	links
e2e	all	0.398	0.192	0.259	827
	-pron	0.441	0.259	**0.327**	677
	-nest	0.363	0.203	0.260	713
	-both	0.363	0.253	0.298	573
baseline	all	0.480	0.182	0.264	827
	-pron	0.480	0.223	**0.304**	677
	-nest	0.363	0.203	0.260	713
	-both	0.391	0.214	0.277	573

Table 4: Baseline and e2e results on WikiGUM test set.

The results in 4 show that *e2e*, even when trained on the largest available Wikification dataset (AIDA, $\approx$1,000 documents, 18K links) does not generalize well to the domains found in our corpus, barely outperforming a naive lookup baseline. Comparing the scenarios, we see that best performance for both systems is achieved when removing pronouns, which is unsurprising since neither strategy can be expected to link them. However removing nested mentions does not result in higher scores: this is because some common targets, such as places, are often nested in larger names (organizations, office-holders), and removing them disrupts score gains from their correct identification. Nevertheless, the most lenient possible evaluations are in the low 30s, as opposed to a score of 82.6 on AIDA (Kolitsas et al., 2018, 524). This suggests that, unsurprisingly, the corpus covers a range of entities and contexts that are under- or unrepresented in previous benchmarks.

5 Conclusion

This paper presented WikiGUM, the first exhaustive Wikification dataset for named entity linking, including nested and pronominal mentions in 12 genres of English text. Our evaluation suggests a high level of agreement, as well as coverage for a significant amount of entities not retrieved by a SOTA neural linking system. We hope that this dataset will enable further research on entity linking and increase coverage for all types of linkable named entities across a broad spectrum of genres, both spoken and written.

References

Laura Banarescu, Claire Bonial, Shu Cai, Madalina Georgescu, Kira Griffitt, Ulf Hermjakob, Kevin Knight, Philipp Koehn, Martha Palmer, and Nathan Schneider. 2013. Abstract meaning representation for sembanking. In *Proceedings of the 7th linguistic annotation workshop and interoperability with discourse*, pages 178–186.

Silviu Cucerzan. 2007. Large-scale named entity disambiguation based on Wikipedia data. In *Proceedings of the 2007 joint conference on empirical methods in natural language processing and computational natural language learning (EMNLP-CoNLL)*, pages 708–716.

Xiang Dai. 2018. Recognizing complex entity mentions: A review and future directions. In *Proceedings of ACL 2018, Student Research Workshop*, pages 37–44.

Leon Derczynski, Diana Maynard, Giuseppe Rizzo, Marieke Van Erp, Genevieve Gorrell, Raphaël Troncy, Johann Petrak, and Kalina Bontcheva. 2015. Analysis of named entity recognition and linking for tweets. *Information Processing & Management*, 51(2):32–49.

Goran Glavaš and Jan Šnajder. 2014. Constructing coherent event hierarchies from news stories. In *Proceedings of TextGraphs-9: the workshop on Graph-based Methods for Natural Language Processing*, pages 34–38.

Johannes Hoffart, Stephan Seufert, Dat Ba Nguyen, Martin Theobald, and Gerhard Weikum. 2012. KORE: keyphrase overlap relatedness for entity disambiguation. In *Proceedings of the 21st ACM international conference on Information and knowledge management*, pages 545–554.

Johannes Hoffart, Mohamed Amir Yosef, Ilaria Bordino, Hagen Fürstenau, Manfred Pinkal, Marc Spaniol, Bilyana Taneva, Stefan Thater, and Gerhard Weikum. 2011. Robust disambiguation of named entities in text. In *Proceedings of the 2011 Conference on Empirical Methods in Natural Language Processing*, pages 782–792.

Yu Hong, Tongtao Zhang, Tim O'Gorman, Sharone Horowit-Hendler, Heng Ji, and Martha Palmer. 2016. Building a cross-document event-event relation corpus. In *Proceedings of the 10th Linguistic Annotation Workshop held in conjunction with ACL 2016 (LAW-X 2016)*, pages 1–6.

Heng Ji, Joel Nothman, Ben Hachey, and Radu Florian. 2015. Overview of TAC-KBP2015 tri-lingual entity discovery and linking. In *TAC*.

Nikolaos Kolitsas, Octavian-Eugen Ganea, and Thomas Hofmann. 2018. End-to-end neural entity linking. In *Proceedings of the 22nd Conference on Computational Natural Language Learning*, pages 519–529, Brussels, Belgium. Association for Computational Linguistics.

Sayali Kulkarni, Amit Singh, Ganesh Ramakrishnan, and Soumen Chakrabarti. 2009. Collective annotation of Wikipedia entities in web text. In *Proceedings of the 15th ACM SIGKDD international conference on Knowledge discovery and data mining*, pages 457–466.

William C Mann and Sandra A Thompson. 1988. Rhetorical Structure Theory: Toward a functional theory of text organization. *Text*, 8(3):243–281.

David Milne and Ian H Witten. 2008. Learning to link with Wikipedia. In *Proceedings of the 17th ACM conference on Information and knowledge management*, pages 509–518.

Khalil Mrini, Franck Dernoncourt, Quan Hung Tran, Trung Bui, Walter Chang, and Ndapa Nakashole. 2020. Rethinking self-attention: Towards interpretability in neural parsing. In *Findings of the Association for Computational Linguistics: EMNLP 2020*, pages 731–742, Online. Association for Computational Linguistics.

Joakim Nivre, Marie-Catherine De Marneffe, Filip Ginter, Yoav Goldberg, Jan Hajic, Christopher D Manning, Ryan McDonald, Slav Petrov, Sampo Pyysalo, Natalia Silveira, et al. 2016. Universal Dependencies v1: A multilingual treebank collection. In *Proceedings of the Tenth International Conference on Language Resources and Evaluation (LREC'16)*, pages 1659–1666.

Andrea Giovanni Nuzzolese, Anna Lisa Gentile, Valentina Presutti, Aldo Gangemi, Darío Garigliotti, and Roberto Navigli. 2015. Open knowledge extraction challenge. In *Semantic Web Evaluation Challenges*, pages 3–15, Cham. Springer International Publishing.

Andrea Giovanni Nuzzolese, Anna Lisa Gentile, Valentina Presutti, Aldo Gangemi, Robert Meusel, and Heiko Paulheim. 2016. The second open knowledge extraction challenge. In *Semantic Web Evaluation Challenge*, pages 3–16. Springer.

Lev Ratinov, Dan Roth, Doug Downey, and Mike Anderson. 2011. Local and global algorithms for disambiguation to Wikipedia. In *Proceedings of the 49th annual meeting of the association for computational linguistics: Human language technologies*, pages 1375–1384.

Nicky Ringland, Xiang Dai, Ben Hachey, Sarvnaz Karimi, Cecile Paris, and James R Curran. 2019. NNE: A dataset for nested named entity recognition in English newswire. *arXiv preprint arXiv:1906.01359*.

Michael Röder, Ricardo Usbeck, Sebastian Hellmann, Daniel Gerber, and Andreas Both. 2014. N^3-A collection of datasets for named entity recognition and disambiguation in the NLP interchange format. In *LREC*, pages 3529–3533.

Ilya Shnayderman, Liat Ein-Dor, Yosi Mass, Alon Halfon, Benjamin Sznajder, Artem Spector, Yoav Katz, Dafna Sheinwald, Ranit Aharonov, and Noam Slonim. 2019. Fast end-to-end wikification. *arXiv preprint arXiv:1908.06785*.

Amir Zeldes. 2017. The GUM corpus: Creating multilayer resources in the classroom. *Language Resources and Evaluation*, 51(3):581–612.

Shuo Zhang and Amir Zeldes. 2017. GitDOX: A linked version controlled online XML editor for manuscript transcription. In *FLAIRS Conference*, pages 619–623.

Association for Computational Linguistics
209 N. Eighth Street
Stroudsburg, Pennsylvania 18360

ISBN 978-1-7138-9168-0

CURRAN ASSOCIATES INC.
proceedings.com